HTML, CSS & JavaScript
FOR COMPLETE BEGINNERS

A Step by Step Guide to Learning HTML5, CSS3 and the JavaScript
Programming Language

IKRAM HAWRAMANI

STEWARDS PUBLISHING

STEWARDS PUBLISHING

Copyright © 2018 Ikram Hawramani

First Edition

First Published in 2018 in the United States

Hawramani.com

This book incorporates and expands upon the author's *HTML & CSS for Complete Beginners* and *JavaScript for Complete Beginners*.

About the Author

Ikram Hawramani is a veteran web designer and developer who has been building websites since 2001. He has worked as a full stack web developer and lead engineer for startups and runs his own web publishing business. His other technical works include *Cloud Computing for Complete Beginners* and *Object-Oriented PHP Best Practices*.

This page intentionally left blank

Contents

Part 1
HTML & CSS

This page intentionally left blank

1. An Introduction to HTML and CSS

HTML stands for Hypertext Markup Language, while CSS stands for Cascading Style Sheets. HTML and CSS were designed to solve the problem of telling computers how to display a document. Below is a typical computer file before the invention of HTML and CSS. The file was created almost 50 years ago, on April 7, 1969. It belongs to a series of documents called RFCs which have continued to this day. These documents are used by the maintainers of the Internet to discuss the development of the infrastructure and technologies related to it.

```
Network Working Group                          Steve Crocker
Request for Comments: 1                                 UCLA
                                               7 April 1969


                   Title:   Host Software
                   Author:  Steve Crocker
                   Installation:   UCLA
                   Date:   7 April 1969
         Network Working Group Request for Comment:   1

CONTENTS

INTRODUCTION

   I. A Summary of the IMP Software

      Messages

      Links

      IMP Transmission and Error Checking

      Open Questions on the IMP Software

  II. Some Requirements Upon the Host-to-Host Software

      Simple Use
```

Notice how bland the document looks. This is because it is a "plaintext" document. It is made up of alphabetical characters, numbers, spaces and a few other things. There is no room for creating borders, colors and beautiful and complex designs with such a limited technology.

To illustrate what HTML is and how it works, we will start by creating a similarly bland plaintext file, then transform it to an HTML file with a few simple steps. On a Windows system, you can create a plaintext file in any folder by right-clicking on an empty area and choosing New -> Text Document (shown below).

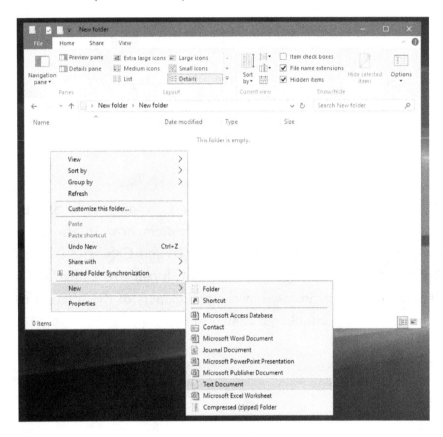

Below is our newly created document:

Name	Date modified	Type	Size
New Text Document.txt	2/2/2018 8:46 AM	Text Document	0 KB

In the above screenshot, if instead of "New Text Document.txt" you see "New Text Document" (without the ".txt" part), this means your computer is set up to hide file extensions. It is important to make file extensions visible for the purposes of the rest of this book. A file extension like ".txt" tells you that this is a text document and affects what program will be used to open the document. In order to make file extensions visible, open any folder, go to the View tab, then click the "Options" button:

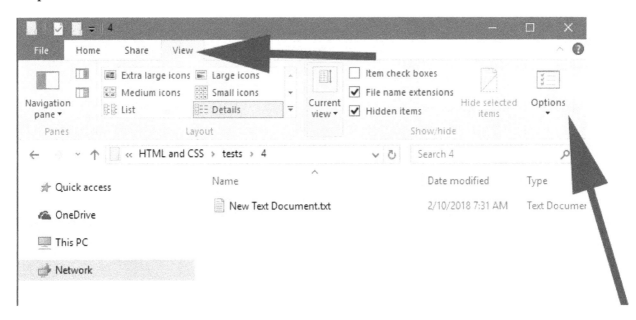

Next, click "Change File and Folder Options" in the little menu that opens up:

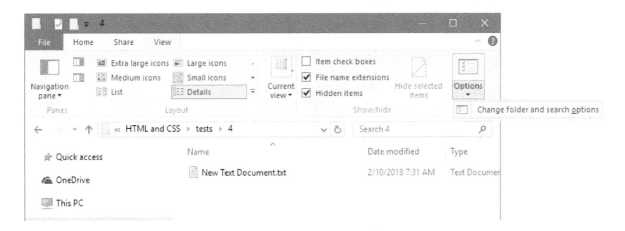

The "Folder Options" window opens up as below, click on the "View" tab at the top of the window:

Uncheck "Hide extensions for known file types":

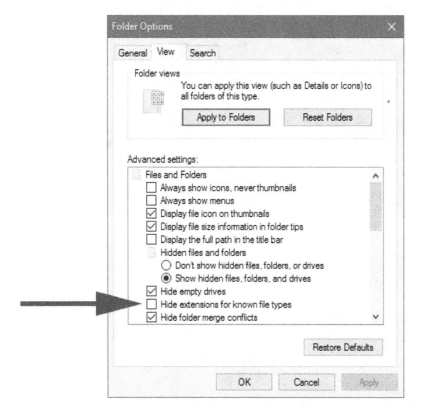

Now, click the OK button at the bottom left and you should be able to start seeing extensions.

Creating an HTML Document

If you open New Text Document.txt, you are presented with a text-editing program called Notepad that lets you type anything you want:

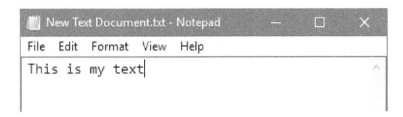

The problem with this program is that it doesn't let you add any formatting. You can't make anything bold, italic, or colorful. You are limited to 'plain' text. If you wanted to draw something, you'd be forced to use dashes and pipes to make crude drawings, as follows:

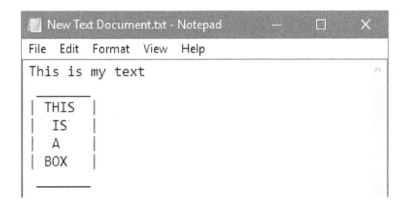

HTML and CSS give us a way of going beyond the limits of plain text. They help us create the sophisticated and occasionally beautiful designs we see on the websites we visit daily.

In the screenshot below, I add HTML 'markup' to the sentence shown earlier:

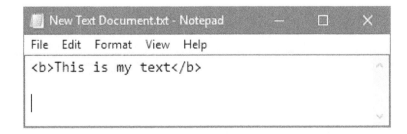

Markup is a way of giving the computer hints for how to understand and show a piece of text or other data. The markup above is HTML that tells the computer this text should be 'understood' as bold text. In HTML, anything enclosed between a <b> and a </b> is bold and will be displayed as bold in a web browser.

If we save the text document, close Notepad and open it again, the text will not become bold, because Notepad continues to assume we are dealing with plain text. In order for the HTML markup to 'come to live', we need to open the file in a program that actually understands HTML. First, we save the file as an HTML file:

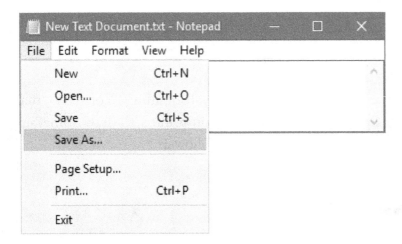

Below, the 'Save As' dialog box opens and here we type 'My New HTML Document.html' in the 'File name' box. Note the ".html" at the end, this lets the computer know that this file is an HTML file.

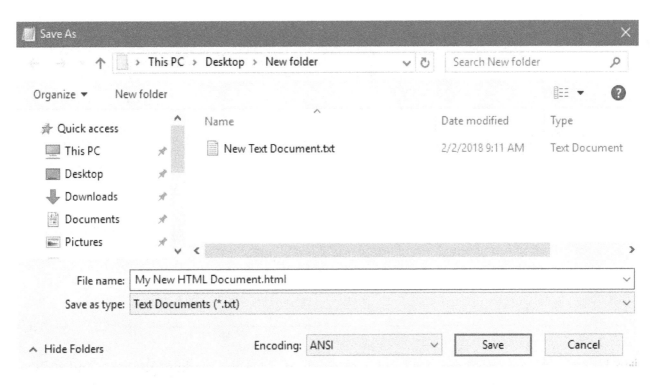

If we look inside the folder, we will now see a new HMTL document:

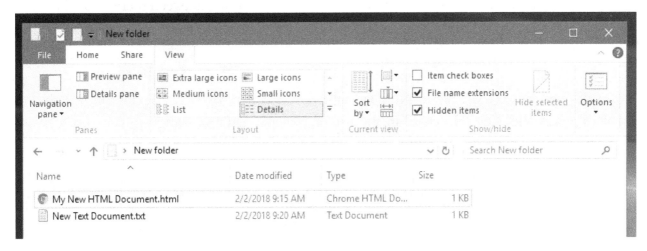

If we open this document by double-clicking on it, this is what shows up:

As can be seen, the text now appears bold, and we do not see the markup (the <b> and </b>), because this markup has been 'interpreted' by the program[1]. When the program sees the <b> and </b> markup, it interprets this as an instruction to display everything between them as bold text.

In this way, we are, in effect, programming the computer. We are telling it 'what to think' about the text.

We can still open the HTML file in Notepad in order to edit it, by right-clicking on it, going to 'Open with', then choosing 'Notepad' in the list (if Notepad isn't showing up, click on 'Choose another app' and you will find it there).

---

[1] The program shown in the screenshot is Chromium, which is a web browser used for…browsing websites. Other browsers include Firefox, Safari, Microsoft Edge, Microsoft Internet Explorer and Opera. A website is merely a bunch of HTML documents linked to one another.

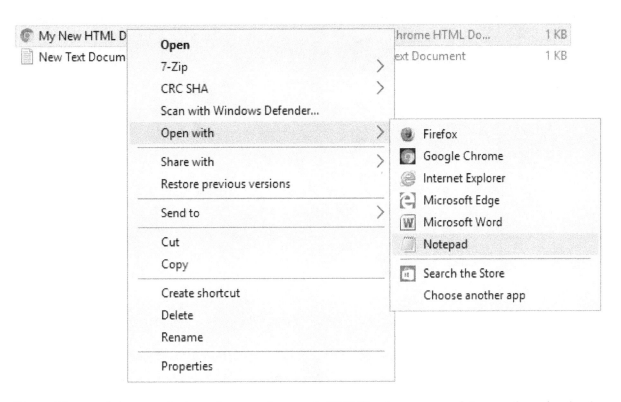

Since Notepad is not designed to understand HTML, the text and its markup both show up, as already mentioned:

We can now add a new line, this time giving it italic markup using the <i> HTML tag:

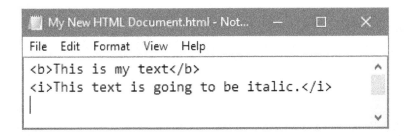

We can now save this document by going to File -> Save.

Now, opening the file again by double-clicking on it, we see the following:

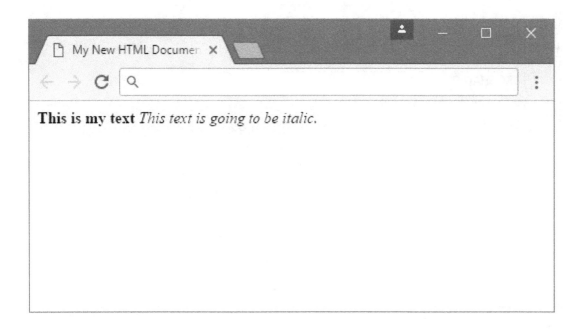

The italic text and the bold text show up on the same line, despite being on different lines when we open the document in Notepad. This is because HTML ignores new lines. The way to create a new line in HTML is to tell HTML to show a new line. There are various ways of achieving this. One way is to use the <br> tag, which tells the program to show a 'break', i.e. a line break or new line. Opening the HTML document in Notepad, we add a '<br>' to the end of the bold line:

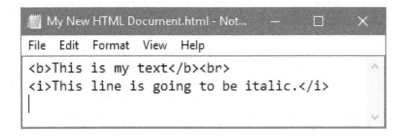

Now, opening the HTML file again in the browser, we see the difference that the <br> tag made:

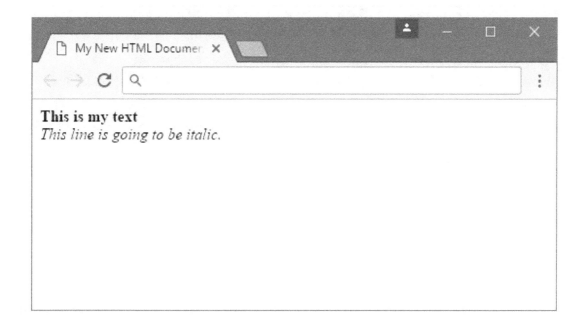

JSTinker

It gets tiresome to have to keep going back and forth between Notepad and the web browser in order to see the results of our changes. Instead, we can use one of many programs that enable us to edit HTML in 'real time' and see its effects immediately. Among such sites are CodePen.io and JSFiddle.net. There is also an open source program called JSTinker that has the same functionality which I will use in this book. You can use this program at my website and other websites.[2] These programs give us a 'playground' or 'sandbox' in which we can play with HTML and CSS, making them very useful for learning. You can follow along by opening the JSTinker link in the footnote below. You can even invite a friend to play along with you by clicking the "collaborate" button shown below.

Opening JSTinker, we see a page with four boxes on it:

---

[2] See http://hawramani.com/wp-content/jstinker/index.html

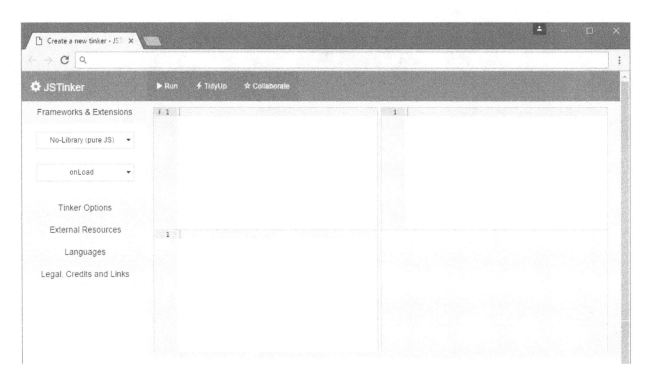

The top left box is where we type our HTML, and the bottom right box is where we see the result.[3] Below is a screenshot of JSTinker with the HTML pasted in the top left box:

Now, if we click the 'Run' button, the program 'interprets' the HTML and displays the result in the bottom right box:

---

[3] The bottom-left box is for JavaScript, which is a language used by coffee-gorging programmers and does not concern us in this book.

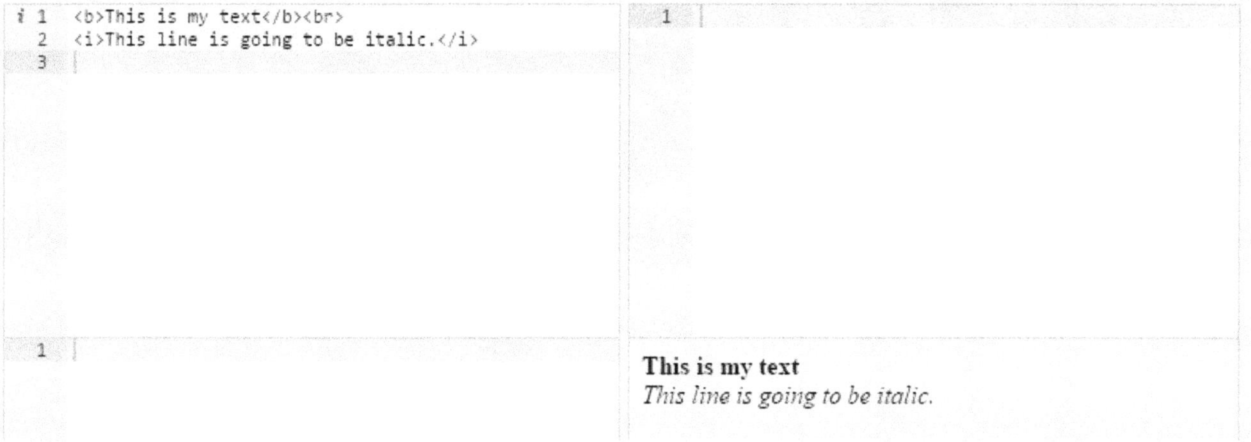

```
i 1  <b>This is my text</b><br>
  2  <i>This line is going to be italic.</i>
  3
```

```
1
```

```
1
```

This is my text
This line is going to be italic.

The numbers you see on the left of the HTML merely tells us the number of that line, which can be helpful when writing code. Let's now add a heading to our HTML. In HTML we use the 'h' tags for headings. These tags start at <h1>, used for the main heading of the document:

```
i 1  <h1>Title</h1>
  2  <b>This is my text</b><br>
  3  <i>This line is going to be italic.</i>
  4
  5
```

```
1
```

```
1
```

Title

This is my text
This line is going to be italic.

For a subtitle, we can use the <h2> tag, as follow (line 2 of the HTML):

```
i  1   <h1>Title</h1>
   2   <h2>Subtitle</h2>
   3   <b>This is my text</b><br>
   4   <i>This line is going to be italic.</i>
   5
   6   |
```

```
   1   |
```

Title

Subtitle

This is my text
This line is going to be italic.

Above, you may have noticed that the title and the subtitle are showing up on separate lines in the bottom right box even though we didn't add a line break between them. The reason for this is that some tags are interpreted as 'blocking' (taking up a whole line) and other tags are interpreted as non-blocking or inline, meaning that they do not take up whole lines.

At this point we can introduce CSS. CSS, which stands for Cascading Style Sheets, is a language that helps us add 'styling' to an HTML document. HTML by itself is only for 'markup'. It enables us to add a few instructions to a document that helps the computer know the difference between a title and a paragraph for example. In technical terms, HTML is for 'semantics', it is not for styling. HTML merely defines the structure of the document, so that we can separate the title from the subtitle, and one section of a document from another. Without HTML or another markup language, a computer would have no way of telling the difference between a title and a subtitle. Both of them are merely lines of text. But thanks to the <h1> and <h2> tags, a computer knows that the <h1> is the main title, the <h2> is the subtitle, and the (as of yet unused) <p> tag is a paragraph.

HTML doesn't do much beyond defining the structure of document. If we want to do more, to add complex grids, borders, backgrounds and other nifty things, we need CSS. The simplest way to add CSS to a document is using the 'style' attribute, as follows (line 1 of the HTML below):

```
i 1   <h1 style="color:gray">Title</h1>
  2   <h2>Subtitle</h2>
  3   <b>This is my text</b><br>
  4   <i>This line is going to be italic.</i>
  5
```

Note how the word 'style' is *inside* the <h1> tag. This tells the browser that we are adding CSS styling to this particular tag. The style we have added is "color:gray". In the CSS language, this means that the tag's content (the heading) should be shown in gray. The CSS is enclosed in quotes, without the quotes the program doesn't know where the CSS ends and the HTML resumes again. Below is the result of the code, which we see once we click the "Run" button mentioned earlier:

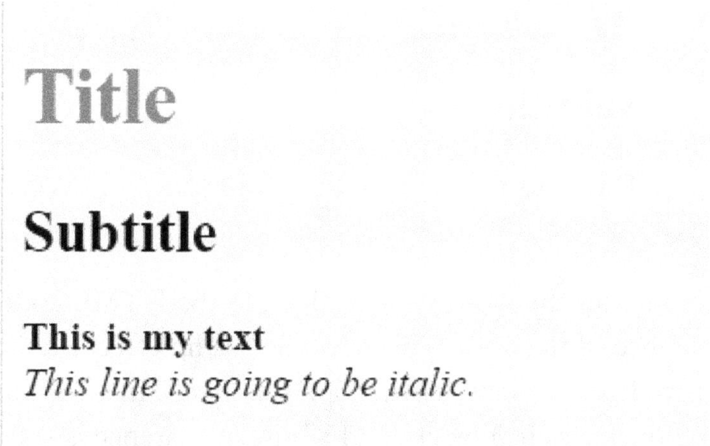

Title

Subtitle

This is my text
This line is going to be italic.

We can now also add a border (lines 1 and 2 of the HTML below):

```
i 1 ▾   <h1 style="color:gray;
  2     border:3px solid red">Title</h1>
  3     <h2>Subtitle</h2>
  4     <b>This is my text</b><br>
  5     <i>This line is going to be italic.</i>
  6
  7     |
```

```
1 |
```

```
1 |
```

Title

Subtitle

This is my text
This line is going to be italic.

We expand the "style" tag by adding a semicolon after the word "gray". Here, in the HTML code, we add a new line in order to tidy up the appearance of the code. This new line has no effect on the appearance of the document. On the next line we have the text "border:3px solid red". In CSS, this means that the tag should have a border whose thickness is 3 pixels, and whose appearance is solid (rather than dashed, for example).

Looking at the appearance of the border, we can see how the <h1> tag is 'blocking' and takes up the whole line. The border does not merely enclose the word 'Title', it encloses the whole of the line, since it does not care about the text, it only cares about the space that is technically taken up by the <h1> tag. That space, as said, is the whole line.

Another way of adding CSS to a document is to use the <style> tag, as shown (lines 1-4 of the HTML below):

```
i  1 ▾ <style>
   2 ▾  h1 {color:gray;
   3    border:3px solid red
   4    }
   5    </style>
   6    <h1>Title</h1>
   7    <h2>Subtitle</h2>
   8    <b>This is my text</b><br>
   9    <i>This line is going to be italic.</i>
  10
  11
```

```
1
```

```
1
```

Title

Subtitle

This is my text
This line is going to be italic.

The result of the above is exactly the same as before. Inside the <style> tag, we use the CSS language to tell the web browser that the <h1> tag should have the color gray and a red border. Everything enclosed in the curly braces { } applies to the tag mentioned before it.

On a new line, we can add styling to <h2> tag, as follows (line 5):

```
i  1 ▾ <style>
   2 ▾  h1 {color:gray;
   3    border:3px solid red
   4    }
   5    h2 {font-style:italic}
   6    </style>
   7    <h1>Title</h1>
   8    <h2>Subtitle</h2>
   9    <b>This is my text</b><br>
  10    <i>This line is going to be italic.</i>
  11
  12
```

```
1
```

```
1
```

Title

Subtitle

The word 'Subtitle' is now in italics. In CSS, it does not matter how we organize the code, for example the code below has the same meaning as the one above:

```
i  1 ▾ <style>
   2 ▾   h1 {color:gray;border:3px solid red
   3    } h2 {font-style:italic}
   4    </style>
   5    <h1>Title</h1>
   6    <h2>Subtitle</h2>
   7    <b>This is my text</b><br>
   8    <i>This line is going to be italic.</i>
```

We generally add new lines in order to make the code more readable. However, we cannot break words, as this would change the meaning of the CSS. For example if we write "ita lic" (with a space between "ita" and "lic"), this breaks the CSS:

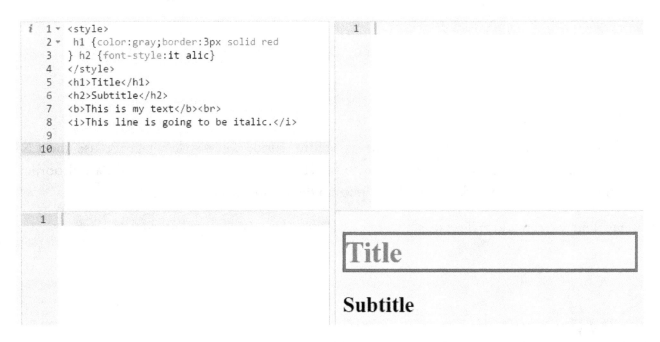

The word 'Subtitle' is now no longer italic. Web browsers are designed to be resilient to broken HTML and CSS, therefore as you can see, the rest of the HTML and CSS continue to function as expected.

JSTinker allows us to separate the HTML from the CSS as follows by putting the CSS inside the box on the right. This helps us keep the code better organized:

Below, I have reorganized the CSS to make it easier to read. This does not affect the meaning of the code.

```
1 ▾ h1 {
2       color:gray;
3       border:3px solid red;
4   }
5 ▾ h2 {
6       font-style:italic;
7   }
8
```

Below, I change the border of the <h1> from solid to dashed (line 3 below):

```
1 ▾ h1 {
2       color:gray;
3       border:3px dashed red;
4   }
5 ▾ h2 {
6       font-style:italic;
7   }
```

Here is the result:

Below, I add a 'dotted' border to the <h2> (line 7):

```
1 ▾ h1 {
2       color:gray;
3       border:3px dashed red;
4   }
5 ▾ h2 {
6       font-style:italic;
7       border:1px dotted black;
8   }
```

Here is the result:

Title

Subtitle

Paragraphs

Earlier, we used the <br> tag to create a line break between the bold and the italic sentences that we wrote:

```
<b>This is my text</b><br>
<i>This line is going to be italic.</i>
```

Another way of achieving the same effect is to use the <p> tag, which stands for "paragraph":

```
<p><b>This is my text.</b></p>
<p><i>This line is going to be italic.</i></p>
```

Above, I have added two paragraphs. Each line begins with a <p> and ends with a </p>, which in HTML means each line is a paragraph. Note the way that at the end of each line, there is a </p> tag, this is a 'closing tag', it tells the computer that this paragraph ends there. After it, a new <p> starts ands ends at the end of the line. This causes each line to be in its own paragraph:

This is my text.

This line is going to be italic.

A paragraph, however, is more than just a line-break. Note how there is no some space between the two lines, when earlier there wasn't. This is because in CSS, by default, paragraphs have a 'margin' associated with them. A margin is space associated with a tag that is outside the tag's 'box'. We can check this out by giving the <p> tag a border in our CSS:

```
 9 ▼ p {
10       border:1px solid black;
11    }
12    |
```

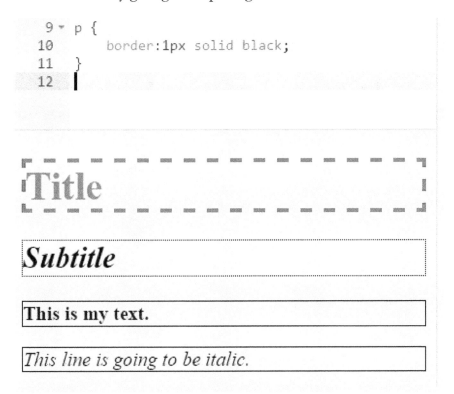

See the way each box has some space under it. We can take away this space by setting the 'margin' CSS property to 0 in the CSS section:

```
 9 ▾  p {
10        border:1px solid black;
11        margin:0;
12    }
13
```

Title

Subtitle

This is my text.
This line is going to be italic.

Now, the boxes are collapsed onto each other. The border between the two boxes is thicker than the rest because that is where the two borders meet, each one adds 1 pixel of length, so that the two together make a thickness of two pixels.

We can now hide the borders to see only the texts by removing the border definition from the CSS for the <p> tag, as follows. I have kept the margin definition.

```
 9 ▾  p {
10        margin:0;
11    }
12
```

Title

Subtitle

This is my text.
This line is going to be italic.

Now, the two paragraphs have no additional space between them. It is as if the two lines are separated by a <br> only.

Spans and Classes

You may remember the <b> tag which we used to create bold text. HTML also offers the <span> tag, which allows to enclose a piece of text to style it. By default, the <span> has no styling of its own, unless we give it a style.

```
i 1    <span>Cat</span> <span>Apple</span>
  2    <span>Dog</span> <span>Orange</span>
  3
```

```
1
```

```
1
```

Cat Apple Dog Orange

In the top left box where the HTML is, we have written the names of four items on two lines. Since this is HTML, the fact that they are on two lines doesn't matter, on the bottom right box they all show up as one line. The way to make them show up on two lines would be to add a <br> tag at the end of the first line, or enclose each line in a <p> and </p>, to turn them into separate paragraphs.

Let's say we want the animal names to have a distinct appearance compared to the fruit names. We can do this through the use of classes:

```
<span class="animal">Cat</span>
<span>Apple</span>
<span class="animal">Dog</span>
<span>Orange</span>
```

In the above, we tell the computer that the stuff inside two of the <span> tags belong to the class 'animal'. Note how the class is enclosed in double quotes. Without that, the computer does not know where the class name begins and where it ends.

By giving the <span> tags class names, we accomplish nothing as of yet. The appearance of the text remains the same. What we need to do is add the CSS that will give the class "animal" a distinct appearance, as follows:

```
1  <span class="animal">Cat</span>
2  <span>Apple</span>
3  <span class="animal">Dog</span>
4  <span>Orange</span>
5
6
7
```

```
1  .animal {
2      font-weight:bold;
3      font-size:150%;
4  }
5
```

Cat Apple **Dog** Orange

In the CSS box, we create a new definition that starts with a dot. In CSS, this denotes that the thing that follows is a class. Without this dot, CSS will think that the thing is a tag name. Inside the curly braces, we give the animal class a bold appearance and we also increase its font size by giving it a font size of 150%, which means one and a half times larger than default.

We can repeat the same process for the fruits:

```
1  <span class="animal">Cat</span>
2  <span class="fruit">Apple</span>
3  <span class="animal">Dog</span>
4  <span class="fruit">Orange</span>
5
6
7
```

```
1 ▾ .animal {
2       font-weight:bold;
3       font-size:150%;
4  }
5 ▾ .fruit {
6       font-style:italic;
7       text-transform:uppercase;
8  }
9
```

```
1
```

Cat *APPLE* **Dog** *ORANGE*

Using the font-style CSS property, we give the fruits an italic appearance. Using text-transform, we turn the fruit names into all-caps text. Note how in the HTML, the words "Apple" and "Orange" are not in all-caps. But using CSS, we can make them appear as if they are in all-caps. We can also make them all-small:

```
1  <span class="animal">Cat</span>
2  <span class="fruit">Apple</span>
3  <span class="animal">Dog</span>
4  <span class="fruit">Orange</span>
5
6
7
```

```
1 ▾ .animal {
2       font-weight:bold;
3       font-size:150%;
4  }
5 ▾ .fruit {
6       font-style:italic;
7       text-transform:lowercase;
8  }
9
```

```
1
```

Cat *apple* **Dog** *orange*

Note that above, the text-transform property is given a value of "lowercase", meaning the text should be transformed to all-lowercase when it is displayed.

An HTML tag can have more than one class, as follows:

```
<span class="animal thing">Cat</span>
<span class="fruit thing">Apple</span>
<span class="animal thing">Dog</span>
<span class="fruit thing">Orange</span>
```

A cat is an animal and a thing, while an apple is a fruit and a thing. We can now give a distinct style to the class "thing", as follows:

```
 1 ▾ .animal {
 2        font-weight:bold;
 3        font-size:150%;
 4   }
 5 ▾ .fruit {
 6        font-style:italic;
 7        text-transform:lowercase;
 8   }
 9 ▾ .thing {
10        text-decoration:underline;
11   }
12   |
```

Cat *apple* Dog *orange*

Since all four <span> tags have the class "thing", all four words get an underlined appearance.

A class name cannot begin with a number, although it can contain numbers elsewhere. For example if we add the number zero before the class name "animal", even if we do everything else correctly, the class stops working:

```
i 1  <span class="0animal thing">Cat</span>
  2  <span class="fruit thing">Apple</span>
  3  <span class="0animal thing">Dog</span>
  4  <span class="fruit thing">Orange</span>
  5
  6
  7  |
```

```
⊠ 1 ▾ .0animal {
⊠ 2      font-weight:bold;
⊠ 3      font-size:150%;
⊠ 4   }
  5 ▾ .fruit {
  6      font-style:italic;
  7      text-transform:lowercase;
  8   }
  9 ▾ .thing {
 10      text-decoration:underline;
 11   }
 12   |
```

```
1  |
```

Cat *apple* Dog *orange*

We can, however, start a class name with a dash or underscore.

Class Conflict

If we give the class "animal" bold styling, while giving the "thing" class normal styling, the two cancel each other out. The computer takes the last definition (the one at the bottom) as the final word.

```
1 ▾ .animal {
2      font-weight:bold;
3   }
4 ▾ .thing {
5      font-weight:normal;
6   }
7  |
```

Cat Apple Dog Orange

We can define the same class multiple times in the same CSS passage. Below, while the "thing" class's normal styling cancels out the "animal" class's bold styling, the final "animal" class definition has the final word, making the words appear bold.

```
1 ▾ .animal {
2        font-weight:bold;
3   }
4 ▾ .thing {
5        font-weight:normal;
6   }
7 ▾ .animal {
8        font-weight:bold;
9   }
10  |
```

Cat Apple Dog Orange

Using the keyword "!important", we can force one of the definitions to become the final word, as follows:

```
1 ▾ .animal {
2        font-weight:bold;
3   }
4 ▾ .thing {
5        font-weight:normal !important;
6   }
7 ▾ .animal {
8        font-weight:bold;
9   }
10  |
```

Cat Apple Dog Orange

!important tells the computer that this definition should be treated as the final word. The use of !important is useful when solving problems, but it is bad practice to use it when doing professional work, and it can make life very difficult, because you can end up with a situation where everything is "important", so that the word loses its meaning.

Romeo and Juliet

Juliet. O Romeo, Romeo! wherefore art thou Romeo?
Deny thy father and refuse thy name;
Or, if thou wilt not, be but sworn my love,
And I 'll no longer be a Capulet.
　　Romeo. [*Aside*] Shall I hear more, or shall I speak at this?
　　Juliet. 'T is but thy name that is my enemy;
Thou art thyself, though not a Montague.
What 's Montague? it is nor hand, nor foot,　　　　　　40
Nor arm, nor face, nor any other part
Belonging to a man.　O, be some other name!
What 's in a name? that which we call a rose
By any other name would smell as sweet;

The above design is taken from a 1881 print of Shakespeare's *Romeo and Juliet*. Using HTML and CSS, we can recreate the design so that we can put it on a website. You may notice the number "40" at the center right of the excerpt, we will ignore that. We will begin with the first part.

We use a <p> tag to enclose each character's set of lines. Inside it, we use <span> tags to differentiate between different parts of the text. The character names are given a "character-name" class (line 1 of the HTML below), while the things they speak are given a "text" class (line 2 of the HTML below). Using <br> tags, we can separate lines as needed (line 3 of the HTML):

```
1   <p><span class="character-name">Juliet.
2   </span><span class="text">O Romeo, Romeo!
3   wherefore art thou Romeo?<br>
4   Deny thy father and refuse thy name;</span></p>
5
6
```

```
Juliet. O Romeo, Romeo! wherefore art thou
Romeo?
Deny thy father and refuse thy name;
```

So far, we have not given any styling to the text, therefore, as can be seen above on the bottom right, the text doesn't have anything special going for it. We give the "character-name" class an italic appearance; we also give it a new font:

```
1 ▼ .character-name {
2       font-style:italic;
3       font-family:'Monotype Corsiva';
4 }
5
```

The result is as folows:

Juliet. O Romeo, Romeo! wherefore art thou Romeo?
Deny thy father and refuse thy name;

The font we used is Monotype Corsiva. This is not exactly the font used in the 1881 print, but it is a good enough approximation. When using fonts, we must take into account the fact that some users may not have that particular font on their computers. Monotype Corsiva is a commonly available font on most computers, while if we used a rarer but more ornate font, it may not show up properly on most users' computers since they will not have the font.[4]

You may notice that the word 'Juliet' is smaller than the rest of the text, which causes it to have an unbalanced appearance. This happens because this word is in a different font compared to the rest, and each font has its own peculiar size. When using multiple fonts side-by-side, we must correct for any imbalance using the font-size CSS property, as follows:

```
1 ▼ .character-name {
2       font-style:italic;
3       font-family:'Monotype Corsiva';
4       font-size:118%;
5 }
```

Here is the result:

Juliet. O Romeo, Romeo! wherefore art thou
Romeo?
Deny thy father and refuse thy name;

Above, the word "Juliet" is now slightly larger (18% larger, to be exact) then before.

---

[4] To get beyond this restriction, we can use the technology known as 'web fonts', which enables a website to carry its own font with it so that it shows up correctly regardless of the user's computer.

You may recall that the word "Juliet" had some space before it in the 1881 design. We can recreate that using the "padding" CSS property, as follows on line 5:

```
1 ▾ .character-name {
2       font-style:italic;
3       font-family:'Monotype Corsiva';
4       font-size:118%;
5       padding-left:15px;
6   }
```

Above, we added 15 pixels of padding to the left of the <span>. If we had used "padding:15px" rather than "padding-left:15px", the padding would have been added all around the <span>. Using "padding-left" we restrict the padding only to the left of the <span>.

Juliet. O Romeo, Romeo! wherefore art thou
Romeo?
Deny thy father and refuse thy name;

Padding is similar to margins in that it adds space around a tag. It is different from it in that padding adds space *inside* the tag, while margin adds space outside of it. We can see this visually by adding a border around the tag, as follows on line 6:

```
1 ▾ .character-name {
2       font-style:italic;
3       font-family:'Monotype Corsiva';
4       font-size:118%;
5       padding-left:15px;
6       border:1px solid black;
7   }
8
```

The result is as follows:

Juliet. O Romeo, Romeo! wherefore art thou
Romeo?
Deny thy father and refuse thy name;

The space created by the "padding-left" propety is inside the border. If we were using a margin, the space would be outside the border, as follows. Below, I have replaced "padding-left" with "margin-left":

```
1 ▾  .character-name {
2        font-style:italic;
3        font-family:'Monotype Corsiva';
4        font-size:118%;
5        margin-left:15px;
6        border:1px solid black;
7    }
```

Juliet. O Romeo, Romeo! wherefore art thou Romeo?
Deny thy father and refuse thy name;

Whether one uses margins or padding can make all the difference in the outcomes of certain designs. For now it is sufficient to know that the two things are distinct. Their different effects will be made clearer throughout this book.

Below is the 1881 design for comparison:

Juliet. O Romeo, Romeo! wherefore art thou Romeo?
Deny thy father and refuse thy name ;

Note how there is some space *after* the word "Juliet", not just before it. We can add this using "padding-right" (line 6 below):

```
1 ▾  .character-name {
2        font-style:italic;
3        font-family:'Monotype Corsiva';
4        font-size:118%;
5        padding-left:15px;
6        padding-right:5px;
7    }
```

Juliet. O Romeo, Romeo! wherefore art thou Romeo?
Deny thy father and refuse thy name;

Below, I use CSS to reduce the size of the font of the <p> tag to 80%, this makes all of the text smaller so that the first line has enough space to show up as one line (line 10 below):

```
 1 ▾ .character-name {
 2        font-style:italic;
 3        font-family:'Monotype Corsiva';
 4        font-size:118%;
 5        padding-left:15px;
 6        padding-right:5px;
 7    }
 8
 9 ▾ p {
10        font-size:80%;
11    }
12    |
```

Juliet. O Romeo. Romeo! wherefore art thou Romeo?
Deny thy father and refuse thy name:

The word "Juliet" retains its 118% size. What is happening is that the style on the <p> tag reduces everything so that it is only 80% as large as before, then Juliet's 118% size, starting from this reduced size, increases it by 18%. In this case, the two size definitions do not conflict, they merely change one another. This is because we are using percentages. If we were using pixels, then one font size would overwrite the other (lines 4 and 10):

```
 1 ▾ .character-name {
 2        font-style:italic;
 3        font-family:'Monotype Corsiva';
 4        font-size:17px;
 5        padding-left:15px;
 6        padding-right:5px;
 7    }
 8
 9 ▾ p {
10        font-size:14px;
11    }
12    |
```

Juliet. O Romeo. Romeo! wherefore art thou Romeo?
Deny thy father and refuse thy name:

Even though the 14 pixel font size on the <p> tag is last, it does not have the final word. The size of "Juliet" remains at 17 pixels. This is because in CSS, a style added to a *class name* takes precedence over a style added to a *tag name*. Whatever we add to "character-name" is considered more important by CSS than whatever we added to the <p> tag, and for this reason it overrules it.

We gave the "character-name" class italic styling. We could have instead used an <i> tag, as follows (line 1 of the HTML):

```
1  <p><i class="character-name">Juliet.
2  </i><span class="text">O Romeo, Romeo!
3  wherefore art thou Romeo?<br>
4  Deny thy father and refuse thy name;</span></p>
5
6
```

```
1  .character-name {
2      font-family:'Monotype Corsiva';
3      font-size:17px;
4      padding-left:15px;
5      padding-right:5px;
6  }
7
8  p {
9      font-size:14px;
10 }
11
```

Juliet. O Romeo, Romeo! wherefore art thou Romeo? Deny thy father and refuse thy name;

Notice that above the word Juliet is enclosed in an <i> tag rather than a <span>. But the <i> tag continues to have the "character-name" class, so that it continues to have the CSS properties (like the Monotype Corsiva font) that we gave to this class.

In the CSS, I removed the "font-style:italic" property. The <i> tag has default italic styling, therefore this is no longer needed.

It is, however, better not to use the <i> and <b> tags for styling. It is best to use <span> tags and add the styling in the CSS. This allows us more leverage in the future. Maybe in the future we decide to change the appearance of the character names to bold instead of italic. If we had used <i> tags for all the character names, we would have had to go through thousands of lines of HTML to remove every <i> tag and change it to a <b> tag. But thanks to using <span> tags and CSS, changing one or two lines or CSS can change the appearance of every single character name in the text.

Now, we are ready to add two more lines of poetry:

```
i 1 ▾ <p><i class="character-name">Juliet.
  2    </i><span class="text">O Romeo, Romeo!
  3    wherefore art thou Romeo?<br>
  4    Deny thy father and refuse thy name;<br>
  5    Or, if thou wilt not, be but swon my love,<br>
  6    And I'll no longer be a Capulet.</span></p>
  7
  8 |
```

```
 1 ▾ .character-name {
 2        font-family:'Monotype Corsiva';
 3        font-size:17px;
 4        padding-left:15px;
 5        padding-right:5px;
 6    }
 7
 8 ▾ p {
 9        font-size:14px;
10    }
11
```

1 |

Juliet. O Romeo, Romeo! wherefore art thou Romeo?
Deny thy father and refuse thy name:
Or, if thou wilt not, be but swon my love,
And I'll no longer be a Capulet.

Since the two lines belong to the same passage, we add them inside the earlier <span> and <p> tags, rather than creating new ones for them.

As a reminder, here is the 1881 design again:

Juliet. O Romeo, Romeo! wherefore art thou Romeo?
Deny thy father and refuse thy name;
Or, if thou wilt not, be but sworn my love,
And I 'll no longer be a Capulet.
Romeo. [*Aside*] Shall I hear more, or shall I speak at this?
Juliet. 'T is but thy name that is my enemy;
Thou art thyself, though not a Montague.
What 's Montague? it is nor hand, nor foot,   40
Nor arm, nor face, nor any other part
Belonging to a man.   O, be some other name!
What 's in a name? that which we call a rose
By any other name would smell as sweet;

Let's now add Romeo's line:

```
i 1 ▾ <p><span class="character-name">Juliet.
  2    </span><span class="text">O Romeo, Romeo!
  3    wherefore art thou Romeo?<br>
  4    Deny thy father and refuse thy name;<br>
  5    Or, if thou wilt not, be but swon my love,<br>
  6    And I'll no longer be a Capulet.</span></p>
  7 ▾ <p><span class="character-name">Romeo.</span>
  8 ▾ <span class="text">[Aside] Shall I hear more,
  9    or shall I speak at this?</span></p>
```

```
  1 ▾ .character-name {
  2        font-style:italic;
  3        font-family:'Monotype Corsiva';
  4        font-size:17px;
  5        padding-left:15px;
  6        padding-right:5px;
  7    }
  8
  9 ▾ p {
 10        font-size:14px;
 11    }
 12
```

```
  1  |
```

Juliet. O Romeo, Romeo! wherefore art thou Romeo?
Deny thy father and refuse thy name:
Or, if thou wilt not, be but swon my love,
And I'll no longer be a Capulet.

Romeo. [Aside] Shall I hear more, or shall I speak at this?

I created a new <p> tag for Romeo's line. The <p> tag, as has already been mentioned, has a margin below it by default, as can be seen in the excessive amount of space between Juliet and Romeo's parts. We can undo the space by setting the "margin" CSS property to zero:

```
i 1 ▾ <p><span class="character-name">Juliet.
  2    </span><span class="text">O Romeo, Romeo!
  3    wherefore art thou Romeo?<br>
  4    Deny thy father and refuse thy name;<br>
  5    Or, if thou wilt not, be but swon my love,<br>
  6    And I'll no longer be a Capulet.</span></p>
  7 ▾ <p><span class="character-name">Romeo.</span>
  8 ▾ <span class="text">[Aside] Shall I hear more,
  9    or shall I speak at this?</span></p>
```

```
  1 ▾ .character-name {
  2        font-style:italic;
  3        font-family:'Monotype Corsiva';
  4        font-size:17px;
  5        padding-left:15px;
  6        padding-right:5px;
  7    }
  8
  9 ▾ p {
 10        font-size:14px;
 11        margin:0;
 12    }
 13    |
```

```
  1  |
```

Juliet. O Romeo, Romeo! wherefore art thou Romeo?
Deny thy father and refuse thy name:
Or, if thou wilt not, be but swon my love,
And I'll no longer be a Capulet.
Romeo. [Aside] Shall I hear more, or shall I speak at this?

Due to certain technicalities, if we had merely done "margin-bottom:0", this wouldn't have accomplished anything. We rather have to set the entire "margin" property to zero, then, if desired, we can add back some margin:

```
 9 ▾ p {
10      font-size:14px;
11      margin:0;
12      margin-bottom:2px;
13   }
14
```

Juliet. O Romeo, Romeo! wherefore art thou Romeo?
Deny thy father and refuse thy name;
Or, if thou wilt not, be but swon my love,
And I'll no longer be a Capulet.

Romeo. [Aside] Shall I hear more, or shall I speak at this?

The "margin:0" takes effect first, removing all margins. The "margin-bottom:2px" takes effect next, adding two pixels of margin underneath each paragraph. This is quite minimal and barely visible.

Below is the rest of the poem marked up in HTML:

```
 1 ▾ <p><span class="character-name">Juliet.
 2   </span><span class="text">O Romeo, Romeo!
 3   wherefore art thou Romeo?<br>
 4   Deny thy father and refuse thy name;<br>
 5   Or, if thou wilt not, be but swon my love,<br>
 6   And I'll no longer be a Capulet.</span></p>
 7 ▾ <p><span class="character-name">Romeo.</span>
 8 ▾ <span class="text">[Aside] Shall I hear more,
 9   or shall I speak at this?</span></p>
10 ▾ <p><span class="character-name">Juliet.
11   </span><span class="text">'T is but thy name
12   that is my enemy;<br>
13   Thou art thyself, though not a Montague.<br>
14   What's Montague? it is nor hand, nor foot,<br>
15   Nor arm, nor face, nor any other part<br>
16   Belonging to a man. O, be some other name!<br>
17   What's in a name? that which we call a rose<br>
18   By any other name would smell as sweet;
19   </span></p>
```

You may note that the HTML is quite hard to read. We can't easily see where one thing begins and another ends. We can make it somewhat more readable by separating different sections:

```
 i  1 ▾  <p>
    2 ▾      <span class="character-name">Juliet.
    3    </span>
    4
    5 ▾      <span class="text">O Romeo, Romeo!
    6    wherefore art thou Romeo?<br>
    7    Deny thy father and refuse thy name;<br>
    8    Or, if thou wilt not,
    9    be but swon my love,<br>
   10    And I'll no longer be a Capulet.</span>
   11    </p>
   12
   13 ▾  <p>
   14 ▾      <span class="character-name">Romeo.
   15    </span>
   16 ▾      <span class="text">[Aside] Shall I
   17        hear more, or shall I
   18        speak at this?</span>
   19    </p>
```

Tidying up code to make it easier to read is known as 'code formatting' and 'code styling' and has no effect on the final product.

Juliet. O Romeo, Romeo! wherefore art thou Romeo?
Deny thy father and refuse thy name;
Or, if thou wilt not, be but swon my love,
And I'll no longer be a Capulet.

Romeo. [Aside] Shall I hear more, or shall I speak at this?

Juliet. 'T is but thy name that is my enemy:
Thou art thyself, though not a Montague.
What's Montague? it is nor hand, nor foot,
Nor arm, nor face, nor any other part
Belonging to a man. O, be some other name!
What's in a name? that which we call a rose
By any other name would smell as sweet;

If you look at the 1881 original, you will notice that there is a somewhat large space in front of the "O" in "O, be some other name!". We can enclose the "O" in a new <span> and give it an "extra-space" class:

```
25   that is my enemy;<br>
26   Thou art thyself, though
27   not a Montague.<br>
28   What's Montague? it is
29   nor hand, nor foot,<br>
30   Nor arm, nor face, nor any other part<br>
31   Belonging to a man.
32   <span class="extra-space">O</span>,
33   be some other name!<br>
```

```
15   .extra-space {
16       padding-left:5px;
17   }
18
```

In the CSS, we gave the "extra-space" class a left padding of 5 pixels. The result is as follows:

Nor arm, nor face, nor any other part
Belonging to a man. O, be some other name!
What's in a name? that which we call a rose
By any other name would smell as sweet:

Another solution would be to use a non-breaking-space entity, as follows (line 32 of the HTML):

```
31   Belonging to a man.
32     O,
33   be some other name!<br>
34   What's in a name? that
35   which we call a rose<br>
36   By any other name would smell as sweet;
37   </span>
38   </p>
```

```
1
```

Juliet. O Romeo, Romeo! wherefore art thou Romeo?
Deny thy father and refuse thy name;
Or, if thou wilt not, be but swon my love,
And I'll no longer be a Capulet.
   Romeo. [Aside] Shall I hear more, or shall I speak at this?
   Juliet. 'T is but thy name that is my enemy;
Thou art thyself, though not a Montague.
What's Montague? it is nor hand, nor foot,
Nor arm, nor face, nor any other part
Belonging to a man. O, be some other name!
What's in a name? that which we call a rose
By any other name would smell as sweet:

The " " (starting with an ampersand and ending with a semicolon) is a special instruction to the computer to create a space at this location.[5] Using two of them back-to-back tells the computer to add two spaces here. The end result is that the "O" now has more space to its left.

Using " " is not good practice because it reduces your leverage to make changes in the future. If, in the future, you wanted these extra spaces to be much larger or smaller, you would have to go through all of your HTML and make changes. If, however, you had used <span> and an "extra-space" class, you would have been able to change everything by making a few changes to the CSS.

_____

[5] These special instructions are known as "HTML entities", and there are thousands of them, although you generally only have use for a few of them.

Divs

The <div> tag (standing for "division") enables us to divide an HTML document into multiple sections. <div> tags are often the starting point for any sophisticated design project. <div> tags are like <span> tags in that they do not carry any default styles. Their difference is that while <span> tags are *inline*, meaning that they can used in the middle of a paragraph to add some style to a word, a <div> tag is *blocking*, it is a block or rectangle that takes up a whole line of space, similar to a <p> tag. Unlike a <p> tag, it doesn't come with any pre-defined margins.

```
1    <div class="division-a"></div>
2    <div class="division-b"></div>
3
```

Above, we have defined two <div> tags with nothing inside them. If you run this code, you will get a blank output, because <div> tags by default have zero height and are therefore invisible. To explore what <div> tags are like, we will first give them a solid black border in the CSS and see what happens:

```
1    <div class="division-a"></div>
2    <div class="division-b"></div>
3
4
```

```
1 ▾ div {
2        border:1px solid black;
3    }
4
5
```

```
1
```

The <div> tags show up as nothing but a black bar. This is because each <div> tag takes up a whole line. Since we have given each div a 1 pixel border, what ends up showing are two bars, each two pixels high. They are basically long borders with nothing inside them.

Let's now give the <div> tags some height:

```
i 1    <div class="division-a"></div>          1 ▾ div {
  2    <div class="division-b"></div>         ⚠ 2        border:1px solid black;
  3                                              3        height:50px;
  4    |                                         4   }
                                                 5
                                                 6   |
```

```
  1   |
```

Now the true appearance of the <div> tags becomes apparent. They are rectangles that take up whole lines. Below, I have given the <div> tag a margin of 20 pixels in the CSS definition. This margin applies to all sides of each div, adding 20 pixels of margin above, below and to the right and left of each div. The end result is that the <div> tags are separated and made smaller as 20 pixels of margin are added on all sides. Their height does not change because the CSS definition continues to force a height of 50 pixels.

```
i 1    <div class="division-a"></div>          1 ▾ div {
  2    <div class="division-b"></div>         ⚠ 2        border:1px solid black;
  3                                              3        height:50px;
  4    |                                         4        margin:20px;
                                                 5   }
                                                 6
                                                 7
                                                 8   |
```

```
  1   |
```

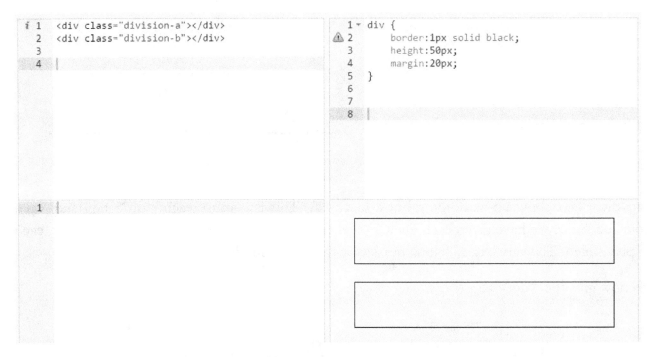

We will now add some content to each <div> tag (lines 2-3 and 6-7 of the HTML):

```
 i  1 ▾ <div class="division-a">
    2       <h1>Main Title</h1>
    3       <p>This is the main text.</p>
    4  </div>
    5 ▾ <div class="division-b">
    6       <h2>Subsidiary Title</h2>
    7       <p>Cautionary tale.</p>
    8  </div>
    9
   10  |
```

```
    1 ▾ div {
 ⚠  2       border:1px solid black;
    3       height:50px;
    4       margin:20px;
    5  }
    6
    7
    8  |
```

Main Title

This is the main text.
Subsidiary Title

Cautionary tale.

It can be seen that the content has a broken appearance. This is because in the CSS, we are forcing each <div> to have a height of 50 pixels, which is not high enough to contain the new content we added. The result is that the content "overflows", it pours out of the top <div> tag and spills over the next one. Using CSS, we can prevent overflow from taking place (line 5 of the CSS below):

```
 i  1 ▾ <div class="division-a">
    2       <h1>Main Title</h1>
    3       <p>This is the main text.</p>
    4  </div>
    5 ▾ <div class="division-b">
    6       <h2>Subsidiary Title</h2>
    7       <p>Cautionary tale.</p>
    8  </div>
    9
   10  |
```

```
    1 ▾ div {
 ⚠  2       border:1px solid black;
    3       height:50px;
    4       margin:20px;
    5       overflow:hidden;
    6  }
    7
    8
    9  |
```

Main Title

Subsidiary Title

Using "overflow:hidden", we cause the overflowed content to disappear. This is not ideal, since now the paragraphs cannot be seen.

Another thing we can do is use "overflow:scroll" (line 5 of the CSS below):

```
1 ▾ div {
⚠ 2        border:1px solid black;
3          height:50px;
4          margin:20px;
5          overflow:scroll;
6    }
7
```

In this case, scroll bars appear to the left of the <div> tags if the content is too large, allowing the user to scroll through the content.

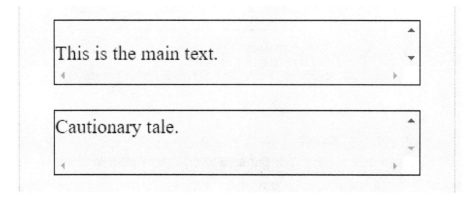

We can also spare ourselves all this trouble by simply removing the "height" property in the CSS. This will allow each <div> to expand in height so that all of the content can be seen:

```
i  1 ▾ <div class="division-a">
   2      <h1>Main Title</h1>
   3      <p>This is the main text.</p>
   4  </div>
   5 ▾ <div class="division-b">
   6      <h2>Subsidiary Title</h2>
   7      <p>Cautionary tale.</p>
   8  </div>
   9
  10  |
```

```
1 ▾ div {
2      border:1px solid black;
3      margin:20px;
4  }
5
6
7  |
```

```
1  |
```

Main Title

This is the main text.

Subsidiary Title

Cautionary tale.

An empty <div> tag that does not have a height will be invisible. But if the <div> has visible content inside it, we can take away the height property and it will continue showing up.

We can now make use of the <div> tags' classes by making the second <div> tag's contents smaller (lines 6-8 of the CSS):

```
1 ▾ div {
2      border:1px solid black;
3      margin:20px;
4  }
5
6 ▾ .division-b {
7      font-size:70%;
8  }
```

Here is the result:

Main Title

This is the main text.

Subsidiary Title

Cautionary tale.

Using <div> tags, I can give all the paragraphs in a specific part of an HTML document follow a certain style while leaving other paragraphs alone (lines 9-11 below):

```
1 ▾ div {
2        border:1px solid black;
3        margin:20px;
4   }
5
6 ▾ .division-b {
7        font-size:70%;
8   }
9 ▾ .division-b p {
10       font-style:italic;
11  }
12
```

The CSS definition ".division-b p" (line 9 above) tells the web browser to apply the style that follows to every paragraph contained inside the class ".division-b". This has no effect on the paragraphs contained outside of it, such as the paragraph "This is the main text" inside division-a.

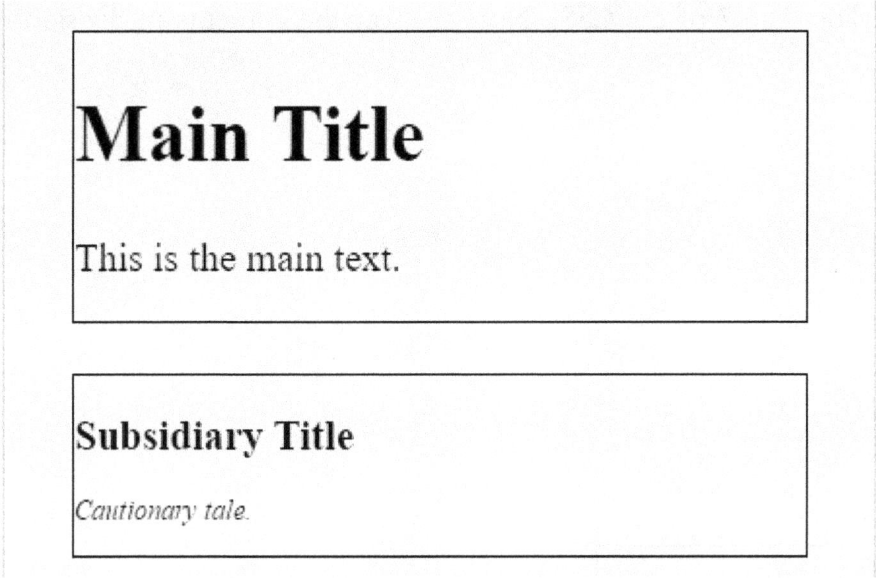

Main Title

This is the main text.

Subsidiary Title

Cautionary tale.

An important use of <div> tags is nesting, where we put one <div> inside another like Russian dolls. Below, I have moved division-b inside division-a

```
1  <div class="division-a">
2      <h1>Main Title</h1>
3      <p>This is the main text.</p>
4      <div class="division-b">
5          <h2>Subsidiary Title</h2>
6          <p>Cautionary tale.</p>
7      </div>
8  </div>
```

The result is as follows:

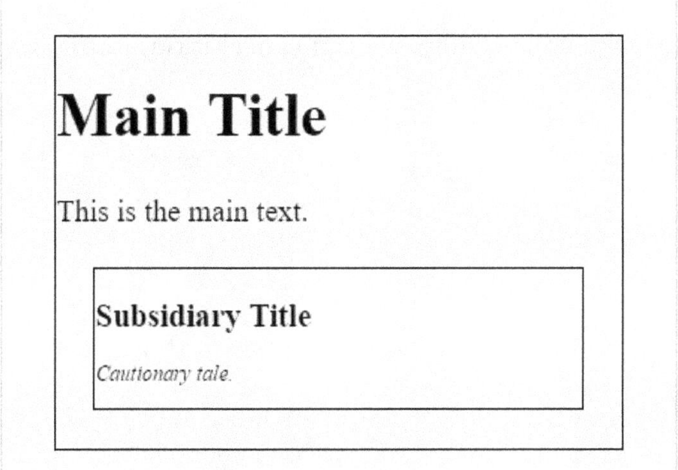

Main Title

This is the main text.

Subsidiary Title

Cautionary tale.

Thanks to the "cascading" nature of CSS (remember that CSS stands for Cascading Style Sheets), styles I add to division-a will also cascade down to the <div> tags contained inside it. Below, I make division-a have an italic styling (line 7 of the CSS). Note the way the contents of division-b also become italic:

```
1 ▾ div {
2      border: 1px solid black;
3      margin: 20px;
4   }
5
6 ▾ .division-a {
7      font-style:italic;
8   }
```

Here is the result:

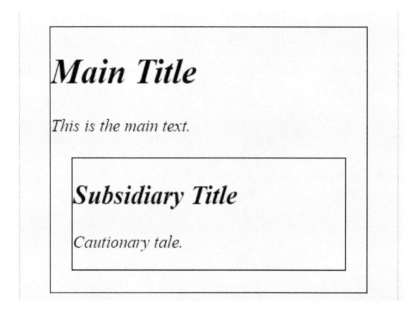

If we do not want the content of division-b to get the italic styling, we can cancel it out in this way (line 10 of the CSS):

```
1 ▾ div {
2      border: 1px solid black;
3      margin: 20px;
4   }
5
6 ▾ .division-a {
7      font-style:italic;
8   }
9 ▾ .division-b {
10     font-style:normal;
11  }
```

Here is the result:

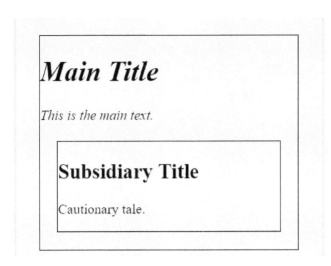

Above, on line 7 we declare that everything inside division-a should be italic. On line 10, we declare that everything inside division-b should be normal rather than italic. These two styles conflict, since now division-b is being told by line 7 to be italic and by line 10 to be normal. The normal style wins because it is *more specific*, since it applies directly to division-b. The italic styling only applies to division-b by chance, due to it being inside division-a. But the normal styling is specifically attached to division-b, therefore it takes precedence.

Styling Divs

We can now better study what padding is. Above, we added a margin of 20 pixels to each rectangle. You can see that the texts are uncomfortably close to the borders. What if we wanted to add space between the text and the borders that enclose them? We cannot do that with margin, since the margin is outside the borders. Padding allows us to do this. Padding is space *inside* the borders:

Below, I have added 10 pixels of padding to the CSS for the <div> tag (line 4 of the CSS), meaning it applies to both rectangles, since both of them are <div> elements.

```
1 ▾ div {
2       border: 1px solid black;
3       margin: 20px;
4       padding:10px;
5   }
```

Here is the result:

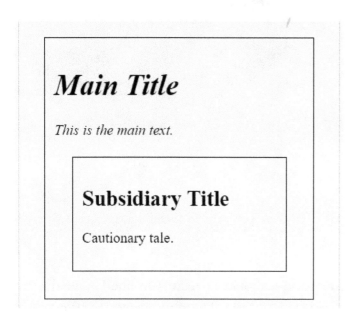

You can see that now the word "Main Title" has more space to its left. The same applies to the "Subsidiary Title".

Below, I have added some shadow to division-b using the "box-shadow" CSS property (line 12 of the CSS):

```
10 ▼  .division-b {
11        font-style:normal;
12        box-shadow:5px 5px 1px gray;
13    }
14    |
```

Main Title

This is the main text.

Subsidiary Title

Cautionary tale.

The pixels defined in the "box-shadow" property define the nature of the shadow. It is five pixels to the right, five pixels down, and larger by 1 pixel from the original rectangle, and its color is gray. You can play around with these numbers to produce various interesting effects (line 12 below):

```
10 ▾  .division-b {
11        font-style:normal;
12        box-shadow:15px 5px 21px gray;
13    }
14
```

The result is as follows:

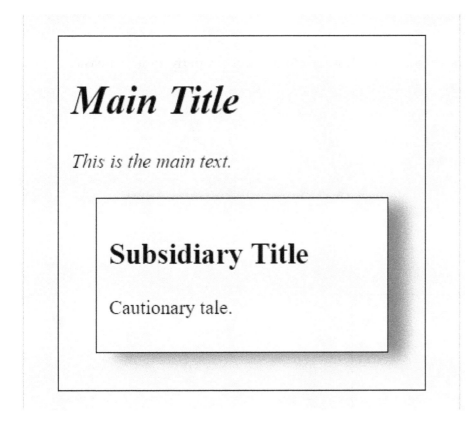

By taking away the border defined in the CSS on line 2, we can give a somewhat artistic appearance to the arrangement:

```
1 ▾  div {
2        margin: 20px;
3        padding:10px;
4    }
5
```

The result is as follows:

Main Title

This is the main text.

Subsidiary Title

Cautionary tale.

Below, I bring back the borders to show the border-radius CSS property (line 3 below), which allows us to create curved borders:

```
1 ▾ div {
2       border: 1px solid black;
3       border-radius:10px;
4       margin: 20px;
5       padding:10px;
6   }
```

The result is as follows:

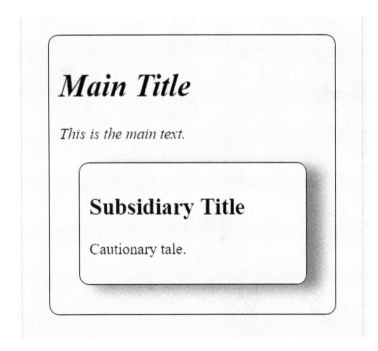

Even if we take the borders away again, the effect of the border-radius remains, as seen in the curvedness of the shadow below:

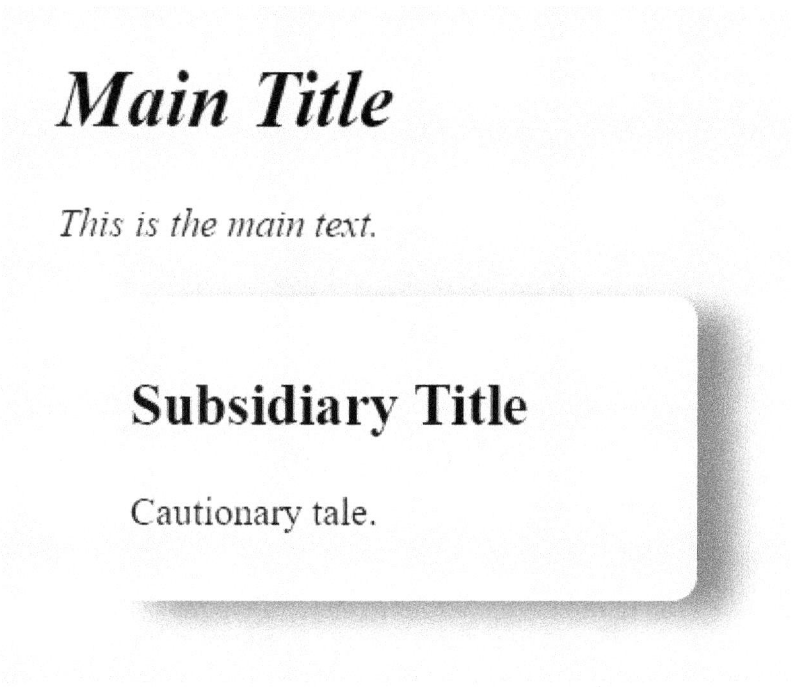

Main Title

This is the main text.

Subsidiary Title

Cautionary tale.

Below, I have given a gray background to division-a:

```
 7 ▾  .division-a {
 8        font-style:italic;
 9        background:#ccc;
10    }
```

The CSS property "background:#ccc" assigns a background to the division (and to any divisions contained inside it). The color code #ccc refers to a specific location on the RGB color spectrum that happens to be gray. In order to easily find out the code for a color, you can Google "CSS color chooser" and you will find many websites that let you pick colors and give you the RGB "hex" code for it.

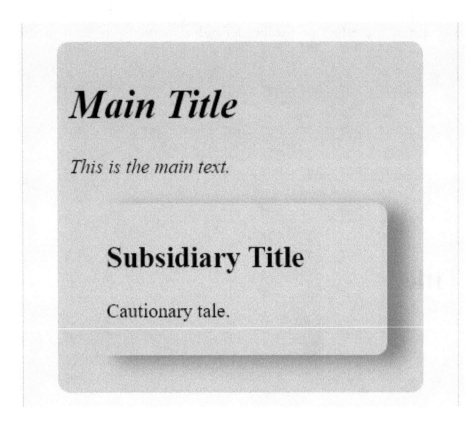

By default, <div> elements have a transparent background.[6] Since division-b is transparent, the gray background of division-a shows through it. Below, I have given division-b a white background that overrides that gray background of division-a (line 14 of the CSS):

---

[6] The difference between a tag and an element is that the word "tag" refers to the HTML, while the word "element" refers to the *result* of the HTML that is displayed in a browser. When we see a <p>, this is a paragraph tag. But when we see that actual paragraph in an article, that is a paragraph element. Sometimes they are used interchangeably, especially when working with HTML. When working with CSS and JavaScript, usually the word "element" is used rather than tag, because CSS and JavaScript generally deal with the result of the HTML.

```
 7 ▾ .division-a {
 8        font-style:italic;
 9        background:#ccc;
10   }
11 ▾ .division-b {
12        font-style:normal;
13        box-shadow:15px 5px 21px gray;
14        background:white;
```

Main Title

This is the main text.

Subsidiary Title

Cautionary tale.

Instead of writing 'white' for the background, I could have written its RGB hex code, which is #fff.

This page intentionally left blank

2. Understanding Lists

Lists are an important part of HTML with many uses. There are two types of lists, ordered and unordered.

```
1  <ol>
2      <li>First item.</li>
3      <li>Second item.</li>
4      <li>Third item.</li>
5  </ol>
6
```

```
1
```

```
1
```

1. First item.
2. Second item.
3. Third item.

Above is an ordered list, which is created using the <ol> tag. Ordered lists are automatically numbered by the browser, as can be seen in the output in the bottom right. Inside the <ol> tag, we use <li> ("list item") tags to add items to the list.

Using the "type" attribute, we can change the numbering system used by the <ol> tag, as follows (line 1 below):

```
1  <ol type="i">
2      <li>First item.</li>
3      <li>Second item.</li>
4      <li>Third item.</li>
5      <li>Fourth item.</li>
6  </ol>
7
```

Above, I have set the type to 'i', which means lower-case Roman numerals:

i. First item.
ii. Second item.
iii. Third item.
iv. Fourth item.

Changing the type to "A" makes the browser show the items given alphabetic 'numbering':

```
1  <ol type="A">
2      <li>First item.</li>
3      <li>Second item.</li>
4      <li>Third item.</li>
5      <li>Fourth item.</li>
6  </ol>
7
```

A. First item.
B. Second item.
C. Third item.
D. Fourth item.

We will introduce various of these numbering types throughout this chapter.

The <ol> tag, like a <div> tag, is *block* element that takes up the whole line, as can be seen below, where I have given the <ol> tag a border (line 2 of the CSS):

```
1  <ol type="A">
2      <li>First item.</li>
3      <li>Second item.</li>
4      <li>Third item.</li>
5      <li>Fourth item.</li>
6  </ol>
7
```

```
1  ol {
2      border:1px solid #000;
3  }
4
```

A. First item.
B. Second item.
C. Third item.
D. Fourth item.

The border color I have used is #000 (three zeroes), which is the same as "black". Beginners sometimes mistakenly type capital letter O's ("O" as in "Oscar") instead of zeroes. Coding programs like JSTinker help us distinguish between zeroes and capital O's by adding a diagonal slash inside zeroes, as seen below:

```
Three zeroes:
000
Three capital O's:
OOO
```

To continue our analysis, below I have given a dashed border to the <li> tags (lines 4-6 of the CSS).

```
1 ▾ ol {
2       border:1px solid #000;
3   }
4 ▾ li {
5       border:1px dashed #000;
6   }
7 |
```

See what happens:

```
A. First item.
B. Second item.
C. Third item.
D. Fourth item.
```

The numbering (the A, B, C and D) are part of the <ol> tag, but they are outside the <li> tags. Yet, they are attached to the <li> tags. Let's give the <li> tag a left margin of 20 pixels (line 6 of the CSS below):

```
i 1 ▾ <ol type="A">
  2       <li>First item.</li>
  3       <li>Second item.</li>
  4       <li>Third item.</li>
  5       <li>Fourth item.</li>
  6  </ol>
  7  |

  1  |
```

```
1 ▾ ol {
2       border:1px solid #000;
3  }
4 ▾ li {
5       border:1px dashed #000;
6       margin-left:20px;
7  }
8  |
```

A.	First item.
B.	Second item.
C.	Third item.
D.	Fourth item.

We have now increased the distance between the <li> tags and the <ol> tag that contains them. Yet the numbering has moved right along with the <li> tags.

In order to increase the distance between the list items and their numbering, we will have to use left padding (line 6 of the CSS below):

```
i 1 ▾ <ol type="A">
  2       <li>First item.</li>
  3       <li>Second item.</li>
  4       <li>Third item.</li>
  5       <li>Fourth item.</li>
  6  </ol>
  7  |

  1  |
```

```
1 ▾ ol {
2       border:1px solid #000;
3  }
4 ▾ li {
5       border:1px dashed #000;
6       padding-left:20px;
7  }
8  |
```

A.	First item.
B.	Second item.
C.	Third item.
D.	Fourth item.

Taking away the borders by setting them to zero (lines 2 and 5 of the CSS), the list now appears as follows:

```
i 1▾ <ol type="A">
  2       <li>First item.</li>
  3       <li>Second item.</li>
  4       <li>Third item.</li>
  5       <li>Fourth item.</li>
  6  </ol>
  7  |
```

```
  1▾ ol {
i 2       border:0px solid #000;
  3  }
  4▾ li {
i 5       border:0px dashed #000;
  6       padding-left:20px;
  7  }
  8  |
```

```
  1  |
```

A. First item.
B. Second item.
C. Third item.
D. Fourth item.

Instead of deleting the border definitions in the CSS, I have set the borders to zero pixels, which means that they will not show up. It is the same as deleting the definitions, except that now I can bring the borders back more easily, merely by changing the zero again to 1 or some other number, instead of having to type the border definitions again.

If we give a specific style to the <li> tags, this also affects the style of their numbering. Below, I have made the list items italic (line 7 of the CSS):

```
  1▾ ol {
i 2       border:0px solid #000;
  3  }
  4▾ li {
i 5       border:0px dashed #000;
  6       padding-left:20px;
  7       font-style:italic;
  8  }
  9  |
```

This makes their numbering also italic:

A. *First item.*
B. *Second item.*
C. *Third item.*
D. *Fourth item.*

This is not always ideal. Sometimes you want the numbering to have one style and the text itself another style. We can create our own custom numbering to get around this issue and create our own self-styled numbering.

To do that, first we hide the existing numbering by adding a line of CSS to the <ol> tag (line 3 below):

```
i 1▼ <ol type="A">
  2      <li>First item.</li>
  3      <li>Second item.</li>
  4      <li>Third item.</li>
  5      <li>Fourth item.</li>
  6  </ol>
  7  |




  1 |
```

```
     1▼ ol {
i    2      border:0px solid #000;
     3      list-style:none;
     4  }
     5▼ li {
i    6      border:0px dashed #000;
     7      padding-left:20px;
     8      font-style:italic;
     9  }
    10  |




              First item.
              Second item.
              Third item.
              Fourth item.
```

The CSS property "list-style:none" tells the browser not to show any numbering. Next, using some advanced features of CSS, we create our own "counter" (lines 5, 11 and 15 of the CSS):

```
     1
     2▼ ol {
i    3      border:0px solid #000;
     4      list-style:none;
     5      counter-reset:mylist;
     6  }
     7▼ li {
i    8      border:0px dashed #000;
     9      padding-left:20px;
    10      font-style:italic;
    11      counter-increment: mylist;
    12  }
    13
    14▼ li:before {
    15    content: counter(mylist);
    16  }
    17
```

At the top of the CSS, we have added a new CSS counter, "counter-reset:mylist" creates a 'variable' called 'mylist'. CSS gives this variable a default value of zero. In the <li> tag's CSS, we have added "counter-increment: mylist". This tells the browser to increase the "mylist" counter for every <li> tag that it creates. Finally, we have created an entirely new definition, which starts with "li:before". This is known as a CSS pseudo-selector, and it is a way of adding content before a particular element.[7] Here, we are saying that before every <li> tag, we want to add the content "counter(mylist)". This tells the browser that before every <li> tag, the value of a CSS counter named "mylist" should be printed.

1First item.
2Second item.
3Third item.
4Fourth item.

The end result, as seen, is that certain numbers are printed before each list item. They don't look good, but now we have great power to change their appearance.

If you found the idea of a variable and a counter confusing, there is no need to worry. Most people learn CSS by copying code from other people on the Internet, often while only half understanding what they are doing. It is sufficient to be able to copy the code above and use it in your own project. It will work even if you do not understand it. You need to add a "counter-reset" property to the <ol> tag, a "counter-increment" property to the <li> tag, and create a new CSS definition (li:before), in which you add a "content" property, and its content is "counter(mylist)". Instead of using the word "mylist", we could have used any word we wanted. It could have been "Jakes_list" or "cat". Whatever name you choose, you must stick with it on lines 5, 11 and 15.

Now, we are ready to add some nifty styling to our numbering (line 16 below):

---

[7] Anything we declare inside CSS in order to give a style to a specific element (such as ".division-a" which we used in the past) is known as a "selector". In the CSS above, the word "ol" on line 2, the word "li" on line 7 and the word "li:before" on line 14 are all selectors. A selector that has a colon inside it is known as a pseudo-selector.

```
14 ▾ li:before {
15        content: counter(mylist);
16        border:1px solid #000;
17 }
18
19
20 |
```

```
1|First item.
2|Second item.
3|Third item.
4|Fourth item.
```

Our styling efforts will focus on the "li:before" selector. Above, I have added a 1 pixel border to the numbering.

Notice how the numbering is in italics. I can now cancel this out (line 18 below):

```
 8 ▾ li {
i  9       border:0px dashed #000;
  10       padding-left:20px;
  11       font-style:italic;
  12       counter-increment: mylist;
  13 }
  14
  15 ▾ li:before {
  16       content: counter(mylist);
  17       border:1px solid #000;
  18       font-style:normal;
  19 }
  20 |
```

```
1|First item.
2|Second item.
3|Third item.
4|Fourth item.
```

In the <li> tag's definition, we added "font-style:italic" to make the list items italic, which also affected the list items' numbering. In the "li:before" selector, we add "font-style:normal" to overrule this style, forcing the numbering to not be italic.

Let's now increase the space between the numbering and the list items. Even though there is a "padding-left:20px" definition on the <li> tag (line 10 above), the new numbering we created is not affected by it.

Below, I have removed the padding on the <li> definition, while adding a right margin of five pixels on "li:before" (line 18). Now the numbering is separated from the items.

```
 8 ▾ li {
i  9        border:0px dashed #000;
   10       font-style:italic;
   11       counter-increment: mylist;
   12   }
   13
   14 ▾ li:before {
   15       content: counter(mylist);
   16       border:1px solid #000;
   17       font-style:normal;
   18       margin-right:5px;
   19   }
   20   |
```

1 *First item.*
2 *Second item.*
3 *Third item.*
4 *Fourth item.*

Below, I have added a "border-radius" of 100%, meaning to make the borders as circular as possible (line 19):

```
   14 ▾ li:before {
   15       content: counter(mylist);
   16       border:1px solid #000;
   17       font-style:normal;
   18       margin-right:5px;
   19       border-radius:100%;
   20   }
```

(1) *First item.*
(2) *Second item.*
(3) *Third item.*
(4) *Fourth item.*

65

To make the numbers look better, we can make the numbering wider, so that the borders look less like eggs and more like circles.

```
14 ▾  li:before {
15        content: counter(mylist);
⚠ 16       border:1px solid #000;
17        font-style:normal;
18        margin-right:5px;
19        border-radius:100%;
20        width:10px;
21    }
22
23    |
24
25
26
27
28
29                                               ▾
```

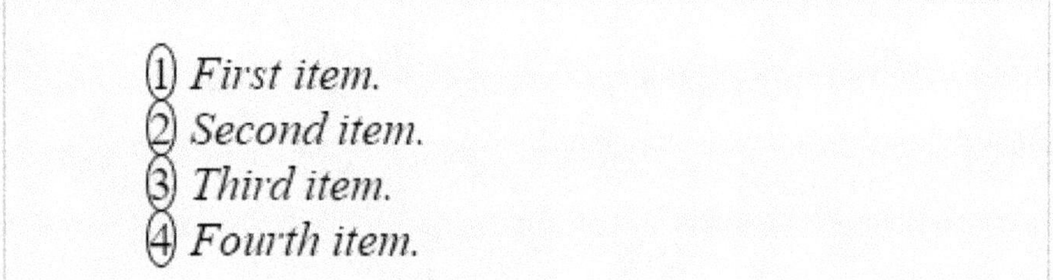

① *First item.*
② *Second item.*
③ *Third item.*
④ *Fourth item.*

Above, I have added a "width:10px" definition (line 20), but it is not having any effect. The reason is that the numbering that we artificially created are "inline" elements (similar to <span> tags), so that they cannot take a width. Inline elements have their width decided for them by the browser.

To get around this, we need to make the numbering stop being inline (line 21 below):

```
14 ▾  li:before {
15        content: counter(mylist);
⚠ 16       border:1px solid #000;
17        font-style:normal;
18        margin-right:5px;
19        border-radius:100%;
20        width:10px;
21        display:block;
22    }
```

Above, I have used the "display" property to turn the numbering into "block" elements, meaning they can now take widths.

① First item.
② Second item.
③ Third item.
④ Fourth item.

You can see that the numbers have more space inside their egg-shaped borders. The problem is that a block takes up a whole line, forcing the list items to appear on the next line. What we need is for the numbers to act like block elements so that they can take a width, but we also do not want them to take up a whole line. The solution is to use the "inline-block" value for the "display" property, creating a hybrid element that has the properties we desire:

```
14 ▾ li:before {
15       content: counter(mylist);
16       border:1px solid #000;
17       font-style:normal;
18       margin-right:5px;
19       border-radius:100%;
20       width:10px;
21       display:inline-block;
22  }
23
24  |
```

① First item.
② Second item.
③ Third item.
④ Fourth item.

An inline-block element has some of the properties of a block element (it can take a width, for example), but it does not take up a whole line.

Now that that problem is out of the way, we can focus on the width of the numbering. Instead of using pixels for the width, we can use another unit known as an "em" (line 20 below).

```
14 ▾  li:before {
15        content: counter(mylist);
⚠ 16       border:1px solid #000;
17        font-style:normal;
18        margin-right:5px;
19        border-radius:100%;
20        width:1em;
21        display:inline-block;
22    }
23
24
```

① First item.
② Second item.
③ Third item.
④ Fourth item.

An "em" refers to the "point" size of a specific font. If I give the numbering a width of 1 em, it means the width of the numbering will be equal to the average size of a letter (or number) in the present font that is being used. Think of "em" as "size of a capital M". 1 em means "as wide as a capital M".[8]

You can see that the eggs are more like circles now. They have expanded to the size of 1 em, meaning the size of an average letter or number. That' still not exactly like a circle, so we will increase it to 1.2 ems (line 20 below):

```
14 ▾  li:before {
15        content: counter(mylist);
⚠ 16       border:1px solid #000;
17        font-style:normal;
18        margin-right:5px;
19        border-radius:100%;
20        width:1.2em;
21        display:inline-block;
22    }
```

Here is the result:

---

[8] This is not absolutely accurate. For more information see the Wikipedia article about the em: https://en.wikipedia.org/wiki/Em_(typography)

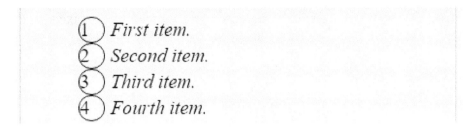

The cool thing about an em is that it expands and shrinks with the font size. If I reduce the font size to 10 pixels as follows (line 12 below), the circles shrink with the font size.

```
 8 ▾ li {
 9        border:0px dashed #000;
10        font-style:italic;
11        counter-increment: mylist;
12        font-size:10px;
13 }
14
15 ▾ li:before {
16        content: counter(mylist);
17        border:1px solid #000;
18        font-style:normal;
19        margin-right:5px;
20        border-radius:100%;
21        width:1.2em;
22        display:inline-block;
23 }
24
```

① First item.
② Second item.
③ Third item.
④ Fourth item.

Above, I have added a "font-size:10px" definition to the <li> tag. As can be seen, the numbering and the circle around it have also shrunk.

If instead of using an em, we had used pixels, the result would have been as follows:

① First item.
② Second item.
③ Third item.
④ Fourth item.

The circles have become deformed. To see this better, let's increase the font size to 30 pixels (line 12 below):

```
  8 ▾  li {
i 9        border:0px dashed #000;
  10       font-style:italic;
  11       counter-increment: mylist;
  12       font-size:30px;
  13  }
  14
  15 ▾  li:before {
  16       content: counter(mylist);
⚠ 17      border:1px solid #000;
  18       font-style:normal;
  19       margin-right:5px;
  20       border-radius:100%;
  21       width:10px;
  22       display:inline-block;
  23  }
  24
```

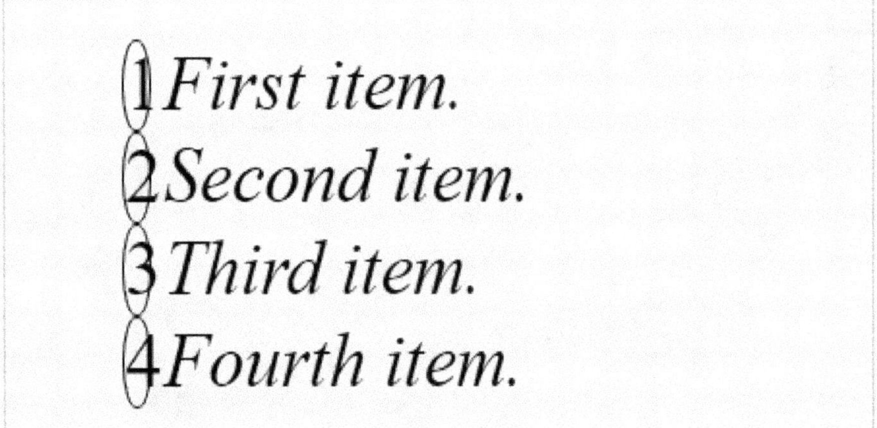

①First item.

②Second item.

③Third item.

④Fourth item.

Above, the font size of the list items and the numbering has increased. But the "width" of the numbers remains 10 pixels, so that the numbering starts to overflow outside the borders. Changing the width to 1.2 ems again (line 21 below), the circles come back again in their proper shape:

```
15 ▾ li:before {
16        content: counter(mylist);
17        border:1px solid #000;
18        font-style:normal;
19        margin-right:5px;
20        border-radius:100%;
21        width:1.2em;
22        display:inline-block;
23    }
24
```

① First item.
② Second item.
③ Third item.
④ Fourth item.

If this talk of ems and pixels has confused you, it is sufficient to know that ems are a unit of size that shrink and grow according to the font size currently in effect. Changing the font size makes the size of an "em" change.

Now that the text is larger, the space between the numbering and the list items has shrunk. They are again uncomfortably close. This is because we used a margin of 5 pixels between the numbering and the list items (line 19 above). As you make the font size larger, the 5 pixels remain 5 pixels, meaning that visually the space appears smaller, similar to the way a truck appears small when it is standing next to one of those massive mining trucks. We can fix this too by using ems for the margin (line 19 below):

```
15 ▾  li:before {
16        content: counter(mylist);
⚠ 17      border:1px solid #000;
18        font-style:normal;
19        margin-right:0.6em;
20        border-radius:100%;
21        width:1.2em;
22        display:inline-block;
23
24    }
```

① First item.
② Second item.
③ Third item.
④ Fourth item.

Above, I have changed the "margin-right" property's value to "0.6em". This tells the browser to keep a space between the numbering and the list items that equals a little over half the size of an average letter. As the size of the letters grows and shrinks, this margin will grow and shrink with it.

Let's now center the numbers inside their circular borders. To do so, we use the "text-align" property (line 23 below):

```
15 ▾  li:before {
16        content: counter(mylist);
⚠ 17      border:1px solid #000;
18        font-style:normal;
19        margin-right:0.6em;
20        border-radius:100%;
21        width:1.2em;
22        display:inline-block;
23        text-align:center;
24    }
```

Here is the result:

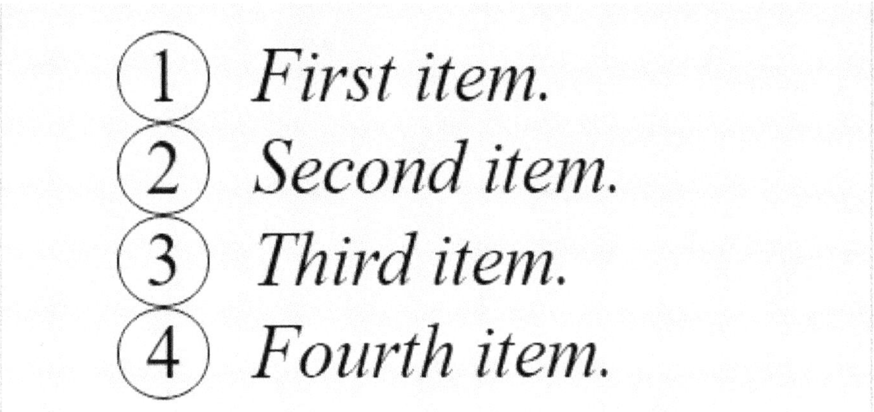

① *First item.*
② *Second item.*
③ *Third item.*
④ *Fourth item.*

The "text-align" property takes the values of "left", "right" and "center".

To make the circles stop touching each other, we will give the "li:before" selector a bottom margin (line 24 below):

```
15 ▾ li:before {
16        content: counter(mylist);
⚠ 17      border:1px solid #000;
18        font-style:normal;
19        margin-right:0.6em;
20        border-radius:100%;
21        width:1.2em;
22        display:inline-block;
23        text-align:center;
24        margin-bottom:0.1em;
25     }
26     |
```

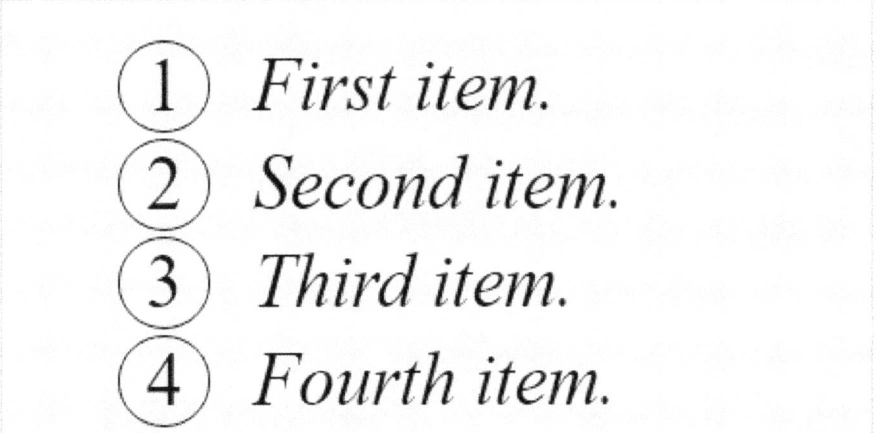

① *First item.*
② *Second item.*
③ *Third item.*
④ *Fourth item.*

Going on with our styling efforts, below I will make the text white and its background dark gray (lines 25 and 26 below):

```
15 ▾  li:before {
16         content: counter(mylist);
⚠ 17        border:1px solid #000;
18         font-style:normal;
19         margin-right:0.6em;
20         border-radius:100%;
21         width:1.2em;
22         display:inline-block;
23         text-align:center;
24         margin-bottom:0.1em;
25         color:#fff;
26         background:#666;
27    }
28    |
```

1 *First item.*
2 *Second item.*
3 *Third item.*
4 *Fourth item.*

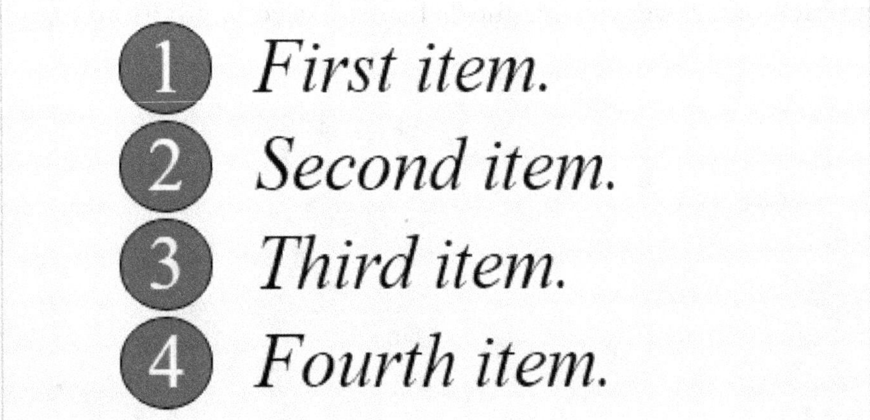

We can now change the font size of the <li> tag back to default by removing the "font-size:30px" definition that we added earlier on line 12 of the CSS:

```
 8 ▾  li {
i 9        border:0px dashed #000;
10        font-style:italic;
11        counter-increment: mylist;
12    }
```

As can be seen below, everything shrinks appropriately thanks to our use of ems rather than pixels:

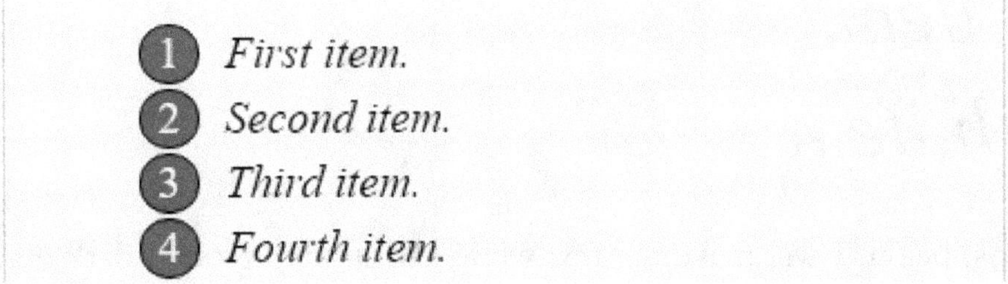

1 *First item.*
2 *Second item.*
3 *Third item.*
4 *Fourth item.*

To show the interplay between our new numbers and the list tags, below I have made the fourth item longer (lines 5 and 6 of the HTML) and I have brought back the borders I hid a while back (lines 3 and 9 of the CSS):

```
1   <ol type="A">
2       <li>First item.</li>
3       <li>Second item.</li>
4       <li>Third item.</li>
5       <li>Roses are red, violets are blue.<br>
6       The fourth item is relatively long.</li>
7   </ol>
8
```

```
1
2   ol {
3       border:1px solid #000;
4       list-style:none;
5       counter-reset:mylist;
6   }
7
8   li {
9       border:1px dashed #000;
10      font-style:italic;
11      counter-increment: mylist;
12  }
13
14  li:before {
15      content: counter(mylist);
16      border:1px solid #000;
17      font-style:normal;
18      margin-right:0.6em;
19      border-radius:100%;
20      width:1.2em;
21      display:inline-block;
```

1. First item.
2. Second item.
3. Third item.
4. Roses are red, violets are blue.
The fourth item is relatively long.

You may note how the <ol> tag is now wasting space on the left, since the numbers are no longer inside that space but are inside the <li> tags. To prevent this waste, we set the left-padding of the <ol> tag to zero on line 6 of the CSS:

```
2   ol {
3       border:1px solid #000;
4       list-style:none;
5       counter-reset:mylist;
6       padding-left:0;
7   }
```

Here is the result:

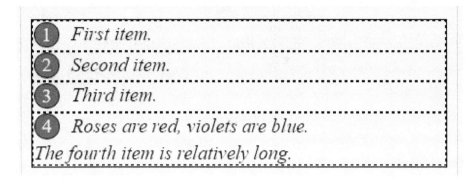

Now, the list items take up the whole of the <ol> tag.

In the HTML, the <ol> tag continues to have the type="A" attribute, which means that its numbering should be made of ABCs rather than decimals. This is no longer having an effect because we hid the default numbering on line 4 above in the CSS. Our new numbering is custom-made on line 16.

In order to create Roman numbering, we have to make a change to line 16 of the CSS:

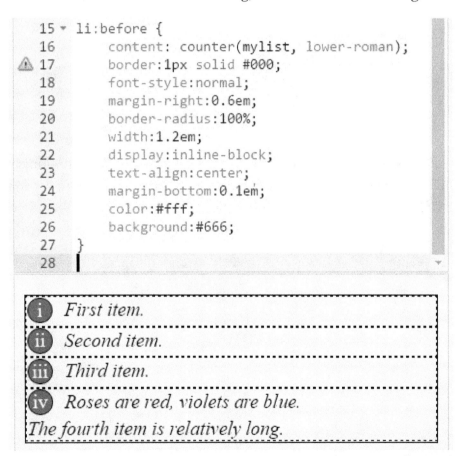

We have changed the value of the "content" property on line 16 so that it now has the word "lower-roman" in it. Note the comma separating "mylist" from "lower-roman", this is necessary.

Instead of Roman numbering, we can use Greek (line 16 below):

```
15 ▾ li:before {
16        content: counter(mylist, lower-greek);
⚠ 17      border:1px solid #000;
18        font-style:normal;
```

The result is as follows:

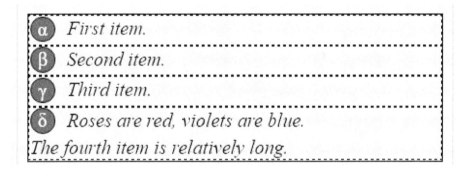

Other possible number formats to use are decimal, decimal-leading-zero, lower-roman, upper-roman, lower-greek, lower-latin, upper-latin, armenian, georgian, lower-alpha and upper-alpha.

Instead of using a number format, we can also use 'static' content to turn the list into a bullet list (line 16 below):

```
15 ▾ li:before {
16        content: '*';
⚠ 17        border:1px solid #000;
18        font-style:normal;
19        margin-right:0.6em;
20        border-radius:100%;
21        width:1.2em;
22        display:inline-block;
23        text-align:center;
24        margin-bottom:0.1em;
25        color:#fff;
26        background:#666;
27   }
28
```

First item.

Second item.

Third item.

Roses are red, violets are blue.
The fourth item is relatively long.

On line 16 above, I have changed the 'content' property to '*', meaning to use an asterisk as the content. We can also use one of many thousands of Unicode symbols[9], such as the snowman symbol on line 16 below:

```
15 ▾ li:before {
16        content: '☃';
⚠ 17        border:1px solid #000;
```

The result is as follows:

---

[9] Google "Unicode symbols" to find one of many sites that let you find all kinds of symbols and copy paste them into your code. Your HTML document must be formatted as a Unicode document. This is the default format on most modern systems.

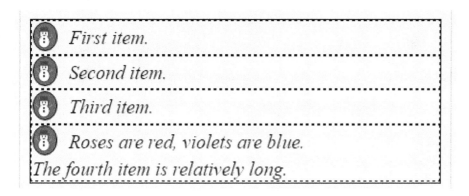

To make the snowmen more visible, I have removed the dark gray background, the circular border and the dashed border on the list items and increased the font size on the list items:

```
 9 ▾ li {
10      font-style:italic;
11      counter-increment: mylist;
12      font-size:20px;
13 }
14
15 ▾ li:before {
16      content: '☃';
17      font-style:normal;
18      margin-right:0.6em;
19      border-radius:100%;
20      width:1.2em;
21      display:inline-block;
22      text-align:center;
23      margin-bottom:0.1em;
24      color:#fff;
25 }
26 |
```

Here is the result:

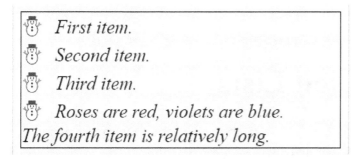

Since we are no longer using a CSS counter, we can remove the 'counter-reset' and 'counter-increment' properties from the <ol> and the <li> tags respectively in the CSS:

```
 2 ▾  ol {
 3        border:1px solid #000;
 4        list-style:none;
 5        padding-left:0;
 6     }
 7     |
 8 ▾  li {
 9        font-style:italic;
10        font-size:20px;
11     }
12
13 ▾  li:before {
14        content: '☃';
15        font-style:normal;
16        margin-right:0.6em;
17        border-radius:100%;
18        width:1.2em;
19        display:inline-block;
20        text-align:center;
21        margin-bottom:0.1em;
```

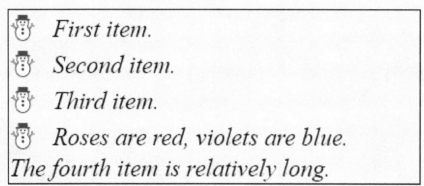

Counters are only useful if you want the browser to automatically number your list items for you. If no numbering is involved, if the content is static as in the snowman above, you no longer have a need for counters.

Unordered Lists

Unordered lists are very much like the ordered lists covered above, except that they do not use numbers, they use bullet points instead. Unordered lists are created using the <ul> tag (instead of the <ol> tag):

```
i  1 ▾ <ul>
   2        <li>First item.</li>
   3        <li>Second item.</li>
   4        <li>Third item.</li>
   5 ▾      <li>Roses are red, violets are blue.<br>
   6        The fourth item is relatively long.</li>
   7   </ul>
   8
```

```
1
```

```
1
```

- First item.
- Second item.
- Third item.
- Roses are red, violets are blue.
  The fourth item is relatively long.

Note how we are not using any CSS. The browser automatically adds the bullets to the list items. Adding borders to the <ul> and <li> tags, we can see the interplay between the list items and the bullets:

```
i  1 ▾ <ul>
   2        <li>First item.</li>
   3        <li>Second item.</li>
   4        <li>Third item.</li>
   5 ▾      <li>Roses are red, violets are blue.<br>
   6        The fourth item is relatively long.</li>
   7   </ul>
   8
```

```
1 ▾ ul {
2       border:1px solid #000;
3   }
4 ▾ li {
5       border:1px dashed #000;
6   }
7
```

```
1
```

- First item.
- Second item.
- Third item.
- Roses are red, violets are blue.
  The fourth item is relatively long.

We can make the bullets part of the list items using "list-style:inside" (line 6 below):

```
4 ▾ li {
5       border:1px dashed #000;
6       list-style:inside;
7 }
8 |
```

```
• First item.
• Second item.
• Third item.
• Roses are red, violets are blue.
The fourth item is relatively long.
```

Using "list-style", we can also determine the shape of the bullets (line 6 below):

```
4 ▾ li {
5       border:1px dashed #000;
6       list-style:circle;
7 }
8 |
```

```
o First item.
o Second item.
o Third item.
o Roses are red, violets are blue.
  The fourth item is relatively long.
```

To make the circles go inside the list items, we can do as follows (line 6 below):

```
4 ▾ li {
5       border:1px dashed #000;
6       list-style:circle inside;
7   }
8   |
```

```
o     First item.
o     Second item.
o     Third item.
o     Roses are red, violets are blue.
The fourth item is relatively long.
```

Note that there is a space (but no comma) between "circle" and "inside".

We can also turn the bullet list into a numbered list, although there is no good reason for doing so, by giving the "list-style" property the name of a numbering format:

```
4 ▾ li {
5       border:1px dashed #000;
6       list-style: decimal inside;
7   }
8   |
```

```
1. First item.
2. Second item.
3. Third item.
4. Roses are red, violets are blue.
The fourth item is relatively long.
```

We can also use an image file to use it as a bullet, as follows:

```
4 ▾  li {
5        border:1px dashed #000;
6        list-style: url("flower_small.png");
7    }
8    |
```

The property definition "url('flower_small.png')" tells the browser to look for an image file named "flower_small.png", located inside the JSTinker folder, and to use that image for the bullet point. If the image we wanted to use was an internet image, we'd have to spell out the image's full URL. For example this is the URL of an image on my personal website:

http://hawramani.com/wp-content/uploads/2018/02/flower_small.png

The full CSS would be as follows:

list-style: url("http://hawramani.com/wp-content/uploads/2018/02/flower_small.png");

If you are not sure what all of this means, there is no need to worry. The details of URLs, links and images will be covered in detail later.

Back to the list, you can see how the flowers are too large. Unfortunately, CSS doesn't allow us much control over the appearance of stuff we add through "list-style".

In order to change the size of the flowers so that they show up properly, we need to get creative like we did with the snowman.

First, we have to set the "list-style" property to none (line 6 of the CSS below):

```
i 1 ▾ <ul>
  2        <li>First item.</li>
  3        <li>Second item.</li>
  4        <li>Third item.</li>
  5 ▾      <li>Roses are red, violets are blue.<br>
  6        The fourth item is relatively long.</li>
  7    </ul>
  8    |
```

```
1 ▾ ul {
2        border:1px solid #000;
3    }
4 ▾ li {
5        border:1px dashed #000;
6        list-style: none;
7    }
8    |
```

```
1    |
```

```
┌─────────────────────────────────────┐
│First item.                          │
├ ─ ─ ─ ─ ─ ─ ─ ─ ─ ─ ─ ─ ─ ─ ─ ─ ─ ─ ┤
│Second item.                         │
├ ─ ─ ─ ─ ─ ─ ─ ─ ─ ─ ─ ─ ─ ─ ─ ─ ─ ─ ┤
│Third item.                          │
├ ─ ─ ─ ─ ─ ─ ─ ─ ─ ─ ─ ─ ─ ─ ─ ─ ─ ─ ┤
│Roses are red, violets are blue.     │
│The fourth item is relatively long.  │
└─────────────────────────────────────┘
```

Next, we add back the flowers using a new selector, the "li:before" that we used for the snowman (lines 8-10 below):

```
 4 ▾ li {
 5       border:1px dashed #000;
 6       list-style: none;
 7   }
 8 ▾ li:before {
 9       content:url('flower_small.png');
10   }
11   |
```

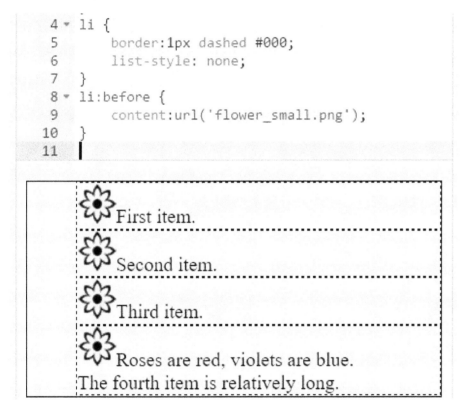

Note that in the "li:before" definition, we are not using a "list-style" property, we are using a "content" property (line 9 above). This gives us some control over the flowers, but it does not let us change their size.

Instead, we set the 'content' property to a blank string, then make use of the 'background-image' property:

```
 8 ▾ li:before {
 9        background-image:url('flower_small.png');
10        content:'';
11    }
12
13    |
```

```
First item.
Second item.
Third item.
Roses are red, violets are blue.
The fourth item is relatively long.
```

A blank string is what you get when you take out the stuff enclosed in quotes. For example if you have the string 'word', if you delete *word*, what remains are the quotes. In computer parlance, we call that a blank string. Above, I have added the flower as a "background-image". Nothing shows up because the "li:before" has a size of zero at the moment, since the content specified on line 10 is empty. This is similar to the way that a <div> shows up as nothing unless we give it a size and border or put some stuff inside it.

Below, I will give the "li:before" selector a height and width of 1 em (lines 10 and 11), and I will also switch its "display" property to the hybrid "inline-block" value (line 12):

```
 8 ▾ li:before {
 9        background-image:url('flower_small.png');
10        height:1em;
11        width:1em;
12        display:inline-block;
13        content:'';
14    }
15
16
```

```
First item.
Second item.
Third item.
Roses are red, violets are blue.
The fourth item is relatively long.
```

Above, everything is working perfectly now, except not. The problem is that the image is still too large. The "li:before" is small, but the image underneath is large, similar to a large flower being seen through a small window. We can visualize this more clearly by giving the "li:before" a border (line 14 below):

```
 8 ▾ li:before {
 9        background-image:url('flower_small.png');
10        height:1em;
11        width:1em;
12        display:inline-block;
13        content:'';
14        border:3px solid #000;
15    }
16    |
```

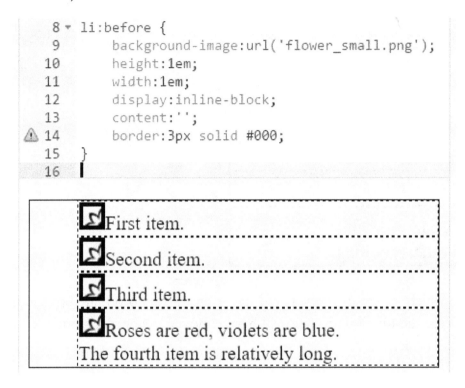

We need to make the image itself smaller. In computer speak, we call this "scaling" an image. To do so, we use the "background-size" CSS property (line 10 below):

```
 8 ▼  li:before {
 9        background-image:url('flower_small.png');
10        background-size:1em 1em;
11        height:1em;
12        width:1em;
13        display:inline-block;
14        content:'';
⚠15        border:3px solid #000;
16    }
```

```
┌──────────────────────────────────────────┐
│ ┌──────────────────────────────────────┐  │
│ │ ❁ First item.                         │  │
│ ·······································  │  │
│ │ ❁ Second item.                        │  │
│ ·······································  │  │
│ │ ❁ Third item.                         │  │
│ ·······································  │  │
│ │ ❁ Roses are red, violets are blue.    │  │
│  The fourth item is relatively long.   │  │
└──────────────────────────────────────────┘
```

Now, both the window through which we see the flower, and the image of the flower, are both 1em high and wide. This allows us to see the full flowers. Below, I have removed the border from line 15 above so that only the flowers can be seen:

```
 8 ▼  li:before {
 9        background-image:url('flower_small.png');
10        background-size:1em 1em;
11        height:1em;
12        width:1em;
13        display:inline-block;
14        content:'';
15    }
16
```

```
┌──────────────────────────────────────────┐
│ ❁First item.                              │
│·······································     │
│ ❁Second item.                             │
│·······································     │
│ ❁Third item.                              │
│·······································     │
│ ❁Roses are red, violets are blue.         │
│ The fourth item is relatively long.       │
└──────────────────────────────────────────┘
```

Below, I have given the "li:before" a right margin of 0.6 ems (line 15 below). I have also hidden the borders on the <ul> and <li> tags by setting them to zero (on lines 2 and 5 below) in order to see the result of our work:

```
 1 ▾ ul {
 2       border:0px solid #000;
 3 }
 4 ▾ li {
 5       border:0px dashed #000;
 6       list-style: none;
 7 }
 8 ▾ li:before {
 9       background-image:url('flower_small.png');
10       background-size:1em 1em;
11       height:1em;
12       width:1em;
13       display:inline-block;
14       content:'';
15       margin-right:0.6em;
16 }
```

❀ First item.
❀ Second item.
❀ Third item.
❀ Roses are red, violets are blue.
The fourth item is relatively long.

Thanks to using ems for the "background-size" and "height" and "width" properties on the "li:before", if we increase the font size on the <li> tag (line 7 below), the flowers will grow larger too:

```
 4 ▾ li {
 5        border:0px dashed #000;
 6        list-style: none;
 7        font-size:30px;
 8 }
 9 ▾ li:before {
10        background-image:url('flower_small.png');
11        background-size:1em 1em;
12        height:1em;
13        width:1em;
14        display:inline-block;
15        content:'';
16        margin-right:0.6em;
```

❋ First item.
❋ Second item.
❋ Third item.
❋ Roses are red,
violets are blue.
The fourth item is
relatively long.

Since the flowers are from an image, if we make the font too large (as above), the flowers get blurry. This is due to the nature of images on computers and there is no cure for it. To avoid it, one should either make sure the font is always at the right size for the image, or they should use non-image glyphs, such as the Unicode snowman earlier.[10]

---

[10] Using Unicode comes with its own issues, as some systems may not be able to display the Unicode glyphs properly. The solution to that is to use a web font that comes with its own glyphs. Web fonts will be covered later.

3. Floating

Using the CSS mechanism of 'floating', we can make a blocking element stop taking up a whole line. This enables us to have multiple <div> or <li> tags show up side-by-side.

Let's look at the unordered list from the last chapter:

```
i 1▾ <ul>
  2       <li>First item.</li>
  3       <li>Second item.</li>
  4       <li>Third item.</li>
  5▾      <li>Roses are red, violets are blue.<br>
  6       The fourth item is relatively long.</li>
  7  </ul>
  8  |
```

```
  1▾ ul {
i 2       border:0px solid #000;
  3  }
  4▾ li {
  5       border:1px dashed #000;
  6       list-style: none;
  7  }|
  8▾ li:before {
  9       background-image:url('flower_small.png');
 10       background-size:1em 1em;
 11       height:1em;
 12       width:1em;
 13       display:inline-block;
 14       content:'';
 15       margin-right:0.6em;
 16  }
 17
 18
 19
```

```
  1  |
```

```
⚙ First item.
⚙ Second item.
⚙ Third item.
⚙ Roses are red, violets are blue.
The fourth item is relatively long.
```

Below, on line 7, I add the "float" property and give it a value of "left":

```
4 ▼ li {
5       border:1px dashed #000;
6       list-style: none;
7       float:left;
8   }
```

Here is the result:

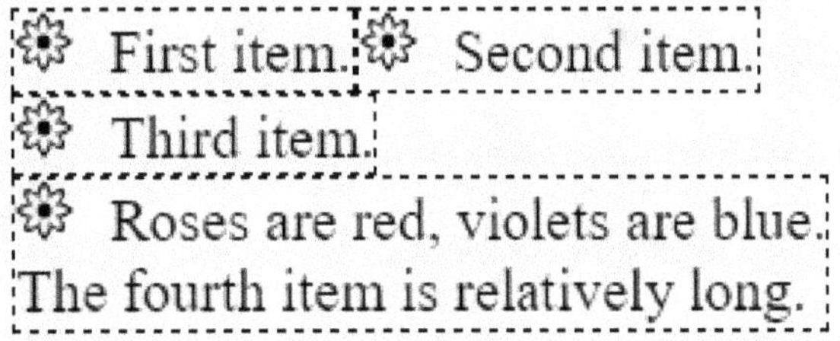

Now, each list item, instead of taking up the whole line, only takes up as much space as its contents require. This makes the first and the second list item show up side-by-side, because the first list item shrinks so much that sufficient space is left on its right to allow the second list item to show up there.

If we make the font size really small (line 8 below), all of the list items will show up side-by-side:

```
4 ▼ li {
5       border:1px dashed #000;
6       list-style: none;
7       float:left;
8       font-size:8px;
9   }
10 ▼ li:before {
11      background-image:url('flower_small.png');
12      background-size:1em 1em;
13      height:1em;
14      width:1em;
15      display:inline-block;
16      content:'';
17      margin-right:0.6em;
18  }
19  |
```

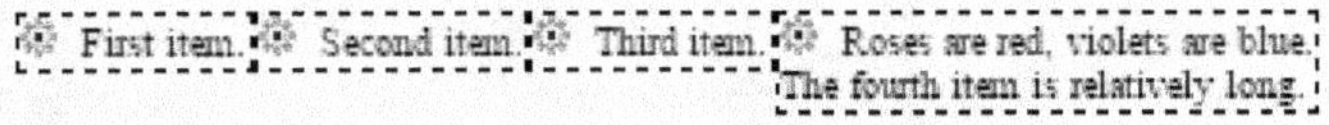

We can now use margins (line 8 below) to space out the list items so that they are not all mashed together:

```
4 ▾ li {
5       border:1px dashed #000;
6       list-style: none;
7       float:left;
8       margin:5px;
```

The result is as follows:

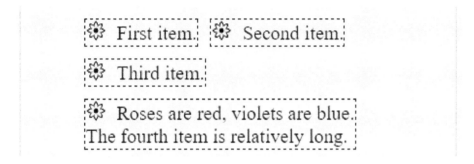

To make the list items look less disorganized, we can give them all a certain width (line 9 below):

```
4 ▾ li {
⚠ 5       border:1px dashed #000;
6       list-style: none;
7       float:left;
8       margin:5px;
9       width:40%;
```

The result is as follows:

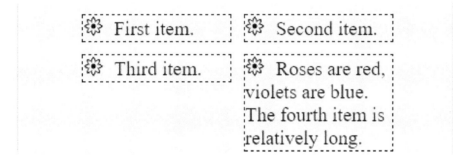

The 40% width means that each list item should take up 40% of the available horizontal space. This "available" space changes depending on the outer context. For example, if we give the <ul> tag a width of 200 pixels (line 3 below), the list items will shrink to each take up 40% of the available 200 pixels:

```
 1 ▾ ul {
 2       border:0px solid #000;
 3       width:200px;
 4  }
 5 ▾ li {
 6       border:1px dashed #000;
 7       list-style: none;
 8       float:left;
 9       margin:5px;
10       width:40%;
```

The result is as follows:

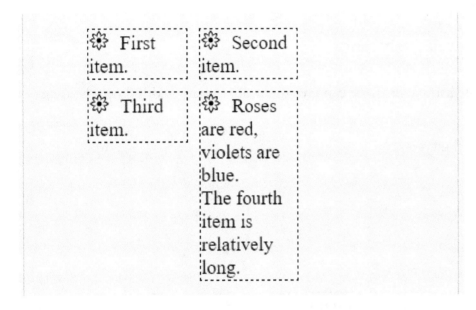

To give our list items a uniform height, we have to specify the height too (line 10 below):

```
 8       margin:5px;
 9       width:40%;
10       height:5em;
```

Here is the result:

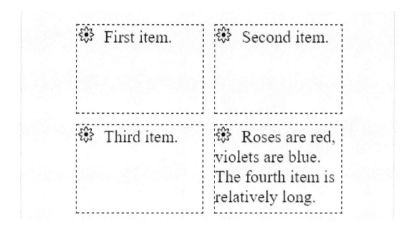

We cannot give floating things heights in percentages because an HTML document technically has infinite height.[11] The height must always be in some absolute or relative unit, like pixels or ems.

When setting a height, you must ensure that it provides sufficient space for the content. If we set the height to 3.5em (line 10 below), the first three items have no issue with it, but the fourth item overflows:

```
4 ▾ li {
5       border:1px dashed #000;
6       list-style: none;
7       float:left;
8       margin:5px;
9       width:40%;
10      height:3.5em;
```

The result is as follows:

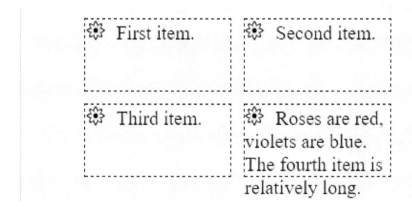

Even if we set the height to 5 ems (line 10 below), a change in font size (line 11 below) can cause the content to spill:

---

[11] Unless the container has a specific height, in which case a percentage height works. This will be seen later.

```
 9        width:40%;
10        height:5em;
11        font-size:17px;
```

Here is the result:

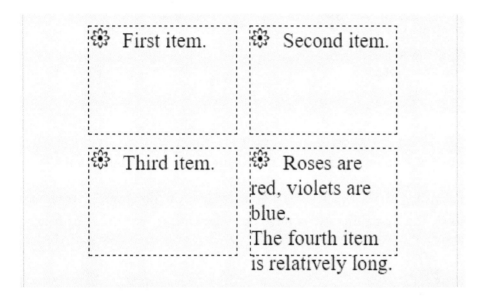

Perhaps you may think spilling wouldn't be an issue if we hide the borders. But if there were more items below the fourth item, the spillage would cause the text of the fourth item to merge with the text of the item below it, causing a broken appearance.

Below, I have removed the flower bullet point in order to simplify the example:

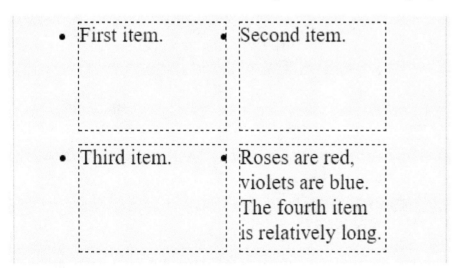

It can be seen that the bullets for the list items on the right are overflowing onto the items on the left. One way to fix this is to make the bullets appear inside the list items using "list-style:inside" (line 11 below):

```
4 ▾ li {
5      border:1px dashed #000;
6      float:left;
7      margin:5px;
8      width:40%;
9      height:5em;
10     font-size:17px;
11     list-style:inside;
```

The result is as follows:

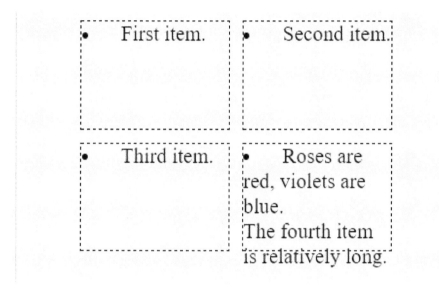

Another way is to prevent the bullets from intruding on their neighbors is to increase the left margin (line 8 below, I have removed the "list-style:inside" definition from earlier):

```
4 ▾ li {
5      border:1px dashed #000;
6      float:left;
7      margin:5px;
8      margin-left:1em;
9      width:40%;
10     height:5em;
11     font-size:17px;
```

Above, on line 7, we give the list items a margin of 5 pixels all round. On the next line, we modify the left margin, which overwrites the 5 pixels on line 7 with the "1em" on line 8. The 1 em of space is sufficient to prevent the bullets from merging into the items on the left.

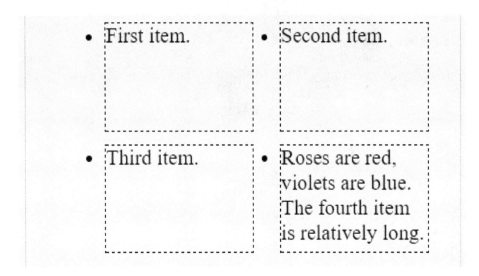

Instead of floating the items to the left, we could have floated them to the right as follows (line 6):

```
1 ▾ ul {
2       border:0px solid #000;
3   }
4 ▾ li {
5       border:1px dashed #000;
6       float:right;
7       margin:5px;
8       margin-left:1em;
9       width:40%;
10      height:5em;
11      font-size:17px;
12  }
13
```

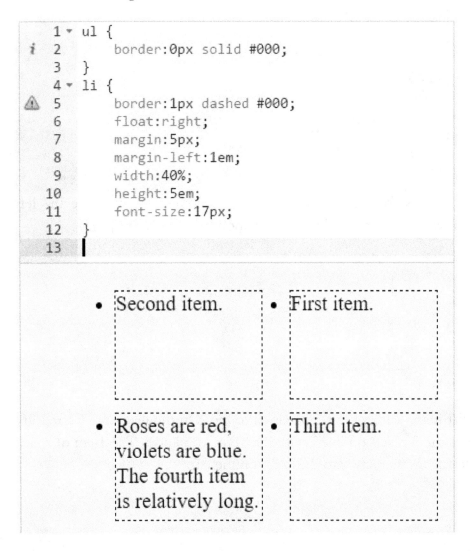

Floating items to the right causes the first item to appear on the top right, the next one on the top left, the third on the bottom right, and so on. Due to the fact that English-speakers are used to a left-to-right language, floating items to the right feels unnatural and is rarely used on a collection of items. It is, however, common to use it on individual elements, as follows:

```
1  <div class="division-a">Division A</div>
2  <div class="division-b">Division B</div>
```

```
1 ▾ div {
2      border:1px solid #000;
3      width: 5em;
4  }
5 ▾ .division-a {
6      float:left;
7  }
8 ▾ .division-b {
9      float:right;
10  }
11  |
```

```
1  |
```

Division A   Division B

Above, division-a is floated to the left (line 6) while division-b is floated to the right (line 9).

Below, I have put the two <div> tags inside another <div> tag with the class "container":

```
1 ▾ <div class="container">
2      <div class="division-a">Division A</div>
3      <div class="division-b">Division B</div>
4  </div>
5  |
```

```
1 ▾ div {
2      border:1px solid #000;
3      width: 5em;
4  }
5 ▾ .division-a {
6      float:left;
7  }
8 ▾ .division-b {
9      float:right;
10  }
11  |
```

```
1  |
```

Division A
Division B

There is a problem, however. The container <div> tag is too small, because in the CSS we have declared that all <div> tags should have a width of 5 ems (CSS line 3 above). In order to fix this, we will cause the width to only apply to the two inner <div> tags:

```
1 ▾ <div class="container">
2        <div class="division-a">Division A</div>
3        <div class="division-b">Division B</div>
4   </div>
5   |
```

```
1 ▾ div {
2        border:1px solid #000;
3   }
4 ▾ .division-a, .division-b {
5        width:5em;
6   }
7 ▾ .division-a {
8        float:left;
9   }
10 ▾ .division-b {
11       float:right;
12  }
13  |
```

| Division A | Division B |

Above, I have created a new CSS selector (line 4 of the CSS), which applies equally to both division-a and division-b (note the way their names are separated by a comma). Now, only division-a and division-b have a width of 5 ems, meaning the container <div> retains its default width (which is to take up the whole line).

You may notice the black bar on top of the texts "Division A" and "Division B". That is the container <div>'s borders. The issue is that since the container <div> tag is not floating (only division-a and division-b are floating, as determined by the CSS on lines 8 and 11), it does not have any content that can give it a height. CSS ignores the height of contained elements if they are floating, *unless* the container element is floating too.

Below, I have added a new CSS selector for the container <div> tag to make it float (line 14 below):

```
1 ▾ div {
2        border:1px solid #000;
3   }
4 ▾ .division-a, .division-b {
5        width:5em;
6   }
7 ▾ .division-a {
8        float:left;
9   }
10 ▾ .division-b {
11       float:right;
12  }
13 ▾ .container {
14       float:left;
15  }
16  |
```

| Division A | Division B |

Above, due to the fact that floating elements do not take up a whole line, the container <div> tag is now as small as it can possibly get. Its width is decided by the width of the stuff inside it, which means the width of division-a and division-b. This makes division-a and division-b touch, because the space between them is shrunk as much as possible. They are still floating apart, but the container div is too small to let them separate.

We can change this by giving the container <div> tag a width (CSS line 15 below):

```
13 ▾ .container {
14        float:left;
15        width:70%;
16    }
```

Division A		Division B

The container <div> tag now has a width of 70%, meaning that it takes up 70% of the available horizontal space. This increased space allows the right-floating division-b to separate from the left-floating division-a. We can also give the container <div> tag a width of 100% to make it take up the whole line:

```
13 ▾ .container {
14        float:left;
15        width:100%;
16    }
```

Division A		Division B

Let's now give the container <div> tag a padding, in order to separate its border from the borders of the elements inside it (CSS line 16 below):

```
13 ▾ .container {
14        float:left;
15        width:100%;
⚠ 16        padding:1em;
17    }
```

Division A		Division B

Notice how the right border of the container <div> element and division-b is "clipped". That's because the container <div> element is too large to be contained in its line, so it spills outside of it.

The reason for this is that the padding we added on line 16 is added onto the 100% width on line 15, increasing the width beyond 100%, meaning the container div is now too large to show up on one line. This is fixed by reducing the width of the container <div> element as follows (line 15 below):

```
13 ▾  .container {
14         float:left;
15         width:91%;
⚠ 16       padding:1em;
17    }
```

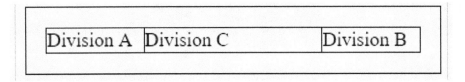

The width is now 91%, which, along with the container <div> element's padding, does not take up the whole line, allowing us to properly see the whole <div>.

Now, let's add a new division, named division-c (line 4 of the HTML below):

```
i 1 ▾ <div class="container">
  2       <div class="division-a">Division A</div>
  3       <div class="division-b">Division B</div>
  4       <div class="division-c">Division C</div>
  5   </div>
  6   |
```

The result is as follows:

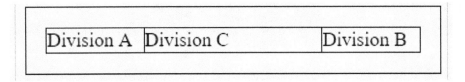

This new division is *not* floating, therefore it will have a strange relationship with the other <div> tags. It will try to take up the whole of the available horizontal space, so that it appears to the right of division-a and takes up everything until the left of division-b.

```
i  1 ▾ <div class="container">
   2        <div class="division-a">Division A</div>
   3        <div class="division-b">Division B</div>
   4 ▾      <div class="division-c">Division C
   5        contains more text than the other
   6        divisions. Roses are red, violets are
   7        blue.
   8        </div>
   9  </div>
  10
```

Above, I have added more text inside division-c. The result is as follows:

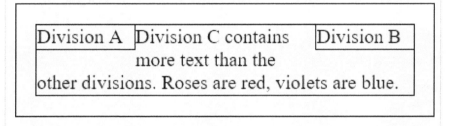

Notice how the content of division-c expands to take up all the available horizontal space Notice also that now the border of division-c appears to contain both divisions a and b, although in reality it does not contain them. This is merely the browser's best effort to make sense of the HTML and CSS that we have given it.

Making division-c also float will change everything. Below, I have added division-c to line 7, so that the left float will also apply to it:

```
 4 ▾ .division-a, .division-b {
 5        width:5em;
 6  }
 7 ▾ .division-a, .division-c {
 8        float:left;
 9  }
10 ▾ .division-b {
11        float:right;
12  }
```

The result is as follows:

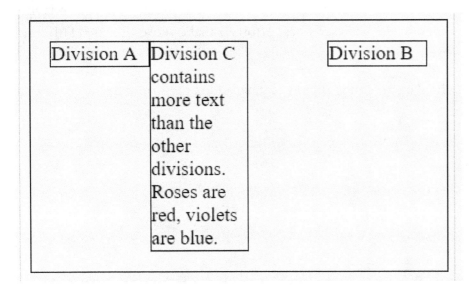

Now, division-c is on an equal footing with divisions a and b. Its width is determined by its contents, therefore it is so wide that it cannot fit between divisions a and b, so it is shown below them.

Below, I have added division-c to line 4, giving it a width of 5 ems similar to divisions a and b:

```
4 ▾ .division-a, .division-b, .division-c {
5       width:5em;
6   }
7 ▾ .division-a, .division-c {
8       float:left;
9   }
```

Here is the result:

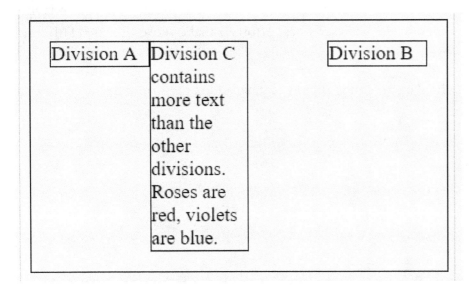

Now, since all three <div> tags have the same same width of 5 ems, there is sufficient space to show them all on the same line, so the browser does that. But since the contents of division-c are long, they automatically expand downwards.

There is no space between division-a and division-c. Since they are both floating left, they touch and stick together. We can change this by giving division-a a right margin (CSS line 11 below):

```
10 ▾ .division-a {
11       margin-right:1em;|
12   }
```

Now, the space between divisions-a and division-c is controlled by our CSS, while the space between divisions b and c is automatic., determined by the width of the container <div>.

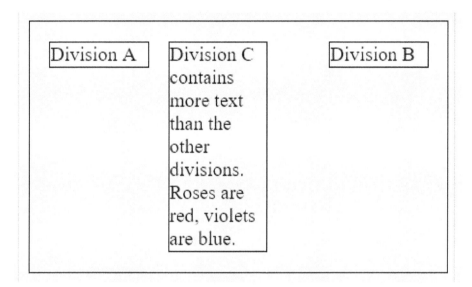

If the width of the container is reduced, the space is reduced or eliminated (CSS line 18 below):

```
16 ▾ .container {
17       float:left;
18       width:77%;|
⚠ 19      padding:1em;
```

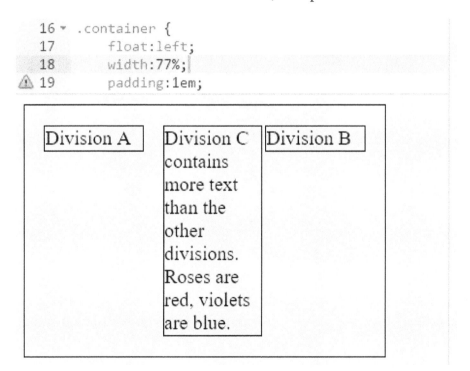

If we reduce the space too much, division-c is forced onto the next line because there is no longer sufficient space to show it side-by-side with divisions a and b (CSS line 18 below):

```
16 ▾  .container {
17        float:left;
18        width:67%;
19        padding:1em;
```

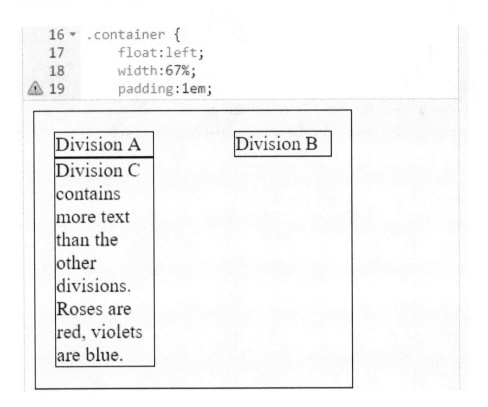

If we wanted to make divisions a, b and c to always have the same amount of space between them regardless of the width of the container <div> tag, this can only be accomplished by giving them all the same float. Below, I have removed all the CSS that applied to floating and have moved the float property to line 3, so that it applies to all four <div> tags (the container <div> tag and the other three):

```
 1 ▾  div {
 2        border:1px solid #000;
 3        float:left;
 4    }
 5 ▾  .division-a, .division-b, .division-c {
 6        width:5em;
 7    }
 8
 9 ▾  .division-a {
10        margin-right:1em;
11    }
```

Now, all divisions are floating left. Since division-a has a right margin of 1 ems (line 10 above), the result is that there is some space between divisions a and b, but no space between divisions b and c:

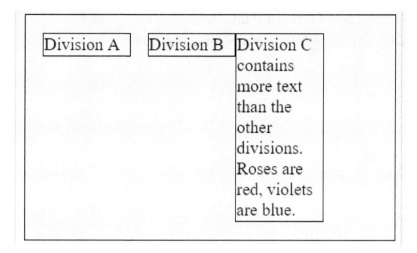

Below, I have moved the margin definition that used to be on line 10 onto line 7, so that it applies to all three <div> tags:

```
 1 ▾ div {
 2       border:1px solid #000;
 3       float:left;
 4   }
 5 ▾ .division-a, .division-b, .division-c {
 6       width:5em;
 7       margin-right:1em;
 8   }
 9 ▾ .container {
10       float:left;
11       width:91%;
12       padding:1em;
13   }
```

The result is as follows:

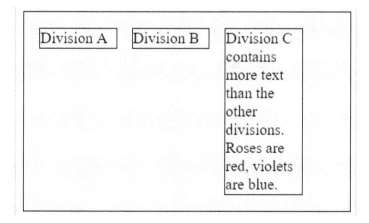

We could prevent the <div> tags from being forced onto new lines when the container <div> tag's width is shrunk by giving everything widths and margins in percentages, as follows:

```
 1 ▾ div {
 2       border:1px solid #000;
 3       float:left;
 4  }
 5 ▾ .division-a, .division-b, .division-c {
 6       width:30%;
 7       margin-right:2%;
 8  }
 9 ▾ .container {
10       float:left;
11       width:91%;
12       padding:1em;
13  }
```

Division A	Division B	Division C contains more text than the other divisions. Roses are red, violets are blue.

Above, on lines 6 and 7, I have changed the widths and margins to percentages. This means that each <div> tag will take up 30% of the available space regardless of how large or small that space is, and that each <div> will have a right margin that amounts to 2% of the available space.

Now, if I were to shrink the container <div> element's width, the rest of the <div> elements will shrink with it (line 11 below):

```
 9 ▾  .container {
10        float:left;
11        width:61%;
⚠12        padding:1em;
13     }
14  |
```

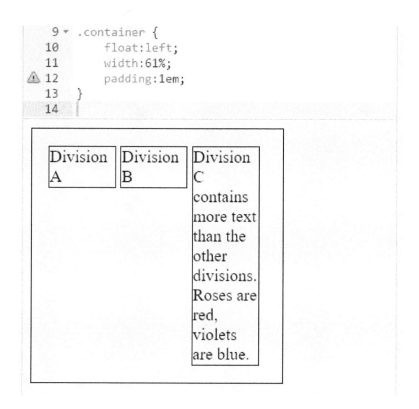

Below, I have increased the container <div> element's width again and given it a border-radius:

```
 9 ▾  .container {
10        float:left;
11        width:91%;
⚠12        padding:1em;
13        border-radius:1em;
14     }
15  |
```

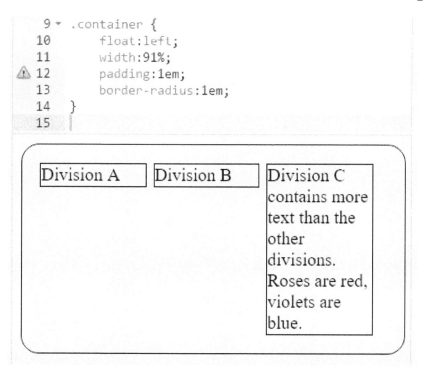

The border-radius property is purely aesthetic and does not affect the contained elements, but it can clip them. This is best illustrated by giving the border-radius a value of 100% (line 13 below):

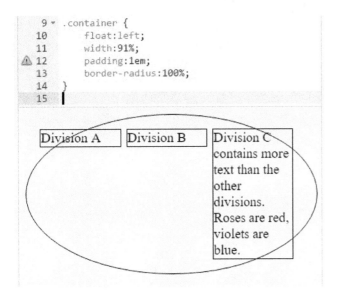

Below, I have given the three divisions a white background (line 8) in order to illustrate their relationship with the border-radius:

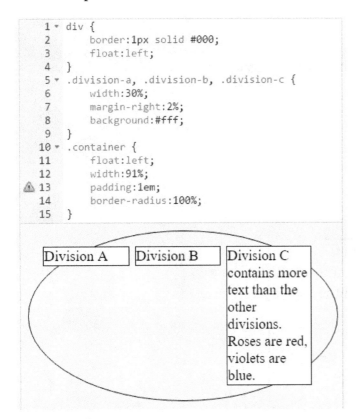

By giving the container <div> an "overflow:hidden" property (line 12 below), we can cause the border radius to clip the contained <div> elements (I have changed the border-radius and the width and padding of the three <div> elements for decorative reasons):

```
11 ▼ .container {
12       overflow:hidden;
13       float:left;
14       width:91%;
⚠ 15       padding:1em;
```

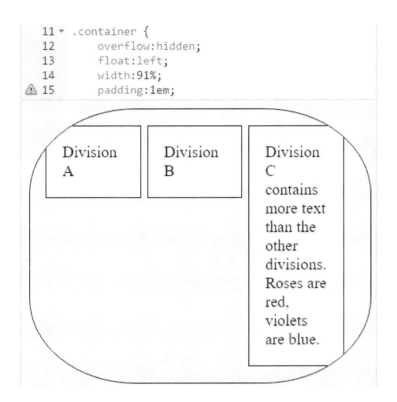

Moving on, below I have removed the border radius and the new styling I added to divisions a, b and c (but I have kept the white background). I have also added a new division-d element (line 9 of the HTML). Here is the new HTML:

```
i  1 ▼ <div class="container">
   2       <div class="division-a">Division A</div>
   3       <div class="division-b">Division B</div>
   4 ▼     <div class="division-c">Division C
   5       contains more text than the other
   6       divisions. Roses are red, violets are
   7       blue.
   8       </div>
   9       <div class="division-d">Division D</div>
  10   </div>
```

I have made division-d have the same styling as the rest of the divisions a, b and c by adding it to the selector on line 6 of the CSS:

```
 1 ▾ div {
 2        border:1px solid #000;
 3        float:left;
 4    }
 5    .division-a, .division-b, .division-c,
 6 ▾ .division-d {
 7        width:20%;
 8        margin-right:2%;
 9        background:#fff;
10    }
11 ▾ .container {
12        float:left;
13        width:91%;
⚠ 14        padding:1em;
15    }
```

Division A	Division B	Division C contains more text than the other divisions. Roses are red, violets are blue.	Division D

If we increase the width of the <div> elements (line 7 below), division-d will be forced onto a new line:

```
 5    .division-a, .division-b, .division-c,
 6 ▾ .division-d {
 7        width:25%;
 8        margin-right:2%;
 9        background:#fff;
10    }
```

Here is the result:

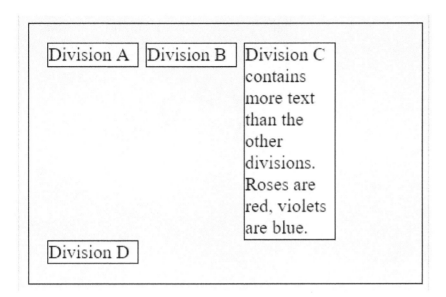

Above, notice that division-d is below the lowest point of division-c. Division-c is forcing its own line to expand vertically due to its large amount of content. There is, unfortunately, no way to avoid this and make the browser understand that we want division-d to show up right below division-a. We can, however, achieve this by making division-c float on the right:

```
 5    .division-a, .division-b, .division-c,
 6 ▾  .division-d {
 7        width:25%;
 8        margin-right:2%;
 9        background:#fff;
10    }
11 ▾  .division-c {
12        float:right;
13    }
```

The result is as follows:

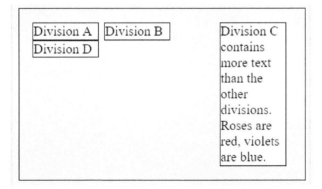

Above, now that division-c is floating on the right, it acquires its own "context" that is independent from divisions existing on the left. We can now add any number of left-floating divisions without them being affected by division-c. Below, I have added division-e and division-f, and I have added them to the CSS on line 6 so that they have the same styles as the other left-floating divisions:

```
 1 ▾ <div class="container">
 2       <div class="division-a">Division A</div>
 3       <div class="division-b">Division B</div>
 4 ▾     <div class="division-c">Division C
 5       contains more text than the other
 6       divisions. Roses are red, violets are
 7       blue.
 8       </div>
 9       <div class="division-d">Division D</div>
10       <div class="division-e">Division E</div>
11       <div class="division-f">Division F</div>
12   </div>
13
```

```
 1 ▾ div {
 2       border:1px solid #000;
 3       float:left;
 4   }
 5   .division-a, .division-b, .division-c,
 6 ▾ .division-d, .division-e, .division-f {
 7       width:25%;
 8       margin-right:2%;
 9       background:#fff;
10   }
11 ▾ .division-c {
12       float:right;
13   }
14 ▾ .container {
15       float:left;
```

Division A	Division B		Division C
Division D	Division E		contains
Division F			more text
			than the
			other
			divisions.
			Roses are
			red, violets
			are blue.

Below I have added a new paragraph (<p> tag) underneath the <div> tags with some Shakespeare lines:

```
11       <div class="division-f">Division F</div>
12 ▾     <p>'Tis but thy name that is my enemy;<br>
13   Thou art thyself, though not a Montague.<br>
14   What's Montague? It is nor hand, nor foot,<br>
15   Nor arm, nor face, nor any other part</p>
16   </div>
```

Here is the result:

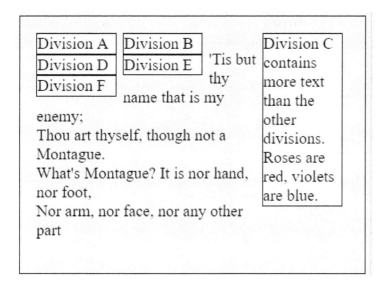

Since the new paragraph is not floating, the browser tries to make it fill the available space wherever that space may be.

To pin down the real location of the <p> element, below I have given it a 3-pixel dashed border (line 20 of the CSS):

```
19 ▾ p {
20        border:3px dashed #000;
21    }
22
```

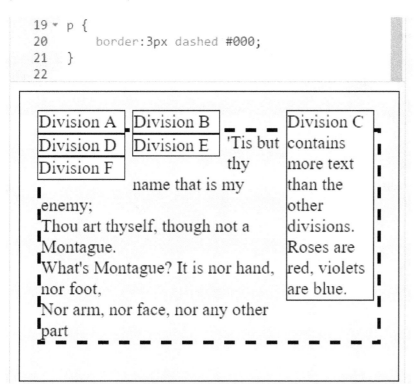

Even if we give the <p> tag a width of 100% (line 21 below), it will not get on its own line, because the floating <div> elements exist in their own parallel reality, they are "floating", they hover over the <p> element, except that they change the <p> element's appearance. The browser makes sure none of the text of the <p> element gets underneath the floating elements.

```
19 ▾  p {
20         border:3px dashed #000;
21         width:100%;
22    }
```

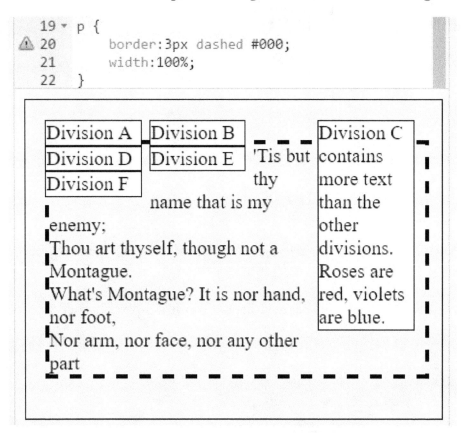

We can now introduce the "clear" property. Below, I have given the <p> element a "clear:left" property (CSS line 22):

```
19 ▾  p {
20         border:3px dashed #000;
21         width:100%;
22         clear:left;
```

The result is as follows:

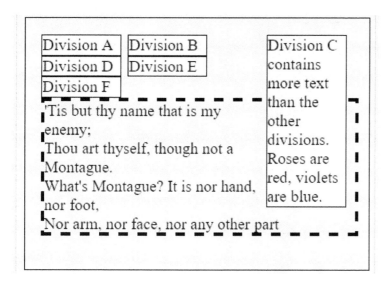

The "clear:left" property tells the browser that we do not want anything on the left of our paragraph. If there is something on the left, as there was earlier, the browser forces the <p> element onto a new line so that its left remains empty of all other elements. Note how the paragraph has not cleared division-c, since we have only instructed the left side to be cleared, the right side remains open for elements like division-c.

We can change this by also giving the <p> element a "clear:right" property (line 23 below):

```
19 ▾ p {
20      border:3px dashed #000;
21      width:100%;
22      clear:left;
23      clear:right;
```

Here is the result:

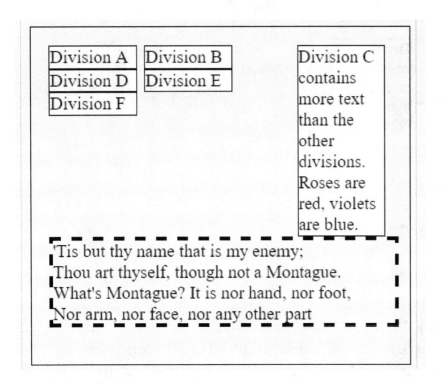

Above, both the left and right sides of the <p> element are not cleared. We can shorten the CSS by using the "clear:both" shorthand (line 22 below):

```
19 ▾  p {
⚠ 20        border:3px dashed #000;
21          width:100%;
22          clear:both;
23    }
24
```

Rules of Nesting and Inheritance

Below, I have switched things up by removing most of the <div> tags. I have placed a <div> element inside the paragraph, causing a broken appearance:

```
i 1 ▾ <div class="container">
  2 ▾     <p>'Tis but thy name that is my enemy;<br>
  3     Thou art thyself, though not a Montague.<br>
  4     <div class="division-a">Division A</div>
  5     What's Montague? It is nor hand, nor foot,<br>
❌ 6     Nor arm, nor face, nor any other part</p>
  7     </div>
```

Here is the result:

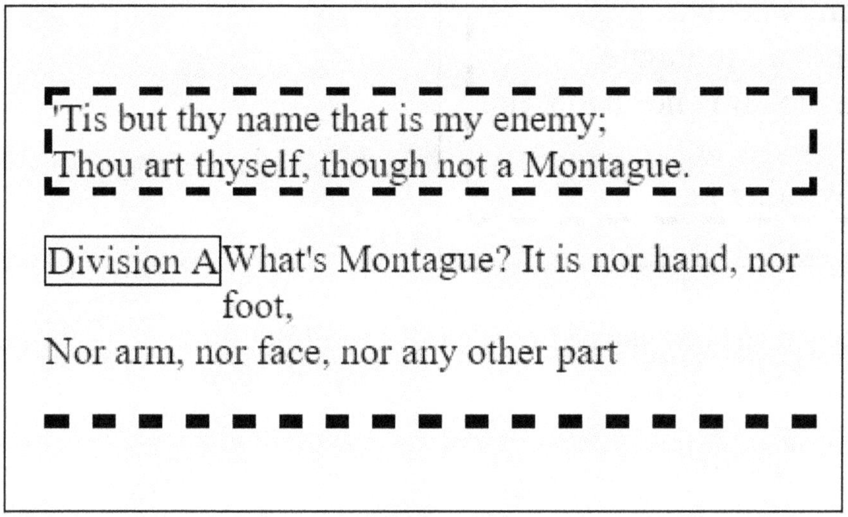

The reason for the broken appearance is that putting a <div> element inside a <p> element breaks the laws of HTML. A <p> element is only allowed to contain *inline* elements (such as <span> and <b>), it is not allowed to contain block elements like a <div>. To fix things, I change the <p> element to a <div> element with a class of "poem":

```
1 ▼ <div class="container">
2 ▼     <div class="poem">'Tis but thy name
3        that is my enemy;<br>
4  Thou art thyself, though not a Montague.<br>
5  <div class="division-a">Division A</div>
6  What's Montague? It is nor hand, nor foot,<br>
7  Nor arm, nor face, nor any other part</div>
8  </div>
9  |
```

In the CSS, I change the "p" selector to ".poem" (line 11):

```
11 ▼ .poem {
12       border:3px dashed #000;
13       width:100%;
14   }
```

Now, the broken appearance is fixed:

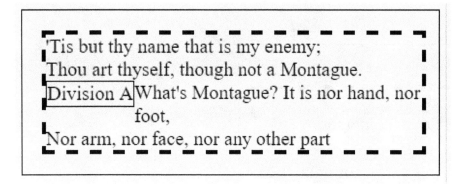

Below, I have given division-a a margin and padding of 1 em (lines 12 and 13):

```
 6 ▾  .container {
 7         float:left;
 8         width:91%;
 9         padding:1em;
10     }
11 ▾  .division-a {
12         padding:1em;
13         margin:1em;
14     }
15 ▾  .poem {
16         border:3px dashed #000;
```

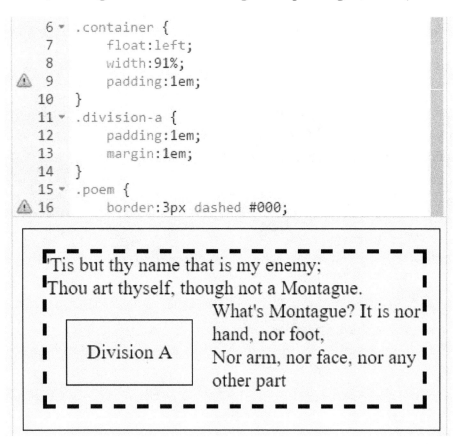

The browser rearranges the text so that it makes room for division-a's increased size.

Below, I add some more lines of poetry:

```
  1 ▾  <div class="container">                          2       border:1px solid #000;
  2 ▾      <div class="poem">'Tis but thy name          3       float:left;
  3         that is my enemy;<br>                        4  }
  4     Thou art thyself, though not a Montague.<br>     5
  5     <div class="division-a">Division A</div>         6 ▾ .container {
  6     What's Montague? It is nor hand, nor foot,<br>   7       float:left;
  7     Nor arm, nor face, nor any other part<br>        8       width:91%;
  8     Belonging to a man. O, be some other name!<br>   9       padding:1em;
  9     What's in a name?                               10  }
 10     That which we call a rose<br>                   11 ▾ .division-a {
 11     By any other word would smell as sweet;</div>   12       padding:1em;
 12  </div>                                             13       margin:1em;
 13                                                      14  }
                                                         15 ▾ .poem {
  1  |                                                   16       border:3px dashed #000;
```

Note the way that the text resumes being on the left once it clears division-a. In this way, we can add side notes or images to a main text, useful for many purposes. Below, I have made division-a float on the right (line 14 of the CSS) instead of left:

```
 11 ▾ .division-a {
 12       padding:1em;
 13       margin:1em;
 14       float:right;
 15  }
```

Since division-a is inside the poem, any styling we add to the poem class will also affect division-a. Above, I have added italic styling on line 19 to the poem class:

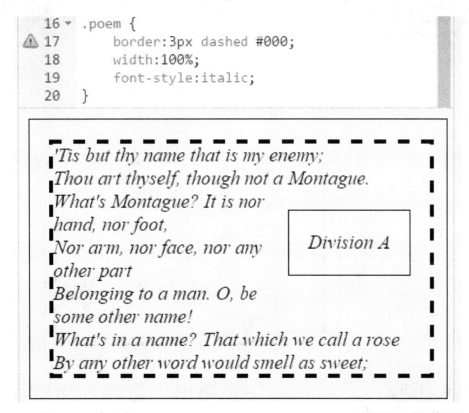

However, only some CSS properties are inheritable. Even if we remove the solid border of the <div> element, division-a will not get the poem class's dashed border. Below, I have deleted the "border:1px solid #000" property that used to be on line 2. The result is that division-a loses its border. But it does not end inheriting the border of the poem class (defined on line 16), despite being contained inside it and inheriting its italic styling. Margins and padding are also not inheritable.

```
 1 ▾ div {
 2        float:left;
 3    }
 4
 5 ▾ .container {
 6        float:left;
 7        width:91%;
 8        padding:1em;
 9    }
10 ▾ .division-a {
11        padding:1em;
12        margin:1em;
13        float:right;
14    }
15 ▾ .poem {
16        border:3px dashed #000;
17        width:100%;
18        font-style:italic;
19    }
```

'Tis but thy name that is my enemy;
Thou art thyself, though not a Montague.
What's Montague? It is nor
hand, nor foot,
Nor arm, nor face, nor any
other part   Division A
Belonging to a man. O, be
some other name!
What's in a name? That which we call a rose
By any other word would smell as sweet;

When a <div> is inside another <div>, we call the outer <div> the "parent" element and the inner <div> a "child" element. In the above example, the <div> that has the "poem" class is the parent of division-a, and division-a is the child of "poem". And both of them are "descendants" of "container", and "container" is their "ancestor".

To clarify these concepts further, below I have created a situation where we have three <div> elements, one inside another:

```
i 1 ▾ <div class="division-a">Division A
  2 ▾    <div class="division-b">Division B
  3 ▾       <div class="division-c">Division C
  4         </div>
  5      </div>
  6 </div>
  7
```

```
1 ▾ div {
2       border:1px solid #000;
3       padding:1em;
4  }
5
6
7
8
9
```

```
1
```

```
Division A

   Division B

      Division C
```

The parent-child relationship only applies to elements that are directly related. The element division-a is the parent of division-b, but it is not the parent of division-c, because division-c's parent is division-b. Instead, division-a is the *grandparent* or *ancestor* of division-c. Using the parent-child metaphor is useful when talking about HTML elements.

Note the way that the border and padding we defined on lines 2 and 3 affected all three <div> elements. This is because on line 1 we have declared that this styling should apply to *all* <div> elements. No inheritance is involved here, regardless of where a particular <div> is located, the styling will apply to it.

If, instead of applying the styling to the <div> selector we had applied it to division-a, the styling wouldn't have affected the other <div> elements, as seen below:

```
i 1 ▾ <div class="division-a">Division A
  2 ▾    <div class="division-b">Division B
  3 ▾       <div class="division-c">Division C
  4         </div>
  5      </div>
  6 </div>
  7
```

```
1 ▾ .division-a {
2       border:1px solid #000;
3       padding:1em;
4  }
5
6
7
8
9
```

```
1
```

```
Division A
Division B
Division C
```

The border and padding affect division-a but do not affect division-b and c. This is because, as mentioned, border and padding are not inheritable. If, instead, we add a font family or some other property, this ends up affecting all the <div> elements, even though this is only added to the division-a selector:

```
1 ▾ .division-a {
2       border:1px solid #000;
3       padding:1em;
4       font-size:25px;
5       font-family:'Monotype Corsiva';
6       text-decoration:underline;
7    }
```

Here is the result:

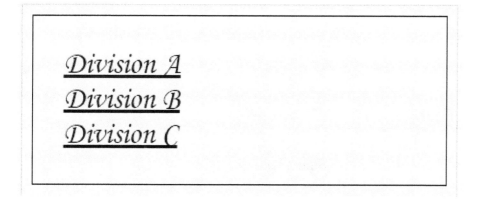

Learning which CSS properties are inheritable and which ones are not happens with practice and trial and error. There is no need to worry about memorizing them.

If we give the <div> tag a left padding of 1 em (line 2 below), the following situation is created:

```
1 ▾ div {
2       padding-left:1em;
3 }
4 ▾ .division-a {
5       border:1px solid #000;
6       padding:1em;
7       font-size:25px;
8       font-family:'Monotype Corsiva';
9       text-decoration:underline;
```

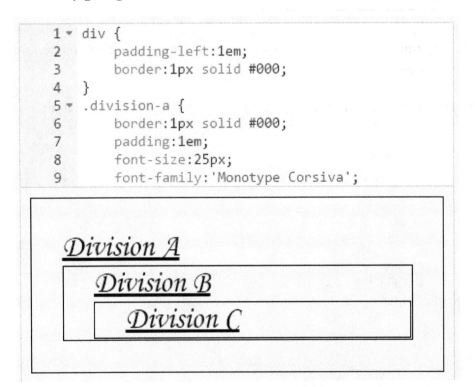

This happens because each <div> element's padding affects the ones inside it. This can be clarified further by giving all of the <div> elements a border (line 3 below):

```
1 ▾ div {
2       padding-left:1em;
3       border:1px solid #000;
4 }
5 ▾ .division-a {
6       border:1px solid #000;
7       padding:1em;
8       font-size:25px;
9       font-family:'Monotype Corsiva';
```

The padding on division-a forces everything inside it to move rightward by 1em. The same process repeats between divisions b and c. If you feel somewhat confused by this, there is no need to worry.

Even skilled web designers get confused by the complex relationships that sometimes get created inside HTML documents. Sometimes they happen on the correct design without fully understanding how it works.

This page intentionally left blank

4. Positioning

Besides floating, there is another way of making HTML elements appear where we want them, and that way is known as positioning, which uses the "position" CSS property.

Below, we have two <div> elements:

```
i 1    <div class="division-a">Division A</div>
  2    <div class="division-b">Division B</div>
  3 |
  4
```

```
1 ▾ div {
2       border:1px solid #000;
3       margin:1em;
4 }
5 |
```

```
1 |
```

```
Division A

Division B
```

Below, I give division-a the CSS property "position:absolute" (line 6 below):

```
1 ▾ div {
2       border:1px solid #000;
3       margin:1em;
4  }
5 ▾ .division-a {
6       position:absolute;
7  }
```

Here is the result:

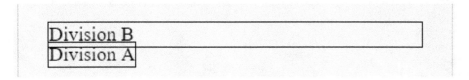

Absolute positioning causes the element to "hover" over the document. Unlike in floating, the element stops having any relationship whatsoever with the stuff underneath it. The broken appearance above is due to division-a hovering, causing the browser to put division-b up where division-a used to be.

Now that we have given division-a absolute positioning, we can move it wherever we want using CSS, as follows (lines 7 and 8):

```
1 ▾ div {
2       border:1px solid #000;
3       margin:1em;
4   }
5 ▾ .division-a {
6       position:absolute;
7       top:2em;
8       left:2em;
9   }
```

Division B

Division A

The "top" property determines the distance of division-a from the top edge, and the "left" property determines its distance from the left edge.

Below, I have reduced the top distance while increasing the left distance:

```
1 ▾ div {
2       border:1px solid #000;
3       margin:1em;
4   }
5 ▾ .division-a {
6       position:absolute;
7       top:1em;
8       left:7em;
9   }
```

Division B

Division A

We can also determine these distances in percentages, as follows:

```
i 1   <div class="division-a">Division A</div>
  2   <div class="division-b">Division B</div>
  3 |
  4

  1 |
```

```
1 ▾ div {
2       border:1px solid #000;
3       margin:1em;
4   }
5 ▾ .division-a {
6       position:absolute;
7       top:50%;
8       left:40%;
9   }
```

Division B

Division A

The property "top:50%" tells the browser to show division-a at or near the middle of its containing element. If there isn't a container, it refers to the browser window. To illustrate this, below I have created a new file on my computer called test.html:

Name	Date modified	Type	Size
🌐 test.html	2/6/2018 9:12 AM	Chrome HTML Do...	1 KB

131

Opening this file in Notepad, I paste into it the HTML and CSS from above:

```
test.html - Notepad
File  Edit  Format  View  Help
<style>
div {
    border:1px solid #000;
    margin:1em;
}
.division-a {
    position:absolute;
    top:50%;
    left:40%;
}
</style>

<div class="division-a">Division A</div>
<div class="division-b">Division B</div>
```

Note that I had to create a new <style> tag which now contains the CSS. Without this, the browser does not know that this is CSS and interprets it as text. To illustrate, below I have removed the <style> tag:

```
test.html - Notepad
File  Edit  Format  View  Help

div {
    border:1px solid #000;
    margin:1em;
}
.division-a {
    position:absolute;
    top:50%;
    left:40%;
}


<div class="division-a">Division A</div>
<div class="division-b">Division B</div>
```

Now, if I were to open this test.html document in a browser, this is what I get:

Below, I have added the <style> tag back, getting the following result:

If I increase the height of the browser window (by using my mouse to drag its bottom border), division-a goes down with it:

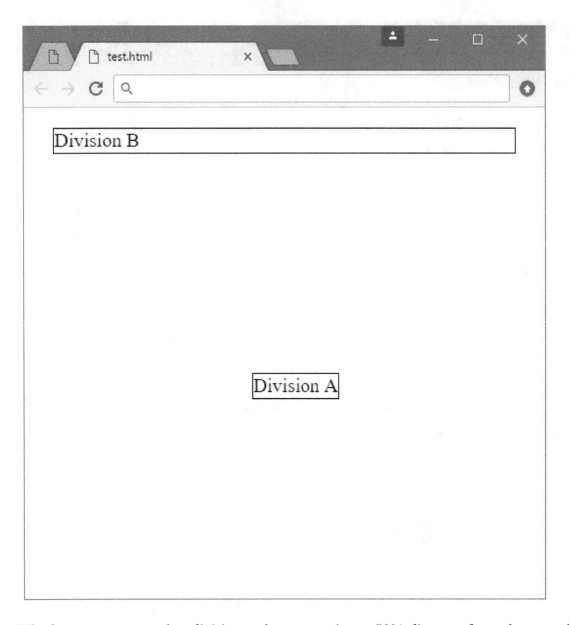

The browser ensures that division-a always remains at 50% distance from the top of the window. If the window is made larger, that 50% distance also becomes larger, so that division-a moves downward. If I shrink the window, division-a moves up:

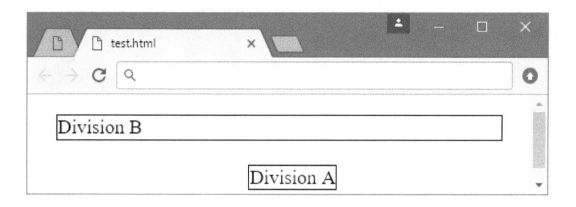

Going back to JSTinker, below I have given division-b absolute positioning by adding it to division-a's CSS selector on line 5. I have also changed the "top" and "left" properties to ems rather than percentages (lines 7 and 8):

```
 1 ▾ div {
 2       border:1px solid #000;
 3       margin:1em;
 4   }
 5 ▾ .division-a, .division-b {
 6       position:absolute;
 7       top:2em;
 8       left:2em;
 9   }
10
```

Division B

Something strange takes place because we have declared that both divisions should appear at the exact same location, which forces them to get overlaid on each other. It is like having a piece of glass with text written on it and putting another piece of glass on it that also has text on it. The two texts get merged.

If, however, we give the <div> elements a background (currently their background is transparent), one of the elements ends up occluding the other (line 9 below):

```
 1 ▾ div {
 2       border:1px solid #000;
 3       margin:1em;
 4   }
 5 ▾ .division-a, .division-b {
 6       position:absolute;
 7       top:2em;
 8       left:2em;
 9       background:#fff;
10   }
```

Division B

Above, the white background of division-b causes division-a (which is exactly underneath it) to hide. We can check this by moving division-b slightly down (line 12 below):

```
 5 ▾ .division-a, .division-b {
 6       position:absolute;
 7       top:2em;
 8       left:2em;
 9       background:#fff;
10   }
11 ▾ .division-b {
12       top:2.5em;
13   }
14
```

Division B

On line 11, I have added a new CSS selector specifically for division-b. On line 12, I have given division-b a top distance of 2.5 ems (rather than the 2 ems declared on line 7). The result is that we see division-a peeking from under division-b.

Instead of using "top" and "left", we can also use "right" and "bottom", as follows (lines 14 and 15):

```
 9 ▾  .division-a {
10        top:2em;
11        left:2em;
12    }
13 ▾  .division-b {
14        bottom:2em;
15        right:2em;
16    }
```

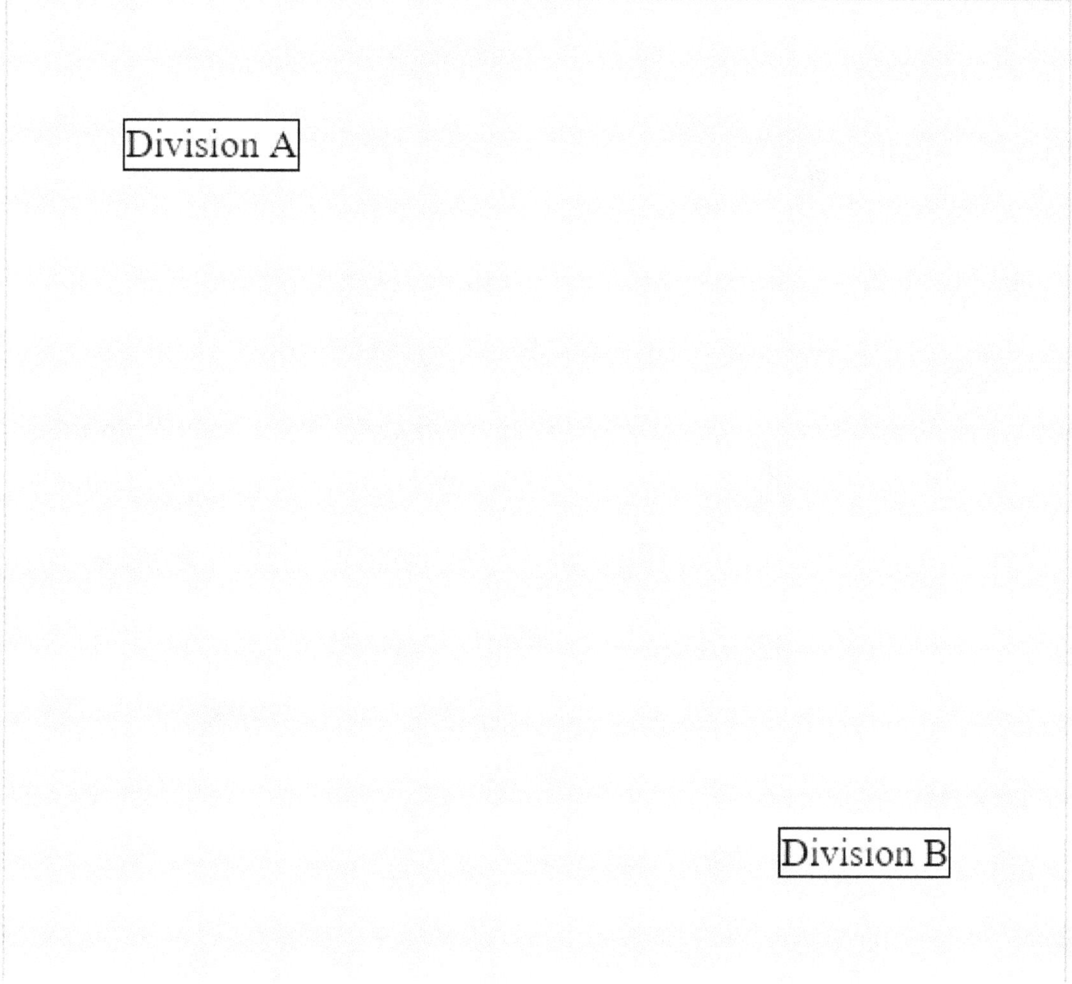

Division A

Division B

Above, division-a is 2 ems distant from the left and top, while division-b is 2 ems distant from the right and bottom.

Below, I have changed division-b's CSS so that it is now 2 ems distant from the top rather than bottom (lines 14 and 15):

```
 5 ▾ .division-a, .division-b {
 6        position:absolute;
 7        background:#fff;
 8   }
 9 ▾ .division-a {
10        top:2em;
11        left:2em;
12   }
13 ▾ .division-b {
14        top:2em;
15        right:2em;
16   }
```

Division A   Division B

Above, both elements are 2 ems distant from the top, but division-a is 2 ems distant from the left while division-b is 2 ems distant from the right, causing them to be at the same position vertically.

Below, I have increased the left distance of division-a and the right distance of division-b:

```
 9 ▾ .division-a {
10        top:2em;
11        left:8em;
12   }
13 ▾ .division-b {
14        top:2em;
15        right:8em;
16   }
```

Division A Division B

If I keep increasing both of these distances, the two divisions run into each other:

```
 9 ▾ .division-a {
10      top:2em;
11      left:9em;
12 }
13 ▾ .division-b {
14      top:2em;
15      right:9em;
16 }
```

DivisioDivision B

Above, division-b wins out and division-a goes underneath it. This is because division-b is declared further down in the HTML, causing it to have precedence. We can, however, declare that one division should be in front of another using the "z-index" property (lines 12 and 17):

```
 9 ▾ .division-a {
10      top:2em;
11      left:9em;
12      z-index:2;
13 }
14 ▾ .division-b {
15      top:2em;
16      right:9em;
17      z-index:1;
18 }
```

Division Aision B

The "z-index" property determines at what "depth" the element should appear compared to other elements. The higher the value, the less depth the element will have, meaning the higher it will be. Above, division-a has a z-index of 2, while division-b has a z-index of 1. This makes division-a "higher", so that it shows on top of division-b.

The values we give to the "z-index" property are arbitrary. We could have given division-a a z-index of 999 and division-b a z-index of 998 and the result would be the same:

```
 9 ▾  .division-a {
10        top:2em;
11        left:9em;
12        z-index:999;
13     }
14 ▾  .division-b {
15        top:2em;
16        right:9em;
17        z-index:998;
18     }
```

Division A|sion B

Playing with Coins

At this point, we can use our knowledge to create some interesting though crude drawings. Below, I have created five divisions:

```
1    <div class="division-a"></div>
2    <div class="division-b"></div>
3    <div class="division-c"></div>
4    <div class="division-d"></div>
5    <div class="division-e"></div>
6
```

Below, I give the <div>s a height, width and border using CSS:

```
i 1  <div class="division-a"></div>
  2  <div class="division-b"></div>
  3  <div class="division-c"></div>
  4  <div class="division-d"></div>
  5  <div class="division-e"></div>
  6
  1  |
```

```
1 ▾ div {
2        height:3em;
3        width:3em;
⚠ 4      border:3px solid #000;
5    }
6
```

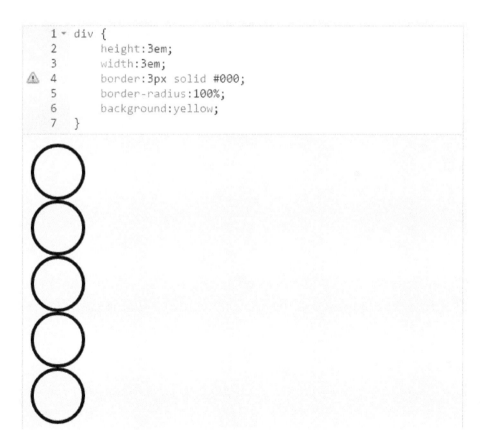

By giving the <div> elements a border-radius of 100%, I turn the rectangles into circles. I have also given them a yellow background (which will not show up if you are reading this in black and white):

```
1 ▾ div {
2        height:3em;
3        width:3em;
⚠ 4      border:3px solid #000;
5        border-radius:100%;
6        background:yellow;
7    }
```

Below, I give the <div> elements absolute positioning (line 7), which makes them all pile on each other due to the fact that they all have the same distance from the top and left by default:

```
1 ▾ div {
2       height:3em;
3       width:3em;
4       border:3px solid #000;
5       border-radius:100%;
6       background:yellow;
7       position:absolute;
8   }
```

Below, I give each <div> its own top and left distance (lines 9 to 13):

```
1 ▾ div {
2       height:3em;
3       width:3em;
4       border:3px solid #000;
5       border-radius:100%;
6       background:yellow;
7       position:absolute;
8   }
9   .division-a {top:1em;left:1em}
10  .division-b {top:1em;left:1.5em}
11  .division-c {top:1em;left:2em}
12  .division-d {top:1em;left:2.5em}
13  .division-e {top:1em;left:3em}
14
```

Above, I have formatted my CSS differently to make it take up less space. The <div> elements appear like a pile of coins, with division-e appearing at the top due to being declared last in the HTML.

By fiddling with the CSS, we can create various designs:

```
 1 ▾ div {
 2       height:3em;
 3       width:3em;
 4       border:3px solid #000;
 5       border-radius:100%;
 6       background:yellow;
 7       position:absolute;
 8   }
 9   .division-a {top:1em;left:1em}
10   .division-b {top:2.5em;left:3em}
11   .division-c {top:1em;left:5em}
12   .division-d {top:2.5em;left:7em}
13   .division-e {top:1em;left:9em}
14
```

Below, using "z-index", I have forced divisions b and d to appear on top of the rest:

```
 9   .division-a {top:1em;left:1em;z-index:1;}
10   .division-b {top:2.5em;left:3em;z-index:2;}
11   .division-c {top:1em;left:5em;z-index:1;}
12   .division-d {top:2.5em;left:7em;z-index:2;}
13   .division-e {top:1em;left:9em;z-index:1;}
14
```

Above, divisions a, c and e have a "z-index" of 1, while divisions b and d have a "z-index" of 2. This means divisions a, c and e appear on a lower "plane" than divisions b and d.

Using scaling, we can make the discs above have varying sizes:

```
 9 ▾  .division-a {top:1em;left:1em;z-index:1;
10        transform:scale(0.5);}
11    .division-b {top:2.5em;left:3em;z-index:2;}
12    .division-c {top:1em;left:5em;z-index:1;}
13    .division-d {top:2.5em;left:7em;z-index:2;}
14    .division-e {top:1em;left:9em;z-index:1;}
15
16
17
```

Above, on line 10, I have made division-a appear smaller using the "transform" property, which is used for applying transformations to an element. The value of the property is "scale(0.5)", meaning to *scale* (i.e. change the size of) the element to 0.5 times its original size. The result is that division-a is now half as large as before.

Below, I have given division-b a scaling of 1.5 (line 12), meaning that it is now one and a half times larger than before:

```
 9 ▾  .division-a {top:1em;left:1em;z-index:1;
10        transform:scale(0.5);}
11 ▾  .division-b {top:2.5em;left:3em;z-index:2;
12        transform:scale(1.5);}
13    .division-c {top:1em;left:5em;z-index:1;}
14    .division-d {top:2.5em;left:7em;z-index:2;}
15    .division-e {top:1em;left:9em;z-index:1;}
```

Scaling an element causes everything about it to change in size, for example any text contained inside it, and the thickness of its border.

Relative Positioning

We have covered the "position:absolute" property, which allows us to give an element an "absolute" position, meaning that its location is unaffected by anything around it.[12] Instead of that, we can also use *relative* positioning. This allows us to have some control over the position of something while also having it be affected by things around it.

```
i 1 ▾ <div>
  2       "Power attracts the corruptible.
  3       Suspect all those who seek it."
  4   </div>
  5   <div>Frank Herbert</div>
  6 |
```

```
1 ▾ div {
2       font-size:20px;
3   }
4
```

```
1 |
```

"Power attracts the corruptible. Suspect all those who seek it."
Frank Herbert

Above, we have a quotation from Frank Herbert, writer of the *Dune* series of sci-fi books. We will go about improving the appearance of this quotation and through this process, learn the use of relative positioning.

First, I will give the quote author's name a class so that I can give it a style (line 5 below):

```
i 1 ▾ <div>
  2       "Power attracts the corruptible.
  3       Suspect all those who seek it."
  4   </div>
  5   <div class="author">Frank Herbert</div>
  6 |
```

I will make the author's name appear on the right using the "text-align" property on line 5 of the CSS:

---

[12] There are caveats to this, as will be made clear.

```
1 ▾ div {
2        font-size:20px;
3   }
4 ▾ .author {
5        text-align:right;
6   }
7   |
```

"Power attracts the corruptible. Suspect all those who seek it."

Frank Herbert

Instead of using plain double quotes, I will use curly double quotes which have a better appearance. This is done through using the "“" and "”" HTML entities, as follows:

```
1 ▾ <div>
2        &ldquo;Power attracts the corruptible.
3        Suspect all those who seek it.&rdquo;
4   </div>
5   <div class="author">Frank Herbert</div>
6   |
```

The result is as follows:

"Power attracts the corruptible. Suspect all those who seek it."

Frank Herbert

I will give the quotation its own class and make its text larger (line 1 of the HTML, lines 7-9 of the CSS):

```
i 1▾ <div class="quote-text">
  2      &ldquo;Power attracts the corruptible.
  3      Suspect all those who seek it.&rdquo;
  4   </div>
  5   <div class="author">Frank Herbert</div>
  6   |
```

```
1▾ div {
2      font-size:20px;
3   }
4▾ .author {
5      text-align:right;
6   }
7▾ .quote-text {
8      font-size:150%;
9   }
10  |
```

```
1  |
```

"Power attracts the corruptible. Suspect all those who seek it."

Frank Herbert

I will style the quotation marks by placing them inside <span> tags with the class "qmark", meaning "quotation mark" (lines 2 and 5):

```
i 1▾ <div class="quote-text">
  2      <span class="qmark">&ldquo;</span>Power
  3      attracts the corruptible.
  4      Suspect all those
  5      who seek it.<span class="qmark">&rdquo;</span>
  6   </div>
  7   <div class="author">Frank Herbert</div>
  8   |
```

Below, we will give the quotation marks a font-size of 250% (lines 10-12 of the CSS):

```
1▾ div {
2      font-size:20px;
3   }
4▾ .author {
5      text-align:right;
6   }
7▾ .quote-text {
8      font-size:150%;
9   }
10▾ .qmark {
11     font-size:250%;
```

The result is as follows:

> " Power attracts the corruptible. Suspect "
> all those who seek it.
>
> Frank Herbert

Above, notice how the second line of the quotation has a broken appearance. That's because the end quotation mark is so large that it pushes the whole of the second line down. We can verify this by giving the quotation marks a border (line 12 below):

```
10 ▾ .qmark {
11       font-size:250%;
12       border:1px solid #000;
13   }
14
```

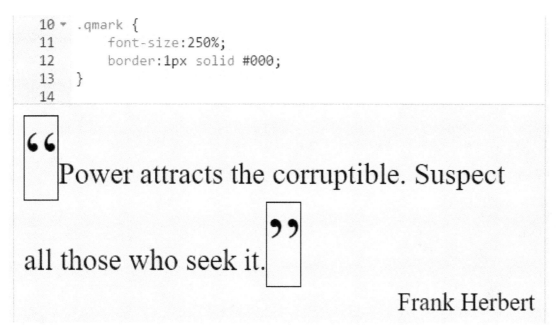

To fix this, we will give the whole quote a "line-height" property. This controls the spacing between lines, as follows (line 9 below):

```
 7 ▾  .quote-text {
 8         font-size:150%;
 9         line-height:1em;
10     }
11 ▾  .qmark {
12         font-size:250%;
13         border:1px solid #000;
14     }
```

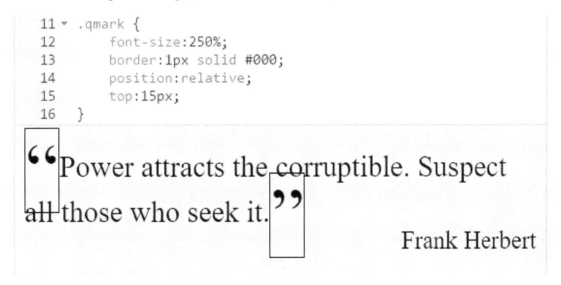

Above, the spacing between the first and second lines of the quote is now appropriate, but the quotation marks are not showing up properly because their larger font size makes not fit properly inside the small font size of the text. We have to force the quotation marks downward, and to do so we use relative positioning (lines 14 and 15 below):

```
11 ▾  .qmark {
12         font-size:250%;
13         border:1px solid #000;
14         position:relative;
15         top:15px;
16     }
```

Above, we are declaring that the quotation marks should be 15 pixels distant from the top of their previous position. The quotation marks move down 15 pixels *relative* to their original position. This makes them adaptable to their environment. For example, below I delete the second sentence of the quotation:

149

```
i 1 ▾ <div class="quote-text">
  2      <span class="qmark">&ldquo;</span>Power
  3      attracts the
  4      corruptible.<span class="qmark">&rdquo;</span>
  5   </div>
  6   <div class="author">Frank Herbert</div>
  7  |
```

```
 1 ▾ div {
 2      font-size:20px;
 3  }
 4 ▾ .author {
 5      text-align:right;
 6  }
 7 ▾ .quote-text {
 8      font-size:150%;
 9      line-height:1em;
10  }
11 ▾ .qmark {
12      font-size:250%;
13      border:1px solid #000;
14      position:relative;
15      top:15px;
16  }
```

```
 1  |
```

"Power attracts the corruptible."

Frank Herbert

Above, notice the way the ending quotation mark has now moved. Its relative positioning means that it is always 15 pixels below where it would be if we hadn't given it positioning.

Below, I bring back the second sentence while hiding the borders by setting the border to zero on line 13 of the CSS:

```
11 ▾  .qmark {
12        font-size:250%;
i 13       border:0px solid #000;
14        position:relative;
15        top:15px;
16     }
```

"Power attracts the corruptible. Suspect all those who seek it."

Frank Herbert

The quotations are a little too close to the text, we can change this with padding (line 16 below):

```
11 ▾  .qmark {
12        font-size:250%;
i 13      border:0px solid #000;
14        position:relative;
15        top:15px;
16        padding:5px;
17    }
```

66 Power attracts the corruptible. Suspect all those who seek it. **99**

Frank Herbert

The styling we create in one font can appear less appealing in another font. For example, below I change the font of the quotation (including the quotation marks) to Monotype Corsiva (line 10 below):

```
7 ▾  .quote-text {
8        font-size:150%;
9        line-height:1em;
10       font-family:'Monotype Corsiva';
11   }
12 ▾  .qmark {
13       font-size:250%;
i 14     border:0px solid #000;
15       position:relative;
16       top:15px;
17       padding:5px;
```

Power attracts the corruptible. Suspect all those who seek it.

Frank Herbert

Now, the ending quotation mark is too far away from the text. To fix this, we give the ending quotation mark a new class while letting it keep the qmark class (line 5 below):

```
i  1 ▾  <div class="quote-text">
   2        <span class="qmark">&ldquo;</span>Power
   3        attracts the corruptible.
   4        Suspect all those
   5        who seek it.<span class="qmark end">&rdquo;</span>
   6    </div>
   7    <div class="author">Frank Herbert</div>
   8    |
```

You can add any number of classes to an element by separating them with spaces (not commas).

Below, I have fixed the appearance of the ending quotation mark on lines 19 to 21:

```
  12 ▾  .qmark {
  13        font-size:250%;
i 14        border:0px solid #000;
  15        position:relative;
  16        top:15px;
  17        padding:5px;
  18    }
  19 ▾  .end {
  20        right:13px;
  21    }
```

“*Power attracts the corruptible. Suspect all those who seek it.*”

Frank Herbert

Above, the ending quotation mark takes its styling from both classes (qmark and end). On the end class, I declare that it should be 13 pixels distant from its previous *right* position, which causes the quotation mark to move leftwards by 13 pixels, making it closer to the text.

Another way of achieving the same would be to give it a *negative* left distance, as follows (line 20 below):

```
19 ▾  .end {
20        left:-13px;
21    }
```

❝ *Power attracts the corruptible. Suspect all*
those who seek it. **❞**

Frank Herbert

Above, the end result is exactly the same as the "right:13px" property. This is because negative distance causes the element to move in the opposite direction.

Absolutes within Relatives

A common usage of relative position is to help us have more control over a certain part of an HTML document. Below, we have a quotation from Shakespeare inside one division, and a Shakespeare portrait inside the other division:

```
 1 ▾ <div class="division-a">
 2        Cowards die many times before their deaths;<br>
 3    The valiant never taste of death but once.<br>
 4    Of all the wonders that I yet have heard,<br>
 5    It seems to me most strange that men should fear;<br>
 6    Seeing that death, a necessary end,<br>
 7    Will come when it will come.
 8
 9    </div>
10 ▾ <div class="division-b">
11        <img src="shakespeare_portrait.gif" />
12    </div>
13
```

```
 1 ▾ .division-a, .division-b {
 2        float:left;
 3        border:1px solid #000;
 4        height:200px;
 5
 6    }
 7 ▾ .division-a {
 8        width:60%;
 9        font-size:90%;
10    }
11 ▾ .division-b {
12        width:35%;
13        margin-left:4%;
14    }
15
```

Cowards die many times before their deaths;
The valiant never taste of death but once.
Of all the wonders that I yet have heard,
It seems to me most strange that men should fear;
Seeing that death, a necessary end,
Will come when it will come.

Inside division-b, we have an <img> tag, which is how we include images inside an HTML document.

When it comes to <div> tags and most other tags, we have an opening and a closing tag. But the <img> tag, similar to the <br> tag, does not have a closing tag, because it has no content besides the image. The "src" attribute on the <img> tag tells the browser where the image is located on your computer or on the Internet.

To illustrate further, below I have a picture (goats_and_girl.jpg) and an html file (test.html) inside the same folder on my computer:

If I open test.html in Notepad, this is what it contains:

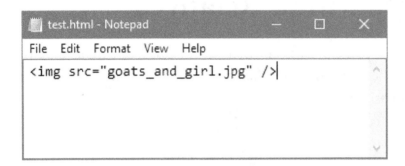

And if I open it in a web browser, I will see this:

When you give only a file name in the "src" tag, the browser will look for the image inside the folder where the html file is.

Below, I have created a new folder and placed the image inside it:

Name	Date modified
my_new_folder	2/7/2018 8:34 AM
test.html	2/7/2018 8:32 AM

Now, if I open "test.html" in a browser, I will only get an icon that tells me the image could not be found:

This is because the "src" tag tells the browser to look for the image inside the same folder as test.html. The browser does just that, but finds nothing. It is not smart enough to look elsewhere for the image. It will only look exactly where we tell it to look. I can tell the browser to look for the image inside the new folder I created that actually contains the image, by modifying "test.html" inside Notepad as follows:

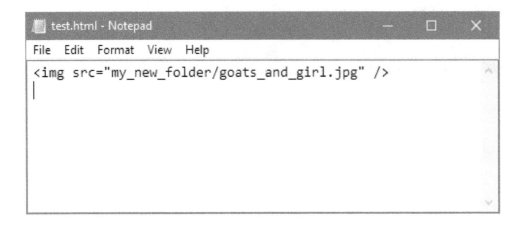

Above, you see what we call a path. "my_new_folder" *slash* "goats_and_girls.jpg" means there is a folder called "my_new_folder", and inside it there is an image file called "goats_and_girl.jpg". If we save the file and open it again in the browser, we will see the image again:

Let us now go back to JSTinker and Shakespeare:

```
 1 ▾ <div class="division-a">
 2       Cowards die many times before their deaths;<br>
 3     The valiant never taste of death but once.<br>
 4     Of all the wonders that I yet have heard,<br>
 5     It seems to me most strange that men should fear;<br>
 6     Seeing that death, a necessary end,<br>
 7     Will come when it will come.
 8
 9   </div>
10 ▾ <div class="division-b">
11       <img src="shakespeare_portrait.gif" />
12   </div>
13 |
```

```
 1 ▾ .division-a, .division-b {
 2       float:left;
⚠ 3       border:1px solid #000;
 4       height:200px;
 5
 6   }
 7 ▾ .division-a {
 8       width:60%;
 9       font-size:90%;
10   }
11 ▾ .division-b {
12       width:35%;
13       margin-left:4%;
14   }
15 |
```

```
 1 |
```

Cowards die many times before their
deaths;
The valiant never taste of death but once.
Of all the wonders that I yet have heard,
It seems to me most strange that men
should fear;
Seeing that death, a necessary end,
Will come when it will come.

Now, if I give the <img> tag absolute positioning and a left distance of 2 ems, the following takes place:

```
15 ▾ img {
16       position:absolute;
17       left:2em;
18   }
19
```

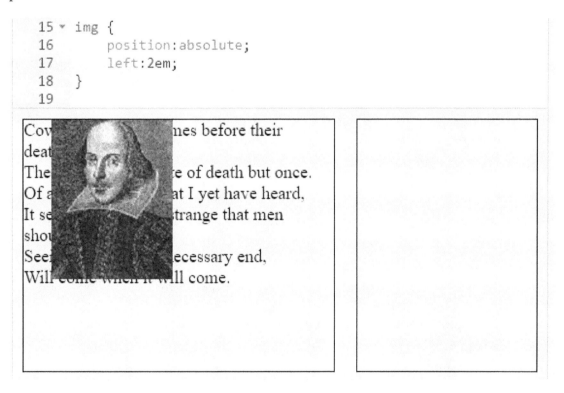

Intuitively, we'd expect the image to stay inside its own box. But the browser interprets the "left" distance as having to do with the whole browser screen, so the image is shown 2 ems distant from the left edge of the whole HTML document. By putting relative positioning on division-b (the box on the right) we can change things (line 14 below):

157

```
11 ▾ .division-b {
12        width:35%;
13        margin-left:4%;
14        position:relative;
15 }
16 ▾ img {
17        position:absolute;
18        left:2em;
```

Here is the result:

Cowards die many times before their
deaths;
The valiant never taste of death but once.
Of all the wonders that I yet have heard,
It seems to me most strange that men
should fear;
Seeing that death, a necessary end,
Will come when it will come.

Above, since division-b has *relative* positioning, the browser interprets the absolute positioning of the <img> element as restricted to division-b. The "left" distance of 2 ems now is calculated from the left edge of division-b rather than the left edge of the whole document.

By giving division-b relative positioning, its appearance or position does not change (unless we give it a "left" property or some other such property). What changes is its authority. Anything inside it that has absolute positioning will now have their position calculated with respect to division-b rather than with respect to the whole document. This allows us to create different zones of authority, i.e. different contexts, within a particular document, helping us create complex designs.

In short, if you give an element absolute positioning, its position is not always calculated with respect to the whole document. If the element is contained inside a <div> that has relative positioning, this forces the absolute position to be calculated with respect to this parent <div>.

To clarify things further, below I have placed Shakespeare's portrait inside three <div> elements:

```
1 ▾ <div class="a">
2 ▾     <div class="b">
3 ▾         <div class="c">
4               <img src="shakespeare_portrait.gif" />
5           </div>
6       </div>
7 </div>
8 }
```

```
1 ▾ div {
2       border: 2px dashed #000;
3       margin:15px;
4 }
5 |
```

```
1 |
```

If I give the portrait absolute positioning and a left and top distance of zero, this takes place:

```
5 ▾ img {
6       position:absolute;
7       left:0;
8       top:0;
9 }
10
```

Above, the image's distance is calculated from the left and top of the whole document, without any respect for the <div> elements, since none of these elements have absolute or relative positioning. The innermost <div> (division "c") appears as collapsed onto itself because we have given its content (the image) absolute positioning, which makes it "hover" over the document without having any influence on other elements. As far as the appearance of division "c" is concerned, it might as well have no contents.

Below, I have given division "a" relative positioning (line 6). The image now changes position, because its top and left distances are now calculated with respect to division "a":

```
5 ▾ .a {
6       position:relative;
7 }
```

Here is the result:

Below, I change things so that now division "b" has relative positioning rather than division "a" (line 5):

```
 5 ▾  .b {
 6        position:relative;
 7    }
 8 ▾  img {
 9        position:absolute;
10        left:0;
11        top:0;
12    }
13
14    |
```

Above, the image's position is calculated with respect to division "b". If we change "b" to "c" (line 5 below), as would be expected, the image moves again:

```
 5 ▼ .c {
 6       position:relative;
 7 }
 8 ▼ img {
 9       position:absolute;
10       left:0;
11       top:0;
12 }
13
14
```

What if two ancestors have relative positioning? Below I have given both divisions "b" and "c" relative positioning. The image's position does not change, because its position is calculated with respect to the *nearest* relative that has relative or absolute positioning, and in this case, that relative happens to be division "c":

```
 5 ▼ .b, .c {
 6       position:relative;
 7 }
 8 ▼ img {
 9       position:absolute;
10       left:0;
11       top:0;
12 }
13
14
```

Absolutes within Absolutes

To clarify the issue of absolutes within absolutes, below I have a single division (division "a") containing Shakespeare's portrait:

```
i  1 ▾ <div class="a">
   2              <img src="shakespeare_portrait.gif" />
   3    </div>
```

Here is the CSS:

```
1 ▾ div {
2        border: 2px dashed #000;
3        margin:15px;
4    }
5 ▾ img {
6        position:absolute;
7        left:0;
8        top:0;
9    }
```

And here is the result:

The division is collapsed onto itself because the image has absolute positioning, meaning it hovers in a way that takes up no height of its parent element. Division "a" is taking up a whole line, which is why it appears as a dashed black bar.

If we give division "a" absolute positioning (line 6 below), something strange takes place:

```
 1 ▾  div {
 2         border: 2px dashed #000;
 3         margin:15px;
 4    }
 5 ▾  .a {
 6         position:absolute;
 7    }
 8 ▾  img {
 9         position:absolute;
10         left:0;
11         top:0;
12    }
13
14
```

Above, division "a" seems to disappear. This is because the absolute positioning makes it collapse horizontally. It stops taking up a whole line, because it is now hovering over the document. The result is that the division becomes as small as it can get. Above, you can actually see it on the top left of Shakespeare's portrait. It looks like a very small square. That is the division's border. It is now a division that is wholly made up of borders, with nothing inside it.

Now, wherever we move division "a", that image will also move there with it, because division "a" is an ancestor of the image and has absolute positioning, so that the image's position is calculated with respect to it. Below, I have given division "a" a left distance of 5 ems and a top distance of 1 em (lines 7 and 8):

```
 1 ▾ div {
 2       border: 2px dashed #000;
 3       margin:15px;
 4   }
 5 ▾ .a {
 6       position:absolute;
 7       top:1em;
 8       left:5em;
 9   }
10 ▾ img {
11       position:absolute;
12       left:0;
13       top:0;
14   }
```

Below, I have given division "a" a width and height, so that it expands in order to appear as if it is the border of the image:

```
 5 ▾ .a {
 6       position:absolute;
 7       top:1em;
 8       left:5em;
 9       height:8em;
10       width:7em;
11   }
```

The result is as follows:

It is difficult to make the image and the border line up perfectly because they are hovering at different planes (as if they are drawn on separate pieces of clear glass that are placed on each other). If we wanted division "a" to properly encapsulate the image, we'd have to make the image relative so that it starts to take up height again.

Below, I have removed the height and width of division "a" and changed the image's positioning to relative:

```
 5 ▾ .a {
 6        position:absolute;
 7        top:1em;
 8        left:5em;
 9   }
10 ▾ img {
11        position:relative;
12        left:0;
13        top:0;
```

Here is the result:

Above, the <div>'s positioning is absolute. But since the image's positioning is relative, it is properly contained inside the <div>, it forces the div to expand around it, creating the effect of a frame.

You may notice, however, that there is some space underneath the image, between the image and the frame. This is caused by the fact that an image is an inline element. I will not go into the details of why this happens, as it gets technical. We can solve it by giving the image a "display:block" property (line 14 below):

```
 5 ▾ .a {
 6        position:absolute;
 7        top:1em;
 8        left:5em;
 9   }
10 ▾ img {
11        position:relative;
12        left:0;
13        top:0;
14        display:block;
15   }
```

We can make the image escape its border by giving its "left" and "top" properties some value, as follows:

```
 5 ▾ .a {
 6        position:absolute;
 7        top:1em;
 8        left:5em;
 9  }
10 ▾ img {
11        position:relative;
12        left:1em;
13        top:1em;
14        display:block;
15  }
```

Note that the "left" and "top" properties of the image are calculated with respect to its place inside the <div>, rather than with respect to the edge of the <div>. To illustrate this, below I have added a <p> element inside the <div> but above the image (HTML line 2):

```
1 ▾ <div class="a">
2       <p>Test</p>
3       <img src="shakespeare_portrait.gif" />
4   </div>
5   |
```

```
 1 ▾ div {
 2        border: 2px dashed #000;
 3        margin:15px;
 4   }
 5 ▾ .a {
 6        position:absolute;
 7        top:1em;
 8        left:5em;
 9   }
10 ▾ img {
11        position:relative;
12        left:1em;
13        top:1em;
14        display:block;
15   }
```

The image moves down because its "left" and "top" distances of 1em are calculated from its natural position inside the <div>. That natural position is somewhere below the <p> element.

If, however, we change the image back to "absolute" (line 11), its position will be calculated with respect to the edge of its parent <div>, without any respect for its natural position inside the <div>:

```
1 ▾ <div class="a">
2       <p>Test test test test test</p>
3       <p>Test test test test test</p>
4       <p>Test test test test test</p>
5       <p>Test test test test test</p>
6       <p>Test test test test test</p>
7       <img src="shakespeare_portrait.gif" />
8   </div>
9   |
```

```
 1 ▾ div {
 2        border: 2px dashed #000;
 3        margin:15px;
 4   }
 5 ▾ .a {
 6        position:absolute;
 7        top:1em;
 8        left:5em;
 9   }
10 ▾ img {
11        position:absolute;
12        left:1em;
13        top:1em;
14        display:block;
15   }
```

Above, I have added a number of additional <p> elements (see the HTML), while giving the image absolute positioning (line 11 of the CSS). The image's position is now calculated with respect to the edges of division "a", without respect for what it contains, so that it hovers over the contents.

Below, I change the image's positioning back to relative (line 11):

```
10 ▾ img {
11        position:relative;
12        left:1em;
13        top:1em;
14        display:block;
15   }
```

Test test test test test

Test test test test test

Test test test test test

Test test test test test

Test test test test test

Above, the image jumps back down to the bottom. The relative positioning makes the image appear where it would without positioning.

Below, I have moved the <img> tag to the middle of the HTML (line 5 of the HTML):

```
i  1 ▾ <div class="a">
   2        <p>Test test test test test</p>
   3        <p>Test test test test test</p>
   4        <p>Test test test test test</p>
   5        <img src="shakespeare_portrait.gif" />
   6        <p>Test test test test test</p>
   7        <p>Test test test test test</p>
   8   </div>
   9   |
```

This causes the image to appear in the middle of the document:

Above, the image's relative positioning continues to exert influence. The image is still 1 em distant from the left and 1 em distant from the top of the image's original position, which is one reason why there is so much space at the top of the image.

In CSS, all elements have 'static' positioning by default. We can disable the effects of positioning by changing the value of the 'position' property to 'static', as follows (line 11 of the CSS):

```
10 ▾  img {
11        position:static;
12        left:1em;
13        top:1em;
14        display:block;
15     }
```

Above, the image now appears exactly where it would appear without positioning. The "top" and "left" properties no longer exert any influence, because 'static' positioning disables the effects of positioning. Now, if we were to take away all the positioning-related CSS, the image will continue to be exactly where it is above:

```
10 ▼ img {
11        display:block;
12 }
13
14 |
15
```

Test test test test test

Test test test test test

Test test test test test

Test test test test test

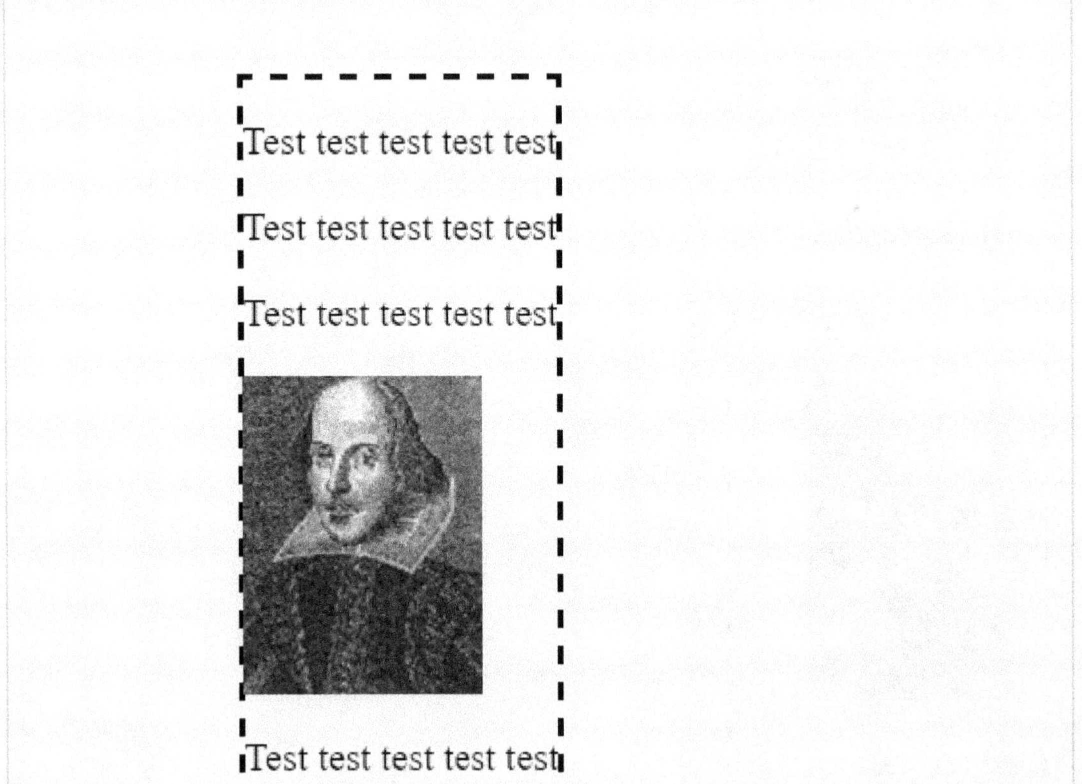

Above, the image stays where it is because if we do not specify any positioning, CSS assumes 'static' positioning by default.

Fixed Positioning

The final type of positioning to talk about is 'fixed' positioning. One of the main tasks of a web designer is to create annoyances for their users, as directed by their bosses. Fixed positioning is one of the main tools for achieving this. Let's say you have a page with an image that people really want to see, but you want to display a reminder that seriously annoys people. We begin with the reminder at the top and the image below it:

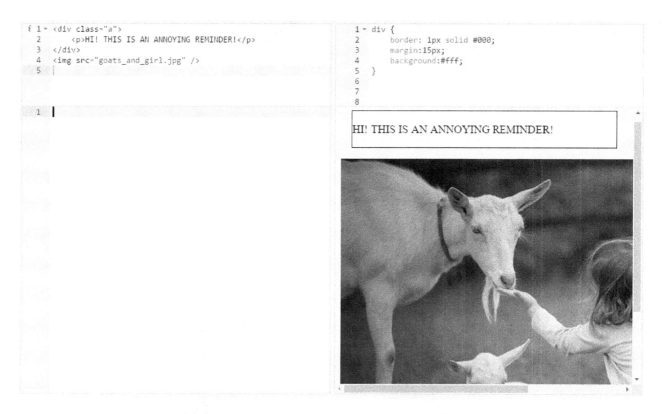

```
i 1 ▾ <div class="a">
  2       <p>HI! THIS IS AN ANNOYING REMINDER!</p>
  3   </div>
  4   <img src="goats_and_girl.jpg" />
  5
```

```
1 ▾ div {
2       border: 1px solid #000;
3       margin:15px;
4       background:#fff;
5   }
6
7
8
```

HI! THIS IS AN ANNOYING REMINDER!

Above, we have a <div> with a paragraph inside it. Below that we have an <img> tag. If the user scrolls down, they will no longer see the reminder, as follows. This will allow them to enjoy the image without having to see the reminder:

```
i 1 ▾ <div class="a">
  2       <p>HI! THIS IS AN ANNOYING REMINDER!</p>
  3   </div>
  4   <img src="goats_and_girl.jpg" />
  5
```

```
1 ▾ div {
2       border: 1px solid #000;
3       margin:15px;
4       background:#fff;
5   }
6
7
8
```

173

Below, we use CSS to give division "a" fixed positioning (lines 6-10):

```
1 ▾ div {
2        border: 1px solid #000;
3        margin:15px;
4        background:#fff;
5 }
6 ▾ .a {
7        position:fixed;
8        top:0;
9        left:0;
10 }
11
```

So far, this appears similar to absolute positioning. What's special about it is that if the user scrolls down, the reminder keeps in view:

```
6 ▼  .a {
7        position:fixed;
8        top:0;
9        left:0;
10     }
```

To further illustrate, below I have added a new image underneath the image shown earlier (HTML line 5):

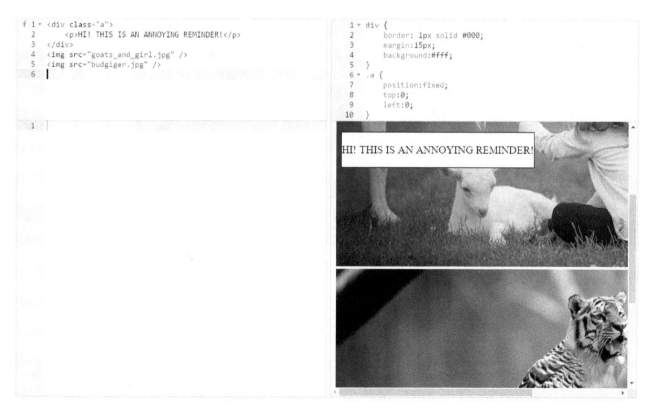

Above, I have scrolled down the document further but the reminder keeps in view.

Instead of top positioning, we can give it bottom positioning to plaster the reminder to the bottom of the screen:

```
1 ▾ div {
2       border: 1px solid #000;
3       margin:15px;
4       background:#fff;
5   }
6 ▾ .a {
7       position:fixed;
8       bottom:0;
9       left:0;
10  }
```

If you have browsed the web on your phone, you have probably run into websites that use fixed positioning to show you an ad at the bottom of the screen which does not go away even if you scroll down.

Below is a picture of a Vietnamese news website that uses fixed positioning to show a 'jump back to top' button on the bottom right of their articles:

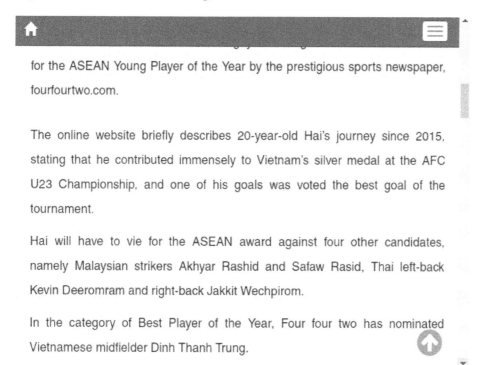

Above, notice the top-facing arrow on the bottom-right. As you scroll down the article, this arrow continues to remain where it is. If you click on it, it takes you back to the top of the page.

This page intentionally left blank

5. Working with Tables

Tables are an important part of HTML. Below I have created a table with two rows and two columns:

```
 1 ▾ <table>
 2 ▾    <tr>
 3          <td>Row 1 Item 1</td>
 4          <td>Row 1 Item 2</td>
 5      </tr>
 6 ▾    <tr>
 7          <td>Row 2 Item 1</td>
 8          <td>Row 2 Item 2</td>
 9      </tr>
10  </table>
```

Row 1 Item 1 Row 1 Item 2
Row 2 Item 1 Row 2 Item 2

We can make it look more like a table by using borders. Below, I have given the <td> tag a border:

```
1 ▾ td {
2       border:1px solid #000;
3   }
4
```

Row 1 Item 1	Row 1 Item 2
Row 2 Item 1	Row 2 Item 2

In HTML, we create tables using the <table> tag. Inside them, we create rows using the <tr> tag (which stands for "table row"), and inside that we use the <td> tag to create individual "cells" of the row.

Below, I have given the <table> element a border (line 5):

```
1 ▾ td {
2       border:1px solid #000;
3   }
4 ▾ table {
5       border:1px solid #000;
6   }
7   |
```

| Row 1 Item 1 | Row 1 Item 2 |
| Row 2 Item 1 | Row 2 Item 2 |

While it looks more like a table now, the double border looks a bit strange. We can fix this using the table-specific property "border-collapse" (line 6):

```
1 ▾ td {
2       border:1px solid #000;
3   }
4 ▾ table {
5       border:1px solid #000;
6       border-collapse:collapse;
7   }
8   |
```

| Row 1 Item 1 | Row 1 Item 2 |
| Row 2 Item 1 | Row 2 Item 2 |

Now, no one can say this is not a proper table. The "border-collapse" property causes the borders on the <td> element to become the borders of the whole table. We can verify this by giving the table a dashed border (line 5 below):

```
1 ▾ td {
2       border:1px solid #000;
3   }
4 ▾ table {
5       border:1px dashed #000;
6       border-collapse:collapse;
7   }
8   |
```

| Row 1 Item 1 | Row 1 Item 2 |
| Row 2 Item 1 | Row 2 Item 2 |

Above, nothing happens because that table's border is hidden behind the <td> border. If, however, we make the table's border thicker, the table's border takes precedence. Below, I have increased the border on the <table> element to 2 pixels:

```
1 ▾ td {
2       border:1px solid #000;
3   }
4 ▾ table {
5       border:2px dashed #000;
6       border-collapse:collapse;
7   }
8   |
```

| Row 1 Item 1 | Row 1 Item 2 |
| Row 2 Item 1 | Row 2 Item 2 |

Above, note the way the inner borders between the cells are not dashed, that is because they are continuing to show the 1 pixel border on the <td> element. If we increase the border on the <td> element so that its thickness equals the border on <table> element, it takes precedence (line 2 below):

```
1 ▾ td {
2       border:2px solid #000;
3   }
4 ▾ table {
5       border:2px dashed #000;
6       border-collapse:collapse;
7   }
8   |
```

Row 1 Item 1	Row 1 Item 2
Row 2 Item 1	Row 2 Item 2

Instead of giving a border to the <td> element, we can give it to the <tr> element, as follows (I've changed the selector on line 1 to "tr" instead of "td"):

```
1 ▾ tr {
2       border:2px solid #000;
3   }
4 ▾ table {
5       border:2px dashed #000;
6       border-collapse:collapse;
7   }
8   |
```

Row 1 Item 1 Row 1 Item 2
Row 2 Item 1 Row 2 Item 2

Above, there is no border between the cells, since the border is on the rows. The border on the <tr> element will not show up unless we are using the "border-collapse:collapse" property on the <table> element. Below, I have deleted the "border-collapse" property from line 6:

```
1 ▾ tr {
2       border:2px solid #000;
3   }
4 ▾ table {
5       border:2px dashed #000;
6   }
7   |
```

┌─ ─ ─ ─ ─ ─ ─ ─ ─ ─ ─ ─ ┐
│ Row 1 Item 1 Row 1 Item 2 │
│ Row 2 Item 1 Row 2 Item 2 │
└─ ─ ─ ─ ─ ─ ─ ─ ─ ─ ─ ─ ┘

Due to the finicky nature of styling the <tr> element, it is best not to use it unless you really have to. Stick to styling the <td> element.

Below, I have changed the "tr" selector back to "td" (line 1):

```
1 ▾ td {
2       border:2px solid #000;
3   }
4 ▾ table {
5       border:2px dashed #000;
6   }
7   |
```

┌─ ─ ─ ─ ─ ─ ─ ─ ─ ─ ─ ┐
│ ┌──────────────┐┌──────────────┐ │
│ │ Row 1 Item 1 ││ Row 1 Item 2 │ │
│ └──────────────┘└──────────────┘ │
│ ┌──────────────┐┌──────────────┐ │
│ │ Row 2 Item 1 ││ Row 2 Item 2 │ │
│ └──────────────┘└──────────────┘ │
└─ ─ ─ ─ ─ ─ ─ ─ ─ ─ ─ ┘

Above, the dashed border on the <table> element and the solid border on the <td> element both show up, since there is no "border-collapse" property to force them to merge.

Below, I have brought back the "border-collapse" property (line 6 of the CSS). I have also added a new cell to the first row (line 5 of the HTML):

```
i  1 ▾ <table>
   2 ▾     <tr>
   3           <td>Row 1 Item 1</td>
   4           <td>Row 1 Item 2</td>
   5           <td>Row 1 Item 3</td>
   6       </tr>
   7 ▾     <tr>
   8           <td>Row 2 Item 1</td>
   9           <td>Row 2 Item 2</td>
  10       </tr>
  11 </table>
   1
```

```
1 ▾ td {
2       border:2px solid #000;
3   }
4 ▾ table {
5       border:2px dashed #000;
6       border-collapse:collapse;
7   }
8
```

Row 1 Item 1	Row 1 Item 2	Row 1 Item 3
Row 2 Item 1	Row 2 Item 2	

Above, since there is no corresponding cell on the second row, it shows up empty. We can fix this by adding a new <td> element on line 10 of the HTML (even if we have no text to put inside it):

```
i  1 ▾ <table>
   2 ▾     <tr>
   3           <td>Row 1 Item 1</td>
   4           <td>Row 1 Item 2</td>
   5           <td>Row 1 Item 3</td>
   6       </tr>
   7 ▾     <tr>
   8           <td>Row 2 Item 1</td>
   9           <td>Row 2 Item 2</td>
  10           <td></td>
  11       </tr>
  12 </table>
   1
```

```
1 ▾ td {
2       border:2px solid #000;
3   }
4 ▾ table {
5       border:2px dashed #000;
6       border-collapse:collapse;
7   }
8
```

Row 1 Item 1	Row 1 Item 2	Row 1 Item 3
Row 2 Item 1	Row 2 Item 2	

Failing to have the same number of cells on each row (i.e. the same number of <td> elements) can cause all kinds of glitches, therefore it is important to make sure to create the same number of <td> elements inside every <tr> element, even if you have nothing to put inside them. This way they show up as empty cells as they should.

Below, I have given the top left cell a class of "a" (line 3 of the HTML). I have also given this class a width of 200 pixels (line 9 of the CSS):

```
i  1 ▾ <table>
   2 ▾     <tr>
   3           <td class="a">Row 1 Item 1</td>
   4           <td>Row 1 Item 2</td>
   5           <td>Row 1 Item 3</td>
   6       </tr>
   7 ▾     <tr>
   8           <td>Row 2 Item 1</td>
   9           <td>Row 2 Item 2</td>
  10           <td></td>
  11       </tr>
  12 </table>
   1
```

```
 1 ▾ td {
 2       border:2px solid #000;
 3   }
 4 ▾ table {
 5       border:2px dashed #000;
 6       border-collapse:collapse;
 7   }
 8 ▾ .a {
 9       width:200px;
10   }
11
```

Row 1 Item 1		Row 1 Item 2	Row 1 Item 3
Row 2 Item 1		Row 2 Item 2	

By giving the top cell in a column a particular width, all the cells underneath it end up getting the same width (notice how the bottom left cell is now as wide as the top left cell).

Instead of giving a cell a particular width, we can give the whole table a certain width, as follows (line 7 of the CSS):

```
1 ▾ td {
2       border:2px solid #000;
3   }
4 ▾ table {
5       border:2px dashed #000;
6       border-collapse:collapse;
7       width:50%;
8   }
```

The result is as follows:

Row 1 Item 1	Row 1 Item 2	Row 1 Item 3
Row 2 Item 1	Row 2 Item 2	

Above, the browser automatically shrinks all the cells so that the table as a whole takes up 50% of the available horizontal space. All the cells retain the same shrunken width. We can still give some cells different widths compared to others, as follows (line 10 of the CSS):

```
 9 ▾ .a {
10       width:100px;
11   }
12   |
```

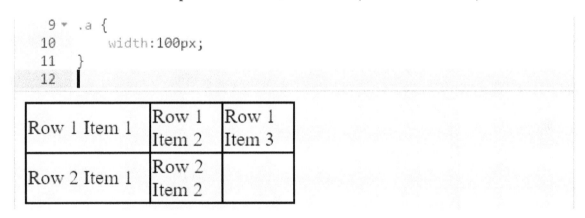

Above, the first column has expanded, but the table as a whole continues to take up 50% of the available horizontal space. The result is that the second and third columns are squeezed. Below, I have given the first column a width of 200 pixels (line 10):

```
 9 ▾  .a {
10        width:200px;
11    }
12
```

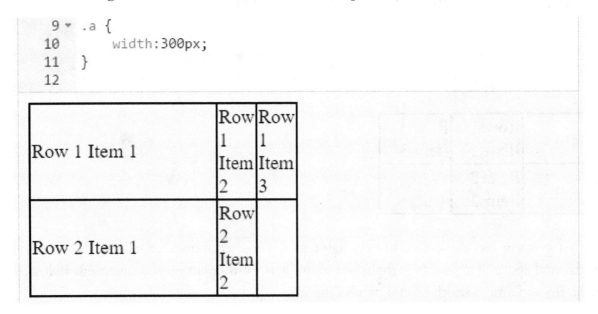

Above, the first column has expanded as much as it can. To put it another way, the second and third columns have shrunk as much as they can. Now, if I tried to further increase the width of the first column nothing will happen, because the second and third columns cannot squeeze further. Below, I have given the first column a width of 300 pixels (line 10):

```
 9 ▾  .a {
10        width:300px;
11    }
12
```

Above, the width of the first column is exactly the same as it was earlier. We cannot stretch a cell indefinitely because the width of the table and the width of the other cells limit its expansion. Table cells cannot shrink more than their contents.

Mr. Batchelor's Expenses

Below, we have the top part of a table of expenses (expressed in pounds, shillings and pennies) found in Thomas Batchelor's General View of the Agriculture of the County of Bedford. Drawn Up by Order of the Board of Agriculture, and Internal Improvement, published in the year 1808. We will now use HTML and CSS to recreate this top part of the table. Throughout this section, we will introduce many new and interesting concepts.

The table has two columns and five rows (there is a row above "Rent and tithes", but it's first cell is empty, while the second cell has the pound, shilling and penny symbols. Below, we have created the table in HTML and added the five rows, but no cells yet:

```
1   <table>
2       <tr></tr>
3       <tr></tr>
4       <tr></tr>
5       <tr></tr>
6       <tr></tr>
7   </table>
8   |
```

We now add the first row's contents:

```
 i   1 ▾ <table>
     2 ▾     <tr>
     3 ▾         <td>
     4               Succession of Crops.
     5           </td>
     6 ▾         <td>
     7               Fallow, one-third Tares.
     8           </td>
     9       </tr>
    10       <tr></tr>
```

Here is the result:

Succession of Crops. Fallow, one-third Tares.

We now add the thick border at the top of the table present in the original:

```
 1 ▾ table {
 2       border-collapse:collapse;
 3       border-top:4px solid #000;
 4   }
 5
```

The result is as follows:

Succession of Crops. Fallow, one-third Tares.

We now add a class of "first-row" to the <td> tags on the first row (lines 3 and 6 below):

```
i  1 ▾ <table>
   2 ▾     <tr>
   3 ▾         <td class="first-row">
   4               Succession of Crops.
   5           </td>
   6 ▾         <td class="first-row">
   7               Fallow, one-third Tares.
   8           </td>
   9       </tr>
  10       <tr></tr>
  11       <tr></tr>
  12       <tr></tr>
  13       <tr></tr>
  14  </table>
```

Using CSS, we give the first row's cells a bottom border (line 6 below):

```
1 ▾ table {
2       border-collapse:collapse;
3       border-top:4px solid #000;
4   }
5 ▾ .first-row {
6       border-bottom:2px solid #000;
7   }
8
```

Succession of Crops. Fallow, one-third Tares.

Let's now take another look at the original table:

Succession of Crops.	Fallow, one-third Tares.		
	£.	s.	d.
Rent and tithes - - -	1	0	0
Poor's-rates - - -	0	3	6
Income tax - - -	0	1	3

Notice how "Succession of Crops" is centered and has a lot of space around it. We recreate this using "text-align" and padding. But first, we need to give the top left cell a new class so that we can target it specifically for padding. Below, we give the top left cell a class of "first-cell" (line 3):

189

```
i   1 ▾   <table>
    2 ▾       <tr>
    3 ▾           <td class="first-row first-cell">
    4                   Succession of Crops.
    5               </td>
    6 ▾           <td class="first-row">
    7                   Fallow, one-third Tares.
```

In the CSS, we add a "text-align" property to the "first-row" class:

```
    5 ▾   .first-row {
    6           border-bottom:2px solid #000;
    7           text-align:center;
    8       }
    9
   10       |
   11
```

Succession of Crops. Fallow, one-third Tares.

Above, the text of both the left and right cells is now center-aligned, but we cannot see it yet due to the small width of their cells.

Next, inside our CSS, we create a brand new selector ".first-row.first-cell":

```
    8       }
i   9 ▾   .first-row.first-cell {
   10           padding:1em;
   11       }
   12
```

Succession of Crops.   Fallow, one-third Tares.

Note that there is no space between the two class names. This selector is something we haven't seen before. This syntax allows us to target an element that has two classes using both classes. It means "give a padding of 1 em to any element that has a class of first-row *and* a class of first-cell". If there was a space between ".first-row" and ".first-cell", the meaning would change. The browser looks at the cells to see if any of them has a class of "first-row" and "first-cell", and finds just such a cell in the top left cell.

The padding we added to the top left cell also affects the top right cell (the cell containing "Fallow…"). This is because the padding expands the top left cell, which forces its whole row to expand, and this expansion affects any other cell on the same row.

Below, I give the top right cell a class of "second-cell" to enable me to target it specifically (line 6):

```
 1 ▾  <table>
 2 ▾      <tr>
 3 ▾          <td class="first-row first-cell">
 4                  Succession of Crops.
 5              </td>
 6 ▾          <td class="first-row second-cell">
 7                  Fallow, one-third Tares.
 8              </td>
 9          </tr>
```

Now, we use the "transform" property to rotate the second cell 270 degrees (line 13 below):

```
12 ▾  .first-row.second-cell {
13          transform:rotate(270deg);
14
15    }
```

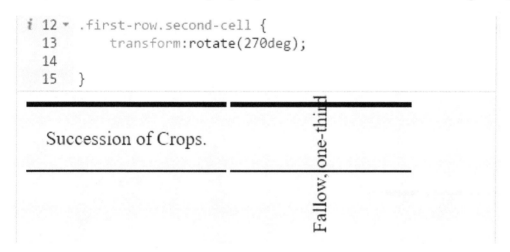

Above, even though we rotated the cell, its borders do not rotate with it. This is because a cell is not allowed to escape the limits of the row and table that contain it. Therefore while the contents rotate, the borders remain in place.

Let's look again at the original table:

Succession of Crops.	Fallow, one-third Tares.		
	£.	s.	d
Rent and tithes - -	1	0	0
Poor'-rates - - -	0	3	6
Income tax - - -	0	1	3

We will now add <br> tags to break up the top right cell's words so that they fit better inside the cell (lines 7-9 below):

```
i  1 ▾  <table>
   2 ▾      <tr>
   3 ▾          <td class="first-row first-cell">
   4                  Succession of Crops.
   5              </td>
   6 ▾          <td class="first-row second-cell">
   7 ▾              <div>Fallow,<br>
   8                  one-third<br>
   9                  Tares.</div>
  10              </td>
  11          </tr>
```

The result is as follows:

Succession of Crops.	Fallow, one-third Tares.

Let's add some padding to make the text stop touching the borders (lines 14 and 15):

```
i  9 ▾  .first-row.first-cell {
  10       padding:1em;
  11  }
i 12 ▾  .first-row.second-cell {
  13       transform:rotate(270deg);
  14       padding-top:0.5em;
  15       padding-bottom:0.5em;
  16  }
```

Succession of Crops.   Fallow, one-third Tares.

Above, even though the cell has been rotated, we still use "padding-top" and "padding-bottom" to add space on the top and bottom, because the rotation does not affect the cell's padding due to the peculiarities of table cells.

Notice that in the original the top right cell's contents are left-aligned (the letter "F" in "Fallow" is directly in line with the "o" in "one"). We recreate this by giving the cell a left alignment (line 16 below):

```
i 12 ▾  .first-row.second-cell {
  13       transform:rotate(270deg);
  14       padding-top:0.5em;
  15       padding-bottom:0.5em;
  16       text-align:left;
  17  }
```

Succession of Crops.   Fallow, one-third Tares.

In the original, there is a border between the first and second cells. We recreate this using the CSS on line 11 below:

```
 i  9 ▾  .first-row.first-cell {
   10        padding:1em;
   11        border-right:2px solid #000;
   12    }
 i 13 ▾  .first-row.second-cell {
   14        transform:rotate(270deg);
   15        padding-top:0.5em;
   16        padding-bottom:0.5em;
   17        text-align:left;
```

Succession of Crops.	Fallow, one-third Tares.

Above, we add a border to the right of the top left cell. The border falls between the two cells, appearing as if it is there to separate the two cells, even though in reality the border belongs to the top left cell.

Let's now work on the second row. We add an empty cell to this second row on line 13 of the HTML. The next cell contains a brand new table of its own:

```
12 ▾        <tr>
13              <td></td>
14 ▾            <td>
15 ▾                <table>
16 ▾                    <tr>
17                          <td>£</td>
18                          <td>s.</td>
19                          <td>d.</td>
20                      </tr>
21                  </table>
22              </td>
23          </tr>
```

The result is as follows:

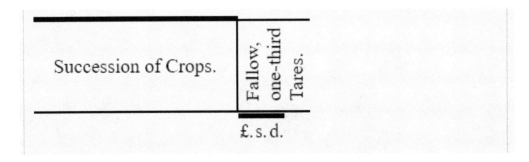

The reason we create a new table to contain the pound, shilling and penny signs is that there is some distance between them in the original, and the best way to create that distance and align the contents properly is to put them in their own table-within-a-table.

This is further clarified when we add the third row (which contains the word "Rent and tithes"):

```
24    <tr>
25        <td>Rent and tithes</td>
26        <td>
27            <table>
28                <tr>
29                    <td>1</td>
30                    <td>0</td>
31                    <td>0</td>
32                </tr>
33            </table>
34        </td>
35    </tr>
```

The result is as follows:

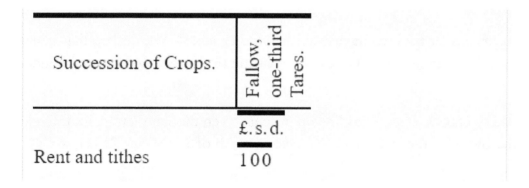

The values for rent and tithes are 1, 0, 0. Together they appear as the number 100, which can confuse people. And they do not line up properly with the symbols above them. The reason we added them to a table within a table is that doing things this way gives us the control necessary to make them line up properly with the stuff above them.

We now have three tables. The "outer" table and two tables on the second column. One inner table contains the symbols, the other contains numbers.

Notice how the new tables have a thick black border at the top. They get this because we declared in the CSS that all tables should have a thick top black border (line 3 below):

```
1 ▾ table {
2       border-collapse:collapse;
3       border-top:4px solid #000;
4 }
```

In order to stop the inner tables from having a border, we create a new selector (line 19 below):

```
19 ▾ table table {
20       border: 0;
21 }
22
23 |
```

Succession of Crops.	Fallow, one-third Tares.
	£.s.d.
Rent and tithes	100

The "table table" selector means "a table contained inside another table". We declare that tables that are inside tables should have no border. The result is that the thick black border on the inner tables disappears.

Next, we need to make the symbols and numbers line up properly even though they are in different cells and tables. We do this by giving the "table table" selector a width of 100% (line 21 below):

```
19 ▾ table table {
20       border: 0;
21       width:100%;
22 }
23 |
```

Succession of Crops.	Fallow, one-third Tares.		
	£.	s.	d.
Rent and tithes	1	0	0

Above, thanks to the fact that all cells belonging to the same column get the same width, when we give the two tables a width of 100%, it means they should expand until they fill all the available horizontal space, and that horizontal space in both cells is exactly the same.

To further clarify things, below we give the cells of the inner tables a dashed border (lines 24-26):

```
19 ▾ table table {
20       border: 0;
21       width:100%;
22 }
23
24 ▾ table table td {
25       border:1px dashed #000;
26 }
27 |
```

Succession of Crops.	Fallow, one-third Tares.	
	£. | s. | d.	
Rent and tithes	1 | 0 | 0	

The selector "table table td" means "a cell that is inside a table that is inside a table". The dashed border helps us see the inner tables clearly. We have a table on the second row which contains the symbols. This table has only one row and three cells. The table on the third row (the "Rent and tithes" row) has one row and three cells, each cell contains a number.

Let's now add the rest of the rows:

```
36 ▾        <tr>
37              <td>Poor-rates</td>
38 ▾            <td>
39 ▾                <table>
40 ▾                    <tr>
41                          <td>0</td>
42                          <td>3</td>
43                          <td>6</td>
44                      </tr>
45                  </table>
46              </td>
47          </tr>
48 ▾        <tr>
49              <td>Income tax</td>
50 ▾            <td>
51 ▾                <table>
52 ▾                    <tr>
53                          <td>0</td>
54                          <td>1</td>
55                          <td>3</td>
56                      </tr>
57                  </table>
58              </td>
59          </tr>
```

And here is the result:

Succession of Crops.	Fallow, one-third Tares.		
	£.	s.	d.
Rent and tithes	1	0	0
Poor-rates	0	3	6
Income tax	0	1	3

In the original table, the numbers corresponding to pounds are left-aligned, those corresponding to shillings are center-aligned, and those corresponding to pennies are right-aligned. Let's now recreate this. There are all kinds of ways of achieving this. We could, for example, give every left cell of the inner tables a class of "left", every middle cell a class of "middle", and so on (lines 17-19 of the HTML and lines 26-34 of the CSS):

```
12      <tr>
13          <td></td>
14          <td>
15              <table>
16                  <tr>
17                      <td class="left">£.</td>
18                      <td class="center">s.</td>
19                      <td class="right">d.</td>
20                  </tr>
21              </table>
22          </td>
23      </tr>
24      <tr>
25          <td>Rent and tithes</td>
26          <td>
27              <table>
28                  <tr>
```

```
19  table table {
20      border: 0;
21      width:100%;
22  }
23  table table td {
24      border:1px dashed #000;
25  }
26  .left{
27      text-align:left;
28  }
29  .center {
30      text-align:center;
31  }
32  .right {
33      text-align:right;
34  }
35
```

Succession of Crops.	Fallow, one-third Tares.		
	£.	s.	d.
Rent and tithes	1	0	0
Poor-rates	0	3	6
Income tax	0	1	3

If the table contains hundreds of tables, adding these classes to every left, center and right cell can be extremely time-consuming, not to mention boring. Whenever you find yourself having to repeat something hundreds of times when doing web design or programming, it usually means there is a better way.

Nth-Child

We use the "nth-child" selector in CSS to apply a style using parent-child relationships. This enables us to address the issue of aligning the contents of a table without having to add classes all over the place. To make the contents of the first column of all the inner tables left-aligned, I can do as follows (line 26 below):

```
19 ▾ table table {
20        border: 0;
21        width:100%;
22 }
23 ▾ table table td {
24        border:1px dashed #000;
25 }
26 ▾ table table td:nth-child(1) {
27        text-align:left;
28 }
29
30 |
```

Succession of Crops.	Fallow, one-third Tares.		
	£.	s.	d.
Rent and tithes	1	0	0
Poor-rates	0	3	6
Income tax	0	1	3

The selector "table table td:nth-child(1)" means: "Apply the following style to every cell that is inside a table that is inside a table, provided that it is the first child of its parent". The "parent" in question is of course the inner rows. And the "first child" merely means the first cell of each inner table. What, therefore, this convoluted syntax means is "the first cell of each inner table", meaning the cells that contain the pound symbol and the numbers below it. Note that above, now, the pound symbol and the numbers below it are all left-aligned.

We can now do the same for the shillings (lines 29-31):

```
29 ▾   table table td:nth-child(2) {
30         text-align:center;
31     }
32
33     |
```

Succession of Crops.	Fallow, one-third Tares.		
	£.	s.	d.
Rent and tithes	1	0	0
Poor-rates	0	3	6
Income tax	0	1	3

Above, the selector on line 29 means "the second cell of every row of every inner table", which naturally applies to all the middle cells of all the inner tables, which means the shilling symbol and all the numbers below it.

If you are finding it difficult to understand these new "nth-child" selectors, there is no need to worry. Even a seasoned web designer will have to exert a lot of mental effort in order to "decode" the meaning of the selector. In practice, the decoding is done through trial and error, for example by quickly adding a border or red color and seeing what happens.

You can simply skim through this section and not worry if things seem to get too complicated. Only with much practice will these selectors become easy to understand. It is sufficient to know that such selectors exist, and if you have a need for them in the future or run into them, you can come back to this section to read up more on them.

Now, we will make the pennies right-aligned (lines 32-34):

```
32 ▾ table table td:nth-child(3) {
33       text-align:right;
34  }
35
36  |
```

Succession of Crops.	Fallow, one-third Tares.		
	£.	s.	d.
Rent and tithes	1	0	0
Poor-rates	0	3	6
Income tax	0	1	3

The new selector means "third child of every row of every inner table", which refers to the pennies.

Let's now hide the dashed border by setting it to zero in order to see what the table really looks like (line 23 below):

```
23 ▾ table table td {
i 24       border:0px dashed #000;
25  }
26 ▾ table table td:nth-child(1) {
27       text-align:left;
28  }
29 ▾ table table td:nth-child(2) {
30       text-align:center;
31  }
32 ▾ table table td:nth-child(3) {
33       text-align:right;
34  }
35  |
36
```

The result is as follows:

Succession of Crops.	Fallow, one-third Tares.		
	£.	s.	d.
Rent and tithes	1	0	0
Poor-rates	0	3	6
Income tax	0	1	3

In the original table below, there is a black border between the symbols and numbers on the right and the text on the left:

Succession of Crops.	Fallow, one-third Tares.		
	£.	s.	d
Rent and tithes	1	0	0
Poor-rates	0	3	6
Income tax	0	1	3

We can add the border using the "nth-child" selector we used earlier (lines 35-37 below):

```
35  table td:nth-child(1) {
36      border-right:2px solid #000;
37  }
38  |
```

Succession of Crops.	Fallow, one-third Tares.		
	£.	s.	d.
Rent and tithes	1	0	0
Poor-rates	0	3	6
Income tax	0	1	3

The selector means "every first cell of every row of every table must have a right border of 2 pixels". We now have a right border that separates the text on the left ("Rent and tithes", etc.) from the symbols and numbers on the right.

Unfortunately, this definition also applies to the inner tables, making their first cells acquire unwanted right borders too (see the borders on the right of the pound symbol and the numbers below it). We hide these unwanted borders as follows (line 28 below):

```
26 ▾ table table td:nth-child(1) {
27        text-align:left;
28        border:0;
29    }
```

The result is as follows:

```
36 ▾ table td:nth-child(1) {
37        border-right:2px solid #000;
38    }
```

Succession of Crops.	Fallow, one-third Tares.		
	£.	s.	d.
Rent and tithes	1	0	0
Poor-rates	0	3	6
Income tax	0	1	3

On line 37, we declare that every first cell of every table should have a right border. But now, on line 28 we have declared that every first cell of every table *that is inside a table* should have no border. This new definition on line 28 is *more specific*, therefore it takes precedence and causes the unwanted borders to go away.

In the original, the pound, penny and shilling symbols have italic formatting. We achieve this as follows (lines 40-42):

```
40 ▾ table tr:nth-child(2) table {
41        font-style: italic;
42   }
43   |
```

Succession of Crops.	Fallow, one-third Tares.		
	£.	s.	d.
Rent and tithes	1	0	0
Poor-rates	0	3	6
Income tax	0	1	3

Above, our brand new selector means "a table that is inside the second row of a table". Which table satisfies this criterion? The table that contains the symbols, of course. Another way of reading the selector is: think of a table, think of the <tr> tags inside it, think of the second one, think of a table inside that. Reading it this way, you can easily pin down what is meant by the selector.

At this point we are nearly done recreating the table. We could do more work on it, but for simplicity's sake we will leave the table as it is.

First and Last Children

Instead of using nth-child(number), CSS also gives us the ":first-child" and ":last-child" pseudo-selectors, as follows.

Below, I have deleted the outer table from the code we used earlier and merged all the inner tables into a single table. I have also deleted most of the CSS:

```
  1 ▾ <table>
  2 ▾     <tr>
  3             <td>£.</td><td>s.</td><td>d.</td>
  4         </tr>
  5 ▾     <tr>
  6             <td>1</td><td>0</td><td>0</td>
  7         </tr>
  8 ▾     <tr>
  9             <td>0</td><td>3</td><td>6</td>
 10         </tr>
 11 ▾     <tr>
 12             <td>0</td><td>1</td><td>3</td>
 13         </tr>
 14 </table>
 15
```

```
  1 ▾ table {
  2       border-collapse:collapse;
  3       width:50%;
  4 }
  5 ▾ table tr {
  6       border-bottom:1px solid #000;
  7       text-align:center;
  8 }
  9
```

£.	s.	d.
1	0	0
0	3	6
0	1	3

Below, I have used the ":first-child" selector to give the first row of the table a black background and white text (lines 9-12):

```
  9 ▾ table tr:first-child {
 10       background:#000;
 11       color:#fff;
 12 }
 13
```

The selector on line 9 should be read as: think of a table, think of its tr tags, think of the one that is a first child. The result is as follows:

£.	s.	d.
1	0	0
0	3	6
0	1	3

Below, I have changed "first-child" to "last-child" on line 9, meaning that we are selecting, of all the rows of the table, the one that is a last child:

```
  9 ▾ table tr:last-child {
 10       background:#000;
 11       color:#fff;
 12 }
 13
```

Here is the result:

£.	s.	d.
1	0	0
0	3	6
0	**1**	**3**

Below, we use "table tr td:first-child" to select every first child of every row:

```
 9 ▾ table tr td:first-child {
10        background:#000;
11        color:#fff;
12   }
13
```

The selector should be read as: think of a table, think of its <tr> tags, think of the <td> tags inside them, think of the ones that are first children. This ends up applying to every first cell of every row. Here is the result:

£.	s.	d.
1	0	0
0	3	6
0	1	3

Changing "first-child" to "last-child", we end up selecting every final cell of every row:

```
 9 ▾ table tr td:last-child {
10        background:#000;
11        color:#fff;
12   }
13
```

Here is the result:

£.	s.	d.
1	0	0
0	3	6
0	1	3

There is no "middle-child" selector to help us select the middle cells. To style the middle column, we have to use the nth-child selector (line 9 below):

```
 9 ▾ table tr td:nth-child(2) {
10       background:#000;
11       color:#fff;
12    }
13
```

The result is as follows:

£.	s.	d.
1	0	0
0	3	6
0	1	3

Above, we use the selector on line 9 to select every second child of every row, which ends up selecting every middle cell.

Below, I have shortened the selector on line 9:

```
 9 ▾ table td:nth-child(2) {
10       background:#000;
11       color:#fff;
12    }
13
```

The result is as follows:

£.	s.	d.
1	0	0
0	3	6
0	1	3

Above, I have changed "table tr td:nth-child(2)" by removing the "tr". The result is the same as earlier, this does not change its meaning. One might have expected this shortened selector to select *the second cell of the table* rather than the second cell of every row of the table. The second cell of the table would have been the top middle cell, the one that contains "s.". But instead, CSS continues to select every second cell of *every row*. This is because CSS interprets the word "child" with respect to its immediate parent. We can even take away the word "table" from the selector and the result would still be the same (line 9 below):

```
 9 ▾ td:nth-child(2) {
10        background:#000;
11        color:#fff;
12    }
13    |
```

£.	s.	d.
1	0	0
0	3	6
0	1	3

Above, the selector on line 9 means "every cell that is a second child". Since each cell's parent is a row, "every cell that is a second child" means "every cell that is the second child of its row" (i.e. every <td> tag inside a <tr> tag).

Even and Odd Children

CSS offers us even and odd selectors that can come in very handy when trying to make a table look pretty, as follows (line 9 below):

```
 1 ▾ table {
 2        border-collapse:collapse;
 3        width:50%;
 4    }
 5 ▾ table tr {
 6        border-bottom:1px solid #000;
 7        text-align:center;
 8    }
 9 ▾ tr:nth-child(even) {
10        background:#000;
11        color:#fff;
12    }
13    |
```

£.	s.	d.
1	0	0
0	3	6
0	1	3

Above, on line 9, I have declared that every row that is even should have a black background with white text. This ends up making the second and fourth rows have this style, without affecting the rest. Below, I have changed the word "even" to "odd" (line 9):

```
 9 ▾ tr:nth-child(odd) {
10       background:#000;
11       color:#fff;
12    }
13    |
```

£.	s.	d.
1	0	0
0	3	6
0	1	3

Now, the first and third rows are affected. "tr:nth-child(odd)" should be read as: Every row that is an odd child of its parent. The table has four rows, we could select each row using tr:nth-child(1), tr:nth-child(2), tr:nth-child(3) and tr:nth-child(4). When we write tr:nth-child(odd), the browser looks at the children and selects nth-child(1) and nth-child(3) of the table, i.e. the ones that have an odd number.

Even and odd formatting is useful when trying to make a large table more readable, as follows:

```
 1 ▾ <table>
 2 ▾    <tr>
 3          <td>£.</td><td>s.</td><td>d.</td>
 4          <td>£.</td><td>s.</td><td>d.</td>
 5          <td>£.</td><td>s.</td><td>d.</td>
 6          <td>£.</td><td>s.</td><td>d.</td>
 7       </tr>
 8 ▾    <tr>
 9          <td>1</td><td>0</td><td>0</td>
10          <td>1</td><td>0</td><td>0</td>
11          <td>1</td><td>0</td><td>0</td>
12          <td>1</td><td>0</td><td>0</td>
13       </tr>
 1    |
```

```
 1 ▾ table {
 2       border-collapse:collapse;
 3       width:50%;
 4    }
 5 ▾ table tr {
 6       text-align:center;
 7    }
 8 ▾ tr:nth-child(even) {
 9       background:#ccc;
10    }
11    |
```

£.	s.	d.	£.	s.	d.	£.	s.	d.	£.	s.	d.
1	0	0	1	0	0	1	0	0	1	0	0
0	3	6	0	3	6	0	3	6	0	3	6
0	1	3	0	1	3	0	1	3	0	1	3
0	1	3	0	1	3	0	1	3	0	1	3
0	1	3	0	1	3	0	1	3	0	1	3

Having the even rows appear different from the odd ones helps the reader avoid losing their place when looking at the table or copying figures from it.

Table Headings

HTML offers us the <th> tag when working with tables. This tag is used to declare column and row headings, as follows (lines 3 and 4 of the HTML):

```
 1  <table>
 2      <tr>
 3          <th>Name</th>
 4          <th>Birth Year</th>
 5      </tr>
 6      <tr>
 7          <td>Geoffrey Chaucer</td>
 8          <td>c. 1343</td>
 9      </tr>
10      <tr>
11          <td>William Shakespeare</td>
12          <td>1564</td>
13      </tr>
14  </table>
```

```
1  table {border-collapse:collapse;}
2  td {
3      border:1px solid #000;
4  }
5
```

Name	Birth Year
Geoffrey Chaucer	c. 1343
William Shakespeare	1564

Above, we have used <th> tags for the "Name" and "Birth Year" cells. This declares that these cells are column headings, meaning that they describe what comes underneath them.

By default, the <th> elements get bold formatting and centered text, to distinguish them from the rest of the cells. Above, we have given table cells a black border. But since the border is applied to the <td> tag (line 2 of the CSS), it does not apply to the <th> tags.

In order to put the <th> tags inside borders too, we add "th" to the selector on line 2:

```
1  table {border-collapse:collapse;}
2  td, th {
3      border:1px solid #000;
4  }
5
```

Name	Birth Year
Geoffrey Chaucer	c. 1343
William Shakespeare	1564

The <th> can also be used for row headings, not just column headings. Below, we have a simple multiplication table:

```
 i  1 ▾ <table>
    2 ▾     <tr>
    3             <th>X</th><th>1</th><th>2</th>
    4         </tr>
    5 ▾     <tr>
    6             <th>1</th><td>1</td><td>2</td>
    7         </tr>
    8 ▾     <tr>
    9             <th>2</th><td>2</td><td>4</td>
   10         </tr>
   11 </table>
    1
```

```
    1    table {border-collapse:collapse;}
    2 ▾  td, th {
    3         border:1px solid #000;
    4         padding:5px;
    5    }
    6 ▾  th {
    7         background:#999;
    8         color:#fff;
    9    }
   10
```

X	1	2
1	1	2
2	2	4

Above, we use <th> tags both for the first row *and* the first column. On line 3 of the HTML, we have only <th> tags. On the next row on line 6, we start out with a <th> tag, then use <td> for the rest of the cells. We repeat the same for line 9 of the HTML. In this way, we create a table that has headings both at the top and to the left. We can give these headings special formatting as we have done above, helping improve the table's appearance and hopefully making it more readable.

6. Links

HTML stands for Hypertext Markup Language. Ted Nelson coined the term "hypertext" in 1963. In 1989, Tim Berners-Lee came up with a way of putting the idea of hypertext into practice, and from this the web was born. At its most basic level, hypertext refers to text that "links" to other text. Imagine you have a magical book that embodies the concept of hypertext. When reading the book's table of contents, if you were to press on any title, the book would immediately start flipping its pages until it gets to the title you pressed. And if you had a hypertext library, if a book referenced a certain page of another book, pressing that reference would immediately cause that other book to come flying through the air and open up at exactly that page.

Hypertext recreates that magical library on a computer. It allows us to have documents that "link to" other documents, and a simple click is sufficient to take us from one document to another document. In the real world, going from one document to another could mean going from one floor of a large library to another. Computers make things easy by instantly bringing up the document we want, except when we have a slow internet connection.

Below, we have folder inside of which there are two HTML documents:

Name	Date modified
document_1.html	2/9/2018 9:36 AM
document_2.html	2/9/2018 9:31 AM

Inside document1.html we have the following:

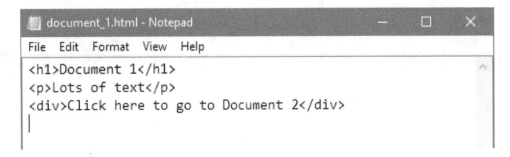

Opening document_1.html in a browser, we get the following:

At the moment, clicking on where it says "Click here" will not do anything, since we haven't created a link yet.

To create the link, we modify the document as follows:

```
document_1.html - Notepad
File  Edit  Format  View  Help
<h1>Document 1</h1>
<p>Lots of text</p>
<div>
<a href="document_2.html">Click here</a> to go to
Document 2
</div>
```

In HTML, we create links using the <a> tag, short for "anchor tag". The "href" attribute of the anchor tag determines what document the tag links to, and the text inside the anchor tag (between the <a> and </a>) determines what the "link text" is going to be.

If we now open the document again in a browser, this is what we see:

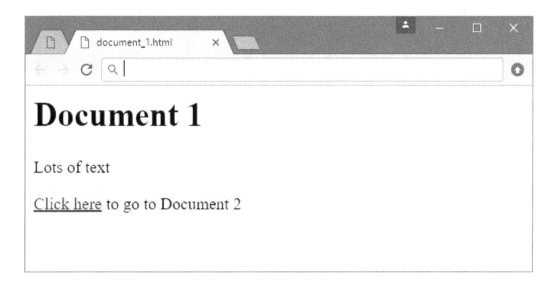

When we click on the underlined text that says "Click here", the browser opens up document_2.html:

We will now edit document_2.html in Notepad to turn the "Click here" into a link:

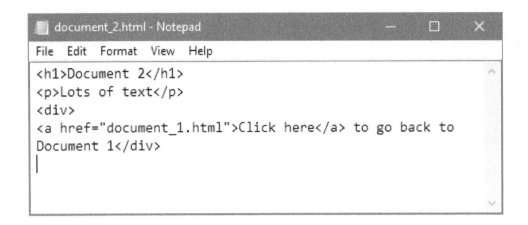

Opening document_2.html again in a browser, this is what we get:

Now, if we click "Click here" above, it opens up Document 1. And inside Document 1, clicking "Click here" takes us again to Document 2. In this way, we have two documents that link to each other.

Let's now go to JSTinker to explore links further. Below, we have an anchor tag that links to Google.com:

```
1    <a href="http://www.google.com">
2        Go to Google</a>
```

Here is what it looks like:

<u>Go to Google</u>

Note the way we have written the URL of Google.com: http://www.google.com. The "http://" is necessary when linking to an "external" document, meaning to a document or web page that is not on your own website or server. Without the "http://" part, the browser will try to find a document on your computer or server that is named www.google.com.

The text that says "Go to Google" has no influence on what happens when a user clicks the link. For example, we can even lie as follows:

```
1  <a href="http://www.google.com">
2      Go to Yahoo.com</a>
3
```

```
1
```

```
1
```

Go to Yahoo.com

Above, the link text says "Go to Yahoo.com", but the "href" tag links to google.com. It is the "href" tag that matters when it comes to the link's behavior, meaning that if you click the link, you will actually go to Google, not Yahoo. This technicality is used by certain deceptive websites to make users think that the link is taking them somewhere where in reality it takes them somewhere completely different.

Links are necessary for "navigation", meaning for letting users go from somewhere in your website to somewhere else. Below, I created a rudimentary website that links to a few pages:

```
i 1   <h1>My Website</h1>
  2   <a href="/home">Home</a>
  3   <a href="/about">About Me</a>
  4   <a href="/portfolio">Portfolio</a>
  5   <a href="/contact">Contact Me</a>
  6   |
```

```
1   |
```

My Website

Home About Me Portfolio Contact Me

The reason the links appear side-by-side is that <a> tags by default are *inline* elements. They do not take up a whole line.

Below, we have taken away the underline formatting of the links (line 2 of the CSS below):

```
1 ▾ a {
2       text-decoration:none;
3   }
4   |
```

My Website

Home About Me Portfolio Contact Me

Below, we add border and padding to the links (lines 3 and 4):

```
1 ▾ a {
2       text-decoration:none;
3       border:1px solid #000;
4       padding:5px;
5   }
6   |
```

My Website

| Home | About Me | Portfolio | Contact Me |

Below, we make the font size of the links smaller (line 5):

```
1 ▾ a {
2       text-decoration:none;
3       border:1px solid #000;
4       padding:5px;
5       font-size:12px;
6   }
```

My Website

Home | About Me | Portfolio | Contact Me

What if we wanted all the rectangles to have the same width? We cannot give the links a width because links are inline. Therefore first we must turn them into block or inline-block elements. Below, we turn them into inline-block (line 6):

```
1 ▾ a {
2       text-decoration:none;
3       border:1px solid #000;
4       padding:5px;
5       font-size:12px;
6       display:inline-block;
7   }
```

My Website

Home | About Me | Portfolio | Contact Me

Below, we give the links a width of 13%:

Above, since the width is too small to contain all of the text of each link, some of the links get broken up into two lines. To make the links look more uniform, we add a height (line 8):

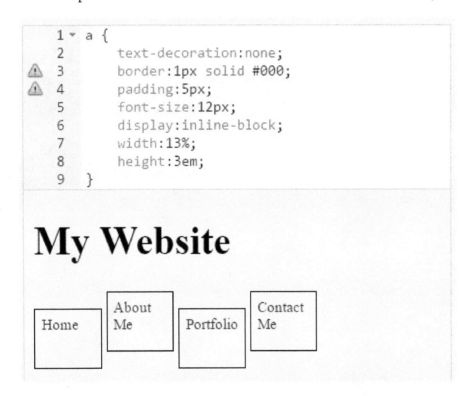

The result is strange because of the "inline-block" display property, which makes the browser make its own choices on how to display the links. In order to have better control over their appearance, we have to use "display:block" instead (line 6 below):

```
1 ▾ a {
2       text-decoration:none;
⚠ 3     border:1px solid #000;
⚠ 4     padding:5px;
5       font-size:12px;
6       display:block;
7       width:13%;
8       height:3em;
9   }
```

Above, we run into a new issue. The "display:block" property makes each link take up a whole line. We therefore have to use floating to make them appear side-by-side (line 7 below):

```
1 ▾ a {
2       text-decoration:none;
⚠ 3     border:1px solid #000;
⚠ 4     padding:5px;
5       font-size:12px;
6       display:block;
7       float:left;
8       width:13%;
9       height:3em;
10  }
```

Here is the result:

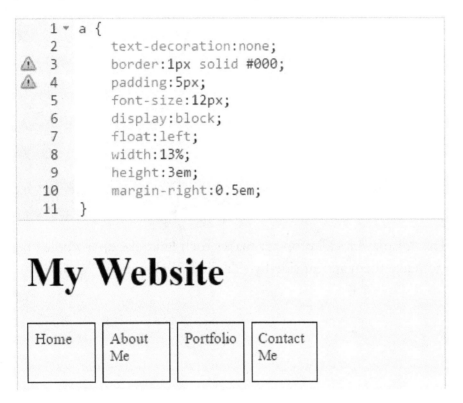

Above, our links are now side-by-side and have a uniform appearance. Below, we add a right margin (line 10) in order to make the links separate:

```
1 ▾ a {
2       text-decoration:none;
3       border:1px solid #000;
4       padding:5px;
5       font-size:12px;
6       display:block;
7       float:left;
8       width:13%;
9       height:3em;
10      margin-right:0.5em;
11  }
```

Using "border-radius" and "text-align", we add some extra styling (lines 11 and 12):

```
10      margin-right:0.5em;
11      text-align:center;
12      border-radius:25%;
13  }
```

Here is the result:

You may notice the way the texts are too close to the top borders (the word "Home" is much closer to the top border of its box than to its bottom border). We can fix this by adding extra top padding, as follows on line 5 below:

```
 1  a {
 2      text-decoration:none;
 3      border:1px solid #000;
 4      padding:5px;
 5      padding-top:20px;
 6      font-size:12px;
 7      display:table;
 8      float:left;
 9      width:13%;
10      height:3em;
11      margin-right:0.5em;
12      text-align:center;
13      border-radius:25%;
```

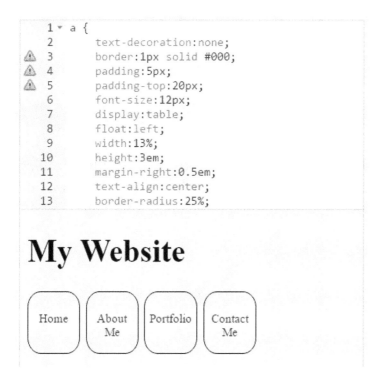

The links are now too tall, because the padding is added onto the existing height of 3 ems. Below I have reduced the height to 2 ems (line 10):

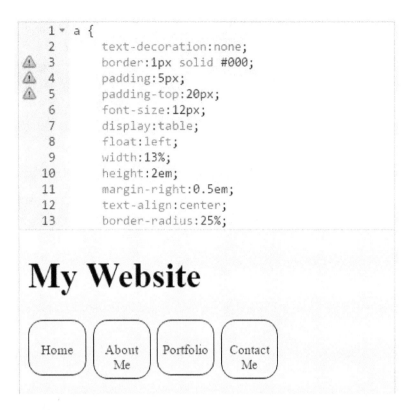

```
1 ▾ a {
2       text-decoration:none;
3       border:1px solid #000;
4       padding:5px;
5       padding-top:20px;
6       font-size:12px;
7       display:table;
8       float:left;
9       width:13%;
10      height:2em;
11      margin-right:0.5em;
12      text-align:center;
13      border-radius:25%;
```

Now the texts are too close to the lower borders. By fiddling with the height and the top padding, we may eventually achieve a decent appearance. We could also simply increase the width of the buttons so that phrases like "About Me" appear on one line instead of two (line 8 below):

```
1 ▾ a {
2       text-decoration:none;
3       border:1px solid #000;
4       font-size:12px;
5       padding:3px;
6       display:table;
7       float:left;
8       width:18%;
9       margin-right:0.5em;
10      text-align:center;
11  }
12  |
```

Above, I have increased the width while reducing the padding and removing the border radius.

You may have run into certain websites where if you hover the mouse over a link or button (buttons are often merely links with added styling), the button's shape changes. This is done using the CSS ":hover" pseudo-selector. Below, I have add hover styling on lines 12 to 15 so that if the user hovers their mouse pointer over one of the links, the link acquires a black background and white text:

```
12 ▾  a:hover {
13         background:#000;
14         color:#fff;
15     }
```

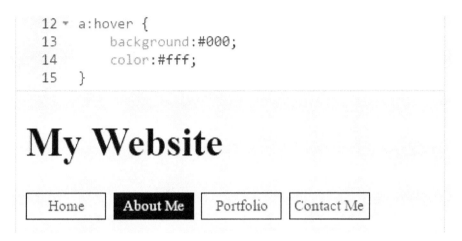

Above, my mouse pointer is hovering over the "About Me" link to make its hover styling visible.

We also have access to the ":visited" pseudo-selector. This enables us to give a visited link a special styling. A visited link is a link that has already been viewed by the user. Below, I have declared that links already visited by the user should appear gray (lines 16-18), and as can be seen, the "About Me" link has become gray because the user has already visited it.

```
12 ▾  a:hover {
13         background:#000;
14         color:#fff;
15     }
16 ▾  a:visited {
17         color:#aaa;
18     }
```

My Website

| Home | About Me | Portfolio | Contact Me |

It is useful to give links visited formatting because it helps users know which links they have visited and which ones they have not. Below is a screenshot from the website opensourceshakespeare.org where Shakespeare's sonnets are listed:

Individual sonnets	1	21	41	61	81	101	121	141
	2	22	42	62	82	102	122	142
	3	23	43	63	83	103	123	143
	4	24	44	64	84	104	124	144
	5	25	45	65	85	105	125	145
	6	26	46	66	86	106	126	146
	7	27	47	67	87	107	127	147
	8	28	48	68	88	108	128	148
	9	29	49	69	89	109	129	149
	10	30	50	70	90	110	130	150
	11	31	51	71	91	111	131	151
	12	32	52	72	92	112	132	152
	13	33	53	73	93	113	133	153
	14	34	54	74	94	114	134	154
	15	35	55	75	95	115	135	
	16	36	56	76	96	116	136	
	17	37	57	77	97	117	137	
	18	38	58	78	98	118	138	
	19	39	59	79	99	119	139	
	20	40	60	80	100	120	140	

Plays + Sonnets + Poems + Concordance + Character Search + Advanced Search + About OSS

Above, the sonnets I have already looked at (such as 1, 16, 30 and 31) have a red color (or gray, if you are viewing this in black and white), while the rest are black. This helps me keep track of the ones I have "visited" (i.e. viewed) and the ones I have not visited yet.

It is, however, unusual to have an item in the navigation menu change its appearance whether the user has visited them or not. We can force the links in our website to not change appearance even if they are visited by adding the ":visited" selector to the main select for the links (line 1 below):

```
 1 ▾ a, a:visited {
 2        text-decoration:none;
⚠ 3        border:1px solid #000;
 4        font-size:12px;
⚠ 5        padding:3px;
 6        display:table;
 7        float:left;
 8        width:18%;
 9        margin-right:0.5em;
10        text-align:center;
11     }
```

My Website

| Home | About Me | Portfolio | Contact Me |

Above, we have declared that links and visited links should both have the same exact styling.

We will now add a paragraph underneath the menu (lines 6-8 of the HTML):

```
𝑖  1    <h1>My Website</h1>
   2    <a href="/home">Home</a>
   3    <a href="/about">About Me</a>
   4    <a href="/portfolio">Portfolio</a>
   5    <a href="/contact">Contact Me</a>
   6 ▾  <p>Welcome to my website. Visit
   7 ▾  <a href="http://example.com">my other
   8    website here</a>.</p>
   9    |
  10
```

Here is the result:

Above, notice the strange appearance of the new link. That is because on line 1 of the CSS, we have declared that *all* links should have such a style, which naturally affects this link too even though it is inside a paragraph. To avoid this issue, we will have to put our navigation links inside their own <div> (lines 2 and 7 below):

```
 1   <h1>My Website</h1>
 2 ▾ <div class="nav">
 3       <a href="/home">Home</a>
 4       <a href="/about">About Me</a>
 5       <a href="/portfolio">Portfolio</a>
 6       <a href="/contact">Contact Me</a>
 7   </div>
 8 ▾ <p>Welcome to my website. Visit
 9 ▾ <a href="http://example.com">my other
10   website here</a>.</p>
```

Above, the new <div> has a class of "nav". We can now use this class to restrict the CSS styling only to links inside this <div> (lines 1 and 12 below):

```
1 ▾ .nav a, .nav a:visited {
2       text-decoration:none;
⚠ 3     border:1px solid #000;
4       font-size:12px;
⚠ 5     padding:3px;
6       display:table;
7       float:left;
8       width:18%;
9       margin-right:0.5em;
10      text-align:center;
11  }
12 ▾ .nav a:hover {
13      background:#000;
14      color:#fff;
15  }
```

My Website

| Home | About Me | Portfolio | Contact Me |

Welcome to my website. Visit <u>my other website here</u>.

Above, our styles now apply to the navigation items, but they leave the link inside the paragraph alone so that it continues to have its default appearance.

Opening Links in New Tabs

When browsing the web, clicking a link takes you to a new page on the same website, making you leave the old page you were looking at. For example, when looking at the Falcon Heavy article on Wikipedia, if I click the link to SpaceX, it will take me to the Wikipedia article about SpaceX. I could also open the link in a new tab by right-clicking on it and choosing "Open link in new tab", as shown below:

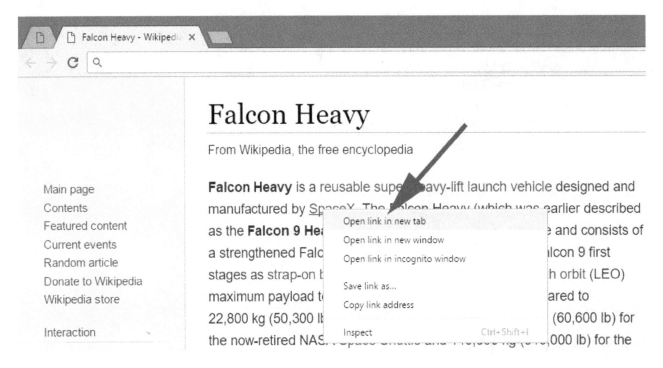

Now, the article about SpaceX opens up in a new tab, meaning the article about Falcon Heavy continues to remain open:

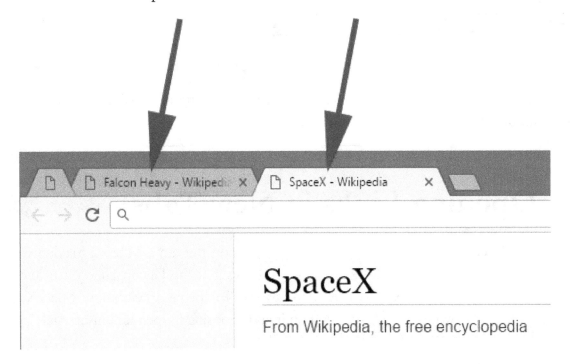

Above, I have placed two arrows. The left one points to the tab for the Falcon Heavy article, and the right arrow points to the newly opened SpaceX article's tab.

When you place a link on your website, by default the link will open in the same tab, rather than in a new tab. We can force a link to open in a new tab using the "target" attribute, as follows:

```
i 1    <h1>Ikram's Website</h1>
  2 ▾  <p>
  3 ▾      <a href="http://example.com"
  4         target="_blank">Click here</a>
  5         to visit some other website.
  6     </p>
  7     |
```

Here is what it looks like:

Ikram's Website

Click here to visit some other website.

Above, on line 3 of the HTML we have an <a> tag that links to example.com. I have broken up the tag into multiple lines for your viewing convenience. On line 4, we have a "target" attribute whose value is "_blank" (note the underscore). This tells the browser to open this link in a new tab. If a user clicks on it, a new tab will open, as if they had chosen "Open link in a new tab" by right-clicking on the link.

It is common practice to make internal links (links on your website that point to other pages on your website) open in the same tab (by not using a "target" attribute), and to make external links (links pointing to other websites) open in a new tab by using the "target" attribute with the "_blank" value.

This page intentionally left blank

7. A New Look at HTML

So far, the HTML documents I have shown you how to create have not been proper HTML documents, even though they show up properly when opened up. In this chapter, I will introduce proper HTML while also introducing various other interesting concepts.

A proper HTML document starts with what is known as a document type declaration. This declaration tells the browser what language our document is written in, since besides HTML, we also have languages like SGML. We also have multiple flavors of HTML, such as XHTML. In this book, we are using the latest version of HTML, which is HTML5. To start an HTML5 document, we declare it as follows:

```
1    <!DOCTYPE HTML>
2
3
4
5
6
```

Above, note the way the tag starts with an exclamation mark. This is not an HTML tag, the HTML tags haven't started yet. Rather, it declares that everything below it is going to be HTML.

In the past, the DOCTYPE declaration was quite long, here is an example (the declaration takes up two lines):

```
1    <!DOCTYPE HTML PUBLIC "-//W3C//DTD HTML 4.01//EN"
2    "http://www.w3.org/TR/html4/strict.dtd">
3
```

With HTML5, it was simplified to merely <!DOCTYPE HTML>.

The next item on the list for creating proper HTML documents is <html> tag. This tag is going to contain everything else we create:

```
1    <!DOCTYPE HTML>
2 ▾  <html>
3
4    </html>
5
6
7
```

Next, we add a <head> and a <body> tag:

```
1    <!DOCTYPE HTML>
2 ▾  <html>
3 ▾      <head>
4
5        </head>
6
7 ▾      <body>
8
9        </body>
10   </html>
```

The <head> tag will contain information about the document, this can include CSS styles and JavaScript code. The <body> tag contains the actual contents of the document, meaning any headings, images, paragraphs, etc. that we have in our document.

The first thing to do in the <head> tag is to declare our "character set", as follows:

```
1    <!DOCTYPE HTML>
2 ▾  <html>
3 ▾      <head>
4            <meta charset="UTF-8">
5        </head>
6
7 ▾      <body>
8
9        </body>
10   </html>
```

You may remember the snowman we used in the chapter about lists. That snowman is "Unicode character" and can only properly show up if the document has a Unicode character set. Above, using the <meta> tag and its "charset" attribute, we declare that our document uses the UTF-8 character set, which is the character set most commonly used on the Internet. If instead of UTF-8 we write "ISO-8859-15" (a character set used for the Latin-derived alphabets), the snowman and other Unicode characters will show up as a jumbled mess of random characters.

There is no need to worry about character sets. It is sufficient to know the meta tag on line 4 in your HTML helps make the world a slightly better place.

The next thing we add is the <title> tag, as follows (line 5 below):

```
1    <!DOCTYPE HTML>
2 ▾  <html>
3 ▾      <head>
4            <meta charset="UTF-8">
5            <title>Welcome!</title>
6        </head>
7
8 ▾      <body>
9
10       </body>
11   </html>
12
13
```

The <title> tag determines the title of your document that is shown as the name of the browser tab where the document is shown, as follows:

Above, the document is empty because we have not added anything to the <body> tag. But notice the "Welcome!" at the very top (above the magnifier icon). That is where the contents of our <title> tag are shown. When doing a web search (such as on Google), it is the contents of the <title> tag that are usually shown to users to tell them what the link contains. For example, below I have done a Google search for "wiki falcon heavy":

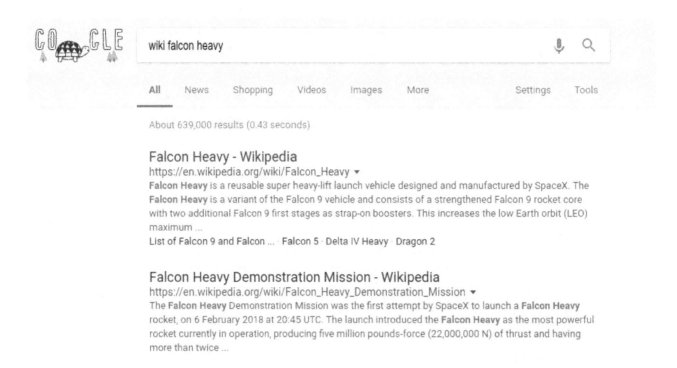

The top search result says "Falcon Heavy - Wikipedia". Clicking on this link, we are taken to a Wikipedia article:

Notice that above, the document's visible title is "Falcon Heavy", it is not "Falcon Heavy - Wikipedia", yet Google shows us the title as "Falcon Heavy - Wikipedia". The reason is the Wikipedia page's <title> tag. If we right-click on an empty area of this article and click "View page source", we will be able to see the HTML for the article:[13]

---

[13] Depending on which browser you are using, the wording for "View page source" can change. The above screenshot is from the Chromium Web Browser.

SpaceX successfully launched the Falcon Heavy on February 6, 2018, at 3:45 p.m. EST (20:45 UTC).[3][9][10] The dummy payload on its maiden flight was SpaceX founder Elon Musk's midnight cherry Tesla Roadster.[11][12]

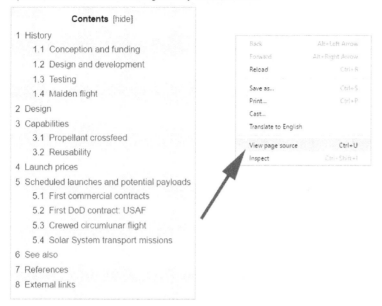

Below is a screenshot of the HTML:

```
1  <!DOCTYPE html>
2  <!-- saved from url=(0042)https://en.wikipedia.org/wiki/Falcon_Heavy -->
3  <html class="client-js ve-not-available" lang="en" dir="ltr"><head><meta
   http-equiv="Content-Type" content="text/html; charset=UTF-8">
4
5  <title>Falcon Heavy - Wikipedia</title>
6  <script>document.documentElement.className =
   document.documentElement.className.replace( /(^|\s)client-nojs(\s|$)/,
   "$1client-js$2" );</script>
7  <script>(window.RLQ=window.RLQ||[]).push(function()
```

Above, note the <title> tag on line 5, whose contents say "Falcon Heavy - Wikipedia". It is based on this <title> tag that in the Google results we saw the page's title as "Falcon Heavy - Wikipedia" rather than merely "Falcon Heavy".

Back to our document, we can now start adding actual content to our document, as follows (lines 9 and 10 of the HTML below):

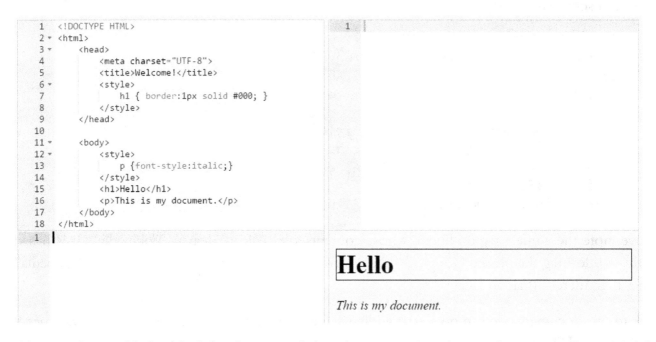

```
1   <!DOCTYPE HTML>
2   <html>
3       <head>
4           <meta charset="UTF-8">
5           <title>Welcome!</title>
6       </head>
7
8       <body>
9           <h1>Hello</h1>
10          <p>This is my document.</p>
11      </body>
12  </html>
13
14
15
```

Hello

This is my document.

All of our HTML document's contents should reside inside the <body> tag. This rule does not apply to CSS. We can add a <style> tag for CSS inside the <head> or the <body> tags, it doesn't matter (lines 7 and 13):

```
1   <!DOCTYPE HTML>
2   <html>
3       <head>
4           <meta charset="UTF-8">
5           <title>Welcome!</title>
6           <style>
7               h1 { border:1px solid #000; }
8           </style>
9       </head>
10
11      <body>
12          <style>
13              p {font-style:italic;}
14          </style>
15          <h1>Hello</h1>
16          <p>This is my document.</p>
17      </body>
18  </html>
```

Hello

This is my document.

Above, I have added a black border around the <h1> tag using the <style> tag on lines 6-8. This tag resides inside the <head> tag. Below that, I have given italic formatting to the <p> tag using the other <style> tag on lines 12-14. This tag resides inside the <body> tag.

We cannot place any contents outside the <head> and <body> tags. Anything you add must either be added to <head> or <body>. Stuff outside these tags is not proper HTML.

Page Backgrounds

The <body> tag gives us a way of applying styles to the whole document. Below, I have a folder with a picture in it called "doodles.png".[14]. I also have an HTML document called "test.html". This document contains the HTML from above.

Name	Date modified
doodles.png	8/9/2017 6:12 AM
test.html	2/10/2018 8:26 AM

Opening "test.html" in a browser, this is what we get:

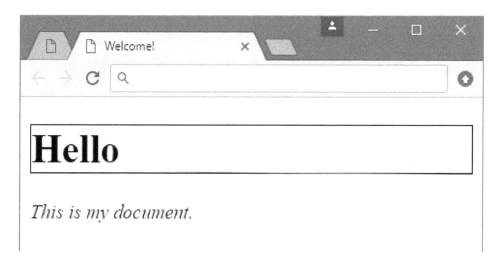

Below, we will add the "doodles.png" picture as a background for the <body> tag (line 8 below):

```
1    <!DOCTYPE HTML>
2 ▾  <html>
3 ▾      <head>
4            <meta charset="UTF-8">
5            <title>Welcome!</title>
6 ▾          <style>
7                h1 { border:1px solid #000; }
8                body {background:url(doodles.png)}
9            </style>
10       </head>
```

The result is that the background is now applied to the whole document:

---

[14] Taken from the free background patterns website subtlepatterns.com.

To work further with the background, I will now put the code inside JSTinker and move the style for the <body> tag into the CSS box:

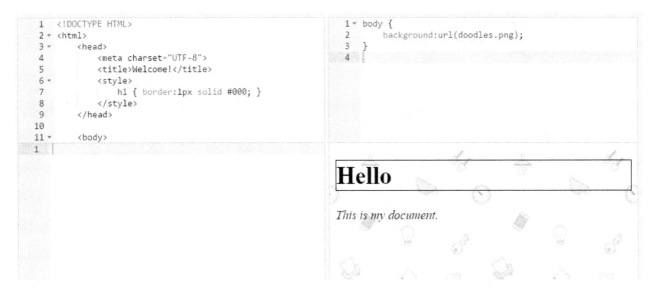

Above, since JSTinker is a playground for HTML and CSS, the background on the <body> only applies to the HTML preview on the bottom right, rather than to JSTinker itself.

Using the "background-size" property, we can make the background image smaller or larger (i.e. we can "scale" it), as follows (line 3):

```
1 ▾ body {
2       background:url(doodles.png);
3       background-size:100px;
4   }
5   |
```

Hello

This is my document.

Above, the "100px" value we gave to the "background-size" property determines the width of the background image. The background's original size (i.e. the size of the image file doodles.png) is 400 pixels, so by declaring it here to be 100 pixels, we force it to become one fourth as large as before. The result is that the doodles are much smaller now.

By default, a background is repeated over and over again to make it fill up all the space it can. We can illustrate this by changing "doodles.png" to "goats_and_girl.jpg" from earlier:

```
1 ▾ body {
2       background:url(goats_and_girl.jpg);
3       background-size:100px;
4   }
5 ▾ h1, p {
6       color:#fff;
7   }
8   |
```

Above, I have also made the <h1> and <p> elements white to make them more visible. Notice the way the picture is repeated over and over again. Also notice the way the picture is smaller than we saw in the past, since the "background-size" property on line 3 is making it have a width of 100 pixels.

Using the "background-repeat" property, we can declare that the background should not be repeated (line 4 below):

```
1 ▾  body {
2        background:url(goats_and_girl.jpg);
3        background-size:100px;
4        background-repeat:no-repeat;
5    }
6 ▾  h1, p {
7        color:#fff;
8    }
```

We can also have the background repeat horizontally by using the "repeat-x" value for the "background-repeat" property (line 4 below):

```
1 ▾  body {
2        background:url(goats_and_girl.jpg);
3        background-size:100px;
4        background-repeat:repeat-x;
5    }
6 ▾  h1, p {
7        color:#fff;
8    }
```

Changing "repeat-x" to "repeat-y", the background is made to repeat vertically:

```
1 ▾ body {
2        background:url(goats_and_girl.jpg);
3        background-size:100px;
4        background-repeat:repeat-y;
5    }
6 ▾ h1, p {
7        color:#fff;
8    }
```

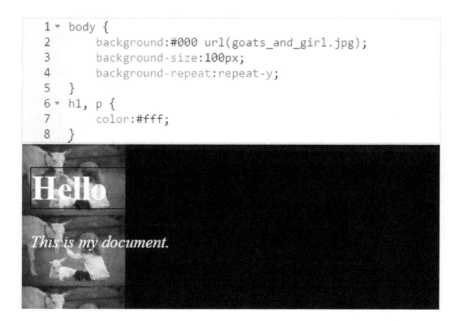

Besides giving the <body> tag an image background, we can also give it a color background while keeping the image, as follows (line 2 below):

```
1 ▾ body {
2        background:#000 url(goats_and_girl.jpg);
3        background-size:100px;
4        background-repeat:repeat-y;
5    }
6 ▾ h1, p {
7        color:#fff;
8    }
```

Above, we have declared that the background of the <body> should be black, we have also given it a URL for an image. This results in a black background except where the image is shown.

Below, I have given the doodles background to the <h1> tag and given the text a black color, while keeping everything else the same (lines 9-13):

```
1 ▾ body {
2       background:#000 url(goats_and_girl.jpg);
3       background-size:100px;
4       background-repeat:repeat-y;
5  }
6 ▾ h1, p {
7       color:#fff;
8  }
⚠ 9 ▾ h1 {
10      background:url(doodles.png);
11      color:#000;
12      background-size:200px;
13  }
```

Above, the background on the <h1> element extends beyond the text, since the background is applied to the <h1> element's box, similar to a border.

Block Quotes

The <blockquote> HTML tag is used to add quotation (i.e. indented paragraphs) to a document, as follows (lines 10-12 of the HTML):

```
1    <!DOCTYPE HTML>
2 ▾  <html>
3 ▾      <head>
4           <meta charset="UTF-8">
5           <title>Welcome!</title>
6       </head>
7
8 ▾      <body>
9           <p>George Eliot said:</p>
10 ▾         <blockquote>Blessed is the man who, having
11          nothing to say, abstains from giving us wordy
12          evidence of the fact.</blockquote>
13      </body>
```

Here is the result:

> George Eliot said:
>
> > Blessed is the man who, having nothing to say, abstains from giving us wordy evidence of the fact.

By default, a <blockquote> element has extra margin on the right and left. We could achieve the same effect by giving a <p> tag extra margin. The benefit of a <blockquote> element is semantics. By using it, even a robot will be able to distinguish the fact that this is a quotation, whereas if we had use a <p> tag, the robot would see it as any other paragraph.

Many websites add special CSS to <blockquote> elements to make the quotations in an article prettier. Below, we have used the ":before" pseudo-selector to add a big curly quote to the beginning of the <blockquote> element:

```
1   blockquote:before {
2       content:"“";
3       font-size:250%;
4   }
5
```

> George Eliot said:
>
> > “
> > Blessed is the man who, having nothing to say, abstains from giving us wordy evidence of the fact.

Above, we have put a curly left quote inside the "content" property and given it a font size of 250%. The result is that there is now a big curly quote at the beginning of the quotation. We can now add further CSS to make it look better:

```
1 ▾ blockquote:before {
2       content:"“";
3       font-size:350%;
4       color:#999;
5       position:relative;
6       top:20px;
7       left:-10px;
8   }
```

George Eliot said:

❝ Blessed is the man who, having nothing to

say, abstains from giving us wordy evidence of
the fact.

Above, I have given the curly quote a gray color. I have also given it relative positioning and increased its distance from the top (forcing it downward) while giving it a negative left distance (forcing it to move leftward). I have also increased the font size to 350%.

The quotation now looks good, but there are some problems. There is now too much space between the quotation and the paragraph above it. This is caused by the very large font size of the quotation mark we added. There is also uneven line spacing inside the quotation. The space between lines one and two is much larger than the space between lines two and three. This, too, is caused by the overly large quotation mark.

We have multiple strategies for dealing with this problem. One way is to give the quotation mark a very small "line-height" property (line 8 below):

```
1 ▾ blockquote:before {
2       content:"“";
3       font-size:350%;
4       color:#999;
5       position:relative;
6       top:20px;
7       left:-10px;
8       line-height:0.1em;
9   }
```

George Eliot said:

> ❝ Blessed is the man who, having nothing to say, abstains from giving us wordy evidence of the fact.

Above, on line 8, we have given the quotation mark a "line-height" of 0.1 ems. This tells the CSS to pretend as if the quotation mark is only one tenth as high as it really is, causing its extreme height to be ignored.

Another strategy would be to give the quotation mark a "display:block' property and make it float:

```
1 ▾ blockquote:before {
2       content:"“";
3       font-size:350%;
4       color:#999;
5       position:relative;
6       top:20px;
7       left:-10px;
8       display:block;
9       float:left;
10   }
```

George Eliot said:

> Blessed is the man who, having nothing to
> say, abstains from giving us wordy
> ❝ evidence of the fact.

By making the quotation mark float, it stops messing with the <blockquote> element's text. The floating has caused the quotation mark's position to be recalculated. Earlier, it was part of the <blockquote>'s text. It is now a block that is no longer part of the text. We can verify this by using a border. Below, I have given a border to the quotation mark while removing the "display:block" and "float:left" properties:

```
1 ▾ blockquote:before {
2       content:"""";
3       font-size:350%;
4       color:#999;
5       position:relative;
6       top:20px;
7       left:-10px;
8       line-height:0.1em;
9       border:1px solid #000;
10  }
```

George Eliot said:

> 66 Blessed is the man who, having nothing to say, abstains from giving us wordy evidence of the fact.

Below, I again change the quotation back to "display:block" and "float:left" (lines 8 and 9):

```
1 ▾ blockquote:before {
2       content:"""";
3       font-size:350%;
4       color:#999;
5       position:relative;
6       top:20px;
7       left:-10px;
8       display:block;
9       float:left;
10      border:1px solid #000;
11  }
```

George Eliot said:

> Blessed is the man who, having nothing to say, abstains from giving us wordy evidence of the fact.
> 66

Notice the way the quotation mark's triangle is on the left of the text, separate from it.

Below, I change the "top" and "left" properties in order to make the quotation mark appear at its proper place (lines 6 and 7):

```
1 ▾ blockquote:before {
2       content:"""";
3       font-size:350%;
4       color:#999;
5       position:relative;
6       top:-15px;
7       left:-10px;
8       display:block;
9       float:left;
10      border:1px solid #000;
```

The result is as follows:

George Eliot said:

 Blessed is the man who, having nothing to say, abstains from giving us wordy evidence of the fact.

Now, setting the border to zero, this is the result we have achieved (line 10 below):

```
1 ▾ blockquote:before {
2       content:"""";
3       font-size:350%;
4       color:#999;
5       position:relative;
6       top:-15px;
7       left:-10px;
8       display:block;
9       float:left;
i 10     border:0px solid #000;
11  }
```

George Eliot said:

 Blessed is the man who, having nothing to say, abstains from giving us wordy evidence of the fact.

249

This is different from the "line-height" fix we used earlier and looks less good. With the "line-height" fix, the quotation mark remained part of the text so that it nudged the word "Blessed" toward the right, giving it a nice stylistic appearance. But now that the quotation mark is a block element that floats, it no longer interacts with the text that way. Now, the word "Blessed" is directly above "say".

IDs

Throughout this book, I have used classes to identify particular elements and give them special styling, as follows:

```
1    <div class="animal dog">Rover</div>
2    <div class="animal dog">Gaspode</div>
3    <div class="animal dog">Sophie</div>
4    <div class="animal cat">Misty</div>
```

Here is the CSS and its result:

```
 1 ▾  .dog:after {
 2         content: "woof";
 3         font-size:80%;
 4         color:#999;
 5         margin-left:10px;
 6         font-style:italic;
 7      }
 8 ▾  .cat:after {
 9         content:"mew";
10         font-size:80%;
11         color:#999;
12         font-style:italic;
13         margin-left:10px;
14      }
15   |
```

Rover *woof*
Gaspode *woof*
Sophie *woof*
Misty *mew*

Above, we have used the ":after" pseudo-selector to add the words "woof" to the end of the dog names and "mew" to the end of the cat name by making use of the "dog" and "cat" classes.

The special thing about classes is that they are *reusable*. You can add the "animal", "dog" or "cat" classes to any number of elements and have them all acquire the same formatting.

Instead of using classes, we can use IDs. For example, below I have given Gaspode the ID of "rons-pet" (line 2 of the HTML):

```
i 1    <div class="animal dog">Rover</div>
  2    <div class="animal dog" id="rons-pet">Gaspode</div>
  3    <div class="animal dog">Sophie</div>
  4    <div class="animal cat">Misty</div>
```

Below, I have used the ID of "rons-pet" to give this element special styling (lines 15-19 of the CSS):

```
15 ▾ #rons-pet {
16       font-size:120%;
17       letter-spacing:0.2em;
18       border:1px solid #000;
19   }
```

Rover *woof*

Gaspode *w o o f*

Sophie *woof*

Misty *mew*

On line 15, we have the selector "#rons-pet". We already know that we use a dot in front of a class name. In front of an ID, we use the hash character (#). On line 17, I use a new propety, "letter-spacing", which is used to increase or decrease the space between each letter of a word. Note how there is a lot of extra space between the letters of "Gaspode", as if it is written as "G a s p o d e". The same has happened to the "woof" for Gaspode.

It is bad practice to use IDs for styling, which is why I have not made use of them in this book.IDs have very high "specificity", leading to something called "specificity wars". I will not go into the details of this, it is sufficient to know that it is best to avoid IDs for styling.

IDs, however, are very useful for another purpose. They enable us to create "jump links" that enable a user to jump from one section of a document to another.

Below, we have two of Shakespeare's sonnets on the same HTML document:

```
 1    <!DOCTYPE HTML>
 2 ▾  <html>
 3 ▾      <head>
 4              <meta charset="UTF-8">
 5              <title>Shakespeare's Sonnets</title>
 6          </head>
 7
 8 ▾      <body>
 9              <h2 style='text-align: center'>SONNET I<br></h2>
10 ▾          <p>From fairest creatures we desire increase,<br>
11    That thereby beauty's rose might never die,<br>
12    But as the riper should by time decease,<br>
13    His tender heir might bear his memory:<br>
14    But thou, contracted to thine own bright eyes,<br>
```

Below, I have scrolled down on the HTML preview to show you the beginning of the second sonnet:

Within thine own bud buriest thy content
And, tender churl, makest waste in niggarding.
   Pity the world, or else this glutton be,
   To eat the world's due, by the grave and thee.

SONNET II

When forty winters shall beseige thy brow,
And dig deep trenches in thy beauty's field,
Thy youth's proud livery, so gazed on now,

Using IDs, we can create a table of contents at the top of the document to help users immediately jump to the sonnet they want. This is helpful for large documents and articles. The title "Sonnet I" is an <h2> tag (see line 9 above), we give it an ID of "sonnet-1" below (line 9 of the HTML):

```
1    <!DOCTYPE HTML>
2 ▾  <html>
3 ▾      <head>
4            <meta charset="UTF-8">
5            <title>Shakespeare's Sonnets</title>
6        </head>
7
8 ▾      <body>
9 ▾          <h2 id="sonnet-1"
10           style='text-align: center'>SONNET I<br></h2>
11 ▾         <p>From fairest creatures we desire increase,<br>
12   That thereby beauty's rose might never die,<br>
13   But as the riper should by time decease,<br>
14   His tender heir might bear his memory:<br>
```

Below, we scroll down to line 29 of the HTML in order to give the title for the second sonnet an id of "sonnet-2":

```
20   And only herald to the gaudy spring, <br>
21   Within thine own bud buriest thy content<br>
22   And, tender churl, makest waste in niggarding.<br>
23       Pity the world, or else this
24   glutton be,<br>
25       To eat the world's due, by
26   the grave and thee.
27   </p>
28
29   <h2 id="sonnet-2" style='text-align: center'>SONNET II<br>
30 ▾          <p>When forty winters shall beseige thy brow,<br>
31   And dig deep trenches in thy beauty's field,<br>
32   Thy youth's proud livery, so gazed on now,<br>
33   Will be a tatter'd weed, of small worth held:<br>
```

Going back to the top of the document, I add two new <a> tags right after the <body> tag (lines 9 and 10):

```
8 ▾      <body>
9            <a href="#sonnet-1">Sonnet I</a>
10           <a href="#sonnet-2">Sonnet II</a>
11
12 ▾         <h2 id="sonnet-1"
```

Notice the special syntax we used for the "href" attribute of the <a> tags on lines 9 and 10. The hash character (#) tells the browser that this is a reference to an ID on the document. Here is what the links look like:

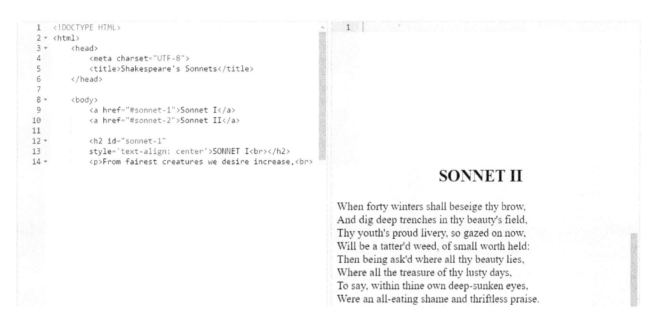

If a user clicks "Sonnet II", the browser will immediately jump to any element on the document that has an ID of "sonnet-2". Below, I have clicked on the Sonnet II link, which causes the browser to scroll down to Sonnet II:

```
1    <!DOCTYPE HTML>
2 ▾  <html>
3 ▾     <head>
4           <meta charset="UTF-8">
5           <title>Shakespeare's Sonnets</title>
6        </head>
7
8 ▾     <body>
9           <a href="#sonnet-1">Sonnet I</a>
10          <a href="#sonnet-2">Sonnet II</a>
11
12 ▾       <h2 id="sonnet-1"
13          style='text-align: center'>SONNET I<br></h2>
14 ▾       <p>From fairest creatures we desire increase,<br>
```

SONNET II

When forty winters shall beseige thy brow,
And dig deep trenches in thy beauty's field,
Thy youth's proud livery, so gazed on now,
Will be a tatter'd weed, of small worth held:
Then being ask'd where all thy beauty lies,
Where all the treasure of thy lusty days,
To say, within thine own deep-sunken eyes,
Were an all-eating shame and thriftless praise.

We can make use of IDs to send users to a specific section of a document that happens to be on another website. Below, I have created a link that takes users to the "Capabilities" section of the Falcon Heavy article on Wikipedia:

```
1 ▾  <a
2    href="https://en.wikipedia.org/wiki/Falcon_Heavy#Capabilities">
3    Click here</a> to view the "Capabilities" section
4    of the Falcon Heavy article on Wikipedia.
5    |
```

Here is what the link looks like:

Click here to view the "Capabilities" section of the Falcon Heavy article on Wikipedia.

If a user clicks that link, the following will open up in their browser:

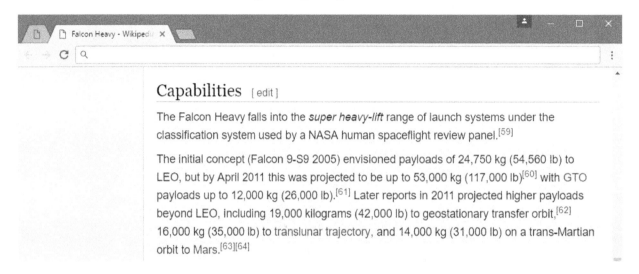

The "href" attribute of the <a> tag is made up of the link to the Wikipedia article:

https://en.wikipedia.org/wiki/Falcon_Heavy

This is followed by the ID of the element that we want to take users to:

#Capabilities

This only works because Wikipedia helpfully adds IDs to its headings. If we look at the HTML for the Wikipedia article, we will see that the id "Capabilities" is defined on a <span> tag inside the <h2> tag for the Capabilities heading (line 383 below):

```
383  <h2><span class="mw-headline" id="Capabilities">Capabilities</span><span class="mw-editsection">
     <span class="mw-editsection-bracket">[</span><a href="https://en.wikipedia.org/w/index.php?
     title=Falcon_Heavy&amp;action=edit&amp;section=7" title="Edit section: Capabilities">edit</a><span
     class="mw-editsection-bracket">]</span></span></h2>
384  <p>The Falcon Heavy falls into the <i>super heavy-lift</i> range of launch systems under the
     classification system used by a NASA human spaceflight review panel.<sup id="cite_ref-hsf200910_59-
     0" class="reference"><a href="https://en.wikipedia.org/wiki/Falcon_Heavy#cite_note-hsf200910-59">
     [59]</a></sup></p>
```

Subscripts and Superscripts

Below, we have an exert from the article on water in *The Standard Electrical Dictionary* by T. O'Conor Sloane (1892):

```
i 1 ▾  <p>A compound whose molecule consists of two atoms of
  2    hydrogen and one atom of oxygen; formula, H2O. Its specific
  3    gravity is 1, it being the base of
  4    the system of specific gravities of solids and liquids. If
  5    pure, it is almost a non-conductor of
  6    electricity.</p>
```

Using the <sub> tag (which stands for "subscript"),we can give the H_2O formula its proper appearance and semantics (line 2 below):

```
i 1 ▾  <p>A compound whose molecule consists of two atoms of
  2    hydrogen and one atom of oxygen; formula, H<sub>2</sub>O.
  3    Its specific gravity is 1, it being the base of
  4    the system of specific gravities of solids and liquids. If
  5    pure, it is almost a non-conductor of
  6    electricity.</p>
  7    |
  8
```

The paragraph now looks thus:

A compound whose molecule consists of two atoms of hydrogen and one atom of oxygen; formula, H_2O. Its specific gravity is 1, it being the base of the system of specific gravities of solids and liquids. If pure, it is almost a non-conductor of electricity.

There is, however, an issue. The <sub> tag forces its line to expand downwards, causing its line to have more space below it than the rest of the lines, leading to an uneven appearance. We can fix this by giving <sub> elements a very small "line-height" property (line 5 below):

```
1 ▾ p {
2       font-size:20px;
3   }
4 ▾ sub {
5       line-height:0.1em;
6   }
7   |
```

A compound whose molecule consists of two atoms of hydrogen and one atom of oxygen; formula, H_2O. Its specific gravity is 1, it being the base of the system of specific gravities of solids and liquids. If pure, it is

Above, the <sub> tag stops exerting influence on the height of its line, making it fit in properly with the rest of the text.

We also have the <sup> tag for creating superscripts, as follows:

```
1   ax<sup>2</sup> + bx + c = 0
```

```
1 ▾ p {
2       font-size:20px;
3   }
4 ▾ sup {
5       line-height:0.1em;
6   }
7   |
```

$$ax^2 + bx + c = 0$$

The <sup> tag, similar to the <sub> tag, messes with the line height of its own line, therefore giving it a small "line-height" property (line 5 above) helps prevent it from messing up the appearance of its paragraph.

Images

Below, we have the picture of a giant rubber duck floating on a river in Hong Kong:

```
1    <img src="rubber_duck.jpg" />
2
```

```
1 ▾ img {
2        width:400px;
3    }
4
```

The rubber duck's picture is too large, therefore in the CSS I have given it a width of 400 pixels (line 2 of the CSS above) to make it appear smaller. By default, images have automatic height; reducing the width will cause the browser to also reduce the height, in this way keeping the image's "aspect ratio" intact.

Below, I have given the image a height besides its width (line 3 below):

```
1 ▾ img {
2        width:400px;
3        height:100px;
4    }
5
```

Above, note the way the image is squished. By giving the image both a width and a height, we are twisting it in order to make it fit this exact width and height. To prevent squishing, we must always either keep the width undefined, or the height undefined, so that the browser may have the freedom to automatically adjust them. Below, I have kept the height of 100 pixels while removing the width defintion:

```
1 ▾ img {
2       height:100px;
3 }
4
```

Above, now that the width definition is gone, the browser adjusts the width of the image to make it smaller *in proportion* to its height, so that the image does not get skewed.

Images take a "height" and "width" attribute that we can use to give them the size we want, as follows:

```
1   <img height="100" src="rubber_duck.jpg" />
2
```

Above, the height attribute of 100 that I added is *not* CSS. It is HTML. Note the way there are no units after the 100, the browser automatically assumes pixels. The result is exactly the same as giving the image a CSS height of 100 pixels. If we define both the width and height, we again run the risk of twisting the image:

```
i 1   <img height="100" width="100" src="rubber_duck.jpg" />
  2
```

```
1
```

```
1
```

The height and width attributes can be useful in cases where you want to quickly determine the width or height of an image without having to bother writing CSS (some systems do not even let you write CSS, limiting you to the use of the width and height attributes). If we had dozens of images and we wanted each one to have a specific width or height, it would be quicker to use the width and height attributes rather than having to add a unique class to each image then write a CSS definition for it.

Alternate Texts

Image tags take an "alt" attribute that we can use to tell search engines and blind people what the image portrays. On line 2 of the HTML below, I have added an "alt" attribute that gives a brief description of the image:

```
  1   <img width="300"
  2   alt="Giant rubber duck floating on river in Hong Kong"
i 3   src="rubber_duck.jpg" />
  4
```

A blind person who is using a screen reader (a program that reads out the contents of web page to them) will now hear this description read out to them, helping them know what the image is even though they cannot see it.

Another benefit is that "alt" attributes help search engines understand the contents of images. If you have web page for a museum that shows dozens of items, if an image has an alt attribute of "Medieval crossbow from Spain", when a user searches on Google for "medieval crossbow from Spain", Google will show them that image from the museum's website (among others). Without the "alt" tag, Google may have no idea what the image portrays, so that the image will not come up in web searches.

Another benefit of an alt attribute is that if for some reason the image fails to load, the user will still see the alt text, helping them know what the image is without seeing it:

Giant rubber duck floating on river in
Hong Kong

8. Beautifying Text

In Latin alphabets, we have two types of fonts; serif fonts and sans-serif fonts:

The letter "A" on the left has serifs, while the letter "A" on the right lacks them. The serifs are the stuff at the bottom of the "A" on the left that make it look like it is wearing slippers. Below, we have a serif "H" on the left and a sans-serif "H" on the right:

Above, the serif "H" on the left has the serifs both at the top and the bottom:

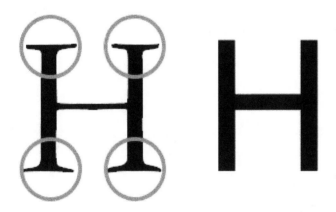

Serif fonts in general have a more classical appearance, while sans-serif fonts ("sans" is French for "lacking", "without") have a more modern appearance. In CSS, we can declare that a certain text should be either serif or sans-serif without specifying the font (line 2 below):

```
1  <p>This is some text</p>
2  |
```

```
1  p {
2      font-family:sans-serif;
3      font-size:30px;
4  }
5  |
```

This is some text

Above, on line 2 of the CSS, I have declared that the <p> element should have a sans-serif font. In general, this declaration is used after specifying a font, as follows:

```
1 ▾ p {
2       font-family:'Roboto Condensed', sans-serif;
3       font-size:30px;
4   }
```

Here is the result:

This is some text

Above, on line 2, I have declared that the <p> element should use the 'Roboto Condensed' font, after which I have written 'sans-serif'. This tells the browser to use the Roboto Condensed font *if the user has this font*, and if they don't have it, it tells the browser to use the default sans-serif font of the user's system.

You can declare as many fonts as you like (separated by commas). The browser will try to use the first one if the user has it. If they don't, the browser will fall back on the second font specified, and if they don't, it will fall back on 'sans-serif'.

Below, on line 2, we have an example of three font declarations, ending with 'serif':

```
1 ▾ p {
2       font-family: 'Goudy Old Style', Centaur, serif;
3       font-size:30px;
4   }
5   |
```

This is some text

Text Shadows

Text "text-shadow" property is used to add a shadow to a text. Below, we have a quotation from Shakespeare:

By the pricking of my thumbs,
Something wicked this way comes.

On line 4 below, I define a text shadow:

```
1 ▾ p {
2       font-family: Centaur, serif;
3       font-size:30px;
4       text-shadow:2px 2px 2px #ccc;
5   }
```

Here is the result:

By the pricking of my thumbs,
Something wicked this way comes.

The "text-shadow" property's value is defined similarly to the "box-shadow" property. We define a top distance, a left distance and a size, followed by a color. Using the interplay between the text color and the shadow, we can create interesting effects, as follows (lines 4 and 5):

```
1 ▾ p {
2       font-family: Centaur, serif;
3       font-size:30px;
4       text-shadow:1px 1px 5px #ccc;
5       color:#ccc;
6   }
```

Here is the result:

By the pricking of my thumbs,
Something wicked this way comes.

Some websites use a very subtle shadow to make their text have a nice-looking sheen, as follows:

```
1 ▾ p {
2       font-family: Centaur, serif;
3       font-size:20px;
4       text-shadow:1px 1px 1px #fff;
5       color:#000;
6   }
7
8   |
```

By the pricking of my thumbs,
Something wicked this way comes.

Above, the HTML preview has a gray background. I have given the text a white "shadow", which creates a very subtle effect where the edges of the black text are brighter than the gray background.

Drop Caps

A drop cap is a large letter that is used at the beginning of a passage. Below is an example of a drop cap from *Stories from Lands of Sunshine* by Eleanor Riggs (1904). The drop cap is the large "J" that takes up multiple lines:

THE MAGNOLIA

JUST beyond New Orleans is a beautiful swamp of tall cypress trees and low palmettoes. It has dark little bayous with strange Indian names, and is the home of hundreds of birds. It is a narrow swamp, and winds like a tattered gray scarf about the shoulders of the old gray lake called Pont'chartrain. In recent years neat cottages have been built

We will now try to recreate something like the above. Below, I have typed some of the paragraph from above:

```
1   <p>Just beyond New Orleans is a beautiful swamp of
2   tall cypress trees and low palmettoes. It has
3   dark little bayous with strange Indian names,
4   and is the home of hundreds of birds. It is a narrow
5   swamp, and winds like a tattered gray scarf about...</p>
6
7
```

```
1   p {
2       font-family: 'Goudy Old Style', serif;
3       font-size:20px;
4   }
5
6
```

Just beyond New Orleans is a beautiful swamp of tall cypress trees and low palmettoes. It has dark little bayous with strange Indian names, and is the home of hundreds of birds. It is a narrow swamp, and winds like a tattered gray scarf about...

In order to add special styling to the letter "J", we put it in a <span> tag and give it a class of its own:

```
1   <p><span class="drop-cap">J</span>ust beyond New Orleans
2   is a beautiful swamp of tall cypress trees and low
```

It may seem strange to put a single letter of a word in a tag of its own, but this is commonly done for styling purposes. It doesn't actually affect the appearance of the text until we add CSS for it:

Just beyond New Orleans is a beautiful swamp of tall cypress trees and low palmettoes. It has dark little bayous with strange Indian names, and is the home of hundreds of birds. It is a narrow swamp, and winds like a tattered gray scarf about...

Let's now give the "drop-cap" class a large font size:

```
6 ▾ .drop-cap {
7       font-size:300%;
8   }
```

Here is the result:

J ust beyond New Orleans is a beautiful swamp of

tall cypress trees and low palmettoes. It has dark little bayous with strange Indian names, and is the home of hundreds of birds. It is a narrow swamp,

Above, the "J" is now much larger. But it causes certain issues for us. It pushes the line right below it down, causing uneven line spacing. We can fix this by giving it a small line height (line 8 below):

```
6 ▾ .drop-cap {
7       font-size:300%;
8       line-height:0.1em;
9   }
```

Here is the result:

Just beyond New Orleans is a beautiful swamp of tall cypress trees and low palmettoes. It has dark little bayous with strange Indian names, and is the

Above, the lines are now evenly spaced.

The next thing to do is to push the "J" downwards. One might think of giving it an inline-block display property and a top margin (lines 9 and 10), as follows, but it doesn't work:

```
 6 ▾  .drop-cap {
 7        font-size:300%;
 8        line-height:0.1em;
 9        display:inline-block;
10        margin-top:20px;
```

Just beyond New Orleans is a beautiful swamp of tall cypress trees and low palmettoes. It has dark little bayous with strange Indian names, and is the

The top margin on line 10 pushes the whole line down, not just the "J".

We can use relative positioning to push it down, as follows (lines 10 and 11):

```
 6 ▾  .drop-cap {
 7        font-size:300%;
 8        line-height:0.1em;
 9        display:inline-block;
10        position:relative;
11        top:20px;
12    }
```

Just beyond New Orleans is a beautiful swamp of tall cypress trees and low palmettoes. It has dark little bayous with strange Indian names, and is the

The trouble is that the "J" gets overlaid onto the line below. If we were to use bottom padding to push the next line down (line 12 below), this would happen:

```
 6 ▾  .drop-cap {
 7         font-size:300%;
 8         line-height:0.1em;
 9         display:inline-block;
10         position:relative;
11         top:20px;
12         padding-bottom:40px;
13    }
```

J ust beyond New Orleans is a beautiful swamp of tall cypress trees and low palmettoes. It has dark little bayous with strange Indian names, and is the home of hundreds of birds. It is a narrow swamp,

Above, all of the second line ends up going down, which is not what we want.

The proper solution is to use "display:block" and a left float:

```
 6 ▾  .drop-cap {
 7         font-size:300%;
 8         line-height:0.1em;
 9         display:block;
10         float:left;
11    }
```

J ust beyond New Orleans is a beautiful swamp of tall cypress trees and low palmettoes. It has dark little bayous with strange Indian names, and is the

Now, if were to give the drop cap a top margin (line 11 below), things will act a little more reasonably:

```
 6 ▼  .drop-cap {
 7        font-size:300%;
 8        line-height:0.1em;
 9        display:block;
10        float:left;
11        margin-top:0.45em;
12    }
```

Just beyond New Orleans is a beautiful swamp of tall cypress trees and low palmettoes. It has dark little bayous with strange Indian names, and is the

Above, the "J" ends up being pushed down, and the line below it makes room for it by moving the word "tall" toward the right. You may notice that the "J" is now running into the word "little" below it. We can fix this by giving the drop cap a bottom margin (line 12 below):

```
 6 ▼  .drop-cap {
 7        font-size:300%;
 8        line-height:0.1em;
 9        display:block;
10        float:left;
11        margin-top:0.45em;
12        margin-bottom:0.5em;
```

Just beyond New Orleans is a beautiful swamp of tall cypress trees and low palmettoes. It has dark little bayous with strange Indian names, and is the home of hundreds of birds. It is a narrow

The bottom margin enlarges the footprint of the drop cap. It tells the browser to reserve this much empty space underneath the drop cap, which forces the text to move away from it.

Below, I have changed the font family of the text to the font known as Georgia (line 2 below):

```
 1 ▼  p {
 2        font-family: Georgia, serif;
 3        font-size:20px;
 4    }
```

Here is the result on our text:

J ust beyond New Orleans is a beautiful swamp of tall cypress trees and low palmettoes. It has dark little bayous with strange Indian names, and is the home of hundreds of birds. It is a narrow swamp, and

Above, notice how there is now a little too much space underneath the drop cap. This is because what looks good in one font does not necessarily work for another font. When changing fonts, we sometimes have to readjust the CSS styling in order to make it look decent again. Below, I reduce the bottom margin (line 12), which reduces the amount of space reserved underneath the drop cap:

```
6 ▾  .drop-cap {
7         font-size:350%;
8         line-height:0.1em;
9         display:block;
10        float:left;
11        margin-top:0.45em;
12        margin-bottom:0.3em;
```

J ust beyond New Orleans is a beautiful swamp of tall cypress trees and low palmettoes. It has dark little bayous with strange Indian names, and is the home of hundreds of birds. It is a narrow swamp, and

This page intentionally left blank

9. Meeting the Inspector

Learning "inspection" is a crucial skill for any learner of HTML and CSS. Web browsers like Chromium, Chrome and Firefox come with an "inspector" that helps you peek into the code of the HTML document you are looking at. Below, inside the Chromium web browser, I have right-clicked on an empty area on the Falcon Heavy article on Wikipedia and chosen to click "Inspect":

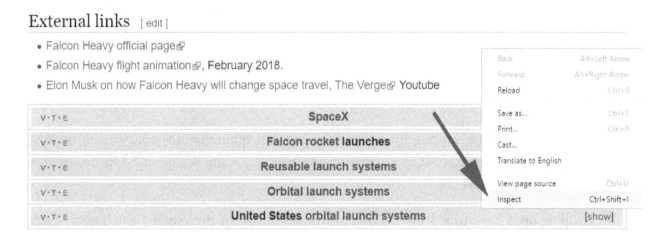

This causes the Chromium Inspector to appear, as follows:

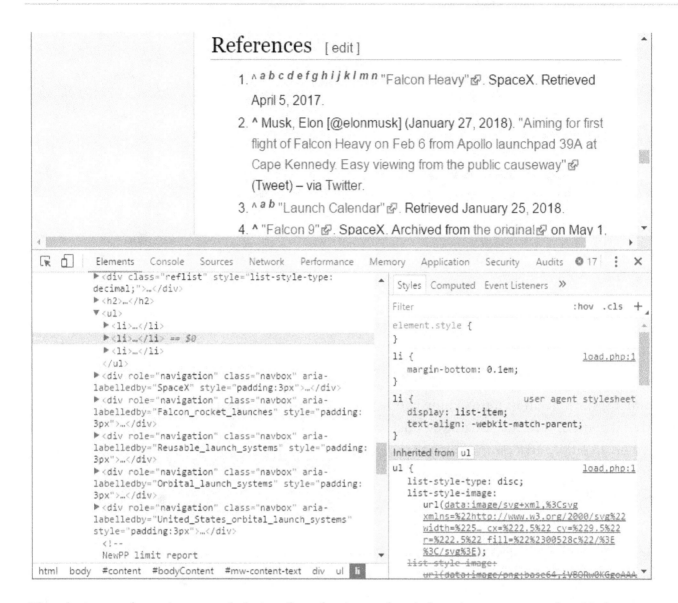

The above can be quite overwhelming for a beginner, but it is quite easy to work with it once you get used to it. On the left, we have direct access to the HTML of the document. On the right, we have access to the document's CSS.

Below, by scrolling up, I have found the HTML for the <h1> tag of the article (which says "Falcon Heavy"):

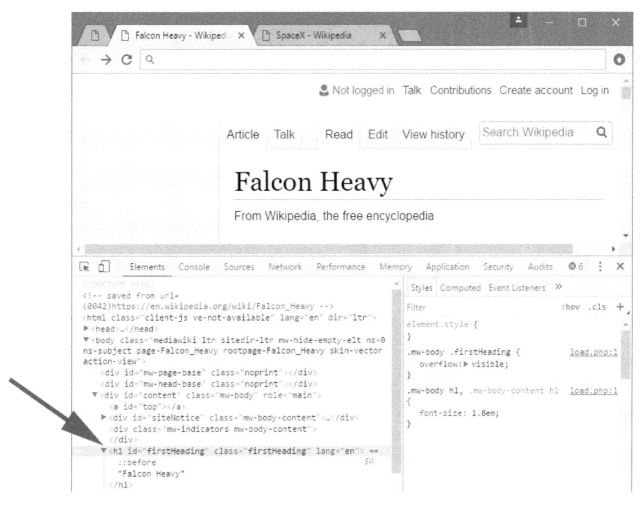

I can now change the word "Falcon Heavy" to anything I want by double-clicking the word "Falcon Heavy" in the inspector:

```
▼<h1 id="firstHeading" class="firstHeading" lang="en">
    ::before
   "Falcon Not So Heavy" == $0
  </h1>
```

Pressing "Enter" ("return" on a Mac) makes my changes show on document:

Do not worry; I am not actually vandalizing Wikipedia. By making changes in the inspector, I only change my own local "copy" of the article. This has no effect on the web page that others see.

Using the inspector, you can now impress your friends by telling them you can make changes to this or that website.

The inspector is also useful for testing our styles on a document in real-time. Below, I have a document open with Shakespeare's first sonnet on it:

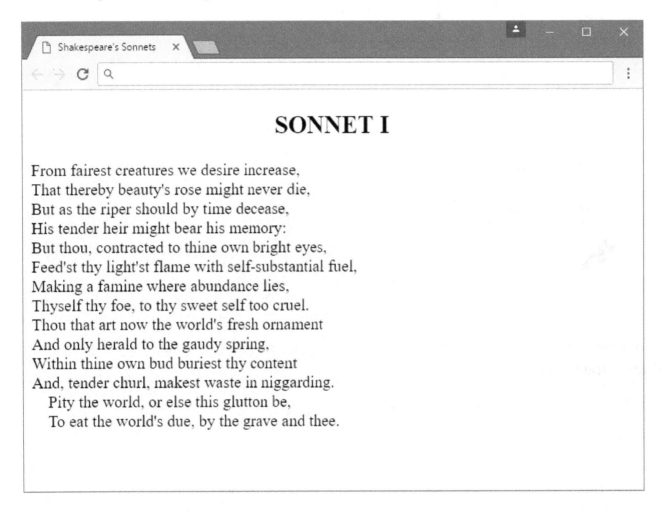

Below, I have opened the inspector:

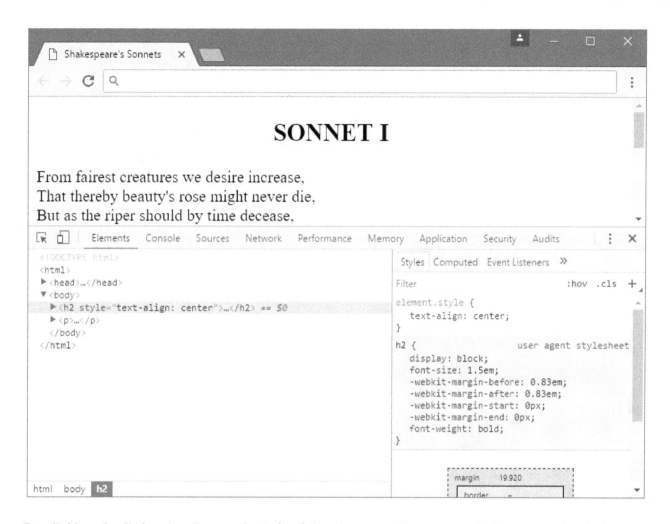

By clicking the little triangles on the left of the elements, I can expand them to make their contents visible. Below, I have clicked the triangle to the left of the <p> tag:

```
<!DOCTYPE html>
<html>
▶ <head>...</head>
▼ <body>
  ▶ <h2 style="text-align: center">...</h2> == $0
    ▼ <p>
        "From fairest creatures we desire increase,"
        <br>
        "
        That thereby beauty's rose might never die,"
        <br>
        "
        But as the riper should by time decease,"
        <br>
        "
        His tender heir might bear his memory:"
```

Let's say we want to test out some styles on the <p> tag. We first have to select it by clicking on it in the inspector:

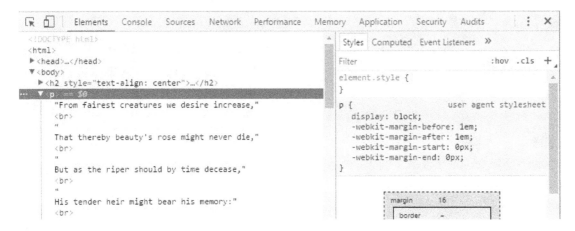

Now, on the right side I can add styles to the <p> tag by clicking the "element.style" box on the right. I start typing "font" and the inspector offers me various CSS properties starting with the word "font":

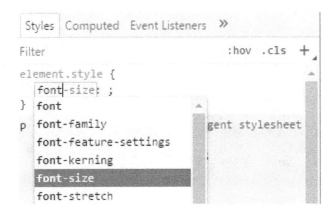

I click on "font-size":

Now, I will press the "tab' button on my keyboard (you can also press Enter/return) and typing "150%" as the new value of the "font-size" property:

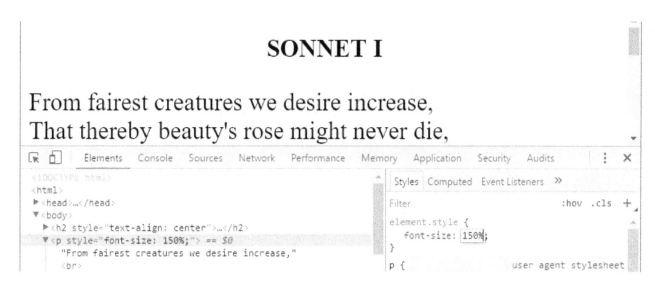

Above, notice the way that the text of the sonnet is now larger. Also notice that in the HTML preview on the left of the inspector, the new style we added is added as a new "style" attribute on the <p> tag. Anything we add in the "element.style" area is added to the element as a style attribute.

Below, I have selected the <h2> tag on the left of the inspector and added a number of CSS properties on the right, changing the appearance of the word "Sonnet I":

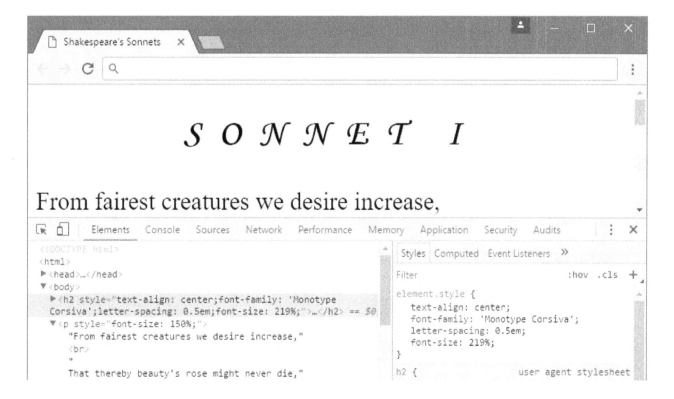

Any changes you make to the document will be lost when you close the tab. There is no way to save the changes you make. Using the inspector is entirely for "inspecting" a document's HTML and CSS to find out more about it.

Below, we have a very simple HTML document with two names on it:

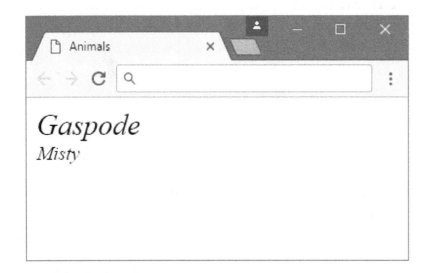

By opening the inspector, I can check what is causing the word "Gaspode" to appear so large:

Above, on the left I have clicked on the <div> tag that contains the word "Gaspode". On the right, I can see the styles that apply to it. The inspector is telling me that there is an italic formatting on the "animal" class, and a 150% font-size on the "dog" class.

We can also make changes to the styles that are on a class. Below, on the right, I have added a 1px border on the "animal" class. The result is that both animal names get a border:

I can even add a brand new class to an element and style that class. On the left side of the inspector, by double-clicking on the class names of an element we can add new classes to it or remove classes. Below, I have added the class "terrier" to the <div> for Gaspode:

```
    </style>
    <div class="animal dog terrier">Gaspode</div> == $0
    <div class="animal cat">Misty</div>
  </body>
</html>
```

Now I can create a new CSS rule for the "terrier" class by lcicking on the plus icon on the top right of the CSS part of the inspector:

Once I click the plus icon, the inspector creates a new CSS section for me and suggests a selector:

I refuse the suggestion and instead type ".terrier" only:

I now add some styles to the "terrier" class. I give it a "font-family" property of "Roboto Condensed' (this is the name of a font) and a padding of 10 pixels. The result can be seen above the inspector.

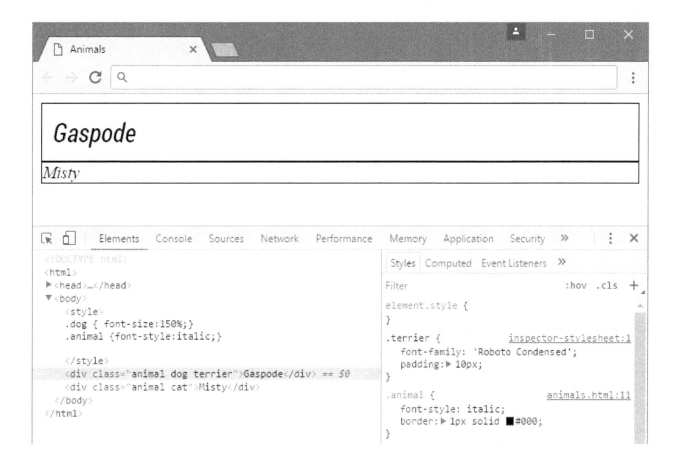

This page intentionally left blank

10. Creating Your First Layout

In this chapter, we will bring together what we have learned so far in order to make a "real" web page. We will study the scenario of turning a non-web design into a web design, which is how professional web designers often do their work. The designs are created on paper or inside a program like Vizio or Photoshop. The design is then given to a web designer who writes the HTML and CSS necessary to recreate the design on the web.

Above, we have a page from a magazine that we will turn into a web page. The page is from a 1836 edition of a London ladies' magazine known as *The Court Magazine*.

Below is a screenshot of the folder in which I will be putting my files:

At the moment, the folder only contains one file. The file is the decorative picture from the magazine page. Below, I have opened the image in Microsoft Paint in order to show you what it looks like:

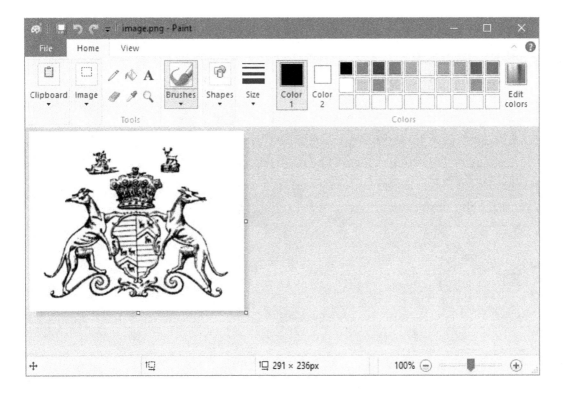

Below, I have created a new file called magazine.html (using the method of clicking an empty area, choosing New -> New Text Document and renaming the Next Text Document.txt to magazine.html):

Name	Date modified
image.png	2/14/2018 11:05 AM
magazine.html	2/14/2018 11:09 AM

Below, I open magazine.html in Notepad++.[15], which is a highly useful (and free!) code editing program:

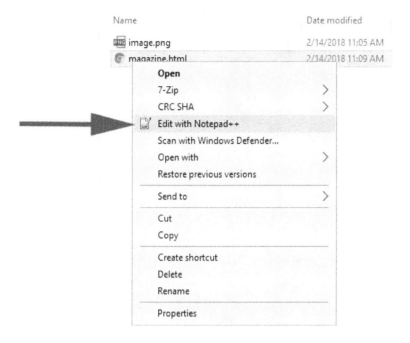

Note: You will not see the option "Edit with Notepad++" until you have downloaded and installed the Notepad++ program..[16]

Below is a picture of the magazine.html file opened in Notepad++:

---

[15] You can download it at notepad-plus-plus.org. If you are using a Mac, you can get a free code editor at brackets.io.
[16] You can Google "How to install notepad++" to find videos and tutorials on installing this program on your computer.

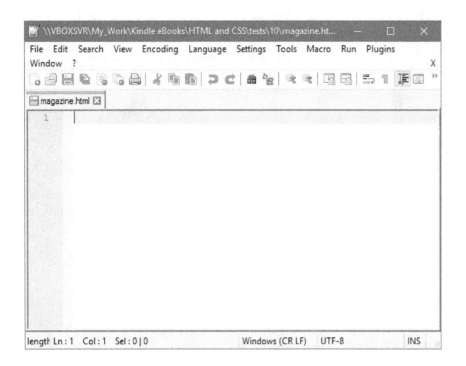

Below, I have entered the code for a barebones HTML document:

It is common to put images in their own folder, there I will create a new folder called "images" and move the image file into it:

It is also common to put CSS in a separate file in its own folder. For this reason, we will create a new folder:

Inside the "css" folder we will create a new file called "styles.css":

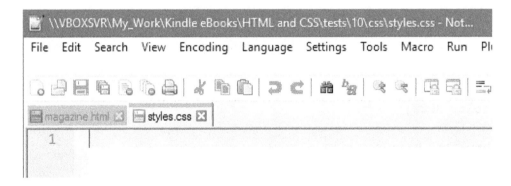

Below, I have also opened the "styles.css" file in Notepad++, so that I can have easy access to it:

We will now tell our html document to get its CSS from this new file, as follows (line 6 below):

```
magazine.html ☒    styles.css ☒
 1        <!DOCTYPE HTML>
 2     ⊟<html>
 3       ⊟    <head>
 4              <meta charset="UTF-8">
 5              <title>The Court Magazine</title>
 6              <link rel="stylesheet" type="text/css" href="css/styles.css"/>
 7           </head>
 8       ⊟   <body>
 9           </body>
10      └</html>
11       |
```

Above, we use the <link> tag that we have not used before. This tag, similar to the <meta> tag, does not have a closing tag. Using the "rel" attribute, we declare that this is a stylesheet. In the "type" attribute, we write "text/css". Using the "href" attribute, we declare where the file is located. The path we declare is "css/styles.css", which tells the browser to look in a folder called "css" and to find a file inside that folder named "styles.css".

We will now test to see if everything is working properly by adding a test <h1> tag on line 9:

```
 8     ⊟    <body>
 9             <h1>TEST</h1>
10           </body>
```

In "styles.css", we will give the <h1> a special formatting, such as a border:

```
magazine.html ☒    styles.css ☒
 1        h1 {border:1px solid #000;}
```

I will now open "magazine.html" in a browser:

Above, we can see that everything is working properly. The title tag "The Court Magazine" can be seen at the top (above the magnifier icon), and the <h1> element now has the black border which we declared inside the "styles.css" file.

We will now work on creating a masthead for our magazine website. A masthead is the top part of a website where the site's logo is shown along with other things. Below is a picture of the website for Britain's Royal Society. The masthead is the top part where you see the word "The Royal Society" on the left and a magnifier and stacked rectangles icon on the right:

The masthead is shown on most pages of a website, depending on the design choices of the creators. Below, I have navigated to the "Grants" page of the Royal Society's website. Notice that the masthead remains the same:

For our website, we will have to take our inspiration from the picture of the magazine page that we saw earlier:

It is complicated to generate curved text in HTML/CSS, therefore for the purposes of this book we will reuse the above title from the picture of the magazine page. Below, I put the above image inside the images folder:[17]

Name	Date modified
image.png	2/14/2018 11:05 AM
magazine_title.png	2/15/2018 10:58 AM

We now use a new tag to create the masthead for our website. This tag is the <header> tag (not to be confused with the <head> tag):

```
 8      <body>
 9          <header>
10              <div class="logo">
11                  <img src="images/magazine_title.png" />
12              </div>
13          </header>
```

The <header> tag does not accomplish anything special when it comes to styling. Instead of <header>, one can merely use a <div>. It is better to use the <header> tag, however, because this is semantically more appropriate. It allows robots (such as search engines) to know this is the masthead of the website, helping them avoid the mistake of thinking the masthead is the actual content of the site.

Inside the <header> tag, I have placed a <div> with a class of "logo", and inside that div, I have placed the <img> tag for the magazine title.

This is what our document looks like now in a browser:

---

[17] Those wishing to follow along can download the image files (and the rest of the files used throughout this chapter) at the author's website here: http://hawramani.com/the-court-magazine

Next, we will define the navigation section of the website:

```
8    <body>
9        <header>
10           <div class="logo">
11               <img src="images/magazine_title.png" />
12           </div>
13           <nav>
14               <a href="">Home</a>
15               <a href="">About</a>
16               <a href="">Contact</a>
17           </nav>
18       </header>
19   </body>
```

Above, I have created a new tag for the navigation. This is the <nav> tag. Similar to the <header> tag, the <nav> is like a <div> and does not come with any special formatting. Inside it I have created a few links. The links at the moment have empty "href" attributes, since we do not yet know where the links should go.

Next will create the contents of the article:

```
13           <nav>
14               <a href="">Home</a>
15               <a href="">About</a>
16               <a href="">Contact</a>
17           </nav>
18       </header>
19       <main>
20           <article>
21
22           </article>
23       </main>
24   </body>
```

To define the main content area of a website, we use the <main> tag. Inside it, we use an <article> tag to define the article area. The <main> tag may also contain ads, videos and other elements not having to do with the article.

Remember that we had an image at the top of the article, below we add that and below it we add the title of the article:

```
20      <article>
21          <img src="images/image.png" />
22          <h1>Genealogical Memoir of Lady Mary Vyner</h1>
23      </article>
```

Here is what our document looks like in the browser:

It does not look very pretty, but we will leave the styling for a little later. It is now time to add the contents of the article. Instead of typing up the contents, I will use some "filler" text. This is used by web designers to test out their designs without having to write out long paragraphs. The most commonly used filler text is "lorem ipsum", which is made up of Latin words. Below is a picture of a number of <p> tags I have added below the <h1> tag filled with the "lorem ipsum" text:

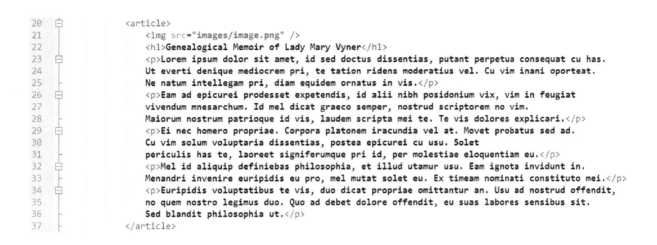

```
20    <article>
21        <img src="images/image.png" />
22        <h1>Genealogical Memoir of Lady Mary Vyner</h1>
23        <p>Lorem ipsum dolor sit amet, id sed doctus dissentias, putant perpetua consequat cu has.
24        Ut everti denique mediocrem pri, te tation ridens moderatius vel. Cu vim inani oporteat.
25        Ne natum intellegam pri, diam equidem ornatus in vis.</p>
26        <p>Eam ad epicurei prodesset expetendis, id alii nibh posidonium vix, vim in feugiat
27        vivendum mnesarchum. Id mel dicat graeco semper, nostrud scriptorem no vim.
28        Maiorum nostrum patrioque id vis, laudem scripta mei te. Te vis dolores explicari.</p>
29        <p>Ei nec homero propriae. Corpora platonem iracundia vel at. Movet probatus sed ad.
30        Cu vim solum voluptaria dissentias, postea epicurei cu usu. Solet
31        periculis has te, laoreet signiferumque pri id, per molestiae eloquentiam eu.</p>
32        <p>Mel id aliquip definiebas philosophia, et illud utamur usu. Eam ignota invidunt in.
33        Menandri invenire euripidis eu pro, mel mutat solet eu. Ex timeam nominati constituto mei.</p>
34        <p>Euripidis voluptatibus te vis, duo dicat propriae omittantur an. Usu ad nostrud offendit,
35        no quem nostro legimus duo. Quo ad debet dolore offendit, eu suas labores sensibus sit.
36        Sed blandit philosophia ut.</p>
37    </article>
```

297

Adding Styles

It is now time to style our creation. The first thing to do is to make the logo smaller, as follows:

```
   magazine.html    styles.css
1  .logo img {
2          width:230px;
3  }
4
```

Above, I have removed the border styling I had added earlier to the <h1>tag. The selector ".logo img" means "an image located inside an element that has the class of 'logo'". The result is as follows:

Home About Contact

Genealogical Memoir of Lady Mary Vyner

Lorem ipsum dolor sit amet, id sed doctus dissentias, putant perpetua consequat cu has. Ut everti denique mediocrem pri, te tation ridens moderatius vel. Cu vim inani oporteat. Ne natum intellegam pri, diam equidem ornatus in vis.

Below, I center-align the logo image by giving the "logo" class a "text-align" property of "center" (line 2 below). The "text-align" property applies to all inline elements inside an element, and since the "img" tag inside the "logo" class is inline, it ends up being center-aligned.

```
1    .logo {
2        text-align:center;
3    }
4    .logo img {
5        width:230px;
6    }
7
```

Here is the result:

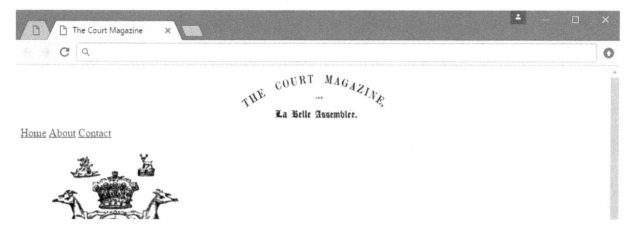

If we had placed the "text-align: center" property inside the ".logo img" selector (as follows on line 6), nothing would have happened:

```
1    .logo {
2
3    }
4    .logo img {
5        width:230px;
6        text-align:center;
7    }
8
```

The reason is that the "text-align" property applies to the *contents* of an element. If we want the image to be center-aligned inside the "logo" div (as we do), we have to declare the "text-align" property on the "logo" <div> on line 2. Declaring "text-align" on line 6 above means "center the image's contents inside the <img> tag", which means nothing when it comes to the image's position inside its container <div>. It's like saying "Hang this painting centered inside its own frame on the wall." This tells you nothing about where it should go on the wall. If you are a little confused, there is no need to worry. I have seen seasoned web designers put "text-align" on inline elements then wonder why nothing happens.

We will now add a subtle border underneath the logo <div> (line 3 below):

```
1   .logo {
2       text-align:center;
3       border-bottom:1px solid #ccc;
4   }
5   .logo img {
6       width:230px;
7   }
8
```

Here is the result:

Below, I center-align the navigation links:

```
9    nav {
10       text-align:center;
11   }
```

Note that I did not write ".nav" but merely "nav" as the selector. This is because in our HTML we are using a <nav> tag, the word "nav" here is a tag name rather than a class name. To refresh your memory, here is what we have in the HTML:

```
<header>
    <div class="logo">
        <img src="images/magazine_title.png" />
    </div>
    <nav>
        <a href="">Home</a>
        <a href="">About</a>
        <a href="">Contact</a>
    </nav>
</header>
```

Here is the result of the center-align we declared above:

The center-aligning works because the <a> tags are inline elements. If we turn them to block elements and make them float as follows, the center-aligning will stop working:

```
 9  ⊟nav {
10        text-align:center;
11   └}
12
13  ⊟nav a {
14        display:block;
15        float:left;
16   └}
```

Here is the result:

HomeAboutContact

If we take away the "float:left" on line 15 but keep "display:block", this takes place:

Home
About
Contact

Above, each <a> tag takes up a full line due to the "display:block". But they *inherit* the "text-align:center" property from the container, so that they end up being centered inside their own boxes. *They are not centered inside the <nav> tag.* We can verify this by adding a border to the <a> tags (line 15 below):

```
13  ⊟nav a {
14        display:block;
15        border:1px solid #000;
16   └}
```

Here is the result:

Above, each <a> tag takes up a whole line and is not centered inside <nav>. But the text of the <a> tags themselves are centered within their own boxes due to inheritance.

Centering things inside things leads to much confusion among web designers due to interplay between block elements, inline elements and inheritance. It takes months of experience to get a "feel" for how these things work together. I am afraid that for now, you are doomed to hundreds of hours of trial and error before things start to make intuitive sense. When confused, it is almost always useful to put a border on the elements you are working with (as I did on line 15 above). This helps you know where the elements begin and end and can help you visualize the problem.

Back to our regular programming, below I have removed the "display:block" property and the border and given a top margin to the <a> tags (line 14):

```
 9   nav {
10        text-align:center;
11   }
12
13   nav a {
14        margin-top:5px;
15   }
```

Here is the result:

Nothing happened because the <a> tags are inline elements. Inline elements do not take margins. What we can do instead is give a top margin to the <nav> tag (line 11 below), which is a block tag and can take a margin:

```
 9   ▢nav {
10   |      text-align:center;
11   |      margin-top:5px;
12   └}
13
14   ▢nav a {
15   |
16   └}
```

Here is the result:

Notice how there is some space above the navigation links now, separating them from the border above them.

Below, I have added a large number of CSS properties to the navigation links:

```
14   ▢nav a {
15   |      text-decoration:none;
16   |      text-transform:uppercase;
17   |      letter-spacing:2px;
18   |      color:#999;
19   |      text-shadow:1px 1px 1px #ccc;
20   |      padding-left:0.6em;
21   |      padding-right:0.6em;
22   └}
```

Here is the result:

Below, I use the ":hover" pseudo-selector to give the links a special appearance when a user hovers their mouse pointer over them:

```
24   ⊟nav a:hover {
25        text-shadow:3px 3px 3px #ccc;
26   └}
```

Below is a picture of what the "ABOUT" link looks like with a mouse hovering over it:

The CSS I added on line 25 above causes the shadow of the text to become wider and longer, making the links have a dynamic appearance when a user hovers their mouse pointer over them.

I will now add a border underneath the navigation as follows (line 12 below):

```
 9   ⊟nav {
10        text-align:center;
11        margin-top:5px;
12        border-bottom:1px solid #ccc;
13   └}
```

Here is the result:

The bottom border we added is too close to the links. There are various ways of fixing this. Below I add bottom padding to the <nav> element (line 13 below):

```
 9   ⊟nav {
10        text-align:center;
11        margin-top:5px;
12        border-bottom:1px solid #ccc;
13        padding-bottom:5px;
14   └}
```

Here is the result:

The bottom padding I added means there should be a space of 5 pixels on the bottom of the <nav> element between this element and its contents. This ends up creating a 5 pixel space between the navigation links and their container (the <nav> element).

Next we turn our attention to the article. Currently, this is what it looks like:

Genealogical Memoir of Lady Mary Vyner

Lorem ipsum dolor sit amet, id sed doctus dissentias, putant perpetua consequat cu has. Ut everti denique mediocrem pri, te tation ridens moderatius vel. Cu vim inani oporteat. Ne natum intellegam pri, diam equidem ornatus in vis.

We have to center the image inside the article. Here is what the HTML looks like:

```
<main>
    <article>
        <img src="images/image.png" />
        <h1>Genealogical Memoir of Lady Mary Vyner</h1>
```

Unfortunately, we cannot center-align the image at the moment because, as already mentioned, putting "text-align:center" on an <img> tag does nothing. And if we were to put "text-align:center" on the <article> tag, this will work, except that it will make everything else inside it center-aligned also, which is not something we necessarily want. In order to get around this issue, we put the <img> tag inside a container (lines 21-23 below):

```
19      <main>
20          <article>
21              <div class="image-contaier">
22                  <img src="images/image.png" />
23              </div>
24              <h1>Genealogical Memoir of Lady Mary Vyner</h1>
```

Now, we can declare the contents of the "image-container" <div> to be center-aligned, which will center-align the image:

```
30  .image-container {
31      text-align:center;
32  }
```

Here is the result:

Genealogical Memoir of Lady Mary Vyner

Lorem ipsum dolor sit amet, id sed doctus dissentias, putant perpetua consequat cu has. Ut everti denique mediocrem pri, te tation ridens moderatius vel. Cu vim inani oporteat. Ne natum intellegam pri, diam equidem ornatus in vis.

The image is a bit too big, so we will change its size using the "width" HTML attribute (rather than CSS) (line 22 below):

```
20          <article>
21              <div class="image-container">
22                  <img src="images/image.png" width="200" />
23              </div>
24              <h1>Genealogical Memoir of Lady Mary Vyner</h1>
```

The benefit of doing things this way is that, as has already been mentioned, it helps us quickly set the size of an image inside an article without having to write CSS, and sometimes editing CSS can require a lot of extra work, for example if you are using a content management system like WordPress or Drupal.

Here is the result:

Genealogical Memoir of Lady Mary Vyner

Next we move on to the title of the article. Below I have added some CSS to styles.css using the selector "article h1", meaning "<h1> tags that happen to be inside <article> tags".

```
34  article h1 {
35      text-align:center;
36      text-transform:uppercase;
37      font-size:15px;
38      letter-spacing:3px;
39  }
```

Here is the result:

HOME   ABOUT   CONTACT

GENEALOGICAL MEMOIR OF LADY MARY VYNER

Lorem ipsum dolor sit amet, id sed doctus dissentias, putant perpetua consequat cu has. Ut everti denique mediocrem pri, te tation ridens moderatius vel. Cu vim inani oporteat. Ne natum intellegam pri, diam equidem ornatus in vis.

Let's now take a look at the original article and see what is left to be done:

We are actually done. The article's text is in two columns, but we do not recreate this because columns are not suited to the web and introduce various styling and readability issues.

Adding a Wrapper

Below, I have placed all of the contents of the <body> inside a div with the class of "outer-wrapper" (lines 9 and 42 below):

```
 8    <body>
 9        <div class="outer-wrapper">
10            <header>
11                <div class="logo">
12                    <img src="images/magazine_title.png" />
13                </div>
14                <nav>
15                    <a href="">Home</a>
16                    <a href="">About</a>
17                    <a href="">Contact</a>
18                </nav>
19            </header>
20            <main>
21                <article>
22                    <div class="image-container">
23                        <img src="images/image.png" width="200" />
24                    </div>
25                    <h1>Genealogical Memoir of Lady Mary Vyner</h1>
26                    <p>Lorem ipsum dolor sit amet, id sed doctus dissentias, putant perpetua consequat cu has.
27                    Ut everti denique mediocrem pri, te tation ridens moderatius vel. Cu vim inani oporteat.
28                    Ne natum intellegam pri, diam equidem ornatus in vis.</p>
29                    <p>Eam ad epicurei prodesset expetendis, id alii nibh posidonium vix, vim in feugiat
30                    vivendum mnesarchum. Id mel dicat graeco semper, nostrud scriptorem no vim.
31                    Maiorum nostrum patrioque id vis, laudem scripta mei te. Te vis dolores explicari.</p>
32                    <p>Ei nec homero propriae. Corpora platonem iracundia vel at. Movet probatus sed ad.
33                    Cu vim solum voluptaria dissentias, postea epicurei cu usu. Solet
34                    periculis has te, laoreet signiferumque pri id, per molestiae eloquentiam eu.</p>
35                    <p>Mel id aliquip definiebas philosophia, et illud utamur usu. Eam ignota invidunt in.
36                    Menandri invenire euripidis eu pro, mel mutat solet eu. Ex timeam nominati constituto mei.</p>
37                    <p>Euripidis voluptatibus te vis, duo dicat propriae omittantur an. Usu ad nostrud offendit,
38                    no quem nostro legimus duo. Quo ad debet dolore offendit, eu suas labores sensibus sit.
39                    Sed blandit philosophia ut.</p>
40                </article>
41            </main>
42        </div>
43    </body>
```

Wrappers are commonly used in order to give websites a more defined appearance. Below I add a border on the "outer-wrapper" div inside styles.css:

```
magazine.html    styles.css

1    .outer-wrapper {
2        border:1px solid #ccc;
3    }
```

Now, the whole web page is enclosed in a border:

Below, I add a margin to the "outer-wrapper" <div>, which increases the space between it and the browser window:

```
1   .outer-wrapper {
2       border:1px solid #ccc;
3       margin:25px;
4   }
```

Here is the result:

Below, I give the wrapper some more styling:

```
1  .outer-wrapper {
2      border:1px solid #ccc;
3      margin:25px;
4      border-radius:15px;
5      box-shadow:5px 5px 15px #000;
6  }
```

Here is what the design looks like now:

In order to give the website a more professional appearance, below I add a background pattern (taken from subtlepatterns.com) to the <body> tag (lines 1-3 below):

```
1   body {
2       background:url("../images/symphony.png");
3   }
4
5   .outer-wrapper {
6       border:1px solid #ccc;
7       margin:25px;
8       border-radius:15px;
9       box-shadow:5px 5px 15px #000;
10  }
```

Here is what the design looks like now:

GENEALOGICAL MEMOIR OF LADY MARY VYNER

Lorem ipsum dolor sit amet, id sed doctus dissentias, putant perpetua consequat cu has. Ut everti denique mediocrem pri, te tation ridens moderatius vel. Cu vim inani oporteat. Ne natum intellegam pri, diam equidem ornatus in vis.

It doesn't look good because the "outer-wrapper" <div> is transparent, so that the background on the <body> tag shows through it. We remedy the situation by adding a white background to the "outer-wrapper" (line 10 below):

```
1   body {
2       background:url("../images/symphony.png");
3   }
4
5   .outer-wrapper {
6       border:1px solid #ccc;
7       margin:25px;
8       border-radius:15px;
9       box-shadow:5px 5px 15px #000;
10      background:white;
11  }
```

Here is the result:

Now, there is a patterned background *outside* the website's contents. The background is applied to the <body> tag, but since the "outer-wrapper" div has a white background, the patterned background does not show through it, it ends up only showing up on the outer edge of the website.

On line 2 of the CSS above, you may have noticed the strange URL we used ("../images/symphony.png"). This is known as a relative path. The two dots tell the browser to go to the parent folder, look for a folder named "images", then look for a file named "symphony.png". It is necessary to do this because we have written this CSS inside the file "styles.css". If you remember, this file is inside its own folder:

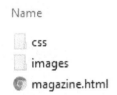

Name

css

images

magazine.html

If we had not written the two dots, the browser would have tried to find the "images" folder inside the "css" folder, which is wrong. The two dots inside "style.css" tell the browser "don't look inside the folder where I am located, but go outside me and look down from there". The browser goes outside the folder for "styles.css", ending up looking at the folder that contains "magazine.html" and the two folders "css" and "images". It then starts looking from there for a folder named "images" and inside that for a file named "symphony.png". This is like telling someone who is looking for something to go look in another room.

In the screenshot of the design shown earlier, notice the way the magazine logo is too close to the top edge. We fix this by giving the "logo" div some top padding (line 17 below):

```
13   .logo {
14       text-align:center;
15       border-bottom:1px solid #ccc;
16       padding-top:20px;
17   }
```

Here is the result:

The same issue exists in the article:

Notice the way the "Loerm ipsum" is too close to the left edge. We fix this by giving the <article> tag some padding:

```
48   article {
49       padding:0 10px;
50   }
```

Here is the result:

> **GENEALOGICAL MEMOIR OF LADY MARY VYNER**
>
> Lorem ipsum dolor sit amet, id sed doctus dissentias, putant perpetua consequat cu has. Ut everti denique mediocrem pri, te tation ridens moderatius vel. Cu vim inani oporteat. Ne natum intellegam pri, diam equidem ornatus in vis.
>
> Eam ad epicurei prodesset expetendis, id alii nibh posidonium vix, vim in feugiat vivendum mnesarchum. Id mel dicat graeco semper, nostrud scriptorem no vim. Maiorum nostrum patrioque id vis, laudem scripta mei te. Te vis dolores explicari.

Now there is some nice space between the paragraphs and their left and right edges. On line 49 above, I used a CSS shorthand to define the padding. The shorthand "0 10px" means zero pixels of padding on the top and bottom, and 10 pixels of padding on the left and right. It is similar to writing "padding: 0 10px 0 10px", just shorter.

Adding a Sidebar

Most websites have a sidebar which provides extra links and information. Below is a picture of the Royal Society's website. The page being displayed is the "Mission and priorities" page. The main content of the page is on the left, while there is a picture and download links on the right. This right section is the sidebar:

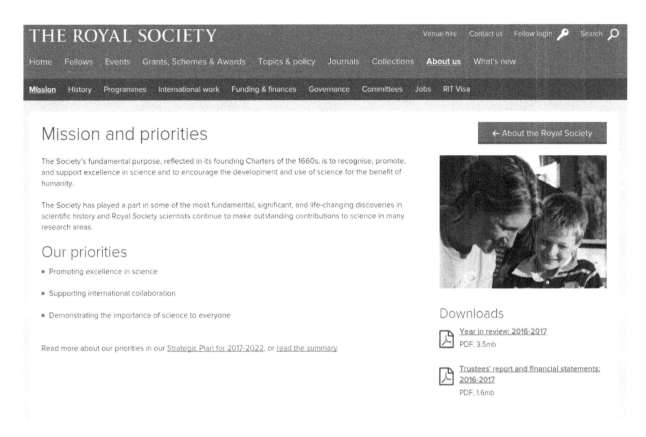

Below, we add a new <div> with a class of "sidebar" to our HTML document (see the bottom):

```
<main>
    <article>
        <div class="image-container">
            <img src="images/image.png" width="200" />
        </div>
        <h1>Genealogical Memoir of Lady Mary Vyner</h1>
        <p>Lorem ipsum dolor sit amet, id sed doctus dissentias, putant perpetua consequat cu has.
        Ut everti denique mediocrem pri, te tation ridens moderatius vel. Cu vim inani oporteat.
        Ne natum intellegam pri, diam equidem ornatus in vis.</p>
        <p>Eam ad epicurei prodesset expetendis, id alii nibh posidonium vix, vim in feugiat
        vivendum mnesarchum. Id mel dicat graeco semper, nostrud scriptorem no vim.
        Maiorum nostrum patrioque id vis, laudem scripta mei te. Te vis dolores explicari.</p>
        <p>Ei nec homero propriae. Corpora platonem iracundia vel at. Movet probatus sed ad.
        Cu vim solum voluptaria dissentias, postea epicurei cu usu. Solet
        periculis has te, laoreet signiferumque pri id, per molestiae eloquentiam eu.</p>
        <p>Mel id aliquip definiebas philosophia, et illud utamur usu. Eam ignota invidunt in.
        Menandri invenire euripidis eu pro, mel mutat solet eu. Ex timeam nominati constituto mei.</p>
        <p>Euripidis voluptatibus te vis, duo dicat propriae omittantur an. Usu ad nostrud offendit,
        no quem nostro legimus duo. Quo ad debet dolore offendit, eu suas labores sensibus sit.
        Sed blandit philosophia ut.</p>
    </article>
</main>
<div class="sidebar">

</div>
```

Below, I add a test <h2> tag to the sidebar <div> (line 43 below):

317

```
42      <div class="sidebar">
43          <h2>Test</h2>
44      </div>
```

Below is the result. The sidebar <div> shows up at the bottom the page, as follows:

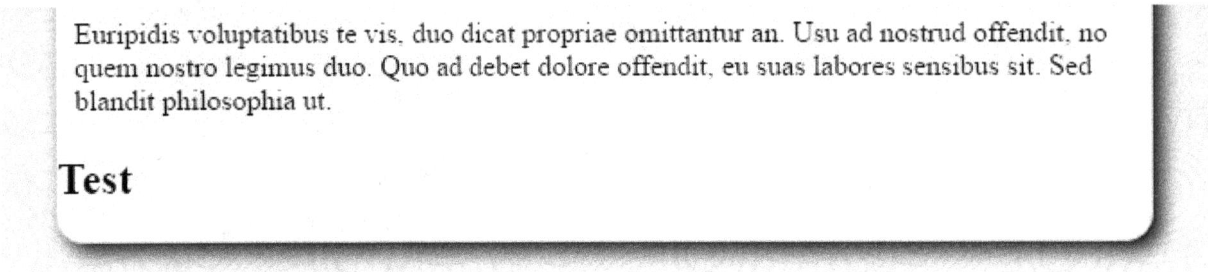

Euripidis voluptatibus te vis, duo dicat propriae omittantur an. Usu ad nostrud offendit, no quem nostro legimus duo. Quo ad debet dolore offendit, eu suas labores sensibus sit. Sed blandit philosophia ut.

Test

In order to make the sidebar show up on the right side of the page, we need to use floating.

```
59  main {
60      float:left;
61      width:65%;
62  }
63  .sidebar {
64      float:right;
65      width:30%;
66  }
```

Here is the result:

Above, the sidebar is now showing up properly on the right. Except that now the wrapper <div> has collapsed, causing the patterned background of the <body> tag to show through.

The solution to this is to use what is known as a "clear fix". The clear fix solves a problem inherent to floating, the problem of the container collapsing. We need to something to force the container not to collapse, but to stretch it so that it can encapsulate the whole design as it is supposed to. In order to create this fix, we need to add a new <div> outside our floating elements (i.e. outside the <main> tag and the sidebar <div>). The new <div> has to be outside these and after them (lines 45-47 below):

```
41      </main>
42      <div class="sidebar">
43          <h2>Test</h2>
44      </div>
45      <div class="clearfix">
46
47      </div>
```

In the CSS, we give the clearfix <div> a "clear:both" property:

```
67   .clearfix {
68       clear:both;
69   }
```

Here is the result:

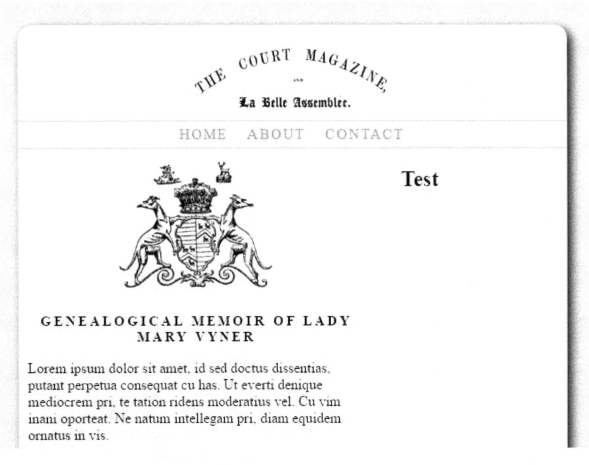

Above, now everything shows up perfectly. If you are a bit unclear on why the clear fix is needed, do not worry, it takes a lot of practice before these things start to make intuitive sense..[18]

Above, notice the way the image above the article's title is now not in the center of the whole page. The reason is that we shrunk the <main> tag's contents to 65%, so the image is now centered within the context of this shrunken <main> tag. The same applies to the <h1> tag inside the <article> tag. It too is centered with respect to the <main> tag. This is a good thing since we do not want the contents of the <main> tag to spill over onto the sidebar.

---

[18] The clear fix I used above is good enough for most cases, but there are far more complicated solutions that are sometimes needed. You can do a web search for "clear fix" to read more on them.

We will now add some real content to the sidebar <div>. I have removed the test <h2> tag and added a "Popular Right Now" section which links to various popular articles on the magazine to encourage readers read them. I use an unordered list for the links:

```
42    <div class="sidebar">
43        <h2>Popular Right Now</h2>
44        <ul>
45            <li><a href="">The Christmas Cattle Show for 1835</a></li>
46            <li><a href="">A Day in the Val D'Aosta</a></li>
47            <li><a href="">Proverbs Out of Use</a></li>
48            <li><a href="">Literature of the Month</a></li>
49        </ul>
50    </div>
```

Here is the result:

Below I add some styling to the <h2> tag inside the sidebar:

```
71   .sidebar h2 {
72       font-size:16px;
73       font-weight:bold;
74       font-style:italic;
75       letter-spacing:2px;
76       color:#666;
77   }
```

Here is the result:

To make the list prettier, I remove the default bullet points (line 80 below) and add my own custom Unicode bullet using the ":before" pseudo-selector:

```
79   .sidebar ul {
80       list-style:none;
81   }
82   .sidebar li:before {
83       content:"❀"
84   }
```

This is what the links look like now:

Popular Right Now

❀The Christmas Cattle
Show for 1835
❀A Day in the Val
D'Aosta
❀Proverbs Out of Use
❀Literature of the
Month

Above, there is a lot of space between the links and the left side. This is caused by the default padding that the browsers adds on the <ul> tag. In order to cancel it out, we do as follows:

```
79    .sidebar ul {
80        list-style:none;
81        padding:0;
82    }
```

Here is our sidebar now:

Popular Right Now

❀ The Christmas Cattle Show
for 1835
❀ A Day in the Val D'Aosta
❀ Proverbs Out of Use
❀ Literature of the Month

Below, we use padding to increase the space between the bullet points and the text:

```
83    .sidebar li:before {
84        content:"❀";
85        padding:5px;
86    }
```

Here is the result:

Popular Right Now

❀ The Christmas Cattle
Show for 1835
❀ A Day in the Val D'Aosta
❀ Proverbs Out of Use
❀ Literature of the Month

Below, I add some styling to the sidebar links:

```
88    .sidebar li a {
89        font-family: Centaur, serif;
90        color:#000;
91        font-size:1.3em;
92        text-decoration:none;
93    }
```

Here is the result:

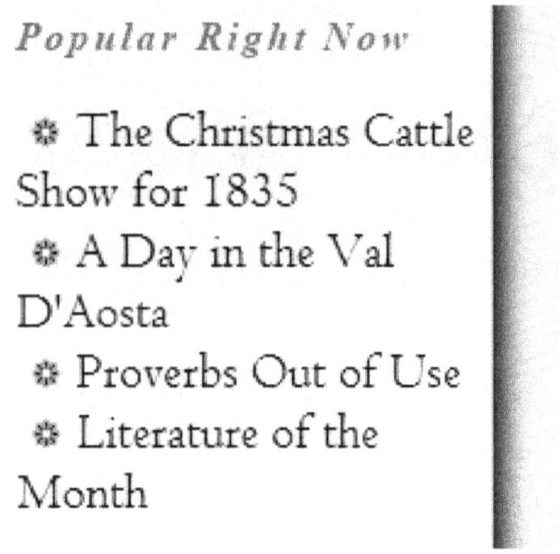

Popular Right Now

❋ The Christmas Cattle
Show for 1835
❋ A Day in the Val
D'Aosta
❋ Proverbs Out of Use
❋ Literature of the
Month

To increase the spacing between each link and the next, I add a bottom margin to the <li> tags:

```
83    .sidebar li {
84        margin-bottom:10px;
85    }
```

Here is the result:

Popular Right Now

❋ The Christmas Cattle
Show for 1835

❋ A Day in the Val
D'Aosta

❋ Proverbs Out of Use

❋ Literature of the
Month

Now, we add a new section to the sidebar called "Drawing of the Month", as follows (lines 51 and 52 below):

```
42    <div class="sidebar">
43        <h2>Popular Right Now</h2>
44        <ul>
45            <li><a href="">The Christmas Cattle Show for 1835</a></li>
46            <li><a href="">A Day in the Val D'Aosta</a></li>
47            <li><a href="">Proverbs Out of Use</a></li>
48            <li><a href="">Literature of the Month</a></li>
49        </ul>
50
51        <h2>Drawing of the Month</h2>
52        <img class="drawing-of-the-month" src="images/drawing_of_the_month.png" />
53    </div>
```

Here is what it looks like:

Above, the drawing is too big and spills out of the sidebar. We fix this with a bit of CSS:

```
97    .sidebar img.drawing-of-the-month {
98        width:200px;
99    }
```

Above, we have declared that an <img> tag inside the sidebar <div> that has the class name of "drawing of the month" should have a width of 200 pixels. The selector "img.drawing-of-the-month" (note the lack of a space between "img" and ".drawing-of-the-month") means an <img> tag having a class of "drawing-of-the-month". If there was a space between "img" and ".drawing-of-the-month", that would have meant "an element with a class of drawing-of-the-month". But without the space, the meaning is that the class name should be on the <img> tag itself.

Here is the result:

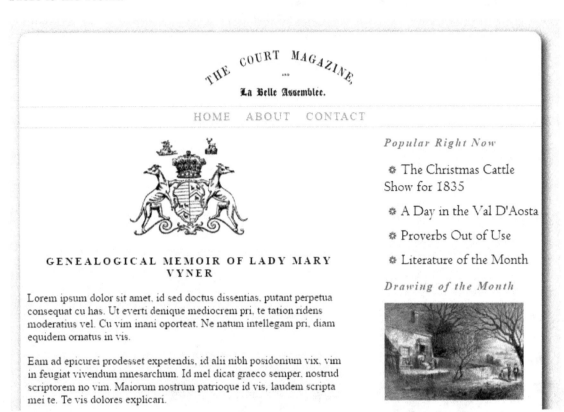

We could help users see a bigger version of the drawing by clicking on it if we put the <img> tag inside an <a> tag that links to the image itself, as follows (lines 52 and 54 below):

```
51        <h2>Drawing of the Month</h2>
52        <a href="images/drawing_of_the_month.png">
53           <img class="drawing-of-the-month" src="images/drawing_of_the_month.png" />
54        </a>
```

Above, we have an <a> tag that links to the image file. If a user clicks on it, they will see the full image in their browser window, as follows:

The appearance of the sidebar does not change in any way when we put the image inside an <a> tag:

The only thing that changes is that when a user clicks on the image, they will be taken to the full image..[19]

---

[19] Note that in a professional design people usually do not link to image files. They would instead link to a new page on their website that has the image on it shown in a larger size. In this way users will continue to see the website's logo and the rest of its design while viewing the picture.

Let's now add a border to the left of the sidebar to separate it from the main content (line 66 below):

```
63    .sidebar {
64        float:right;
65        width:30%;
66        border-left:1px solid #ccc;
67    }
```

Here is the result:

GENEALOGICAL MEMOIR OF LADY MARY VYNER

Lorem ipsum dolor sit amet, id sed doctus dissentias, putant perpetua consequat cu has. Ut everti denique mediocrem pri, te tation ridens moderatius vel. Cu vim inani oporteat. Ne natum intellegam pri, diam equidem ornatus in vis.

Eam ad epicurei prodesset expetendis, id alii nibh posidonium vix, vim in feugiat vivendum mnesarchum. Id mel dicat graeco semper, nostrud scriptorem no vim. Maiorum nostrum patrioque id vis, laudem scripta mei te. Te vis dolores explicari.

Ei nec homero propriae. Corpora platonem iracundia vel at. Movet probatus sed ad. Cu vim solum voluptaria dissentias, postea epicurei cu usu. Solet periculis has te, laoreet signiferumque pri id, per molestiae eloquentiam eu.

Popular Right Now

❀ The Christmas Cattle Show for 1835

❀ A Day in the Val D'Aosta

❀ Proverbs Out of Use

❀ Literature of the Month

Drawing of the Month

Above, the sidebar's border is too close to the sidebar's contents. We fix this by giving the sidebar a left padding (line 67 below):

```
63    .sidebar {
64        float:right;
65        width:30%;
66        border-left:1px solid #ccc;
67        padding-left:10px;
68    }
```

Here is the result:

There is, however, an issue. If we look lower down on the page, we see that the sidebar's border does not extend fully to the bottom as we would expect:

Lorem ipsum dolor sit amet, id sed doctus dissentias, putant perpetua consequat cu has. Ut everti denique mediocrem pri, te tation ridens moderatius vel. Cu vim inani oporteat. Ne natum intellegam pri, diam equidem ornatus in vis.

Eam ad epicurei prodesset expetendis, id alii nibh posidonium vix, vim in feugiat vivendum mnesarchum. Id mel dicat graeco semper, nostrud scriptorem no vim. Maiorum nostrum patrioque id vis, laudem scripta mei te. Te vis dolores explicari.

Ei nec homero propriae. Corpora platonem iracundia vel at. Movet probatus sed ad. Cu vim solum voluptaria dissentias, postea epicurei cu usu. Solet periculis has te, laoreet signiferumque pri id, per molestiae eloquentiam eu.

Mel id aliquip definiebas philosophia, et illud utamur usu. Eam ignota invidunt in. Menandri invenire euripidis eu pro, mel mutat solet eu. Ex timeam nominati constituto mei.

Euripidis voluptatibus te vis, duo dicat propriae omittantur an. Usu ad nostrud offendit, no quem nostro legimus duo. Quo ad debet dolore offendit, eu suas labores sensibus sit. Sed blandit philosophia ut.

Above, the sidebar's border ends a little after the Drawing of the Month image. This is because the sidebar <div> ends there, since it only gets as long as its contents require. There is no simple CSS fix for this to make the sidebar the same height as the article. One thing we could do is give the sidebar a bottom border (line 67 below):

```
63    .sidebar {
64        float:right;
65        width:30%;
66        border-left:1px solid #ccc;
67        border-bottom:1px solid #ccc;
68        padding-left:10px;
69    }
```

Here is the result:

Lorem ipsum dolor sit amet, id sed doctus dissentias, putant perpetua consequat cu has. Ut everti denique mediocrem pri, te tation ridens moderatius vel. Cu vim inani oporteat. Ne natum intellegam pri, diam equidem ornatus in vis.

Eam ad epicurei prodesset expetendis, id alii nibh posidonium vix, vim in feugiat vivendum mnesarchum. Id mel dicat graeco semper, nostrud scriptorem no vim. Maiorum nostrum patrioque id vis, laudem scripta mei te. Te vis dolores explicari.

Ei nec homero propriae. Corpora platonem iracundia vel at. Movet probatus sed ad. Cu vim solum voluptaria dissentias, postea epicurei cu usu. Solet periculis has te, laoreet signiferumque pri id, per molestiae eloquentiam eu.

Drawing of the Month

The bottom border gives the sidebar a completed appearance and does not look too bad (we can add some bottom padding to increase the distance between the drawing and the border.

Another solution is to give the sidebar a minimum height, as follows (line 67 below):

```
63    .sidebar {
64        float:right;
65        width:30%;
66        border-left:1px solid #ccc;
67        min-height:800px;
68        padding-left:10px;
69    }
```

The "min-height" property means the element should never get smaller in height than this. A minimum height of 800 pixels means the sidebar should never be smaller than 800 pixels in height. This is different from giving it a "height" of 800 pixels, because if we give it a "height" of 800 pixels and later on we add extra stuff to the sidebar so that its height increases beyond 800 pixels, the content will spill out of the sidebar since the 800 pixel height does not allow it to grow. But with "min-height", we ensure that it has a minimum height while allowing for future growth.

Here is the result:

Lorem ipsum dolor sit amet, id sed doctus dissentias, putant perpetua consequat cu has. Ut everti denique mediocrem pri, te tation ridens moderatius vel. Cu vim inani oporteat. Ne natum intellegam pri, diam equidem ornatus in vis.

Eam ad epicurei prodesset expetendis, id alii nibh posidonium vix, vim in feugiat vivendum mnesarchum. Id mel dicat graeco semper, nostrud scriptorem no vim. Maiorum nostrum patrioque id vis, laudem scripta mei te. Te vis dolores explicari.

Ei nec homero propriae. Corpora platonem iracundia vel at. Movet probatus sed ad. Cu vim solum voluptaria dissentias, postea epicurei cu usu. Solet periculis has te, laoreet signiferumque pri id, per molestiae eloquentiam eu.

Mel id aliquip definiebas philosophia, et illud utamur usu. Eam ignota invidunt in. Menandri invenire euripidis eu pro, mel mutat solet eu. Ex timeam nominati constituto mei.

Euripidis voluptatibus te vis, duo dicat propriae omittantur an. Usu ad nostrud offendit, no quem nostro legimus duo. Quo ad debet dolore offendit, eu suas labores sensibus sit. Sed blandit philosophia ut.

Drawing of the Month

Above, note the way the sidebar's border extends right to the bottom of the page. Not only that, but the sidebar now pushes the outer wrapper downward, so that there is now space underneath the article too.

Adding a Footer

A footer is the bottom part of a website where the copyright notice and some other items are placed. Below is a picture of the Royal Society's website's footer (the large gray area):

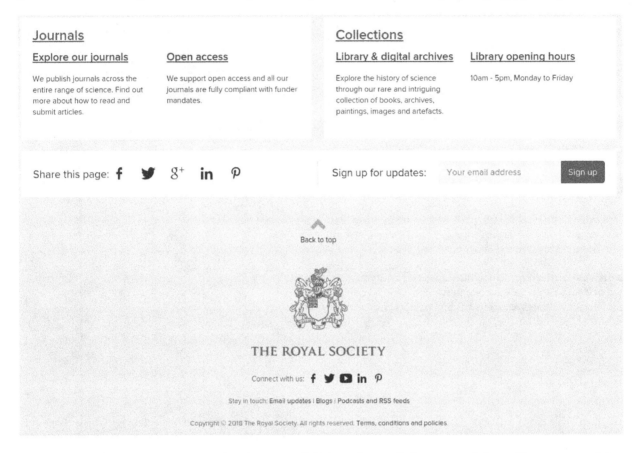

Above, the footer contains a "back to top" link, a logo, links to social media, a copy right notice, and links to the website's terms and conditions.

In HTML, we create footers using the <footer> tag, which is a semantic tag similar to <main> and <header>. Below, I have added a <footer> tag after the clear fix <div>, inside the outer wrapper <div> (lines 60-62):

```
51              <h2>Drawing of the Month</h2>
52              <a href="images/drawing_of_the_month.png">
53                  <img class="drawing-of-the-month" src="images/drawing_of_the_month.png" />
54              </a>
55          </div>
56          <div class="clearfix">
57
58          </div>
59
60          <footer>
61            Copyright &copy; 2018. All Rights Reserved.
62          </footer>
63      </div>
64  </body>
```

Here is the result:

Copyright © 2018. All Rights Reserved.

In the <footer> tag, I used the © HTML entity which stands for the copyright symbol. We will now add some CSS in order to improve the appearance of the footer:

```
104  footer {
105      border-top:1px solid #ccc;
106      text-align:center;
107      font-size:80%;
108  }
```

Here is the result:

Copyright © 2018. All Rights Reserved.

Let's add some padding to give the footer some breathing space (line 108 below):

```
104  footer {
105      border-top:1px solid #ccc;
106      text-align:center;
107      font-size:80%;
108      padding:10px 0;
109  }
```

333

The property "padding:10px 0" is shorthand for creating 10 pixels of padding at the top and bottom and zero pixels on the left and right. Here is the result:

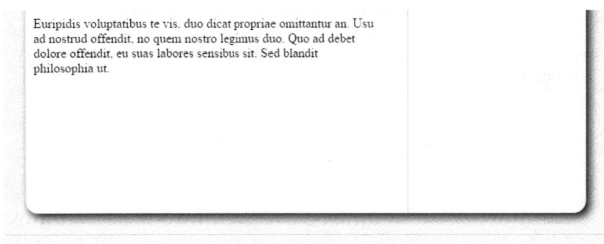

We could also copy the Royal Society's website's design by putting the footer outside the main website's design. We accomplish that by moving the <footer> tag outside the outer wrapper <div>:

```
60        </div>
61        <footer>
62            Copyright &copy; 2018. All Rights Reserved.
63        </footer>
64    </body>
```

Above, the <footer> tag is now right before the <body> tag's closing tag. Here is the result:

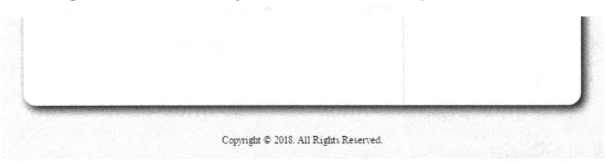

We no longer have a need for the top border on the <footer> tag. Below I have removed it:

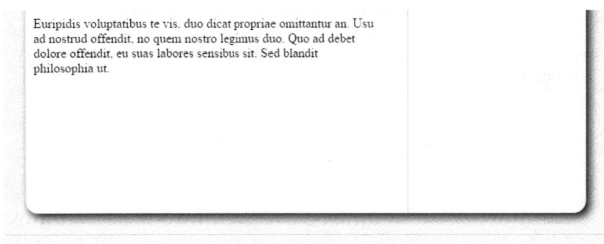

Thanks to using centering and percentages, our site expands and collapses based on the width of the user's browser window. Below is what the site looks like if a user views it on a large screen:

Above, note the way the site's logo and the article's picture continue to be properly centered within the design. And notice how the article's area and the sidebar have both grown in width.

Below is what the site looks like on a small screen:

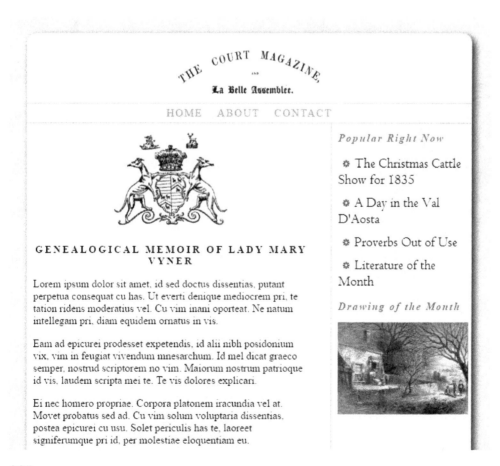

Fixed Width Sites

It is sometimes desirable for a website to have the same width regardless of the size of the screen. We can achieve this by giving the outer wrapper <div> a width (line 11 below):

```
 5    .outer-wrapper {
 6        border:1px solid #ccc;
 7        margin:25px;
 8        border-radius:15px;
 9        box-shadow:5px 5px 15px #000;
10        background:white;
11        width:700px;
12    }
```

Here is the result:

Now, if I view the site on a larger screen, here is what I will see:

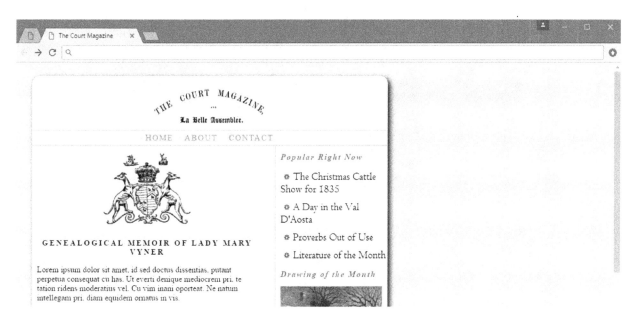

Above, the browser window has expanded, but the contents of the site remain the same width. Generally when doing this, we want the site to be centered rather than being stuck to one side of the screen. This is called "centering a layout" and there are various ways of going about it.

In the present layout, we will accomplish centering using an automatic margin. Currently, the outer wrapper has the following CSS:

```
 5   .outer-wrapper {
 6       border:1px solid #ccc;
 7       margin:25px;
 8       border-radius:15px;
 9       box-shadow:5px 5px 15px #000;
10       background:white;
11       width:700px;
12   }
```

We change line 7 above as follows:

```
 5   .outer-wrapper {
 6       border:1px solid #ccc;
 7       margin:25px auto;
 8       border-radius:15px;
 9       box-shadow:5px 5px 15px #000;
10       background:white;
11       width:700px;
12   }
```

Above, we added the word "auto" to the end of the margin property. This shorthand means that we want 25 pixels of margin at the top and bottom, and *automatic* margins on the left and right.

Automatic margins are calculated by the browser in a way that centers the element. Here is the result:

Above, the website is now properly centered within the browser window.

Centering a layout in CSS is notoriously confusing due to the interactions between one <div> and another and their various properties (floats, positioning).

Another form of centering uses positioning as follows (lines 13-15):

```
 6   .outer-wrapper {
 7       border:1px solid #ccc;
 8       margin:25px auto;
 9       border-radius:15px;
10       box-shadow:5px 5px 15px #000;
11       background:white;
12       width:700px;
13       position:absolute;
14       left:50%;
15       margin-left:-350px;
16   }
```

Above, we use a special trick. We cause the outer wrapper to be 50% distant from the left edge. This by itself is not enough, because this 50% distance pushes the outer wrapper and its contents too far to the left, as follows:

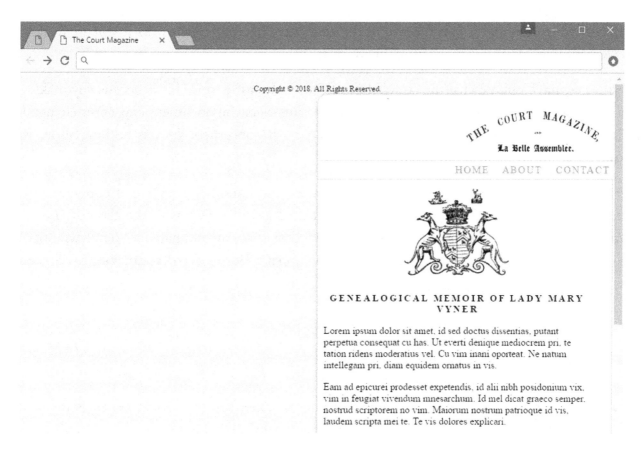

Above, the design is pushes so far to the left that we cannot even see the sidebar. The "margin-left:-350px" fixes this by moving the outer wrapper leftwards by 350 pixels. Here is the result:

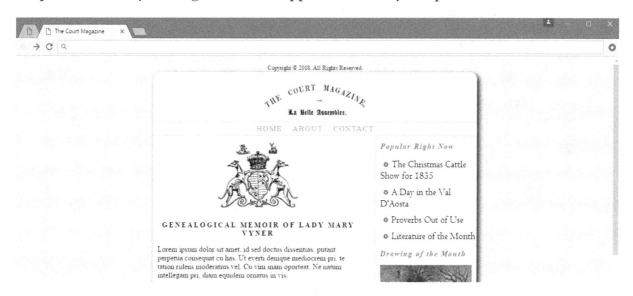

Above, now the website is properly centered. The 350 figure is the width of the outer wrapper div (700 pixels) divided by two. If you are confused about why this works, there is no need to worry. It is sufficient to know that this is a trick that works. You give something a 50% left distance, then give it a negative margin that is half the size of the element. This trick only works if you are dealing with an element that has a specific width defined for it.

Above, you may have noticed that the copyright notice is now at the top. This is because by making the outer wrapper absolutely positioned, it ends up hovering over the document and other elements will entirely ignore its presence. As far as the <footer> tag is concerned, there is nothing above it, so it shows up at the very top of the document.

In order to fix that, we have to put the absolute positioning on another <div> that contains both the outer wrapper and the <footer>. Below, I have created a new <div> with the class of "outer-outer-wrapper". The name is a bit silly, in a professional design you would name it "outer-wrapper" and the old outer wrapper would be renamed "inner-wrapper". But to avoid confusion, I will keep the new <div>'s class name as "outer-outer-wrapper":

```
 8      <body>
 9          <div class="outer-outer-wrapper">
10              <div class="outer-wrapper">
11                  <header>
```

This new <div> contains everything, including the outer wrapper and the footer. Below is the new CSS we add to styles.css for the new outer outer wrapper (lines 5-10 below):

```
 5    .outer-outer-wrapper {
 6        width:700px;
 7        position:absolute;
 8        left:50%;
 9        margin-left:-350px;
10    }
11    .outer-wrapper {
12        border:1px solid #ccc;
13        margin:25px auto;
14        border-radius:15px;
15        box-shadow:5px 5px 15px #000;
16        background:white;
17        width:700px;
18    }
```

Above, the old outer wrapper no longer has absolute positioning. I have moved the absolute positioning definition to the new outer outer wrapper. This new <div> must have a width similar to the outer wrapper in order for the centering calculation to work.

Here is the result:

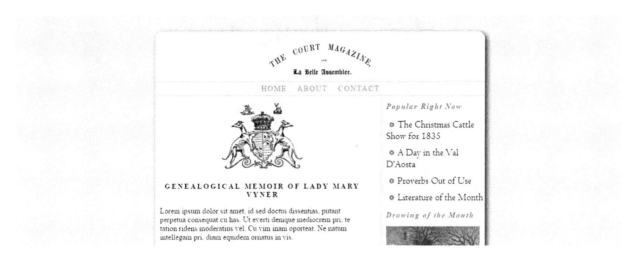

Above, everything is now working perfectly. We have a secret "outer outer" wrapper that is not showing up, but that is causing the whole design to be centered.

Creating a Contact Page

In this section, we will create a new page for the magazine where users can contact the magazine's owners. Here is what our site's folder looks like at the moment:

Below, I create a new empty HTML document named "contact.html":

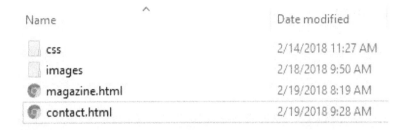

Below, I have opened "contact.html" inside Notepad++:

Now, I will copy and paste all of the contents of "magazine.html" inside "contact.html", as follows:

```
     magazine.html    styles.css    contact.html
 1      <!DOCTYPE HTML>
 2      <html>
 3          <head>
 4              <meta charset="UTF-8">
 5              <title>The Court Magazine</title>
 6              <link rel="stylesheet" type="text/css" href="css/styles.css"/>
 7          </head>
 8          <body>
 9              <div class="outer-outer-wrapper">
10                  <div class="outer-wrapper">
11                      <header>
12                          <div class="logo">
13                              <img src="images/magazine_title.png" />
14                          </div>
15                          <nav>
16                              <a href="">Home</a>
17                              <a href="">About</a>
18                              <a href="">Contact</a>
19                          </nav>
20                      </header>
21                      <main>
22                          <article>
23                              <div class="image-container">
24                                  <img src="images/image.png" width="200" />
25                              </div>
26                              <h1>Genealogical Memoir of Lady Mary Vyner</h1>
27                              <p>Lorem ipsum dolor sit amet, id sed doctus dissentias, putant perpetua consequat cu has.
28                              Ut everti denique mediocrem pri, te tation ridens moderatius vel. Cu vim inani oporteat.
29                              Ne natum intellegam pri, diam equidem ornatus in vis.</p>
```

Copying and pasting saves a lot of work, since we want the contact page to look similar to the rest of the site. Instead of building the page from scratch, we use the HTML for "magazine.html" as a template. Below, I change the title of the new page to "Contact Us – The Court Magazine" (line 5):

```
3      <head>
4          <meta charset="UTF-8">
5          <title>Contact Us - The Court Magazine</title>
6          <link rel="stylesheet" type="text/css" href="css/styles.css"/>
7      </head>
8      <body>
```

Above, notice that on line 6 we refer to the "styles.css" file, which "magazine.html" also refers to. We can have as many HTML documents as we want with all of them using the same CSS file for styling.

Below, I have deleted the contents of the <article> tag, but I have kept everything else, such as the sidebar (and the footer):

```
21     <main>
22         <article>
23
24         </article>
25     </main>
26     <div class="sidebar">
27         <h2>Popular Right Now</h2>
```

Here is what the page looks like when opened in a browser:

Above, we have the site's design showing up properly, with a blank space where the contact page's contents should go.

Below, we add the contact page's title:

```
21    <main>
22        <article>
23            <h1>Contact Us</h1>
24        </article>
25    </main>
```

Here is the result:

Next we will add an explanatory paragraph:

```
21     <main>
22         <article>
23             <h1>Contact Us</h1>
24             <p>Please use the form below to send us a message. You may also contact us
25             by emailing us at contact@example.com.</p>
26         </article>
27     </main>
```

Here is the result:

CONTACT US

Please use the form below to send us a message. You may also contact us by emailing us at contact@example.com.

Popular Right Now

❀ The Christmas Cattle Show for 1835

We can turn "contact@example.com" into an email link, which is a type of link that when clicked, opens up the user's email client (such as Outlook).

```
22     <article>
23         <h1>Contact Us</h1>
24         <p>Please use the form below to send us a message. You may also contact us
25         by emailing us at <a href="mailto:contact@example.com">contact@example.com</a>.</p>
26     </article>
```

Above, notice the special "mailto:" keyword used inside the "href" attribute (line 25). This tells the browser this is an email link. Here is what the page looks like now:

CONTACT US

Please use the form below to send us a message. You may also contact us by emailing us at contact@example.com.

Next, we start creating the contact form using the HTML <form> tag:

345

```
27  ⊟              <form>
28
29  ⊢              </form>
```

Next, I add a text input box to the form:

```
27  ⊟              <form>
28                     <label for="full-name">Full Name</label>
29                     <input type="text" id="full-name" name="full-name" /><br/>
30  ⊢              </form>
```

Here is what it looks like:

CONTACT US

Please use the form below to send us a message. You may also contact us by emailing us at contact@example.com.

Full Name [   ]

The <label> tag on line 28 creates the "label" for the input. The "for" attribute on line 28 determines which input box the label is for, the input box is "full-name", meaning this label is related to an input box that has an ID of "full-name".

The "name" attribute on the <input> tag is used by the server and does not concern us here, it is sufficient to know that on a real website, this attribute matters to the programmers who work on the website's "back-end" (database, etc.).

Without a label, users will only an empty box, as follows:

CONTACT US

Please use the form below to send us a message. You may also contact us by emailing us at contact@example.com.

[   ]

Instead of using a <label> tag, you could use a <div> or <p> tag to contain the word "Full Name", as follows:

```
27  ⊟              <form>
28                     <p>Full Name</p>
29                     <input type="text" id="full-name" name="full-name" /><br/>
30  ⊢              </form>
```

Here is what it looks like:

CONTACT US

Please use the form below to send us a message. You may also contact us by emailing us at contact@example.com.

Full Name

The above will work. The <label> tag, however, has benefits. The first is that blind users will be told by their screen reading program that the input box has a label of "Full Name" associated with it. Another benefit is that if a user clicks on the word "Full Name", the input box will immediately get a typing cursor in it, as follows:

Full Name

Next, we add a <textarea> tag where users can write down the message they want to send to the magazine:

```
27  <form>
28      <label for="full-name">Full Name</label>
29      <input type="text" id="full-name" name="full-name" /><br/>
30
31      <label for="message">Message</label>
32      <textarea id="message" name="message"></textarea>
33  </form>
```

Here is what it looks like:

Full Name

Message

The <textarea> tag allows users to type out a longer message than the <input> tag does, and it allows the use of the Enter/return key so that users can write multiple paragraphs if they want. Note that while the <input> tag is self-closing, the <textarea> tag requires a closing </textarea> tag.

Above, the form doesn't look too pretty, but we will leave styling for later.

Next, we add a submit button as follows (line 34):

```
27      <form>
28          <label for="full-name">Full Name</label>
29          <input type="text" id="full-name" name="full-name" /><br/>
30
31          <label for="message">Message</label>
32          <textarea id="message" name="message"></textarea><br />
33
34          <input type="submit" value="Send Message!" />
35      </form>
```

Here is the result:

CONTACT US

Please use the form below to send us a message. You may also contact us by emailing us at contact@example.com.

Full Name _____

Message _____

Send Message!

On line 34 above, the "type" attribute has a value of "submit", which tells the browser this is a submit button. The "value" attribute is "Send Message!", this determines the text that is shown to users inside the submit button.

We can now turn our attention to styling the form. In order to give our form a uniform appearance, we style the <label> tag as follows:

```
117     label {
118         display:block;
119         width:100px;
120         float:left;
121         text-align:right;
122     }
```

Here is the result:

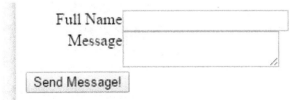

The equal width of the two labels causes the input and the text area to be aligned exactly above each other. We have to give the labels a "display:block" property since we they are inline elements by default and cannot take a width. We cause them to float left otherwise they would take up a whole line. We use "text-align:right" to align the label texts on the right, this helps them stay visually close to the input boxes they describe.

Below, we add a right padding to the <label> tag to create some space between the labels and the input boxes (line 122 below):

```
117    label {
118        display:block;
119        width:100px;
120        float:left;
121        text-align:right;
122        padding-right:10px;
123    }
```

Here is the result:

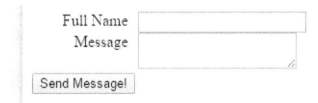

Next, we add some bottom margin to the input box:

```
125    input[type=text] {
126        margin-bottom:10px;
127    }
```

Above, we use a special CSS construct we have not met before. Remember that both the input box and the submit button are created using <input> tags, the only thing that distinguishes them is their "type" attribute in the HTML. In the CSS above, we are declaring that an input that has a "type" attribute of "text" should get a bottom margin of 10 pixels. This means that the CSS will only apply to the input box and not to the submit button.

Here is the result:

Instead of using "input[type=text]", we could have added a bottom margin to the ID of the input (#full-name), or we could have given the input a class name and put the CSS on that class. In CSS, there are usually multiple ways of achieving the same thing. The benefit of using "input[type=text]" is that if we add any new input boxes, the style will automatically apply to them too.

Next, we give the input and the textarea boxes the same width, as follows:

```
129   input[type=text], textarea {
130       width:60%;
131   }
```

Here is the result:

Full Name [   ]

Message [   ]

[Send Message!]

If you look carefully, you will notice that the input and the textarea are not actually the exact same width, despite giving them both a 200 pixel width. This is caused by a technical issue related to the way the browser calculates the width of an input versus the width of a textarea. The solution is to use the "box-sizing" CSS property, as follows (line 131 below):

```
129   input[type=text], textarea {
130       width:60%;
131       box-sizing:border-box;
132   }
```

The CSS property "box-sizing:border-box" property tells the browser to calculate the width of the input and the textarea with respect to their borders rather than their inner contents. The result is that they get the same apparent width:

Full Name [   ]

Message [   ]

[Send Message!]

Notice that the textarea is somewhat small. Below I have written a three-line message, when I go to line 3, line 1 stops showing due to scrolling out of view:

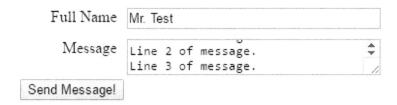

We can provide a better user experience by making the message writing area higher. To do this, we can either define a height in CSS, or use the "rows" attribute as follows:

```
<label for="message">Message</label>
<textarea rows="8" id="message" name="message"></textarea><br />
```

Above, I have created a "rows" attribute with a value of "8". This tells the browser that this textarea should be high enough to show eight lines of text at the same time. Here is what it looks like:

Above, I written down 8 lines, each line with a number on it.

Next, we style the submit button. We give it a left margin of 110 pixels to make it appear underneath the input boxes as follows:

```
134  input[type=submit] {
135      margin-left:110px;
136  }
```

Above, on line 134, I have used the "input[type=submit]" selector, meaning the style will only apply to inputs whose "type" attribute is "submit". Here is the result:

We can add all kinds of styling to a submit button, as follows:

```
134    input[type=submit] {
135        margin-left:110px;
136        border:1px solid #000;
137        color:#fff;
138        background:#666;
139        padding:5px;
140        text-shadow:1px 1px 0px #000;
141        font-size:120%;
142        font-family:Centaur, serif;
143        letter-spacing:2px;
144    }
```

Here is the result:

By now, you may be wondering what happens if you type some stuff in the boxes and press the submit button. Where does the data go? On a real website, when you press the submit button, the data ends up being sent to the server where the website is located. The server has a program that accepts the data and saves it in a database, and perhaps sends an email to the website's owner with the contents of the message in it.

It is outside the scope of this book to teach how form submission works, since that is part of web development rather than HTML and CSS.

This page intentionally left blank

Part 2
JavaScript

This page intentionally left blank

11. An Introduction to Programming

Programming is the art and science of telling computers what to do. Unlike humans, computers in general have no preconceived notions of their own. You cannot command a computer-controlled robot to wash the dishes because it has no ability to understand human language, and even if it could, it has no idea what washing is, what dishes are, and how one goes about performing dish washing. By bringing together dozens of programmers, an entrepreneur can build a robot that can understand human speech and that can wash dishes. Usually each programmer works only on a small part of such a project; one team might work on writing the code that helps the robot's computer understand human speech, another might work on the code that tells the robot how to move its body parts.

Computers are incapable of learning, but they are capable of following instructions. Programming is how we write those instructions. Below we have the screenshot of a web page opened in Notepad. The web page contains a little bit of JavaScript, which can be seen inside the **`<script>`** tag:

```
my_first_web_page.html - Notepad               —    □    ✕

File  Edit  Format  View  Help

<html>
  <head>
    <script>
      alert('Hello there, person!');
    </script>
  </head>
  <body>
  This is a document.
  </body>
</html>
```

Make sure to type the single quotation marks before Hello and after the exclamation mark (the semicolon is not strictly necessary in this specific example). Save the file again and open it again in a browser, and this is what now happens:

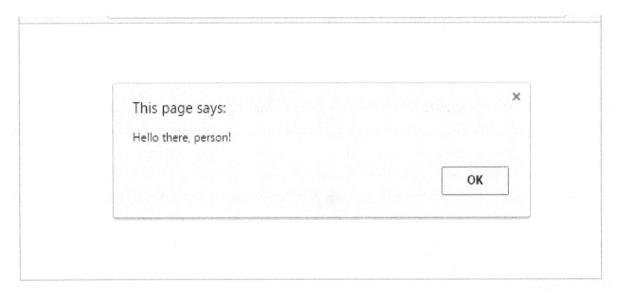

As soon as you open the webpage, a dialog box opens. What you are seeing above is a JavaScript "alert", which is used to notify users about certain things. We have now officially done some JavaScript programming. In the HTML code, everything that goes between **<script>** and **</script>** is JavaScript code. Let's look at it again:

```
<script>
  alert('Hello there, person!');
</script>
```

We have two computer languages interacting with each other here. The first one is HTML, as we discussed. But inside the document, we use **<script>** to tell the computer that everything from there on is JavaScript, then use **</script>**) (note the slash) to tell the computer the JavaScript ends here and the HTML starts again after it.

We have a single line of JavaScript in the above example:

alert('Hello there, person!');

This line tells the computer to show an alert to the user when the user opens the file. If this webpage was placed on a website, any user visiting the site will have seen this alert. If the people at Google put this line of code in the JavaScript section of Google.com, everyone opening the Google homepage would be shown such an alert.

And this is what coding or programming is. By writing a special piece of code (in the above example, by writing **alert('Hello there, person!')**), you command the computer to do a specific thing that you want it to do.

There is no need to worry about memorizing any of the code in this chapter. I am merely showcasing parts of JavaScript for you so that you can get a general feel for the way the language is used.

Let's now see another example. What if you wanted your webpage to show what the square root of 555 is? Below, I have removed the **alert...** inside the JavaScript and changed it as follows:

```
<script>
  document.write(Math.sqrt(555));
</script>
```

The above JavaScript tells the computer: "When a person opens this webpage, write out the square root of 555 at the beginning of the document". If we now open the webpage, this is what we see:

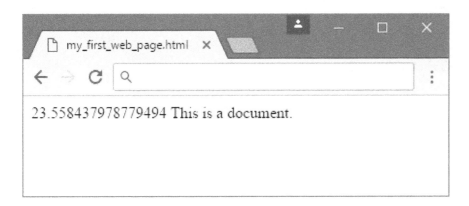

We used a multi-layered JavaScript command (or more correctly, JavaScript "statement") to tell the computer what to do. The **document.write()** command tells the computer: Write out anything you see between the brackets. We could have written **document.write('Hello!')** instead, as follows:

```
<script>
  document.write('Hello!');
</script>
```

And the result would have been as follows:

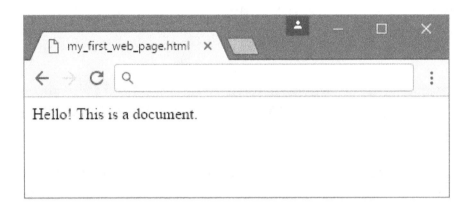

That is not very useful, since we can write a Hello! Without using any JavaScript. But by writing **document.write(Math.sqrt(555))** we use JavaScript's mathematical powers to do a complicated calculation behind the scenes and show people the result inside the webpage when they view it inside a browser. When the browser sees this line of JavaScript code, it knows that what we want is for it to calculate the square root of 555, then to write out the result inside the document. Since we did not tell the computer how to display the results, it showed us the square root of 555 with 15 decimals: **23.558437978779494**, which is a rather unnecessary level of detail. Computers have no common sense, so if we want them to do things a certain way, we have to spell it out for them. For example, we can use JavaScript's mathematical rounding powers to tell the computer to display the result in a more sensible way:

```
<script>
  document.write(Math.sqrt(555).toFixed(2));
</script>
```

Now, if we save the document and reload the webpage:

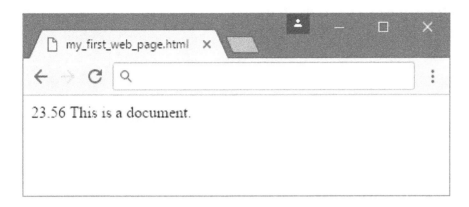

The JavaScript we are using (**document.write(Math.sqrt(555).toFixed(2));**) tells the computer to perform three actions one after the other. The first action is **Math.sqrt(555)**, which tells the computer to find out the square root of 555. The next action is **toFixed(2)**, which tells the computer to round the result of the previous action to two decimal places. The final action is **document.write()**, which tells the computer to write out the result inside the document. Without **document.write()**, the computer still performs the calculations, but it will not show the result:

```
my_first_web_page.html - Notepad          —    □    ✕
File  Edit  Format  View  Help
<html>
  <head>
    <script>
      Math.sqrt(555).toFixed(2);
    </script>
  </head>
  <body>
  This is a document.
  </body>
</html>
```

Here is the result:

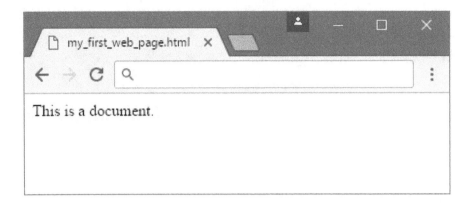

That is quite useless, which is why we have to use some method of *outputting* the result of the calculation. To "output" something means to show users the result of some computer action. Without output, things may happen behind the scenes, but a person viewing the webpage will not be shown anything interesting. This is sometimes useful, for example companies like Google and Facebook use JavaScript to store information about you behind the scenes and send it back to their own computers. They then sell this information to advertisers. Usually when you visit any major website, thousands of lines of JavaScript run behind the scenes, doing all kinds of things that you do not see.

Back to our webpage, instead of using **document.write()**, we can use the **alert()** command that we showed earlier:

```
<script>
  alert(Math.sqrt(555).toFixed(2));
</script>
```

Now, if we reload the webpage:

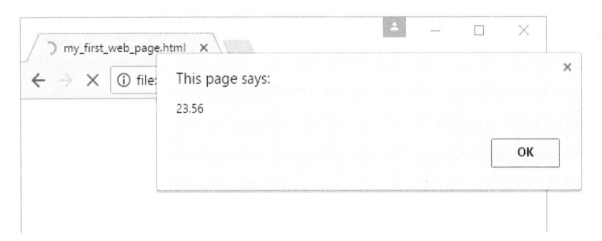

Above, a dialog box opens up that shows the result of **Math.sqrt(555).toFixed(2)**. If the user clicks **OK**, the dialog box closes and they will then see the document in its normal state:

We can show multiple alerts to users. For example:

```
<script>
  alert('Hello!');
  alert('Hello again!');
</script>
```

Now, if we reload the webpage, this is what happens:

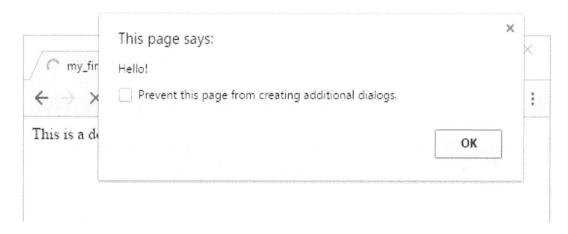

If we press **OK**, we are shown the second alert:

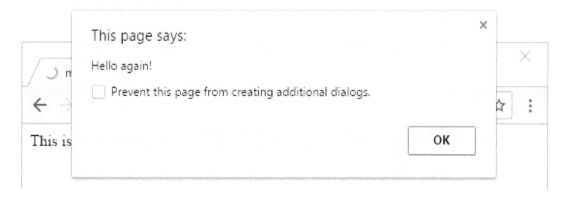

By using multiple alerts website owners can cause serious annoyances to their users, for this reason web browsers such as Google Chrome allow the user to stop the alerts from showing up for that particular web page by ticking the checkbox that says "Prevent this page…".

Tinkering with JavaScript using JS Tinker

We have already made extensive use of JS Tinker for HTML and CSS. We will now make use of for JavaScript. We can either put JavaScript inside the HTML box using **<script>** tags, or we can use the bottom left box that is specially designated for JavaScript.

Instead of having the JavaScript in the HTML box, we can move it to the JavaScript box as follows:

```
 i  1 ▾ <html>
    2 ▾   <head>
    3 ,    </head>
    4 ▾    <body>
    5        This is a document
    6      </body>
    7    </html>
    8
    9  |
 ⚠ 1   document.write('Hello!');
    2  |
```

```
1
```

Hello!

JS Tinker automatically merges the HTML and the JavaScript and displays the result. Due to the way that JS Tinker works, this merging causes **document.write()** to overwrite the entire contents of the document, which is why we no longer see "This is a document". This issue will be clarified later. It is more convenient to use the HTML box for JavaScript, because it allows us to determine where our output shows up. For this reason we will only be making use of the HTML box for both HTML and JavaScript in this book.

12. Outputs and Variables

Check out the HTML code below:

```
i  1 ▾ <html>
   2 ▾   <head>
   3       </head>
   4 ▾   <body>
   5        The word 'king' is made up of x letters
   6       </body>
   7     </html>
   8
   9     |
```

The word 'king' is made up of x letters

I have changed the JS Tinker program to only show the HTML box and the output box since that takes up less space for the purposes of this book. We will now replace the "x" on line 5 with some JavaScript that actually calculates the length of the word and prints it out:

```
i  1 ▾ <html>
   2 ▾   <head>
   3       </head>
   4 ▾   <body>
   5 ▾      The word 'king' is made up of <script>
   6             document.write('king'.length);
   7          </script> letters
   8       </body>
   9     </html>
```

The word 'king' is made up of 4 letters

We injected some JavaScript into the sentence to make it dynamically print out the length of the word "king". We can separate out the JavaScript from the rest of the text as follows. This does not affect the result:

```
i   1▾  <html>
    2▾    <head>
    3     </head>
    4▾    <body>
    5       The word 'king' is made up of
    6▾      <script>
    7           document.write('king'.length);
    8       </script>
    9       letters
   10     </body>
   11   </html>
```

The word 'king' is made up of 4 letters

HTML ignores line breaks, regardless of how many blank lines we add, the result remains the same:

```
i   1▾  <html>
    2▾    <head>
    3     </head>
    4▾    <body>
    5       The word 'king' is made up of
    6
    7
    8▾      <script>
    9           document.write('king'.length);
   10       </script>
   11
   12
   13       letters
   14     </body>
   15   </html>
```

The word 'king' is made up of 4 letters

This is useful for us since it allows us to add JavaScript anywhere we like without worrying about breaking apart sentences and paragraphs. If we *did* want to add line breaks, we can always use tags like **
** in our HTML.

The JavaScript we used to calculate the length of the word king is as follows:

document.write('king'.length);

Above, it does not matter whether you put "king" in single quotes or double quotes. But it must be in quotes.

The **document.write()** part, as you may recall, simply tells the browser to print out whatever is between the brackets. The interesting part of the code is **'king'.length**. If we remove the **.length** part, here is the result:

```
i   1▾  <html>
    2▾    <head>
    3     </head>
    4▾    <body>
    5       The word 'king' is made up of
    6▾      <script>
    7           document.write('king');
    8       </script>
    9       letters
   10     </body>
   11   </html>
```

The word 'king' is made up of king letters

Above, the JavaScript merely prints out the word "king". By using `.length` after `'king'` (without any spaces), we are telling the browser that we are not interested in the word "king" itself, we are only interested in its length. It literally means: 'Access the "length" property of "king"'. When the computer does that, the result is 4, because the `.length` property, unsurprisingly, counts the length of the thing that comes before it. Since "king" is made up of 4 letters, its `.length` property is 4.

We should now clarify something. The JavaScript has no relationship with HTML outside of it. For example if in the HTML I change the word "king" to "elephant", the JavaScript will continue thinking about the word "king":

```
i   1 ▾ <html>
    2 ▾    <head>
    3        </head>
    4 ▾    <body>
    5         The word 'elephant' is made up of
    6 ▾       <script>
    7              document.write('king'.length);
    8          </script>
    9          letters
   10      </body>
   11  </html>
```

The word 'elephant' is made up of 4 letters

Above, the JavaScript code continues to count the length of "king", because that is what we are telling it to do. The command **document.write('king'.length);** has a very specific meaning and has nothing to do with whatever might be outside the JavaScript.

To correct things, we have to change the word "king" to "elephant" inside the JavaScript too (line 7 below):

```
i   1 ▾ <html>
    2 ▾    <head>
    3        </head>
    4 ▾    <body>
    5         The word 'elephant' is made up of
    6 ▾       <script>
    7              document.write('elephant'.length);
    8          </script>
    9          letters
   10      </body>
   11  </html>
```

The word 'elephant' is made up of 8 letters

What if there was a way to write the word "elephant" only once, so that we could avoid having to update the JavaScript every time we update the HTML? In fact we can do that by using JavaScript.

367

```
i   1 ▾  <html>
    2 ▾    <head>
    3        </head>
    4 ▾    <body>
    5 ▾      The word '<script>
    6              document.write('elephant');
    7        </script>' is made up of
    8 ▾      <script>
    9              document.write('elephant'.length);
   10        </script>
   11        letters
   12      </body>
   13  </html>
```

The word 'elephant' is made up of 8 letters

Above, we are using JavaScript in two places. First we use it to print out the word "elephant" (line 6), then we used to print out the length of the word "elephant" (line 9). This so far hasn't solved the problem, if you change the word "elephant" on line 6, line 9 will continue to print out the length of the word "elephant". What we will do is use a *variable* to store the word we are interested in, then we will use the variable where we need to.

```
i   1 ▾  <html>
    2 ▾    <head>
    3        </head>
    4 ▾    <body>
    5 ▾      The word '<script>
    6              var my_word = 'elephant';
    7              document.write(my_word);
    8        </script>' is made up of
    9 ▾      <script>
   10              document.write(my_word.length);
   11        </script>
   12        letters
   13      </body>
   14  </html>
```

The word 'elephant' is made up of 8 letters

Above, on line 6, I declared a variable called **my_word**. A variable acts as a container or box that you can put stuff inside so that you can access it later on. On line 6, I declare that the browser should create a variable named **my_word**, and that inside it there should be the word "elephant".

Let's now look at line 6 closely:

var my_word = 'elephant';

In JavaScript, we declare variables using the keyword **var**. This tells the computer that we are making a new variable. The name we choose for the variable can be anything, it is merely a label. On line 7, we declare that the contents of the variable **my_word** should be printed out. The JavaScript command **document.write()** doe looks inside the container that we have named **my_word** and prints out its contents on the screen. Since on line 6 we placed the word 'elephant' inside the variable, on line 7 **document.write()** ends up bringing out the word 'elephant'.

But things do not stop there. On line 10, we declare that the length of the variable **my_word** should be printed out, and since **my_word** contains the word "elephant", what ends up happening is that JavaScript prints out the length of the word "elephant".

We can now change the word "elephant" to anything we want and JavaScript will correctly print out its length:

```
 1 ▾  <html>
 2 ▾    <head>
 3      </head>
 4 ▾    <body>
 5 ▾      The word '<script>
 6            var my_word = 'xylophone';
 7            document.write(my_word);
 8        </script>' is made up of
 9 ▾      <script>
10            document.write(my_word.length);
11        </script>
12        letters
13      </body>
14    </html>
```

The word 'xylophone' is made up of 9 letters

Note the semicolons we have placed at the end of every line of JavaScript. The semicolon declares that the JavaScript instruction right before it has ended. Without it, the computer thinks that the stuff on the next line is still a continuation of the same instruction, which causes the JavaScript to stop working correctly. JS Tinker is a smart program that automatically corrects some mistakes, therefore even if you leave out a semicolon things will often continue functioning normally. But in real-world JavaScript forgetting the semicolon can cause your JavaScript to stop working.

We may put multiple JavaScript instructions on the same line, as follows:

```
 4 ▾    <body>
 5 ▾      The word '<script>
 6            var my_word = 'xylophone'; document.write(my_word);
 7        </script>' is made up of
 8 ▾      <script>
 9            document.write(my_word.length);
10        </script>
11        letters
12      </body>
```

Above, I have merged the earlier lines 6 and 7 onto a single line 6. We can put any number of instructions on the same line as long as they are separated by semicolons. Here we can see the importance of semicolons. Below, I have removed the semicolon after "xylophone":

```
 1 ▾  <html>
 2 ▾    <head>
 3      </head>
 4 ▾    <body>
 5 ▾      The word '<script>
 6            var my_word = 'xylophone' document.write(my_word);
 7        </script>' is made up of
```

The word " is made up of 9 letters

The result is that the **document.write()** instruction that comes after it ends up doing nothing, so that the variable is not printed out (in the preview area on the right, see the way the word "xylophone" no longer appears).

As already mentioned, we can name our variables anything we want:

```
i  1▾ <html>
   2▾   <head>
   3     </head>
   4▾   <body>
   5▾     The word '<script>
   6           var interesting_word = 'xylophone';
   7           document.write(interesting_word);
   8       </script>' is made up of
   9▾     <script>
  10           document.write(interesting_word.length);
  11       </script>
  12       letters
```

The word 'xylophone' is made up of 9 letters

Above, I have changed the variable name from **my_word** to **interesting_word**. It does not affect the result of the code.

We can declare multiple variables in JavaScript with a single statement (in JavaScript a statement is anything that ends in a semicolon. Above I referred to statements as instructions, since statements *are* instructions to the computer. But the word "statement" is the correct technical term).

```
<script>
    var cat_sound = 'meow',
        dog_sound = 'bark';
</script>
```

In the above code block, we declare two variables, **cat_sound** and **dog_sound**. Notice that at the end of the line for the sound of cats, we do not have a semicolon but a comma. This tells JavaScript that we have another variable to declare. Once we are done declaring all of our variables, we use the semicolon.

The above code block is the same as the following in its meaning:

```
<script>
    var cat_sound = 'meow';
    var dog_sound = 'bark';
</script>
```

Above, we use two separate statements, each of them ending in a semicolon. It is a matter of preference which one you use. The earlier method requires less typing since you have to type **var** only once.

Below we go about making use of the variables:

```
i  1 ▾ <html>
   2 ▾   <head>
   3       </head>
   4 ▾   <body>
   5 ▾     <script>
   6           var cat_sound = 'meow',
   7               dog_sound = 'bark';
   8       </script>
   9       Cats
  10       <script>document.write(cat_sound);</script>
  11       and dogs
  12       <script>document.write(dog_sound);</script>.
  13     </body>
  14  </html>
```

Cats meow and dogs bark.

Above, we use three separate JavaScript code blocks. In the first one, we merely declare the variables without doing anything with them. We use HTML to print out the word "Cats", then the JavaScript code block prints out the value of the **cat_sound** variable. The same is done for the dog sound.

If we write out the same JavaScript statement multiple times, it will be carried out multiple times, as follows:

```
i  1 ▾ <html>
   2 ▾   <head>
   3       </head>
   4 ▾   <body>
   5 ▾     <script>
   6           var cat_sound = 'meow',
   7               dog_sound = 'bark';
   8       </script>
   9       Cats
  10 ▾     <script>
  11         document.write(cat_sound);
  12         document.write(cat_sound);
  13         document.write(cat_sound);
  14       </script>
  15       and dogs
  16       <script>document.write(dog_sound);</script>.
  17     </body>
  18  </html>
```

Cats meowmeowmeow and dogs bark.

Above, on lines 11-13 we have the same statement printing out the cat sound, so that on right-hand side we see "meowmeowmeow" being printed out. There are no spaces between the "meow"s because we have not told JavaScript to put spaces between them. We can do so as follows:

```
i  1 ▾ <html>
   2 ▾   <head>
   3       </head>
   4 ▾   <body>
   5 ▾     <script>
   6           var cat_sound = 'meow',
   7               dog_sound = 'bark';
   8       </script>
   9       Cats
  10 ▾     <script>
  11         document.write(cat_sound);
  12         document.write(' ');
  13         document.write(cat_sound);
  14         document.write(' ');
  15         document.write(cat_sound);
  16       </script>
  17       and dogs
```

Cats meow meow meow and dogs bark.

On lines 12 and 14, I have added the statements **document.write(' ');**. The stuff inside **document.write()** may look strange, but it is merely a space with single quotes on each side of it. It is telling JavaScript to print out a space.

We can accomplish the same effect by using a single **document.write()** command through the use of *concatenation*, as follows on line 11:

```
i  1 ▾ <html>
   2 ▾   <head>
   3       </head>
   4 ▾   <body>
   5 ▾     <script>
   6           var cat_sound = 'meow',
   7               dog_sound = 'bark';
   8       </script>
   9       Cats
  10 ▾     <script>
  11         document.write(cat_sound + ' ' + cat_sound + ' ' + cat_sound);
  12       </script>
  13       and dogs
  14       <script>document.write(dog_sound);</script>.
  15     </body>
  16 </html>
```

Cats meow meow meow and dogs bark.

Above, on line 11 we are using the plus sign to combine different pieces of text together. We are combining a cat sound with a space, and combining that with another cat sound, with another space, with another cat sound, then printing out the result.

The plus sign is known as an "operator" in programming. It performs operations on the thing or things that are before and after it.

Below we have a new example that we will use to showcase some more concatenation. On line 2 we declare a variable by the name of **fruit**, then on line 3 we write out its contents. The result is that we see the word 'apple' on the little preview area on the right-hand side:

```
i  1 ▾ <script>
   2        var fruit = 'apple';
   3        document.write(fruit);
   4    </script>
   5    |
```
apple

Above, to simplify the code, I have only included the **<script>** tag. I skipped the **<html>**, **<head>** and **<body>** tags because they are not strictly necessary for our purposes. JS Tinker automatically adds them behind the scenes. The above example is the same as if we had typed out the following:

```
i   1 ▾ <html>
    2 ▾     <head>
    3        </head>
    4 ▾     <body>
    5 ▾     <script>
    6            var fruit = 'apple';
    7            document.write(fruit);
    8        </script>
    9    </body>
   10    </html>
```
apple

But the first example is shorter and takes up less space.

Below I have added a bit of additional code to the **document.write()** statement:

```
i  1 ▾ <script>
   2        var fruit = 'apple';
   3        document.write('the word ' + fruit);
   4    </script>
```
the word apple

On line 3, we have the text that says **'the word '** concatenated with the variable **fruit** using the **+** operator.

Below, I have placed an illustration of the way the above code works behind the scenes:

```
document.write('the word ' + fruit);
```

↓

```
document.write('the word ' + 'apple');
```

↓

```
document.write('the word apple');
```

At the second stage above, the variable **fruit** has been "evaluated" by the browser, meaning that its contents have been extracted in order to be used in an operation. The operation is concatenation, the result of which can be seen at the last stage.

Notice the way there is a space after "word" and before the single quotation mark in **'the word '**. That is necessary in order to show a space between "the word" and "apple" in the output. Here is what happens if we remove it:

```
1 ▾ <script>
2       var fruit = 'apple';
3       document.write('the word' + fruit);
4   </script>
```
the wordapple

Above, "word" and "apple" merge together because we have not told JavaScript to create a space between them. We can add a space either by adding a space after "word", or as follows:

```
1 ▾ <script>
2       var fruit = 'apple';
3       document.write('the word' + ' ' + fruit);
4   </script>
```
the word apple

Above, we are explicitly adding a space between the two bits of text. In many cases JavaScript ignores any space or new line inside the code, so if we separate out the stuff inside **document.write()** onto their own lines, this does not change anything:

```
1 ▾ <script>
2       var fruit = 'apple';
3       document.write(
4           'the word'
5           + ' '
6           + fruit
7       );
8   </script>
```
the word apple

Above, the closing bracket for **document.write()** has been pushed all the way down to line 7. Any text you wish to print out must be enclosed in quotation marks, otherwise JavaScript will think that it is a JavaScript instruction. Below I have added the word "is" on line 7, but I have neglected to add the quotation marks:

```
1 ▾ <script>
2       var fruit = 'apple';
3       document.write(
4           'the word'
5           + ' '
6           + fruit
7           + is
8       );
9   </script>
```

We see no output in the preview area because the code has stopped working. JavaScript thinks we are trying to access a variable named **is**, which does not exist, so it makes the code crash.

Below, I have corrected the code by adding quotation marks around "is":

```
 i  1 ▾ <script>
    2       var fruit = 'apple';
    3       document.write(
    4           'the word'
    5           + ' '
    6           + fruit
    7           + 'is'
    8       );
    9  </script>
```

the word appleis

Now the code is working, except that the word "apple" and "is" are merged together. This is something that you will run into time and again when concatenating text. To correct it, below I have added a space before "is", but *inside* the quotation mark:

```
 i  1 ▾ <script>
    2       var fruit = 'apple';
    3       document.write(
    4           'the word'
    5           + ' '
    6           + fruit
    7           + ' is'
    8       );
    9  </script>
```

the word apple is

Adding spaces outside the quotation mark has no effect, as follows on line 7:

```
 i  1 ▾ <script>
    2       var fruit = 'apple';
    3       document.write(
    4           'the word'
    5           + ' '
    6           + fruit
    7           +    'is'
    8       );
    9  </script>
```

the word appleis

The reason is that, as has been mentioned, JavaScript ignores spaces inside its code, *unless* the space is part of a piece of text enclosed in quotation marks.

Below we have added some additional detail to our code:

```
i  1 ▾ <script>
   2       var fruit = 'apple';
   3       document.write(
   4           'the word'
   5           + ' '
   6           + fruit
   7           + ' is made up of '
   8           + fruit.length
   9           + ' letters.'
  10       );
  11   </script>
```

the word apple is made up of 5 letters.

On line 8, I use **fruit.length** to get the length of the contents of the variable **fruit**. Let's now talk about what **fruit.length** really means. As you now know, **fruit** is the name of a variable we declared on line 2. As for **length**, it is a *property* of the variable **fruit** that tells us how many letters the variable contains. The dot between them tells JavaScript that what comes after is a property of what comes before it.

Data types

In programming, we have various "data types" that we use for storing information. The main data types we run into are strings and numbers. We have already used strings. So far I have called them "text". A string in JavaScript is the stuff enclosed inside quotation marks, for example **'apple'** below:

```
i  1 ▾ <script>
   2       var fruit = 'apple';
   3       var year = 2018;
   4   </script>
```

Above, on line 2, we have a string variable named **fruit**. It contains the string **'apple'**. We also have a number variable named **year**. It contains the number **2018**. Note the way **2018** does not have quotation marks around it.

We have different data types in programming because some things only make sense when applied to strings, other things only when applied to numbers. The way the computer stores one data type behind the scenes is completely different from the way it stores another data type, and this can make all the difference in the world in the way a program works and how fast it runs.

Below we have an example of a bit of nonsense; we are trying to divide a *string* by 2018:

```
i 1▾ <script>
  2      var fruit = 'apple';
  3      var year = 2018;
  4      document.write(fruit / year);
  5  </script>
```

NaN

When we try to divide **'apple'** by **2018** using the slash on line 4 inside **document.write()**, the result is **NaN** which means "not a number". When you see **NaN**, it means you are trying to do something that does not make sense in JavaScript.

In JavaScript, as seen above, the forward slash (**/**) is used for division. Below we divide the **year** variable by 2, resulting in 1009:

```
i 1▾ <script>
  2      var fruit = 'apple';
  3      var year = 2018;
  4      document.write(year / 2);
  5  </script>
```

1009

The **length** property we spoke of earlier only works on strings (and arrays and objects, which will be discussed later). It does not work on numbers:

```
i 1▾ <script>
  2      var fruit = 'apple';
  3      var year = 2018;
  4      document.write(year.length);
  5  </script>
```

undefined

Above I try to access a supposed **length** property of the **year** variable, but the result is **undefined**. The reason is that JavaScript does not have a **length** property for numbers, so when we try to access it, JavaScript tells us it is not defined.

In the following example, we have a string variable named **fruit** with the string **'apple'** inside it. We also have a number variable named **x** with the number **1000** inside it.

```
i 1▾ <script>
  2      var fruit = 'apple';
  3      var x = 1000;
  4      document.write(fruit + x);
  5  </script>
```

apple1000

Above, on line 4 we are concatenating the two variables. Unlike with division, this does not lead to an error. JavaScript converts the number to a string, and then concatenates it with **'apple'** to result in **apple1000**. It is the context that determines whether we will get an error or not. Dividing a string by a number does not make sense, so it results in an error. But adding a string to a number can be made to make sense. It is a little strange and can confuse people, but this is how JavaScript works. In other languages, such as C, you get an error if you try to add a string and a number. But languages like JavaScript try to be clever and guess what you were trying to do.

Below, I have added a new number variable on line 4 named **y** with the number **2000** inside it:

```
i 1▾ <script>
  2      var fruit = 'apple';                    3000
  3      var x = 1000;
  4      var y = 2000;
  5      document.write(x + y);
  6  </script>
```

On line 5, I use the plus operator to add **x** and **y**. Since both of them are numbers, JavaScript performs mathematical addition, resulting in the number 3000, which is the sum of 1000 and 2000. It is the context that determines what the plus operator will do. If it is dealing with strings, it concatenates the strings together. If it is dealing with numbers, it performs addition. If it is dealing with a mix of strings and numbers, it concatenates them as if they were all strings.

Since both **x** and **y** are numbers, we can do division on them without this leading to an error, as follows on line 5:

```
i 1▾ <script>
  2      var fruit = 'apple';                    0.5
  3      var x = 1000;
  4      var y = 2000;
  5      document.write(x / y);
  6  </script>
```

Below, on line 5, I have created a new variable named **result**. Instead of putting a number or string directly inside it, what I put inside is **x / y**. What this means is that JavaScript will perform this operation and then put the results inside the variable:

```
i 1▾ <script>
  2      var fruit = 'apple';                    0.5
  3      var x = 1000;
  4      var y = 2000;
  5      var result = x / y;
  6      document.write(result);
  7  </script>
```

On line 6, I print out the contents of **result**, which as you might expect, is whatever we get when we divide the contents of **x** by **y** (0.5).

We can use the same variable multiple times in the same calculation. On line 5 below, we add **x** to **x**, then add that to **y**, resulting in the number 4000:

```
i  1▾ <script>
   2      var fruit = 'apple';
   3      var x = 1000;
   4      var y = 2000;
   5      var result = x + x + y;
   6      document.write(result);
   7  </script>
```

4000

Below, on line 5 I do the same calculation as the one above, but on line 6, in a new statement, I do a different calculation and assign the results to the **result** variable:

```
i  1▾ <script>
   2      var fruit = 'apple';
   3      var x = 1000;
   4      var y = 2000;
   5      var result = x + x + y;
   6      result = x + 1;
   7      document.write(result);
   8  </script>
```

1001

What happens is that on line 5 the **result** variable ends up containing the number 4000. But the next statement *overwrites* the variable, causing it to contain the result of **x + 1**.

Below, I overwrite the variable another time on line 7, causing it to become a string:

```
i  1▾ <script>
   2      var fruit = 'apple';
   3      var x = 1000;
   4      var y = 2000;
   5      var result = x + x + y;
   6      result = x + 1;
   7      result = 'banana';
   8      document.write(result);
   9  </script>
```

banana

JavaScript does not care that the **result** variable used to contain a number in the past. When we declare on line 7 that it should contain the string **'banana'**, that is what happens. The results of the previous calculations are discarded, and the **result** variable goes from being a number to a string.

Some languages do not let you do such a thing, if you try to put a number inside a variable that used to contain a string or vice versa, you will get an error. But in JavaScript you can do this. Languages that allow such a thing are known as *dynamically typed* languages; the data types are "dynamic", in one statement a variable might be a string, then the next operation might turn it into a number. Other languages use *static typing*, in such languages trying to put a string inside a number variable causes the program to crash.

Interpolation

The presence of a mix of strings and numbers causes JavaScript to make a guess about whether to treat everything as numbers or as strings. Let's take a look at the following:

```
i  1▾  <script>
   2        document.write('a'  + 500 + 500);
   3  </script>
```
a500500

Above, since the *first* operand in the operation is a string (the string **'a'**, JavaScript treats the entire operation as a string operation. It treats the numbers 500 and 500 as strings, instead of doing mathematical addition on them, it merely puts them side-by-side, performing string concatenation.

Below, we have reversed the order of the operation:

```
i  1▾  <script>
   2        document.write(500 + 500 + 'a');
   3  </script>
```
1000a

Strangely, JavaScript now performs mathematical addition on the numbers, resulting in the number 1000, then it performs concatenation. The reason is that in JavaScript the order of operations goes from left to right, the same as in mathematics. When JavaScript sees two numbers with a plus sign between them, it performs mathematical addition. When it sees a number and a string with a plus sign between them, it performs string concatenation. This can be an endless source of confusion, therefore good programmers do not write code like that above. They first make sure everything is a string or a number before using a plus sign between them. Later we will discuss how this is done.

The above discussion only applies to the plus sign. Since division, multiplication and subtraction are always mathematical, they are only allowed on numbers. For instance, let's look at the following:

```
i  1▾  <script>
   2        document.write(500 * 500 * 'a');
   3  </script>
```
NaN

Above, we are using the multiplication operator ***** to multiply 500 by 500 by the string **'a'**, which results in the **NaN** error. The same happens if we use the minus sign:

```
i  1▾  <script>
   2        document.write(500 - 500 - 'a');
   3  </script>
```
NaN

The same applies to division.

But if we multiply 500 by 500, then use the plus sign to add that to a string, things work, due to the fact that JavaScript performs operations from left to right one after another:

```
i 1 ▾ <script>
  2       document.write(500 * 500 + 'a');          250000a
  3   </script>
```

What happens above is that JavaScript sees two numbers being multiplied, so it performs mathematical multiplication. Next, it sees the number 25000 being added to the string **'a'**, so it switches gears and performs string concatenation.

Variable names

Programming languages have rules for what names you can use for variables. You can use lowercase, uppercase and number characters. You may also use underscores. These are all valid variable names:

my_variable
my_Variable
myVariable
MyVariable
MyVariable1
_my_variable

The last example above actually starts with an underscore. That is perfectly valid. However, the first important rule to remember is that you cannot have numbers at the beginning of a variable name, so the following JavaScript statement is invalid:

```
var 1st_name = 'James';
```

You may not use dashes (i.e. the minus sign), spaces and most special characters (such as the percentage sign) in variable names either. You can use dollar signs, however.

For now, to avoid errors in the code you try, keep using alphabetic letters and underscores to avoid errors.

Checking errors

The piece of code below has an error in it that prevents it from working. But what is the error?

```
1  <script>
2      document.write(Hello);
3  </script>
```

For a beginner to programming, it can be very difficult to find out why their code is not working. However, web browsers provide a useful "error console" that can sometimes help you find out what is wrong with your code. Below, there is a screenshot that shows how to access the error console in the Chrome web browser. In whatever browser you are using, go to the settings menu and find the "Developer tools" item (or something similar). In Chrome this option is actually hidden away, you have to click "More tools" first then you will see it:

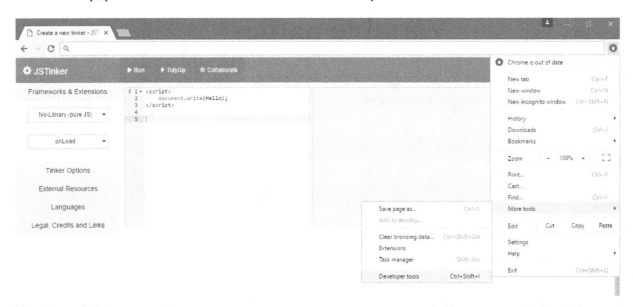

Another way of accessing the error console is to right-click on a blank area of the page and click "Inspect" (the bottom menu item below):

Once you do the above, the browser's developer tools are displayed (see the bottom part of the following screenshot), which can be a bit overwhelming at first:

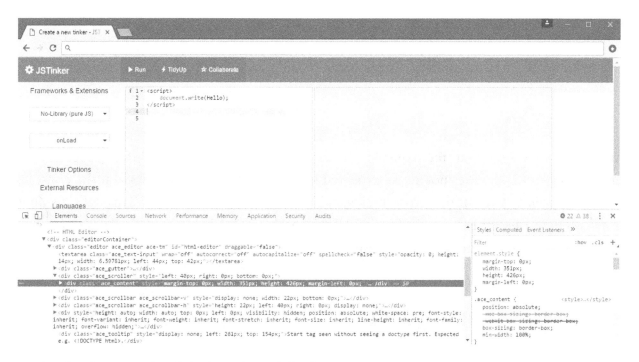

In the developer tools, click the "Console" tab to view JavaScript errors and certain other errors:

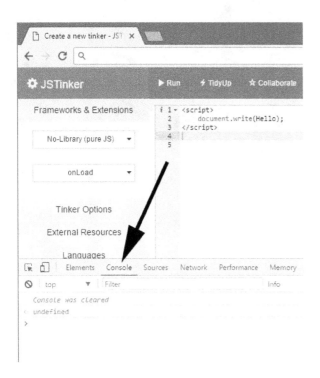

Now, if I click "Run" in JS Tinker to run the erroneous code shown earlier, here is what the console shows:

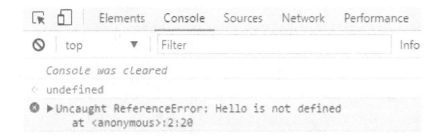

While the error messages that the console shows are not always very helpful (especially to beginners), when your code does not act as expected it can be helpful to take a look at the console. Above, the important part of the error message is "Hello is not defined". This tells us that JavaScript was trying to access a *variable* named **Hello** but failed because the variable was not declared. Let's take a look at the bad code again:

```
i 1▾ <script>
  2      document.write(Hello);
  3  </script>
  4 |
  5
```

In this simple piece of code, we are not dealing with any variables, so what is the console talking about? The problem with the code is that we forgot to put quotation marks before and after the word "Hello", so JavaScript thinks **Hello** is a variable name. To correct the problem, below I have added the necessary quotation marks:

```
i  1 ▾ <script>
   2       document.write('Hello');
   3  </script>
```

Hello

Now the code is working without issue.

Below we have a different example of erroneous code:

```
i  1 ▾ <script>
   2       var 1st_name = 'James';
   3  </script>
```

When running the above code, this is what the console tells us:

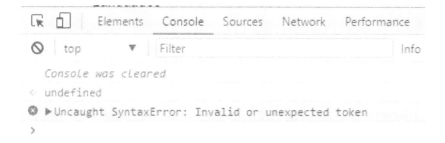

The error this time is "Invalid or unexpected token", which is a generic error message that tells us we have written nonsensical or bad JavaScript. In the above case, the issue is that the variable name **1st_name** starts with a number, which is not allowed.

By now, you have a reasonably good understanding of what a variable is and what strings are. If the rest of the discussion has left you a little bit confused or overwhelmed, there is no need to worry. You will see these concepts many more times in the next few chapters. You do not learn programming by memorizing things, but by running into the same concepts and tinkering with them over and over again in different settings.

This page intentionally left blank

13. Repeated Action

The most important benefit of computers is their ability to perform the same action over and over again. A computer can find the sum of a million numbers in a few seconds, something that would have required a human many days of work.

In programming, we have many ways of telling the computer to perform some action a certain number of times, or to continuously perform it until it reaches some result or condition. Starting from the simplest examples, we will slowly learn how to build complex algorithms. Below, we have the word "hello" inside the variable named **the_word**. Notice how in the preview area on the right we see nothing. That is because we do not have any **document.write()** statements telling the computer to output stuff.

```
i 1▾ <script>
  2      var the_word = 'hello';
  3  </script>
```

Now, imagine if for some strange reason your boss asked you to create a document with the word "hello" written in it 1000 times. Instead of spending half an hour typing or copying and pasting, you can do it in a few seconds by writing a bit of JavaScript. We have already seen that we can do the same thing over and over again by repeatedly writing the same statement, as follows:

```
i 1▾ <script>
  2      var the_word = 'hello';
  3      document.write(the_word);
  4      document.write(the_word);
  5      document.write(the_word);
  6  </script>
```

hellohellohello

But writing or copying the JavaScript statement **document.write(the_word);** a thousand times is not the smartest way of achieving our goal. Instead, we will use a *loop*. A loop in programming is a piece of code that the computer runs over and over again. There are multiple types of loops in JavaScript. We will look at a *while loop* first:

```
i  1▾ <script>
   2      var the_word = 'hello';
   3      var number_of_hellos_printed_so_far = 0;
   4▾     while(number_of_hellos_printed_so_far < 1000) {
   5          document.write('hello');
   6          number_of_hellos_printed_so_far =
   7              number_of_hellos_printed_so_far + 1;
   8      }
   9  </script>
```

hellohellohellohello

Above, you see the complete code for writing out the word "hello" 1000 times. We will spend some time deconstructing it. In the preview areas we see the word "hello" four times. The text actually goes on, extending rightward, until 1000 "hello"s are printed, but there isn't sufficient space to show them all on this page.

In order to print exactly 1000 "hello"s, we need a way of keeping track of how many we have already printed. We do that using the **number_of_hellos_printed_so_far** variable declared on line 2. We first set it to zero, since on line 2 we have not printed anything so far. We next have the **while** loop. The basic structure of a while loop is as follows:

```
while(some_condition_is_true) {
   do something...
}
```

It basically tells the computer: As long as this condition applies, continually run the code below over and over again. The code that the **while** loop should run is enclosed in *curly braces*. These braces **{}** tell the **while** loop where it starts and where it ends.

In our example, the condition we have says that as long the value of the **number_of_hellos_printed_so_far** variable is less than 1000 (notice the mathematical "less than" operator), the code inside the **while** loop should be repeatedly run over and over again.

When running a loop, what JavaScript does is that it carries out the statements inside the loop, then checks the condition again, then, if the condition is still true, it runs the code again.

Inside the **while** loop we have two statements. The first one (on line 5) prints out a "hello" using **document.write()**. The second statement, which takes up two lines (6 and 7) keeps track of how many "hello"s we have printed. I have broken a single statement into two lines only for readability's sake. This:

```
6      number_of_hellos_printed_so_far =
7          number_of_hellos_printed_so_far + 1;
```

is exactly the same as this:

```
number_of_hellos_printed_so_far = number_of_hellos_printed_so_far + 1;
```

We have line 7 slightly indented (it has slightly more spaces before it) to indicate to ourselves that this line continues from the one above it. The spaces do not do anything, they are merely for readability's sake.

We keep track of how many "hello"s we have printed by updating the value of the **number_of_hellos_printed_so_far** variable. We add the number 1 to the value of the variable each time the loop runs. The very first time JavaScript runs the loop, the value of **number_of_hellos_printed_so_far** is zero as we declared on line 2. Then the statement on lines 6 and 7 add one to the value of the variable, so that the variable ends up containing the number 1. Once JavaScript finishes running one *iteration* of the loop (meaning running the code inside it once from top to bottom), it goes back to the top, checks the condition again, and if the condition is true, it then runs the code again. To refresh our memory, let's take another loop at the code for our while loop:

```
4 ▾     while(number_of_hellos_printed_so_far < 1000) {
5           document.write('hello');
6           number_of_hellos_printed_so_far
7             = number_of_hellos_printed_so_far + 1;
8       }
```

Below we have a textual description of what JavaScript is thinking as it runs the loop each time. The numbers at the beginning of each line represent the line number of the code above:

4 (start of while loop). Is the value of the variable number_of_hellos_printed_so_far less than 1000? Yes.

5. Print out a "hello".

6. Increase the value of number_of_hellos_printed_so_far by one. Go back to the top. (Now number_of_hellos_printed_so_far contains the number 1)

4. Is number_of_hellos_printed_so_far less than 1000? Yes.

5. Print out a "hello".

6. Increase the value of number_of_hellos_printed_so_far by one. Go back to the top. (Now number_of_hellos_printed_so_far contains the number 2)

4. Is number_of_hellos_printed_so_far less than 1000? Yes.

5. Print out a "hello".

6. Increase the value of number_of_hellos_printed_so_far by one. Go back to the top. (Now number_of_hellos_printed_so_far contains the number 3)

JavaScript will repeat the above thought process over and over again until it reaches the following, which represent the last two iterations of the loop:

4. Is number_of_hellos_printed_so_far less than 1000? Yes. (at this point number_of_hellos_printed_so_far has 999 inside it)

5. Print out a "hello".

6. Increase the value of number_of_hellos_printed_so_far by one. Go back to the top. (Now number_of_hellos_printed_so_far contains the number 1000)

4. Is number_of_hellos_printed_so_far less than 1000 now? No. Since the condition is now false, we cannot continue. This is the end of the loop.

In the very last iteration of the loop, the variable **number_of_hellos_printed_so_far** ends up containing 1000. When JavaScript next tries out the code **while(number_of_hellos_printed_so_far < 1000) {**, it compares the value of **number_of_hellos_printed_so_far** with 1000 to find out if it is less than it or not. Since **number_of_hellos_printed_so_far** contains 1000, JavaScript is basically asking "Is 1000 less than 1000?". Of course it is not, which means that the *condition* for the loop is no longer true, which means the loop should no longer be run. When the condition is no longer true, JavaScript skips the loop's code and runs any code that comes after the loop.

Infinite loops

The **while** loop runs only as long as its condition is true. The following piece of code will run *forever* (do not try it on your computer):

```
i 1▾ <script>
  2▾     while(5 === 5) {
  3             document.write('hello');
  4         }
  5  </script>
```

Above, each time JavaScript prints out a "hello", behind the scenes it asks the question "Is 5 equal to 5?", and since the answer is always "Yes!" the loop keeps going without end. The weird three equal signs **===** between the two numbers is how we check for equality in JavaScript. Earlier we already saw how we check whether a variable is less than a certain number (using the mathematical "smaller than" sign, **<**). Here we are using the mathematical "is equal to" sign, which requires three equal signs in JavaScript for reasons that will become clear later on.

I recommend that you do not try out the code above because it creates what is known as an *infinite loop*, which can cause your browser to crash. An infinite loop is a loop whose condition is always true. It is similar to telling a robot, "Keep digging holes as long as water is wet".

Below is another infinite loop:

```
i 1▾ <script>
  2▾     while((1 + 1) === 2) {
  3             document.write('hello');
  4         }
  5  </script>
```

Above, we have told JavaScript to continuously print out "hello"s as long as adding the number one to one equals two. Since 1 + 1 will always equal 2, the loop will continue forever.

Below is an example of an infinite loop that involves strings and variables:

```
i 1▾ <script>
  2      var first_name = 'James';
  3▾     while(first_name === 'James') {
  4             document.write('Hello James!');
  5         }
  6  </script>
```

On line 3, we check whether or not the variable **first_name** contains the string **'James'**. Since this variable will always contain this string when JavaScript goes back to the top at the end of every iteration, the loop will go on forever.

Above, the single equal sign on line 2 tells JavaScript to place the string **'James'** inside the variable **first_name**. The triple equal sign on line 3 has a completely different and unrelated meaning. It is a comparison operator that checks whether the stuff on its left and right are exactly the same.

More while loops

Below we are trying to find out the result of continuously multiplying the number 500 by 2:

```
1  <script>
2      var my_number = 500;
3      while(my_number < 10000) {
4          my_number = my_number * 2;
5      }
6      document.write(my_number);
7  </script>
```

16000

With each iteration of the loop, we multiply **my_number** by 2 on line 4 and store the new result inside the same variable. This overwrites the variable's previous value with the new one. On line 4, JavaScript calculates the result of **my_number * 2**, which is 1000 the first time the loop runs. It then puts this result inside the variable, so that once line 4 is finished running, **my_number** will contain the number 1000. The next time the loop runs, the same process repeats. JavaScript calculates the result of **my_number * 2**, which this time is 2000. Each iteration doubles the variable value.

On line 3, we have a condition in order to prevent an infinite loop. The condition tells JavaScript to run the loop as long as **my_number** is less than ten thousand.

On line 6, we print out the final value of **my_number** in the preview area, which is 16000. In order to find out why the end result is 16000, we can tell JavaScript to print out the value of **my_number** with every iteration of the loop:

```
1  <script>
2      var my_number = 500;
3      while(my_number < 10000) {
4          document.write(my_number);
5          document.write('<br>');
6          my_number = my_number * 2;
7      }
8      document.write(my_number);
9  </script>
```

500
1000
2000
4000
8000
16000

Above, every time the loop runs, on line 4 we print out the value of **my_number** which at first is 500 as seen at the top of the preview area. On line 5 we have something new. You do not need to understand what this line means, suffice it to say that it causes the next item to be printed on a new line. It basically means "start a new line at this point in the document". This is why the numbers are neatly stacked on each other; we are telling JavaScript to make a new line for each iteration of the loop (its literal meaning is: create an HTML **\<br\>** tag at this point. The **\<br\>** tag in HTML creates new lines in the document.)

On the next iterations of the loop, **my_number** ends up containing 1000, 2000, 4000 and 8000. On the final iteration, JavaScript checks whether 8000 is less than 10000 (on line 3). Since the answer is "Yes!", the loop continues to run. On line 4 the number 8000 is printed, then on line 6 the number is doubled by multiplying it by 2. JavaScript goes back to the top of the loop and asks, "Is 16000 less than 10000?", since this time the answer is "No!", the loop stops running. On line 8 we print out the final value of **my_number**, which is 16000, as seen at the bottom of the preview area.

The best way to learn programming is to read code and try to make sense of it. This is why I provide numerous examples in which similar concepts are treated. Many educational books overwhelm you with technical details and specifications and leave you to learn on your own. My teaching method is quite different from that. I help you see the same concepts in action in many different contexts, helping you get a natural feel for the way programming works.

This page intentionally left blank

14. Conditionals and Comparisons

In programming, we often have a need to check whether a variable is this way or that way before we perform a certain operation on it.

Below, we are trying to develop a little program for a shopping website that checks whether the user is allowed to buy cigarettes or not based on their age. If they are allowed, the site would let them add cigarettes to their shopping cart, otherwise it will not. We will not actually build the complete code for the whole website's shopping cart mechanism, since that requires very advanced code. We are simply looking at a very small section of such a website's code.

```
1 ▾ <script>
2       var user_age = 28;
3       var can_purchase_cigarettes = false;
4 ▾     if(user_age >= 18) {
5           can_purchase_cigarettes = true;
6       }
7 </script>
```

Above, on line 2 we declare a variable named **user_age** with the number 28 inside it. In a real program the user age will be dynamically retrieved from a database, but that is a topic for another book. Here we are manually setting it to 28 for the sake of the example.

On line 3, we declare a variable named **can_purchase_cigarettes** with the value **false** inside it. This variable is neither a string nor a number. It is a *boolean*. Boolean variables, named after the self-taught English mathematician George Boole (died 1864), can only contain the values **true** or **false**. Note how there are no quotation marks around the word **false** on line 3. If it had quotations, it would merely be a string variable with the word "false" inside it. But when we omit the quotation marks, we are declaring a boolean variable.

At this point in your learning it may seem strange that there is a whole type of variable dedicated to truth and falsehood, but as you progress, you will see that boolean variables are an essential part of programming.

On line 3, by declaring **can_purchase_cigarettes** to be **false**, we are assuming that no one can purchase cigarettes unless it can be proved that they can do so in the lines that follow. On line 4 we have an **if** statement. Similar to the **while** statement, the **if** takes a condition between brackets and has a bunch of code between its curly braces. As you know, JavaScript ignores whitespace, so below is a completely functional **if** statement:

```
if(1 < 2) { document.write('Yes!'); }
```

Above, we are telling JavaScript to print out a "Yes!" if one is less than two. Since one is truly less than two, when the code runs, "Yes!" will be printed out in the document. There is no need to have a semicolon at the end of the curly braces (at the very end of the line above), because in JavaScript *code blocks* do not need semicolons to tell JavaScript the block is finished. The presence of the closing curly brace is sufficient for JavaScript know that this block of code is done. A code block is the stuff in curly braces and can be made up of multiple lines of code as we have seen in the previous examples.

The **while** statement is designed to run a block of code a number of times. The **if** statement, on the other hand, is designed to run the block of code just once, and *only* if the condition is true. If the condition is false, the block of code is ignored and JavaScript goes on running anything else that comes afterwards.

Let's take another look at the example we were working on earlier:

```
1  <script>
2      var user_age = 28;
3      var can_purchase_cigarettes = false;
4      if(user_age >= 18) {
5          can_purchase_cigarettes = true;
6      }
7  </script>
```

On line 4, we are checking whether the **user_age** variable *is greater than or equal to* 18. In JavaScript, **>=** means "greater than or equal to". The greater sign has to be written first, then the equal sign (if you write **=>** , this has a completely different meaning and has nothing to do with comparison).

In the **if** statement's code block, we are setting the value of the **can_purchase_cigarettes** variable to **true** on line 5. Since this code runs *only* if the condition on line 4 is true, what this means is that this variable only gets set to **true** if the user's age is 18 or more.

Now we can add some output to our example:

```
1  <script>
2      var user_age = 28;
3      var can_purchase_cigarettes = false;
4      if(user_age >= 18) {
5          can_purchase_cigarettes = true;
6      }
7
8      if(can_purchase_cigarettes === true) {
9          document.write('Click here to '
10             + 'view the cigarette section');
11
12     }
13     else {
14         document.write('Sorry, you cannot '
15             + 'view the cigarette section');
16     }
17  </script>
```

Click here to view the cigarette section

Above, we have added a new section of code starting from line 8. In this section of code, we are telling JavaScript to print out "Click here to view the cigarette section", but *only if* the value of **can_purchase_cigarettes** is **true**. In the preview on the right, you see that the "Click here…" message was printed out. That is because on line 5 we set the value of **can_purchase_cigarettes** to **true**. Since the condition on line 8 is satisfied, the code underneath it runs. If you click on the message that says "Click here…", nothing actually happens right now since more code is needed to turn the message into something interactive. But we are not adding that code to keep the example simple.

On line 13 we have something new. It is an **else** statement. The **else** statement is the companion of the **if** statement. You do not always need it, but it is handy when you do need it. In the **else** statement's code block we write the code that we want to be executed when the **if** statement's condition is not satisfied. We are saying: If the user can purchase cigarettes then do this, but if not, do this other thing in the **else** section.

Above, the **else** statement does not do anything because the **if** statement's condition is true. We can make the **else** statement run by setting the **user_age** variable to something less than 18, such as 17:

```
 i  1 ▾ <script>
    2       var user_age = 17;
    3       var can_purchase_cigarettes = false;
    4 ▾     if(user_age >= 18) {
    5           can_purchase_cigarettes = true;
    6       }
    7
    8 ▾     if(can_purchase_cigarettes === true) {
    9           document.write('Click here to '
   10           + 'view the cigarette section');
   11
   12       }
   13 ▾     else {
   14           document.write('Sorry, you cannot '
   15           + 'view the cigarette section');
   16       }
   17  </script>
```

Sorry, you cannot view the cigarette section

Above, the code is exactly the same as before except for line 2, where we declare that **user_age** is **17**. By changing line 2, we cause a whole cascade of effects on the rest of the program: The if statement on line 4 no longer runs since when JavaScript checks whether **user_age** is greater or equal to 18 behind the scenes, the answer is "No!". And this means that the code on line 5 is not executed, so that the value of **can_purchase_cigarettes** continues to be **false** because we declared it as **false** on line 3.

On line 8, we check if the variable **can_purchase_cigarettes** has the boolean value **true**. Since it does not, JavaScript ignores the **if** statement's code and jumps immediately to the **else** section. In the **else** section, we print out a message that tells the user they cannot view the cigarette section, and this is what we now see in the preview.

Multi-condition statements

We will now move on to a different example. In demographics, a country's "working age" population is defined as the population of people between the ages of 15 and 64. Below, we write a piece of code that decides whether someone is within the demographic working age or not based on their age.

```
i  1▾  <script>
   2        var user_age = 17;
   3        var is_in_demographic_working_age = false;
   4
   5▾       if(user_age >= 15 && user_age <= 64) {
   6            is_in_demographic_working_age = true;
   7        }
   8
   9▾       if(is_in_demographic_working_age === true) {
  10            document.write('You are in the '
  11                + 'demographic working age.');
  12        }
  13
  14  </script>
```

You are in the demographic working age.

Above, the first two lines of code are simple. We have a variable with a person's age inside it, and another variable that keeps track of whether this person is within the demographic working age range or not. By default, we set this variable to **false**.

On line 5, we have an **if** statement with multiple conditions, which is something new. We have to check if the user's age is at least 15 *and* at most 64. The double ampersand (**&&**) in JavaScript is used to mean "and" in conditionals. We use it when we want to ensure that the condition on both left and right of it are both true at the same time. In our example, the first condition is **user_age >= 15**, which is true, since the age is 17, which is greater than 15. The second condition is **user_age <= 64**, (**<=** means "less than or equal to"), which is also true, since the **user_age** is 17, which is less than 64. On line 6 we set **is_in_demographic_working_age** to **true** if both conditions are met. In the next **if** statement on lines 9 to 12, we print out a message if the user is within the demographic working age.

Below, we expand our code to determine whether the user is in the *legal* working age or not, which is different from the demographic working age. The legal working age is differs according to the country. Here we will use the US federal working age, which is any age 16 or older.

```
i  1 ▼ <script>
   2       var user_age = 17;
   3       var is_in_demographic_working_age = false;
   4       var is_in_legal_working_age = false;
   5
   6 ▼     if(user_age >= 15 && user_age <= 64) {
   7           is_in_demographic_working_age = true;
   8       }
   9
  10 ▼     if(user_age >= 16) {
  11           is_in_legal_working_age = true;
  12       }
  13
  14 ▼     if(is_in_demographic_working_age === true) {
  15           document.write('You are in the '
  16           + 'demographic working age.');
  17       }
  18
  19 ▼     if(is_in_legal_working_age === true) {
  20           document.write('<br>');
  21           document.write('You are in the '
  22           + 'legal working age.');
  23       }
  24
  25 </script>
```

You are in the demographic working age.
You are in the legal working age.

Above, we have added a new variable on line 4 to keep track of whether the user is in the legal working age or not. We also have a new **if** statement on lines 10-12. This statement's condition is simpler than the one before it because we merely need to check if the age is greater or equal to 16. There is no maximum age to worry about. On lines 19-23, we print out a second line that tells the user they are in the legal working age if they truly are. On line 20 I used the statement introduced earlier in the book to print out a new line, so that the second message shows up on its own line.

Below, I have updated the part of the code that prints out messages. I have added **else** statements to tell the user they are not within each age range if they are not.

```
14 ▼     if(is_in_demographic_working_age === true) {
15           document.write('You are in the '
16           + 'demographic working age.');
17       }
18 ▼     else {
19           document.write('You are not in the '
20           + 'demographic working age.');
21       }
22
23 ▼     if(is_in_legal_working_age === true) {
24           document.write('<br>');
25           document.write('You are in the '
26           + 'legal working age.');
27       }
28 ▼     else {
29           document.write('<br>');
30           document.write('You are not in the '
31           + 'legal working age');
32
33       }
```

Below I have set the age to 15 on line 2:

```
i  1 ▾ <script>
   2      var user_age = 15;
   3      var is_in_demographic_working_age = false;
   4      var is_in_legal_working_age = false;
```

> You are in the demographic working age.
> You are not in the legal working age

The age 15 is in the demographic working age but not in the legal working age, so for the second message, it is message in the **else** section (lines 28-33) that shows up.

If I change the user's age to 70, the message switch up, because 70 is not in the demographic working age while it is in the legal working age since the legal working age has no limit:

```
i  1 ▾ <script>
   2      var user_age = 70;
   3      var is_in_demographic_working_age = false;
   4      var is_in_legal_working_age = false;
```

> You are not in the demographic working age.
> You are in the legal working age.

Brackets

In programming, as in mathematics, we can use brackets to ensure that things happen in a certain order.

```
i  1 ▾ <script>
   2      var x = 2 * 4 + 3;
   3      var y = (2 * 4) + 3;
   4      var z = 2 * (4 + 3);
   5      document.write('x is ' + x);
   6      document.write('<br>');
   7      document.write('y is ' + y);
   8      document.write('<br>');
   9      document.write('z is ' + z);
  10  </script>
```

> x is 11
> y is 11
> z is 14

Above, we declare three variables and later print out their values. On lines 3 and 4 we add brackets into the calculation at different places. On line 3, we put **2 * 4** between brackets, telling JavaScript to perform this multiplication before adding the 3 at the end. Since this is what JavaScript would have done anyway whether we told it to or not, these brackets make no difference; the value of **x** and **y** is the same. On line 4, however, we add brackets between **4 + 3**. This makes a difference because now JavaScript carries out this addition operation before the multiplication. The result is that **z** ends up containing the number 14, since two times seven is fourteen.

"Or" conditions

We have already seen the double ampersand (**&&**) which is used to mean "and" in JavaScript conditionals. We also have the double pipe (**||**) which is used to mean "or". You type the pipe character by holding down Shift and pressing the backslash key on most keyboards.

In the following example, we have an imaginary school's website that parents, teachers and students can all use. The **user_type** variable keeps track of the type of user who is currently using the system. Sometimes there is a need to prevent students from seeing parts of the system that teachers and parents are allowed to see. Below, we implement the logic of how this should be done:

```
 i   1 ▾ <script>
     2       var user_type = 'teacher';
     3
     4       if(user_type === 'teacher'
     5 ▾       || user_type === 'parent') {
     6         document.write('Stuff only '
     7         + 'parents and teachers '
     8         + 'can see...');
     9       }
    10 ▾   else {
    11         document.write('Sorry, '
    12           + 'minors are not allowed '
    13           + 'to view this section');
    14       }
    15   </script>
```

Stuff only parents and teachers can see...

Above, we have broken the **if** statement's condition onto two lines (lines 4 and 5) to make it take up less space in the screenshot. Lines 4 and 5 have the exact same meaning as this:

```
if(user_type === 'teacher' || user_type === 'parent') {
```

The if statement's condition says that if the user is a teacher or a parent, then do the stuff that follows. Since we declared the **user_type** as **'teacher'** on line 2, we see that the if statement runs and prints out the message "Stuff only parents and teachers can see...".

If we change the user's type to "parent" on line 2, the same message is still shown:

```
i  1▾ <script>
   2      var user_type = 'parent';
   3      if(user_type === 'teacher'
   4▾        || user_type === 'parent') {
   5        document.write('Stuff only '
   6        + 'parents and teachers '
   7        + 'can see...');
   8      }
   9▾    else {
  10        document.write('Sorry, '
  11        + 'minors are not allowed '
  12        + 'to view this section');
  13      }
  14  </script>
```

Stuff only parents and teachers can see...

When JavaScript evaluates (i.e. runs or executes) the condition in the **if** statement, it first checks the left side of the condition: **user_type === 'teacher'**. This condition fails, since the user type does not equal "teacher". Since we are using the double pipe between the two conditions, JavaScript evaluates the condition on the right-hand side of the pipe: **user_type === 'parent'**. This condition does not fail, because the user type is indeed "parent". Therefore even though the first condition fails, since the second one succeeds, JavaScript executes the code inside the **if** statement's curly braces.

If we now change the user type to "student", the code of the **else** statement ends up running:

```
i  1▾ <script>
   2      var user_type = 'student';
   3      if(user_type === 'teacher'
   4▾        || user_type === 'parent') {
   5        document.write('Stuff only '
   6        + 'parents and teachers '
   7        + 'can see...');
   8      }
   9▾    else {
  10        document.write('Sorry, '
  11        + 'minors are not allowed '
  12        + 'to view this section');
  13      }
  14  </script>
```

Sorry, minors are not allowed to view this section

Now, we see the message "Sorry, minors are not allowed...".

Not equals

We have already seen that we can use the triple equal sign to check whether something is equal to something or not. We also have the "not equals" sign in programming:

```
i 1▾ <script>
  2      var number = 5;
  3▾     if(number !== 6) {
  4          document.write('The number is not six.');
  5      }
  6  </script>
```

The number is not six.

Above, we use JavaScript's "is not equal to" sign, which is an exclamation mark followed by two equal signs (**!==**) to check that **number** is not equal to 6. Since **number** contains the number 5, it really is not equal to six, therefore the condition is true and the code inside the **if** statement runs.

We often have multiple ways of achieving the same thing when programming. For example, below we rephrase the above code so that it no longer needs a "not equals" sign:

```
i 1▾ <script>
  2      var number = 5;
  3▾     if(number < 6 || number > 6) {
  4          document.write('The number is not six.');
  5      }
  6  </script>
```

The number is not six.

On line 3 above, we are saying that **number** should be either smaller than 6 or greater, which means that it should not be equal to six.

Mixed conditionals

We can mix the double pipe and double ampersand in the same conditional when necessary. Below we have an imaginary game where we have a warrior with certain powers. The warrior will be able to perform certain feats if certain conditions are true.

```
i 1▾ <script>
  2      var charisma = 5;
  3      var intelligence = 5;
  4      var strength = 10;
  5      var armor = 10;
  6      var can_defeat_dragon = false;
```

We have the variables **charisma**, **intelligence** and **strength** which keep track of the player's powers. In a real game these variables will change as the user progresses in the game. The **can_defeat_dragon** keeps track of whether the player has the power to defeat dragons or not. In this game, users can defeat dragons either by having high charisma and intelligence (so that they can outwit it), or by having very high strength and armor (so that they can defeat it in battle). We will now go about implementing these conditions in code:

```
i  1▼ <script>
   2      var charisma = 5;
   3      var intelligence = 5;
   4      var strength = 10;
   5      var armor = 10;
   6      var can_defeat_dragon = false;
   7
   8▼     if(charisma > 10 && intelligence > 10) {
   9          can_defeat_dragon = true;
   10     }
   11▼    if(armor > 100 && strength > 100) {
   12         can_defeat_dragon = true;
   13     }
   14
   15     document.write('Can you defeat a dragon? ');
   16
   17▼    if(can_defeat_dragon) {
   18         document.write('Yes');
   19     }
   20▼    else {
   21         document.write('No');
   22     }
   23 </script>
```

Can you defeat a dragon? No

In the **if** statement on lines 8-10, we set **can_defeat_dragon** to **true** if the player has both a **charisma** higher than 10 and an **intelligence** higher than 10. On lines 11-13, in a different if statement, we set **can_defeat_dragon** to **true** if the player has both an **armor** of 100 and **strength** of 100. Below that we have some output statements telling the user whether they can defeat dragons or not.

Now, if we increase both the **charisma** and the **intelligence** to 10 on lines 2 and 3, nothing changes:

```
i  1▼ <script>
   2      var charisma = 10;
   3      var intelligence = 10;
```

Can you defeat a dragon? No

That is because in the condition on line 8, we are requiring that the **charisma** and **intelligence** should be *more than 10*. This means that 10 is not enough, they have to be more. This is a common cause for programming errors, when programmers mistakenly write "greater than" when they mean "greater than or equal to". Below we increase the **charisma** and **intelligence** both to 11, which does satisfy the requirements for defeating dragons:

```
i  1▼ <script>
   2      var charisma = 11;
   3      var intelligence = 11;
```

Can you defeat a dragon? Yes

We can merge the two **if** statements on lines 8 to 13 into a single statement that accomplishes the same thing, as follows:

```
i  1 ▾ <script>
   2       var charisma = 11;
   3       var intelligence = 11;
   4       var strength = 10;
   5       var armor = 10;
   6       var can_defeat_dragon = false;
   7
   8       if((charisma > 10 && intelligence > 10)
   9 ▾        || (armor > 100 && strength > 100)) {
  10           can_defeat_dragon = true;
  11       }
```

Can you defeat a dragon? Yes

Above, we have used brackets to separate the two sets of conditions. Below I have written the **if** statement's condition section on one line and added some extra space to make it easier to understand:

```
if(  (charisma > 10 && intelligence > 10) || (armor > 100 && strength > 100)  ) {
```

JavaScript first evaluates (i.e. checks the value of) the condition on the left of the double pipe: **(charisma > 10 && intelligence > 10)** and since this condition is true, the statement runs. Similar to mathematics, JavaScript first evaluates the stuff inside brackets. If we were to change the positions of the extra brackets, we would get erroneous results:

```
   8       if(charisma > 10 && (intelligence > 10
   9 ▾        || armor > 100) && strength > 100) {
  10           can_defeat_dragon = true;
  11       }
```

Above, I have changed things so that it is now **intelligence** and **armor** that are in brackets: **(intelligence > 10 || armor > 100)**. The meaning of this new **if** statement is that the player should have a **charisma** higher than 10, and an **intelligence** higher than 10 or **armor** higher than 100, and a **strength** greater than 100, in order to be able to defeat a dragon. Now if we set the **charisma** and **intelligence** extremely high, they do nothing to help the player defeat the dragon if they do not also have high strength. By changing the position of brackets, the meaning of the conditionals completely changes.

```
i  1 ▾ <script>
   2       var charisma = 100;
   3       var intelligence = 100;
   4       var strength = 100;
   5       var armor = 10;
   6       var can_defeat_dragon = false;
   7
   8       if(charisma > 10 && (intelligence > 10
   9 ▾        || armor > 100) && strength > 100) {
  10           can_defeat_dragon = true;
  11       }
```

Can you defeat a dragon? No

15. Further Loops

We have already looked at **while** loops, used for making JavaScript repeatedly do something. There are other types of loops that we use in programming, one of which is the **for** loop. But before we talk about **for** loops, we have to talk about incrementing and decrementing.

Incrementing and Decrementing

If you have a variable with a number inside it, such as 5, you can increase its value by 1 (to make it 6) as follows:

```
i  1 ▾ <script>
   2      var my_number = 5;
   3      my_number = my_number + 1;
   4      document.write(my_number);
   5    </script>
```
6

Above, even though we assign the number 5 to **my_number** on line 2, since we add one to it and assign the result back to the variable on line 3, the number 6 gets printed out in the preview area.

JavaScript provides us with a shorthand for doing this, as follows:

```
i  1 ▾ <script>
   2      var my_number = 5;
   3      my_number++;
   4      document.write(my_number);
   5    </script>
```
6

The meaning of the above code is the same as before, but we are now using the *increment operator* (two plus signs without spaces). When we put **++** after a variable name, we tell JavaScript to increase the variable's value by one. Behind the scenes, JavaScript checks the variable's value (which in the above example is the number 5), finds out the result of increasing it by one (which is the number 6), then changes the variable by putting the new number inside it.

We also have the *decrement operator* which is made up of two minus signs. This operator decreases a variable's value by one:

```
i  1 ▾ <script>
   2        var my_number = 5;                        4
   3        my_number--;
   4        document.write(my_number);
   5   </script>
```

Above, the number 4 gets printed out because on line 3 we use the decrement operator to decrease the value of **my_number** by one. Note that on line 3 we have a semicolon at the end. This is necessary since **my_number--** is a complete statement and needs to be terminated by a semicolon like any other statement. If we repeatedly decrement a variable, each time we take one away from it. Below, we turn the variable's value from 5 to zero using five decrement statements:

```
i  1 ▾ <script>
   2        var my_number = 5;                        0
   3        my_number--;
   4        my_number--;
   5        my_number--;
   6        my_number--;
   7        my_number--;
   8        document.write(my_number);
   9   </script>
```

For loops

Below is an example of a very simple **for** loop:

```
i  1 ▾ <script>
   2 ▾    for(var i = 1; i < 5; i++) {           Hello!
   3           document.write('Hello!' + '<br>');  Hello!
   4        }                                      Hello!
   5   </script>                                   Hello!
   6
```

In the above block of code, we tell JavaScript to print out "Hello" four times. To understand what is going on, let's examine the stuff on line 2 in detail. After the for, we have brackets that contain three sections of code, like this:

for(section 1 ; section 2 ; section 3)

Each section is separated from the others by a semicolon. In the first section, we declare a variable we want to use to control how many times the loop will run. This first section is a simple variable declaration like we have already seen numerous times:

var i = 1;

The variable is named **i**. It is common practice to name this variable **i**, but it can be named anything else we want.

In the second section, we declare the condition that JavaScript should check with every iteration of the loop (each time the code of the loop runs). The condition we have provided above is **i < 5**. This means that the loop should run as long as the value of the variable **i** is less than five.

In the third section, we give JavaScript a statement that should run with each iteration of the loop. This section is generally used to make a change to the value of **i** that affects whether the loop continues running or not. The statement we have given it is an increment statement: **i++**. This means that every time the loop runs, the value of **i** should be increased by one.

Let's now take another look at our example **for** loop:

```
1   <script>
2       for(var i = 1; i < 5; i++) {          Hello!
3           document.write('Hello!' + '<br>');  Hello!
4       }                                       Hello!
5   </script>                                   Hello!
6
```

When JavaScript runs the above code, what takes place is that first it creates a variable named **i**. Then it checks whether the variable satisfies the condition **i < 5**. Since it does, JavaScript runs the code inside the **for** loop's curly braces, so that a "Hello!" is printed out followed by a new line. Once JavaScript gets to the bottom of the **for** loop (once it gets to the closing curly brace), it runs the statement in the third section of the code on line 2, increasing the value of **i** by one, so that now **i** will have a value of 2 behind the scenes.

Then JavaScript goes back to the top of the loop, checks the condition on line 2 to see if it is still true (it checks whether two is less than five), then runs the code again, then at the end increases **i** by one, then jumps back to the top, and so on and so forth.

The first section of the code on line 2, where we declare the variable **i**, only runs once at the beginning. The other two sections run with every iteration.

We can make use of the variable **i** inside the loop's code. We can for example check what its value is with each iteration:

```
 i   1 ▾ <script>
     2 ▾     for(var i = 1; i < 5; i++) {
     3             document.write(i + '<br>');
     4             document.write('Hello!' + '<br>');
     5         }
     6   </script>
     7
     8
     9
    10
    11
```

```
1
Hello!
2
Hello!
3
Hello!
4
Hello!
```

Above, we see that at first the value of **i** is 1. It increases with each iteration until it becomes 4. Then the loop ends. The reason the loop ends is that at the end of the fourth iteration, JavaScript runs **i++**, which turns the value of **i** into 5. Then it checks whether **i** is less than five before deciding whether to run the loop another time. Since the value of **i** is no longer less than five, the loop finishes running.

Let's now check out a new example:

```
 i   1 ▾ <script>
     2 ▾     for(var i = 1; i > -5; i--) {
     3             document.write(i + '<br>');
     4         }
     5   </script>
     6
     7
     8
     9
```

```
1
0
-1
-2
-3
-4
```

Above, we start out by declaring **i** to be 1. But the condition is now different, **i > -5** means that the loop should run as long as **i** is greater than minus five. In the third section on line 2, we have **i--** (rather than **i++**). This means that we decrease the value of **i** by one with each iteration. The result, as you see, is that the value of **i** decreases each time until it reaches -4, at which point the loop finishes.

Similar to a **while** loop, **for** loops can lead to infinite loops that never finish running and that cause your browser to crash. Below is an example of an infinite **for** loop:

```
 i   1 ▾ <script>
     2 ▾     for(var i = 1; i > -5; i++) {
     3             document.write(i + '<br>');
     4         }
     5   </script>
```

The problem with this loop is in the third section on line 2 (everything else is similar to the code in the previous screenshot). We are telling JavaScript to print out the value of **i** as long as it is greater than minus five. The problem is that since we are increasing i with each iteration (since it is now **i++** rather than **i--**), *the value of **i** will never stop being greater than -5*. In fact, the value of **i** will continue increasing indefinitely, so that the condition **i > -5** will always be true. The result is that this loop will continue running until your computer uses all the energy in the universe, or until your browser crashes, whichever comes first.

If the syntax of the **for** loop still seems mysterious and difficult to understand, this is perfectly fine. It will take much practice before it starts to make intuitive sense.

Moving on, below we have a for loop that uses neither the increment or decrement operator in the third section on line 2. It rather uses the new statement **i = i * 2**. This means that JavaScript should multiple the value of **i** with every iteration.

```
1 ▾ <script>
2 ▾     for(var i = 1; i < 100; i = i * 2) {
3           document.write(i + '<br>');
4       }
5   </script>
6
7
8
9
10
```

```
1
2
4
8
16
32
64
```

The result is obvious. JavaScript keeps doubling the value of **i** and printing it out until the condition **i < 100** stops being true.

Anything you put in the third section of a **for** loop should be a *complete JavaScript statement*. If we had merely put **i * 2**, we would have caused an infinite loop:

```
1 ▾ <script>
2 ▾     for(var i = 1; i < 100; i * 2) {
3           document.write(i + '<br>');
4       }
5   </script>
```

Above, with each iteration, JavaScript multiplies **i** by two then *throws away the result*, since we do not have **i =** in front of it. We are basically telling JavaScript to run the loop as long as **i** is less than 100 without telling it to do anything to the value of **i**, so that **i** forever remains 1.

To understand this better, consider the following code:

```
1 ▾ <script>
2       var i = 1;
3       i * 2;
4       document.write(i);
5   </script>
```

```
1
```

A beginner might expect the code on line 3 to cause the value of **i** to become 2. But as you can see in the preview, when we print out the value of **i** on line 4, we get 1 rather than 2. The code on line

3 is actually useless, because it should be **i = i * 2**. If we merely write **i * 2**, this tells JavaScript to find out the result of **i** times two, but it does not tell it to do anything with the result, so JavaScript performs the calculation behind the scenes then throws away the result.

Here is an example:

```
i   1▾ <script>
    2       var i = 1;
    3       5 * 5 * 5;
    4       document.write(i);
    5   </script>
```
```
1
```

Above, on line 3 we tell JavaScript to multiply five by five by five. But since we do not tell JavaScript to do anything with the result, the calculation takes place behind the scenes then JavaScript throws away the result. In order for JavaScript not to throw away the result, we have to either tell it to print it out, as follows:

```
i   1▾ <script>
    2       var i = 1;
    3       document.write(5 * 5 * 5);
    4       document.write('<br>');
    5       document.write(i);
    6   </script>
```
```
125
1
```

Or we have to put the result inside some variable, as follows:

```
i   1▾ <script>
    2       var i = 1;
    3       var j = 5 * 5 * 5;
    4       document.write(i);
    5       document.write('<br>');
    6       document.write(j);
    7   </script>
```
```
1
125
```

Below, we have another example of a useless piece of JavaScript:

```
i   1▾ <script>
    2       'hello';
    3   </script>
```

The above is perfectly valid JavaScript code, similar to writing **5 * 5 * 5**. It tells JavaScript to evaluate the value of **'hello'** but without telling it to do anything with it. So JavaScript dutifully looks at the string **'hello'** and sees that it is good, then forgets about it. The code works, it just doesn't do anything we humans would consider useful.

Never loops

A never loop is a loop that never runs. Below is an example:

```
i 1▾ <script>
  2▾     for(var i = 1; i > 50; i++) {
  3            document.write(i + '<br>');
  4        }
  5  </script>
```

On line 3, we tell JavaScript to continue running the loop as long as **i** is greater than 50. But since **i** is 1 at the beginning, the condition is false from the start, so the loop ends immediately without printing anything out.

```
i 1▾ <script>
  2        var my_number = 0;
  3▾     while(my_number === 1) {
  4            document.write(my_number);
  5        }
  6  </script>
```

Above, on line 3, we are saying the loop should run as long as **my_number** equals 1. But since on line 2 we have declared that **my_number** is zero, this condition is false from the start, so the code inside the while loop's curly braces never runs. JavaScript simply ignores it and goes on to run any code that might be below it, as follows:

```
i 1▾ <script>
  2        var my_number = 0;
  3▾     while(my_number === 1) {
  4            document.write(my_number);
  5        }
  6        document.write('Here we are.');
  7  </script>
```

Here we are.

16. Functions

In programming, functions allow us to name a block of code and reuse it later on. Below is an example:

```
 i  1 ▼ <script>
    2 ▼     function newline() {
    3             document.write('<br>');
    4         }
    5
    6         document.write('First line.');
    7         newline();
    8         document.write('Second line.');
    9   </script>
```

First line.
Second line.

On lines 2-4, we define a function named **newline()**. The function name is followed by brackets for reasons that will become clear later on. After the brackets we have curly braces, then the actual code of the function. What this function does is that it prints out a new line. You see the function used on line 7. On line 6, we write out a line. On line 7 we *call* the **newline** function, and on line 8 we write out a second line.

A function name can be anything we want, similar to variable names, and similar to variable names, there are some characters you are not allowed to use in the name, such as dashes.

When we write **newline();** on line 7, it is as if we had written **document.write('<br>');**. Behind the scenes, every time JavaScript sees the statement **newline()**, it performs the action inside the **newline** function.

Below, we call the **newline()** function twice, causing two new lines to be printed out:

```
i  1▾ <script>
   2▾     function newline() {
   3             document.write('<br>');
   4         }
   5
   6         document.write('First line.');
   7         newline();
   8         newline();
   9         document.write('Second line.');
  10  </script>
```

First line.

Second line.

When we define the **newline()** function on lines 2-4, this does not cause anything to happen just yet. JavaScript stores the code inside the function until we *call* it. Above, we call the function twice, on lines 7 and 8.

If we remove the calls to **newline()**, the function will not do anything:

```
i  1▾ <script>
   2▾     function newline() {
   3             document.write('<br>');
   4         }
   5
   6         document.write('First line.');
   7         document.write('Second line.');
   8  </script>
```

First line.Second line.

When you declare a function, you are telling JavaScript to hold this piece of code in memory until you have a need for it later on.

Below we have a little program that greets a user in different ways based on their language. If the user's language is English, the program says "Hello", while if the user's language is French, it says "Bonjour":

```
i  1▾ <script>
   2         var user_name = 'James';
   3         var user_language = 'English';
   4
   5▾     function greetings() {
   6▾         if(user_language === 'English') {
   7                 document.write('Hello');
   8             }
   9▾         else if(user_language === 'French') {
  10                 document.write('Bonjour');
  11             }
  12         }
  13
  14         greetings();
  15         document.write(' ');
  16         document.write(user_name);
  17         document.write('!');
  18  </script>
```

Hello James!

Inside the **greetings()** function on lines 5 to 12, we check the **user_language** variable, and based on its value, we either write out "Hello" or "Bonjour". Above, you see the **else if** statement, which is used to check a condition once the condition before it proves to be false. We are telling JavaScript: If the language is English, then do this, *but if* the language is French, then do this other thing. We could have also added an else at the end to tell JavaScript what to do if the language is neither English nor French.

On lines 14-17, we start to actually write out some stuff. First, we call the **greetings()** function, which ends up writing out a "Hello". Then we write out a space (line 15), the user's name (line 16) and finally an exclamation mark (line 17).

Every time we call the **greetings()** function, JavaScript checks the user's language to see whether it should write out a "Hello" or a "Bonjour".

Below, we have the same code as above while adding some additional lines to it starting from line 20. We change the **user_name** variable to "Marcel" and we change the **user_language** to "French".

```
1 ▾ <script>
2       var user_name = 'James';
3       var user_language = 'English';
4
5 ▾     function greetings() {
6 ▾         if(user_language === 'English') {
7               document.write('Hello');
8           }
9 ▾         else if(user_language === 'French') {
10              document.write('Bonjour');
11          }
12      }
13
14      greetings();
15      document.write(' ');
16      document.write(user_name);
17      document.write('!');
18      document.write('<br>');
19
20      user_name = 'Marcel';
21      user_language = 'French';
22      greetings();
23      document.write(' ');
24      document.write(user_name);
25      document.write('!');
26      document.write('<br>');
27 </script>
```

Hello James!
Bonjour Marcel!

Above, on line 22 we have another call to the **greetings()** function, but note that this time it writes out a "Bonjour", because we changed the user's language on line 21 to French.

Below, I have renamed the greetings() function to **greet_user()** and added some extra code to its end:

```
5    function greet_user() {
6        if(user_language === 'English') {
7            document.write('Hello');
8        }
9        else if(user_language === 'French') {
10            document.write('Bonjour');
11        }
12        document.write(' ');
13        document.write(user_name);
14        document.write('!');
15    }
```

Now, the function checks the user's language and greets them, and *also* prints out a space, the user's name and an exclamation mark. All of these actions happen every time we call **greet_user()**, as follows:

```
1    <script>
2        var user_name = 'James';
3        var user_language = 'English';
4
5        function greet_user() {
6            if(user_language === 'English') {
7                document.write('Hello');
8            }
9            else if(user_language === 'French') {
10                document.write('Bonjour');
11            }
12            document.write(' ');
13            document.write(user_name);
14            document.write('!');
15        }
16
17        greet_user();
18        document.write('<br>');
19
20        user_name = 'Marcel';
21        user_language = 'French';
22        greet_user();
23        document.write('<br>');
24    </script>
```

```
Hello James!
Bonjour Marcel!
```

Above, on line 17 we call **greet_user()**, which prints out "Hello James!". Then we print out a new line on line 18. Next we change the user's name to "Marcel" and the user's language to "French", then call **greet_user()** again on line 22. This time it prints out "Bonjour Marcel!".

The great power of functions is that they help us use the same piece of code in multiple places, which helps make our programs shorter and easier to understand.

Moving on, below we have a different program that calculates an employee's new salary based on their performance rating. The rating can either be A, B, or C.

```
1  <script>
2      var employee_performance = 'A';
3      var salary = 50000;
4
5      function show_new_salary() {
6          document.write('Your new salary is ');
7          if(employee_performance === 'A') {
8              document.write(salary * 1.1);
9          }
10         else if(employee_performance === 'B') {
11             document.write(salary * 1.05);
12         }
13         else {
14             document.write(salary);
15         }
16     }
17
18     show_new_salary();
19 </script>
```

Your new salary is 55000.00000000001

The **show_new_salary()** function writes out "Your new salary is " followed by a number. If the **employee_performance** variable equals "A", the salary is multiplied by 1.1, meaning it is increased by 10%. If the performance is "B", it is instead multiplied by 1.05, meaning it is increased by only 5%. And if their performance is something else, no promotion is applied.

Since on line 2 we declared the performance as "A", when we call **show_new_salary()** on line 18, the promotion on line 8 is applied and printed out, which is what you see in the preview area. The salary shown is 55000, a 10% increase over 50000.

You may notice that the salary shown is not exactly 55000, it is rather 55000.00000000001. That is caused by the way JavaScript performs calculations behind the scenes. JavaScript performs *approximate* calculations when doing things like multiplication and division, which result in strange results like the above. The root cause has to do with the way numbers are represented inside the computer's memory. To avoid that, we have to use certain mathematical operations to round the resulting number to an integer:

419

```
i   1 ▾  <script>
    2        var employee_performance = 'A';
    3        var salary = 50000;
    4
    5 ▾      function show_new_salary() {
    6            document.write('Your new salary is ');
    7            var new_salary = salary;
    8
    9 ▾          if(employee_performance === 'A') {
   10                new_salary = Math.floor(salary * 1.1);
   11            }
   12 ▾          else if(employee_performance === 'B') {
   13                new_salary = Math.floor(salary * 1.05);
   14            }
   15 ▾          else {
   16
   17            }
   18            document.write(new_salary);
   19        }
   20
   21        show_new_salary();
   22  </script>
```

Your new salary is 55000

Above, I have made some changes to the **show_new_salary()** function. On line 7, I declare a new variable called **new_salary** and place inside it the number that is already inside **salary**. This means that we assume the new salary is the same as the old salary unless proven otherwise later on. Since the **employee_performance** is "A", the code on line 10 runs. In this line of code, perform the same calculation as before by multiplying the **salary** by 1.1 to increase it by 10%. But this time we have enclosed the calculation between the **Math.floor()** function. The **Math.floor()** function is a built-in JavaScript function that rounds down a number with decimal points to an integer. It takes a number and shows us what the number is if we take away everything after the decimal point.

Finally, on line 18 we print out **new_salary**, which is 55000.

Notice that on line 16, the **else** statement is now empty. That is because there is nothing for the **else** statement to do anymore. Since on line 7 we assume that **new_salary** is the same as **salary**, if the performance is anything besides "A" or "B", the **new_salary** will be the same as **salary** without any need for additional statements. Since the **else** statement is empty, we can remove it:

```
    9 ▾          if(employee_performance === 'A') {
   10                new_salary = Math.floor(salary * 1.1);
   11            }
   12 ▾          else if(employee_performance === 'B') {
   13                new_salary = Math.floor(salary * 1.05);
   14            }
   15            document.write(new_salary);
   16        }
```

To illustrate that it is still functioning correctly, I will now change the performance to "C":

```
i   1▾ <script>
    2       var employee_performance = 'C';
    3       var salary = 50000;
    4
    5▾     function show_new_salary() {
    6           document.write('Your new salary is ');
    7           var new_salary = salary;
    8
    9▾         if(employee_performance === 'A') {
   10               new_salary = Math.floor(salary * 1.1);
   11           }
   12▾         else if(employee_performance === 'B') {
   13               new_salary = Math.floor(salary * 1.05);
   14           }
   15           document.write(new_salary);
   16       }
   17
   18       show_new_salary();
   19 </script>
```

Your new salary is 50000

As you can see, the salary remains at 50000, because inside the **show_new_salary()** function JavaScript sets **new_salary** to **salary** on line 7, then checks whether the performance is "A" or "B", and since it is not, it ends up writing out **new_salary** without making changes to it.

Below, after printing out the first employee's new salary, we change the variables, presumably dealing with a different employee whose old salary is 75000 and whose performance is "A":

```
   18       show_new_salary();
   19       document.write('<br>');
   20
   21       employee_performance = 'A';
   22       salary = 75000;
   23       show_new_salary();
   24 </script>
```

Here is the result:

Your new salary is 50000
Your new salary is 82500

Functions with inputs

In everyday programming, most functions take *inputs*, something our functions have not done so far. **Math.floor()** is an example of a function that takes inputs: you give it a number, it gives you a result.

Below, we have a function that doubles any number we give to it:

```
1 ▾ <script>
2 ▾     function double_this(number) {
3           var new_number = number * 2;
4           return new_number;
5       }
6
7       document.write(double_this(50));
8 </script>
```

```
100
```

On line 2, we declare a function named **double_this()**. This function takes a variable called **number**. And it *returns* a variable named **new_number**. On line 7, we write out the result of **double_this(50)**, which results in 100 being shown in the preview area.

Let's now look at the function definition. A *function definition* is the term we use for the whole block of code in which we define a function, meaning lines 2-5 above. On line 2, inside the brackets we have the word **number**. This causes a variable to be created inside the function with the name of **number**. JavaScript automatically puts inside this variable anything we *pass* to the function when we make use of the function. Since on line 7 we pass the number 50 to the **double_this()** function, this causes the **number** variable to have 50 inside it.

On line 3, we declare a new variable named **new_number**, which has value of **number** multiplied by two. On line 4 we have something new, the **return** statement. In this statement we tell JavaScript what the function should *return*, meaning what the function should "print out" when we use it. Writing **return new_number;** means "whenever this function is called, give back **new_number** as the result".

This can be a bit difficult for a beginner to understand. This is perfectly fine, since here we are dealing with a very complex part of programming. Once you have understood how functions work, you will have mastered the basics of programming.

To further clarify, below I have kept the function the same as before while changing the stuff after it. The meaning of the code is the same as before:

```
i  1 ▾ <script>
   2 ▾     function double_this(number) {                    100
   3             var new_number = number * 2;
   4             return new_number;
   5         }
   6
   7         var my_number = 50;
   8         var my_doubled_number = double_this(my_number);
   9         document.write(my_doubled_number);
  10  </script>
```

On line 8, I declare the variable **my_doubled_number**. The value we assign to this variable is the result of double_this(my_number). This tells JavaScript to put **my_number** inside the **double_this()** function, then put inside **my_doubled_number** whatever is returned by the function. Think of the function as a machine. Something goes in, something else comes out.

Below we use **double_this()** to double a bunch of different numbers on lines 7, 9 and 11:

```
i  1 ▾ <script>
   2 ▾     function double_this(number) {                    20
   3             var new_number = number * 2;                 40
   4             return new_number;                           66
   5         }
   6
   7         document.write(double_this(10));
   8         document.write('<br>');
   9         document.write(double_this(20));
  10         document.write('<br>');
  11         document.write(double_this(33));
  12  </script>
```

Doubling a number is not a very impressive mathematical operation. Let's create a function that checks whether a number is odd or not:

```
i  1 ▾ <script>
   2 ▾     function is_odd(number) {
   3             var divided_by_two = number / 2;
   4             var rounded = Math.floor(divided_by_two);
   5 ▾         if(rounded === divided_by_two) {
   6                 return false;
   7             }
   8 ▾         else {
   9                 return true;
  10             }
  11         }
```

What we have inside the above function is an *algorithm*, a word named after the Persian mathematician al-Khwarizmi (died 850 CE). An algorithm is a step-by-step set of instructions for discovering the value of something. On line 2 of the function, we divide the **number** variable (the number the user is checking for oddness or evenness) by two. If it is an even number, the division will not lead to a decimal point (for example dividing 20 by two results in 10 without any decimals).

While if it is an odd number, the result will contain stuff after the decimal point (for example, dividing 3 by 2 results in 1.5). We use this fact to detect whether a number is odd or even. On line 4, we round down the divided number to the nearest integer. If **divided_by_two** contains a whole number, rounding will have no effect on it (if we divided 20 by 2, the result would be 10, and rounding it would still give us 10). But if it contains a number with stuff after the decimals, rounding it would cause that stuff to be thrown away, so that the **rounded** number ends up being different from **divided_by_two**.

On line 5, we check whether rounding made a difference or not. If **rounded** is exactly the same as **divided_by_two**, it means rounding made no difference, which means **divided_by_two** had no fractional part, which means the number is even, therefore we return the boolean value of "false", meaning **number** is not odd. In the **else** part, we return "true", meaning **number** is odd. Below is an example of how we can make use of the **is_odd()** function:

```
 i   1 ▾  <script>
     2 ▾     function is_odd(number) {
     3            var divided_by_two = number / 2;
     4            var rounded = Math.floor(divided_by_two);
     5 ▾          if(rounded === divided_by_two) {
     6                return false;
     7            }
     8 ▾          else {
     9                return true;
    10            }
    11        }
    12
    13        var age = 55;
    14        document.write('Your age is ');
    15 ▾      if(is_odd(age) === true) {
    16            document.write('odd');
    17        }
    18 ▾      else {
    19            document.write('even');
    20        }
    21    </script>
```

Your age is odd

On line 15, **is_odd(age) === true** means "does the **is_odd()** function return **true** when you pass it the value of the **age** variable? JavaScript runs the **is_odd()** function by putting the number 55 into the **number** variable and performing the rest of the calculations. If on line 9 the value that is returned is **true**, then the code on line 16 runs. Otherwise the code on line 19 runs. Below we change **age** to 22:

```
i  1▾ <script>
   2▾     function is_odd(number) {
   3           var divided_by_two = number / 2;
   4           var rounded = Math.floor(divided_by_two);
   5▾         if(rounded === divided_by_two) {
   6               return false;
   7           }
   8▾         else {
   9               return true;
  10           }
  11       }
  12
  13       var age = 22;
  14       document.write('Your age is ');
  15▾     if(is_odd(age) === true) {
  16           document.write('odd');
  17       }
  18▾     else {
  19           document.write('even');
  20       }
  21  </script>
```

Your age is even

Below, we have a loop in which we use the **is_odd()** function to check whether the numbers from 1 to 9 are odd or even:

```
i  1▾ <script>
   2▾     function is_odd(number) {
   3           var divided_by_two = number / 2;
   4           var rounded = Math.floor(divided_by_two);
   5▾         if(rounded === divided_by_two) {
   6               return false;
   7           }
   8▾         else {
   9               return true;
  10           }
  11       }
  12
  13▾     for(var i = 1; i < 10; i++) {
  14           document.write('The number ' + i + ' is ');
  15▾         if(is_odd(i) === true) {
  16               document.write('odd');
  17           }
  18▾         else {
  19               document.write('even');
  20           }
  21           document.write('<br>');
  22       }
  23  </script>
```

The number 1 is odd
The number 2 is even
The number 3 is odd
The number 4 is even
The number 5 is odd
The number 6 is even
The number 7 is odd
The number 8 is even
The number 9 is odd

With each iteration of the loop, JavaScript passes the value of **i** to the **is_odd()** function on line 15, which determines whether the word "odd" will be printed out on line 16 or the word "even" on line 19. Before the end of each iteration, we print out a new line on line 21 so that the next line of text should start on a new line.

Below, we have the same loop as the above converted to a while loop:

```
i  1▼ <script>
   2▼     function is_odd(number) {
   3           var divided_by_two = number / 2;
   4           var rounded = Math.floor(divided_by_two);
   5▼          if(rounded === divided_by_two) {
   6               return false;
   7           }
   8▼          else {
   9               return true;
  10           }
  11       }
  12
  13       var number_to_check = 1;
  14▼      while(number_to_check < 10) {
  15           document.write('The number ' +
  16             number_to_check + ' is ');
  17▼          if(is_odd(number_to_check) === true) {
  18               document.write('odd');
  19           }
  20▼          else {
  21               document.write('even');
  22           }
  23           document.write('<br>');
  24
  25           number_to_check++;
  26       }
  27 </script>
```

The number 1 is odd
The number 2 is even
The number 3 is odd
The number 4 is even
The number 5 is odd
The number 6 is even
The number 7 is odd
The number 8 is even
The number 9 is odd

The code should be self-explanatory, except for line 25. Without line 25, the above loop would be an infinite loop, because **number_to_check** will always remain at 1 unless we do something to it inside the loop. If we do nothing to it, the condition on line 14 will always be true. What we do on line 25 is increase the number by one, so that on the next iteration the loop should deal with the number that comes after it. In this way the number eventually reaches 10, which causes the loop to stop running.

Moving on, we can make use of one function to build another function. For example, let's say we want to make an **is_even()** function to check whether a number is even or odd. Instead of building a whole new function from scratch, we can make use of **is_odd()** from before:

```
i   1▾  <script>
    2▾      function is_odd(number) {
    3               var divided_by_two = number / 2;
    4               var rounded = Math.floor(divided_by_two);
    5▾              if(rounded === divided_by_two) {
    6                   return false;
    7               }
    8▾              else {
    9                   return true;
    10              }
    11          }
    12
    13▾     function is_even(number) {
    14▾          if(is_odd(number) === false) {
    15                  return true;
    16              }
    17▾          else {
    18                  return false;
    19              }
    20          }
    21  </script>
```

Above, we have the same code as before from lines 2-11. We then have the new **is_even()** function. This function merely checks whether a number is odd using the **is_odd()** function from before. If it is not odd, it returns **true**, otherwise it returns **false**. In this way, the **is_even()** function does not need to do any mathematical heavy lifting, it leaves it all to the **is_odd()** function.

Moving on, earlier we had the following example for calculating an employee's new salary based on their performance:

```
i   1▾  <script>
    2           var employee_performance = 'C';
    3           var salary = 50000;
    4
    5▾      function show_new_salary() {
    6               document.write('Your new salary is ');
    7               var new_salary = salary;
    8
    9▾              if(employee_performance === 'A') {
    10                  new_salary = Math.floor(salary * 1.1);
    11              }
    12▾             else if(employee_performance === 'B') {
    13                  new_salary = Math.floor(salary * 1.05);
    14              }
    15              document.write(new_salary);
    16          }
    17
    18      show_new_salary();
    19  </script>
```

Your new salary is 50000

The **show_new_salary()** function is not actually a good function in programming because it is making use of variables outside of it. If you move this function to a different web page, the function might fail miserably if someone forgets to declare the **employee_performance** and **salary** variables above it. In real-world programming, the code might go on for thousands of lines and you can never rely on some variable being available. To turn it into a good function, we have to turn it into a function that take the employee performance and salary as inputs, rather than accessing them randomly. Below is the improved example:

```
i  1 ▾ <script>
   2       var employee_performance = 'A';
   3       var salary = 45000;
   4
   5 ▾     function show_new_salary(salary, perf) {
   6           document.write('Your new salary is ');
   7           var new_salary = salary;
   8
   9 ▾         if(perf === 'A') {
  10               new_salary = Math.floor(salary * 1.1);
  11           }
  12 ▾         else if(perf === 'B') {
  13               new_salary = Math.floor(salary * 1.05);
  14           }
  15           document.write(new_salary);
  16       }
  17
  18       show_new_salary(salary, employee_performance);
  19 </script>
```

Your new salary is 49500

Above, we have changed the **show_new_salary()** function so that it now takes two inputs, as declared on line 5. The two inputs are separated by a comma. The first input is **salary**, the second is **perf**, short for performance. Everything else functions like before. On line 18, when using **show_new_salary()**, we now have to pass it the variables **salary** and **employee_performance**. The **show_new_salary()** function is now independent of the code that is outside of it. For example, we can rename the **employee_performance** variable on line 2 to **performance**, we also change the code on line 18 to say performance rather than **employee_performance**. Now the code continues working like before even though we made no changes at all to the show_new_salary() function:

```
i   1▾  <script>
    2       var performance = 'A';
    3       var salary = 45000;
    4
    5▾      function show_new_salary(salary, perf) {
    6           document.write('Your new salary is ');
    7           var new_salary = salary;
    8
    9▾          if(perf === 'A') {
   10               new_salary = Math.floor(salary * 1.1);
   11           }
   12▾          else if(perf === 'B') {
   13               new_salary = Math.floor(salary * 1.05);
   14           }
   15           document.write(new_salary);
   16       }
   17
   18       show_new_salary(salary, performance);
   19  </script>
```

Your new salary is 49500

In the earlier, not-so-good example where the **show_new_salary()** function wasn't taking inputs, if we had changed the names of the variables on lines 2 or 3, we would have also had to change the **show_new_salary()** function. But now that the function operates according to inputs, it does not care about the variable names outside of it. It operates in a separate universe of its own; it has become a machine that takes something and spits something out.

As it should be clear by now, the variable names inside the function are unrelated to those outside. Below we rename **salary** to **pay** inside the function:

```
i   1▾  <script>
    2       var performance = 'A';
    3       var salary = 45000;
    4
    5▾      function show_new_salary(pay, perf) {
    6           document.write('Your new salary is ');
    7           var new_pay = pay;
    8
    9▾          if(perf === 'A') {
   10               new_pay = Math.floor(pay * 1.1);
   11           }
   12▾          else if(perf === 'B') {
   13               new_pay = Math.floor(pay * 1.05);
   14           }
   15           document.write(new_pay);
   16       }
   17
   18       show_new_salary(salary, performance);
   19  </script>
```

Your new salary is 49500

Above, everything continues functioning normally because the function does not care about the variable names outside. It only cares about what is passed to it by JavaScript. Whatever we pass to it on line 18 ends up inside the function's **pay** and **perf** variables.

To clarify further, we have a simpler, although more absurd, example:

```
1  <script>
2      var number = 5;
3      function double_monkey(monkey) {
4          return monkey * 2;
5      }
6      document.write(double_monkey(number));
7  </script>
```

10

Above, we have a **double_monkey()** function that doubles anything number passed to it. When making use of the function on line 6, we have to pass it the **number** variable. But inside the function, the function is free to call this variable anything it wants. In this case, it calls it **monkey**. To make it even simpler, below I remove the **number** variable:

```
1  <script>
2      function double_monkey(monkey) {
3          return monkey * 2;
4      }
5      document.write(double_monkey(5));
6  </script>
```

10

Above, we pass the number 5 to the **double_monkey()** function on line 5, which turns it into 10.

At this point, we have covered the basics of functions. If you are still a bit unclear on how functions exactly work, continue reading and it should become clearer as you see more examples of functions in action.

17. String Manipulation

Performing operations on strings is part of a programmer's daily life. For this reason programming languages offer a vast array of functionality to help us work with strings. In the following example, we print out the first letter of the word "cat":

```
1 ▾ <script>
2       var word = 'cat';
3       var first_letter = word[0];
4       document.write(first_letter);
5   </script>
```

c

On line 3, we use a special syntax that lets us access any character of a string by providing its place in the string. The meaning of **word[0]** is "the character in the **word** variable that is at position zero". In programming, we often start counting up from zero, rather than one, so position zero means the first character. Below, we change **word[0]** to **word[1]**, which ends up printing the second character for the **word** variable (the letter "a" in "cat"):

```
1 ▾ <script>
2       var word = 'cat';
3       var second_letter = word[1];
4       document.write(second_letter);
5   </script>
```

a

Below we have an even simpler example:

```
1 ▾ <script>
2       document.write('Hello there!'[11]);
3   </script>
```

!

When we write **'Hello there!'[11]**, it means "get the character that is at position 11 of this string", which happens to be the exclamation mark.

Changing case

Below, we use JavaScript's built-in **toUpperCase()** function to capitalize a word:

```
i  1 ▾ <script>
   2        var animal = 'dog';
   3        var capital_animal = 'dog'.toUpperCase();
   4
   5        document.write(animal + ' ' + capital_animal);
   6    </script>
```
dog DOG

The syntax **'dog'.toUpperCase()** is unusual because nothing is passed to the **toUpperCase()** function like you would expect. What we have here is a special syntax that we use when calling one of JavaScript's build-in functions on a particular type of data (a string, a number, or something else). The **toUpperCase()** function can only be used with strings, if you use it with a number you get an error:

```
i  1 ▾ <script>
   2        var number = 5;
   3        var number_capitalized = number.toUpperCase();
   4        document.write(number_capitalized);
   5    </script>
```

When we run the above nonsensical code, we get no output. If we look at the console, this is what we see:

```
⊗ ▶ Uncaught TypeError: number.toUpperCase is not a function
       at <anonymous>:3:37
```

JavaScript says **toUpperCase()** is not a function because in the world of numbers, this function does not exist. It only exists in the world of strings.

When calling a function like **toUpperCase()**, it does not matter whether you call it on a variable that contains a string or on a string directly:

```
i  1 ▾ <script>
   2        var my_string = 'This is a line of text.';
   3        var my_string_capitalized = my_string.toUpperCase();
   4        document.write(my_string_capitalized);
   5    </script>
```
THIS IS A LINE OF TEXT.

The above has the same result as this:

```
i  1 ▾ <script>
   2        var my_string_capitalized = 'This is a line of text.'.toUpperCase();
   3        document.write(my_string_capitalized);
   4    </script>
```
THIS IS A LINE OF TEXT.

The counterpart to **toUpperCase()** is **toLowerCase()**. Below we have the same code from above, but we print out a new line of text which is made up of the previous line turned to lowercase:

```
i  1 ▾ <script>
   2        var my_string_capitalized = 'This is a line of text.'.toUpperCase();
   3        document.write(my_string_capitalized);
   4        var my_string_uncapitalized = my_string_capitalized.toLowerCase();
   5        document.write('<br>');
   6        document.write(my_string_uncapitalized);
   7  </script>
```

THIS IS A LINE OF TEXT.
this is a line of text.

Moving on, below we have a function that capitalizes the first letter of any word passed to it. The example brings together much of what we have learned so far and it will require some time to explain, therefore do not worry if at first it looks a bit overwhelming:

```
i  1 ▾ <script>
   2 ▾      function capitalizeFirstLetter(word) {
   3            var first_letter = word[0];
   4            first_letter = first_letter.toUpperCase();
   5            var result = first_letter;
   6 ▾          for(var i = 1; i < word.length; i++) {
   7                result = result + word[i];
   8            }
   9            return result;
  10        }
  11
  12        var word = 'cat';
  13        var first_letter_capitalized
  14            = capitalizeFirstLetter(word);
  15        document.write(first_letter_capitalized);
  16  </script>
```

Cat

Try to read the code and guess how it works before reading my explanation. You should try to do this with every example; the more code you read, the better you will get at understanding how it works.

Inside the **capitalizeFirstLetter()** function, on line 3 we get the first letter of the **word** variable and put it inside the **first_letter** variable. We can check that this is functioning correctly by writing the variable's contents out (line 4 below):

```
i  1 ▾ <script>
   2 ▾      function capitalizeFirstLetter(word) {
   3            var first_letter = word[0];
   4            document.write(first_letter + '<br>');
```

c
Cat

As you see in the preview area, a letter "c" is printed followed by a new line. The letter "c" is still lowercase since the uppercasing is done on the next line. Below I have moved the **document.write()** to line 5, after the **first_letter** is made uppercase. As you see in the preview area, now an uppercase "C" is printed out:

```
i  1 ▾ <script>
   2 ▾     function capitalizeFirstLetter(word) {
   3            var first_letter = word[0];
   4            first_letter = first_letter.toUpperCase();
   5            document.write(first_letter + '<br>');
```

```
C
Cat
```

Let's now take another look at the function without any of the additional document.write() statements we added above:

```
   2 ▾     function capitalizeFirstLetter(word) {
   3            var first_letter = word[0];
   4            first_letter = first_letter.toUpperCase();
   5            var result = first_letter;
   6 ▾         for(var i = 1; i < word.length; i++) {
   7                result = result + word[i];
   8            }
   9            return result;
  10        }
```

On line 5, we declare a new variable named **result**. This variable will be a container for the uppercased word. At first we place the first letter inside it, later on we add the rest of the letters. Next we have a for loop. In this loop, we go over the contents of the **word** variable letter by letter, each time adding the letter to the end of the **result** variable.

Since on line 6 we declare the variable i to be 1, when on line 7 JavaScript reads **result + word[i]** the first time, it sees it as **result + word[1]**. On the next iteration, JavaScript increases **i** to 2, so that this time **word[i]** means **word[2]**. With each iteration the next letter of the **word** variable is added to the end of **result**, until the loop is done.

The loops condition on line 6 is **i < word.length**. This means that the loop should run as long as **i** is less than the length of the word variable.

Below I have added two new **document.write()** statements in order to clarify what is happening inside the loop when JavaScript executes it:

```
i  1 ▾ <script>
   2 ▾     function capitalizeFirstLetter(word) {
   3            var first_letter = word[0];
   4            first_letter = first_letter.toUpperCase();
   5            var result = first_letter;
   6 ▾         for(var i = 1; i < word.length; i++) {
   7                result = result + word[i];
   8                document.write('The value of i is: ' + i + '<br>');
   9                document.write('The value of result is: ' + result + '<br>');
  10            }
  11            return result;
  12        }
```

```
The value of i is: 1
The value of result is: Ca
The value of i is: 2
The value of result is: Cat
Cat
```

As you would expect, at first, meaning during the first iteration of the loop, the value of **i** is 1, since we declared it to be 1 on line 6 when we wrote **var i = 1**. During the first iteration the value of **result** is "Ca". That is because before the loop, on line 5, we put "C" inside it. Then inside the loop, on line 7, we put "a" inside it, so that it becomes "Ca". Once JavaScript reaches the bottom of the loop, it increase **i** by one, then it starts from the top again. As you can see in the preview, the loop only runs twice, since the word "cat" has three letters and the loop is designed to only work on the parts of the word that are supposed to be lowercase, so it only deals with the "at" part. At the end of the second iteration, JavaScript increases **i** by one so that it becomes 3. Once it is three, it no longer satisfies the loop's condition of **i < word.length**, since **i** is now 3 and **word.length** is also 3.

Once the loop stops running, we have a return statement on line 11 that returns the **result** variable. Below, I have changed the word "cat" to "dinosaur" on line 14:

```
1 ▾ <script>
2 ▾     function capitalizeFirstLetter(word) {
3           var first_letter = word[0];
4           first_letter = first_letter.toUpperCase();
5           var result = first_letter;
6 ▾         for(var i = 1; i < word.length; i++) {
7               result = result + word[i];
8               document.write('The value of i is: ' + i + '<br>');
9               document.write('The value of result is: ' + result + '<br>');
10          }
11          return result;
12      }
13
14      var word = 'dinosaur';
15      var first_letter_capitalized
16          = capitalizeFirstLetter(word);
17      document.write(first_letter_capitalized);
18  </script>
19
20
```

The value of i is: 1
The value of result is: Di
The value of i is: 2
The value of result is: Din
The value of i is: 3
The value of result is: Dino
The value of i is: 4
The value of result is: Dinos
The value of i is: 5
The value of result is: Dinosa
The value of i is: 6
The value of result is: Dinosau
The value of i is: 7
The value of result is: Dinosaur
Dinosaur

As you see in the preview area, the loop now runs many more times, since the word "dinosaur" is much longer than "cat'. Thanks to the fact that in the for loop we tell JavaScript to run the loop as long as **i** is less than **word.length**, no matter what word we pass to the function, the loop always runs exactly the number of times needed.

Using a loop is actually the hard way of doing things. We could accomplish the same thing using JavaScript's **substring()** function, which allows us to extract part of a string.

```
1 ▾ <script>
2 ▾     function capitalizeFirstLetter(word) {
3           var first_letter = word[0];
4           first_letter = first_letter.toUpperCase();
5           var rest_of_the_word = word.substring(1, word.length);
6           var result = first_letter + rest_of_the_word;
7           return result;
8       }
9
10      var word = 'dinosaur';
11      var first_letter_capitalized
12          = capitalizeFirstLetter(word);
13      document.write(first_letter_capitalized);
14  </script>
```

Dinosaur

Above, I have replaced the loop with lines 5 and 6. On line 5, we use the **substring()** function to get the rest of the word after getting its first letter. The **substring()** function takes two numbers corresponding to the range of the characters we wish to extract. Below is a simple example of using the **substring()** function to get the first two letters of the word "cat":

```
i  1 ▾ <script>
   2        document.write('cat'.substring(0, 2));
   3    </script>
```
ca

Writing **substring(0, 2)** tells JavaScript to put together **'cat'[0]** and **'cat'[1]** and show us the result. It has the same meaning as this:

```
i  1 ▾ <script>
   2        document.write('cat'[0] + 'cat'[1]);
   3    </script>
```
ca

The second number we give to **substring()** tells JavaScript where it should stop. This number is not inclusive; **substring(0,2)** means "get us the characters at position 0 and 1 but stop before position 2". This can be confusing for programmers, so there is no shame in having to look up this function again and again for months until you get used to it.

Back to our example:

```
i  1 ▾ <script>
   2 ▾      function capitalizeFirstLetter(word) {
   3            var first_letter = word[0];
   4            first_letter = first_letter.toUpperCase();
   5            var rest_of_the_word = word.substring(1, word.length);
   6            var result = first_letter + rest_of_the_word;
   7            return result;
   8        }
   9
  10        var word = 'dinosaur';
  11        var first_letter_capitalized
  12            = capitalizeFirstLetter(word);
  13        document.write(first_letter_capitalized);
  14    </script>
```
Dinosaur

Above, on line 5 we give the **substring()** function **word.length** as its second argument (we call the stuff we pass to a function its "arguments", so **substring()** has two arguments, while **capitalizeFirstLetter()** has only one argument). Since the length of "dinosaur" is 8, JavaScript sees this as **substring(1, 8)**, which means that **substring()** should get the letters starting from the second position and stopping before the 8th position. Below is an illustration of how this works:

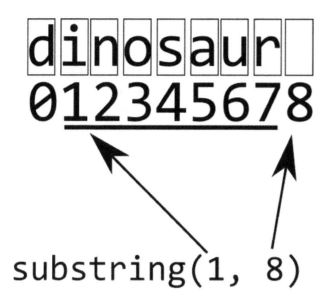

Since JavaScript starts counting the positions from zero rather than one, position 1 is actually the second letter of the word. We tell JavaScript to stop at position 8, which as you see above is empty. So JavaScript ends up getting everything from position 1 to position 7, or "inosaur". The way the **substring()** function works is unintuitive and even experienced programmers will have to occasionally look it up to remember how it works.

On line 6 of our code, we concatenate **first_letter** with **rest_of_the_word**, and place the result inside **result**. On the next line we return the **result** variable.

An experienced programmer can shorten the **capitalizeFirstLetter()** to a single line, as follows:

```
1  <script>
2      function capitalizeFirstLetter(word) {
3          return word[0].toUpperCase() + word.substring(1, word.length);
4      }
5
6      var word = 'dinosaur';
7      var first_letter_capitalized
8          = capitalizeFirstLetter(word);
9      document.write(first_letter_capitalized);
10 </script>
```

Dinosaur

As beginners we sometimes feel tempted to write code like the above because it looks clever. It accomplishes so much in so little space. But clever code is not always good code, since readability matters. Writing a clever piece of code that is nearly impossible for others to understand is not good code, it is actually bad code; programmers often work in teams and other team members should be able to read your code and understand it easily instead of having to waste many minutes trying to decipher what the code is doing. The above is not too bad because what it is doing is relatively simple. But the more complicated the code is, the better it is to break it up into multiple statements to make it easier to understand.

Moving on, below we use the **capitalizeFirstLetter()** function twice in the same statement on lines 8 and 9 in order to capitalize the first letters of both the **first_name** and the **second_name** variables, so that each of "james" and "potter" becomes "James" and "Potter":

```
 i   1 ▾ <script>
     2 ▾     function capitalizeFirstLetter(word) {
     3           return word[0].toUpperCase() + word.substring(1, word.length);
     4       }
     5
     6       var first_name = 'james';
     7       var second_name = 'potter';
     8       document.write(capitalizeFirstLetter(first_name)
     9           + ' ' + capitalizeFirstLetter(second_name));
    10   </script>
```
James Potter

Below we have a different example:

```
 i   1 ▾ <script>
     2 ▾     function capitalizeFirstLetter(word) {
     3           return word[0].toUpperCase() + word.substring(1, word.length);
     4       }
     5
     6       var full_name = 'james potter';
     7       document.write(capitalizeFirstLetter(full_name));
     8   </script>
```
James potter

Above, only "james" ends up being capitalized because we are passing the "james potter" string all in one go to the **capitalizeFirstLetter()** function. The function capitalizes the first letter and returns everything after it unchanged. It does not care about any spaces there might be in the string, so we end up with "James potter".

18. Arrays

We have already spoken of data types. We have strings, numbers and booleans. In this chapter we will cover a new data type known as an array.

If you think of an ordinary variable as a box that holds things, an array is a box that holds other boxes, which in turn hold things.

Below, we have declared an array named **fruits** with two string values inside it. An array is declared using square brackets **[ ]**.

```
1 ▾ <script>
2       var fruits = ['apple', 'orange'];
3   </script>
```

As can be seen on line 2, the two values placed inside the array are separated by a comma.

Below we access the values we placed inside the fruits array:

```
1 ▾ <script>
2       var fruits = ['apple', 'orange'];      apple
3       document.write(fruits[0]);             orange
4       document.write('<br>');
5       document.write(fruits[1]);
6   </script>
```

We already discussed the way you can access the first character of a string variable using **[0]**, and the other characters using their appropriate index values. Arrays, like strings, can be accessed using similar index values. Above, on line 3 we write out the contents of **fruits[0]**, which means "the value that is at index 0 of the array". The result is that the word "apple" gets printed out. On line 5 we write out the word "orange" using **fruits[1]**, because "orange" is at index 1.

Below I have added another value to the array on line 3, writing it out on line 8:

```
i  1 ▾ <script>
   2 ▾     var fruits = ['apple', 'orange',
   3             'banana'];
   4         document.write(fruits[0]);
   5         document.write('<br>');
   6         document.write(fruits[1]);
   7         document.write('<br>');
   8         document.write(fruits[2]);
   9   </script>
```

apple
orange
banana

Since 'banana' is at index 2, we use **fruits[2]** to access it online 8. It is unnatural and confusing to use the number 2 to access the *third* item in the array, this is something you just have to get used to. This leads to mistakes even among experienced programmers when they do not pay sufficient attention to the code they are writing.

Instead of printing out each value on a separate line of code, we can use a **for** loop to do the job for us in a few lines of code regardless of how long the array is:

```
i  1 ▾ <script>
   2 ▾     var fruits = ['apple', 'orange',
   3             'banana'];
   4 ▾     for(var i = 0; i < fruits.length; i++) {
   5             document.write(fruits[i]);
   6             document.write('<br>');
   7         }
   8   </script>
```

apple
orange
banana

On line 4 we declare that the **for** loop should run as long as **i** is less then **fruits.length**. The **length** attribute returns the number of items in the array. If we were dealing with a string, **length** would return how many characters were inside the string. Below I have added a new statement on lines 5-7 that prints out the length of the array in the preview area:

```
i  1 ▾ <script>
   2 ▾     var fruits = ['apple', 'orange',
   3             'banana'];
   4
   5         document.write('length of fruits '
   6             + 'array is: ' + fruits.length +
   7             '<br>');
   8
   9 ▾     for(var i = 0; i < fruits.length; i++) {
  10             document.write(fruits[i]);
  11             document.write('<br>');
  12         }
  13   </script>
```

length of fruits array is: 3
apple
orange
banana

In the **for** loop, since **fruits.length** is 3, the result is that we are practically telling the loop to run as long as the variable **i** is less than three. Since **i** starts at zero (because we wrote **var i = 0** in the loop's condition), this means that the loop will run three times. Each time, it will increase **i** by one (because we wrote **i++** in the loop condition), and once it becomes three, the condition **i < fruits.length** ends up being false, so that loop ends. To illustrate, below on line 6 we print out the value of **i** during every loop:

```
1  <script>
2      var fruits = ['apple', 'orange',
3          'banana'];
4
5      for(var i = 0; i < fruits.length; i++) {
6          document.write('i is ' + i + '<br>');
7          document.write(fruits[i]);
8          document.write('<br>');
9      }
10  </script>
```

```
i is 0
apple
i is 1
orange
i is 2
banana
```

Once the value of **i** becomes 3, the condition **i < fruits.length** becomes false, since **i** will not be less than 3, it will be *equal to* 3.

Now, if we add many new items to the array, they will all get printed out without us having to make changes to the **for** loop:

```
1  <script>
2      var fruits = ['apple', 'orange',
3          'banana', 'lemon', 'strawberry',
4          'mango', 'blackberry'];
5
6      for(var i = 0; i < fruits.length; i++) {
7          document.write('i is ' + i + '<br>');
8          document.write(fruits[i]);
9          document.write('<br>');
10     }
11  </script>
12
13
14
15
16
17
18
19
```

```
i is 0
apple
i is 1
orange
i is 2
banana
i is 3
lemon
i is 4
strawberry
i is 5
mango
i is 6
blackberry
```

Above, on lines 3 and 4 we have added four new fruits to the **fruits** array, but on lines 6-10 we have the same loop as before. Since we have made the array larger, **fruits.length** now equals 7. This means that the loop will run seven times since on line 6, inside the loop condition, we are saying the loop should run as long as **i** is less than **fruits.length**, whatever **fruits.length** might be. Any items we add or remove from the array affect the value of **fruits.length**, which affects how many times the loop will run.

Array functions

Similar to strings, arrays have numerous functions that help programmers operate on them. The first function we will discuss is the **toString()** function.[20] which prints out everything inside the array as a string. This can be useful when you are not sure what is inside the array and you want to quickly take a look at its contents. Below we have an array named **car_makers**, which contains the names of three car companies.

```
i  1 ▾ <script>
   2 ▾     var car_makers = ['Toyota', 'Ford',
   3           'Tesla'];
   4
   5       document.write(car_makers.toString());
   6  </script>
```
Toyota,Ford,Tesla

Above, on line 5, we use **car_makers.toString()** to get the all of the contents of the array as one string.

Below, on lines 6 and 7 I add two new statements. The first one simply prints out the length of the array, which is 3. The second statement, however, prints out the length of the string returned by **.toString()**, which is 17.

```
i  1 ▾ <script>
   2 ▾     var car_makers = ['Toyota', 'Ford',
   3           'Tesla'];
   4
   5       document.write(car_makers.toString() + '<br>');
   6       document.write(car_makers.length + '<br>');
   7       document.write(car_makers.toString().length);
   8  </script>
```
Toyota,Ford,Tesla
3
17

The **car_makers.toString().length** statement is known as a "chain". JavaScript starts reading it from left to right. First it gets the array **car_makers**, then it runs the **toString()** function on it. Next, it gets the length attribute of the result of the **toString()** function.

We are telling JavaScript: turn this array into a string, then get the length of the string.

We can even chain multiple functions:

---

[20] The more technically correct name for this type of function is "method". As we have discussed, functions take an input and return a result. Methods, however, *operate on the thing they are called on* and often do not take any inputs and sometimes do not return any outputs. To avoid over-complicating the matter I will continue referring to the as functions.

```
i  1▾  <script>
   2▾      var car_makers = ['Toyota', 'Ford',
   3            'Tesla'];
   4
   5        document.write(car_makers.toString() + '<br>');
   6        document.write(car_makers.length + '<br>');
   7        document.write(car_makers.toString().toUpperCase());
   8  </script>
```

```
Toyota.Ford.Tesla
3
TOYOTA.FORD.TESLA
```

Above, on line 7, we first turn **car_makers** into a string, then use **toUpperCase()** to turn the string into an all-caps string.

Below, we go further, using the **substring()** string function to only get the word "TOYOTA":

```
i  1▾  <script>
   2▾      var car_makers = ['Toyota', 'Ford',
   3            'Tesla'];
   4
   5        document.write(car_makers.toString() + '<br>');
   6        document.write(car_makers.length + '<br>');
   7        document.write(
   8            car_makers.toString().toUpperCase().substring(0,6)
   9            );
  10  </script>
```

```
Toyota.Ford.Tesla
3
TOYOTA
```

On line 8, we use the **substring()** function (covered in the chapter on strings) to extract everything in the string at indexes 0 to 6, which happens to be the word "TOYOTA".

Note that the only reason we are able to use string functions like **toUpperCase()** and **substring()** on the **car_makers** array is that we are first converting it to a string using **toString()**. Without **toString()**, using string functions on an array would lead to an error.

Back to array functions, the next function we will discuss is the **push()** function. This function allows us to push an element onto the end of an array, as follows:

```
i  1▾  <script>
   2▾      var car_makers = ['Toyota', 'Ford',
   3            'Tesla'];
   4        document.write(car_makers.length + '<br>');
   5        car_makers.push('BMW');
   6        document.write(car_makers.length + '<br>');
   7        document.write(car_makers.toString());
   8  </script>
```

```
3
4
Toyota.Ford.Tesla.BMW
```

On line 3 above we print out the length of the array, which is 3, since it begins with three elements. On line 4 we use the **push()** function to add a new element to the array, which is the string **BMW**. When we print out the array's length again on line 6, this time the length is 4, because we have added a new element to the array. On line 7 we use **toString()** to print out all of the array's contents, which now has **BMW** at the end.

443

The opposite of the **push()** function is the **pop()** function, which causes the last element of the array to be "popped" out.

```
1 ▾ <script>
2 ▾    var car_makers = ['Toyota', 'Ford',
3         'Tesla'];
4      var last_element = car_makers.pop();
5      document.write(last_element);
6      document.write('<br>');
7      document.write(car_makers.toString());
8 </script>
```

Tesla
Toyota,Ford

On line 4, we create a new variable **last_element** and put the result of **car_makers.pop()** inside it. When we print out the value of **last_element** on line 5, we see that the word "Tesla" is printed out in the preview area.

On line 7 we have something interesting. When we print out the array's contents, we see only Toyota and Ford. The array now has only two elements. This is because the **pop()** function does two things at the same time: it returns the last element of the array, *and* it removes that element from the array.

Below, we use a **while** loop to pop out every element of the array:

```
1 ▾ <script>
2 ▾    var car_makers = ['Toyota', 'Ford',
3         'Tesla'];
4      document.write('The length of the '
5      + ' array before the loop is: '
6      + car_makers.length + '<br>');
7
8 ▾    while(car_makers.length > 0) {
9          document.write(car_makers.pop()
10         + '<br>');
11         document.write('Length now: '
12         + car_makers.length + '<br>');
13     }
14
15     document.write('The length of the '
16     + ' array at the end of the loop: '
17     + car_makers.length);
18 </script>
```

The length of the array before the loop is: 3
Tesla
Length now: 2
Ford
Length now: 1
Toyota
Length now: 0
The length of the array at the end of the loop: 0

On lines 4-6, we print out the starting length of the array, which is 3. Inside the **while** loop, the condition we have is **car_makers.length > 0**, which means that the loop should run as long as the length of the **car_makers** array is greater than zero, meaning as long as it is non-empty. On line 9, we have **document.write(car_makers.pop())**. This pops out the last element of the array and immediately passes it to the **document.write()** function, so that it ends up being printed out. On lines 11-12 we print out the new length of the array, which as you can see in the preview area keeps going down during every loop. Once the loop is finished, the length of the array is zero.

We can even use **pop()** to remove elements from an array without doing anything with the popped out element, as follows:

```
i  1 ▾ <script>
   2 ▾     var car_makers = ['Toyota', 'Ford',
   3           'Tesla'];
   4 ▾     while(car_makers.length > 0) {
   5             car_makers.pop();
   6         }
   7
   8         document.write(car_makers.toString());
   9   </script>
```

Above, the loop on lines 4-6 removes all the elements of the array. When we try to print out the contents of the array using **toString()** on line 8, nothing is printed out because the array has nothing in it anymore.

An alternative to **push()** is **unshift()**, which adds an element to the *beginning* of an array rather than to its end:

```
i  1 ▾ <script>
   2 ▾     var car_makers = ['Toyota', 'Ford',
   3           'Tesla'];
   4       car_makers.push('BMW');
   5       document.write(car_makers.toString()
   6         + '<br>');
   7
   8       car_makers.unshift('KIA');
   9       document.write(car_makers.toString());
  10   </script>
```

Toyota.Ford.Tesla.BMW
KIA.Toyota.Ford.Tesla.BMW

Above, on line 4 we use the already-covered **push()** function to add **BMW** as the final element of the **car_makers** array. We then print out the result on lines 5-6. Next, on line 8 we use **unshift()** to add **KIA** as the first element of the array. On printing out the array on line 9, we now see that **KIA** is the first element of the array (second line of the preview).

Do not worry about memorizing the names of these functions. Even experienced programmers have to look them up at times. What is important is to know such functions exist, it is then easy to find them by doing an web search. For example you can search for "javascript remove last item of array" or "javascript add item to beginning of array" and you will find dozens of websites that mention the relevant functions.

What if for some reason we wanted to move the last element of an array to the beginning? We can do that by using **pop()** and **unshift()** together:

```
i  1▾  <script>
   2▾      var car_makers = ['Toyota', 'Ford',
   3            'Tesla'];
   4        car_makers.unshift(car_makers.pop());
   5        document.write(car_makers.toString());
   6  </script>
```

Tesla,Toyota,Ford

Above, on line 4 we are using **car_makers.pop()** to pop out the last element, but since we are doing it inside the brackets of **car_makers.unshift()**, the popped out element ends up inside the array but at the beginning, as seen in the preview. If you are a bit confused by this, we can break it down into more steps to make it clearer:

```
i  1▾  <script>
   2▾      var car_makers = ['Toyota', 'Ford',
   3            'Tesla'];
   4        var last_element = car_makers.pop();
   5        car_makers.unshift(last_element);
   6        document.write(car_makers.toString());
   7  </script>
```

Tesla,Toyota,Ford

The above code does exactly the same thing as before. On line 4 we pop out the last element and put it inside a variable. Then on line 5 we put the value of this variable into the array as its first element. Instead of using the **last_element** variable as an intermediary, we could simply write **car_makers.unshift(car_makers.pop())** to capture the result of **car_makers.pop()** and put it back into the array in one step instead of two.

We also have the **shift()** function which like pop() removes items from the array, but unlike **pop()** it removes from the front of the array rather than the end.

Deconstructing Shakespeare

In this section, we deconstruct a Shakespeare verse from Sonnet 130 and introduce some new operations in the process.

```
i  1▾  <script>
   2        var verse = "I love to hear her speak,"
   3          + " yet well I know "
   4          + "That music hath a far more "
   5          + "pleasing sound;";
   6
   7        document.write(verse);
   8  </script>
```

I love to hear her speak, yet well I know That music hath a far more pleasing sound;

Above, we first have a very long string in which I have placed the verse. The verse is made up of two lines in the original, as follows:

| I | love | to | hear | her | speak, | yet | well | I | know |

That music hath a far more pleasing sound;

But to simplify the example, I have turned the verse into one very long string. In the preview area you see the verse broken into three lines simply because there is not enough space to show it all on one line. If I make my browser window larger, the preview area expands and the browser tries to show all of the verse on one line (I have also zoomed out the browser text in order to get a screenshot that would fit within a book):

> I love to hear her speak, yet well I know That music hath a far more pleasing sound;

The split() function

Back to the business at hand, below I use a new string function called **split()** to split the string and make an array out of it:

```
1  <script>
2      var verse = "I love to hear her speak,"      love
3          + " yet well I know "
4          + "That music hath a far more "
5          + "pleasing sound;";
6
7      var verse_words = verse.split(" ");
8      document.write(verse_words[1]);
9  </script>
```

On line 7, **verse.split(" ")** tells JavaScript to split the string at every space. This means that JavaScript creates a new array with the word "I" as its first element, the word "love" as the second element, "to" as the third element, "hear" as the fourth element, and so on. The stuff between the two quotation marks is what JavaScript will split the string at, at present we have placed a space between the quotation marks. On line 8, we print out the *second* item of the result stored in the **verse_words** variable, which is the word "love".

Below I print out the contents of the **verse_words** array using the **toString()** function:

```
i   1▾  <script>
    2       var verse = "I love to hear her speak,"
    3           + " yet well I know "
    4           + "That music hath a far more "
    5           + "pleasing sound;";
    6
    7       var verse_words = verse.split(" ");
    8       document.write(verse_words.toString());
    9   </script>
```
I,love,to,hear,her,speak,,yet,well,I,know,

Above, the entire array is printed out on one line. Since there isn't enough space available to see the whole line, we can only see until "know".

Below I use a **for** loop to print out all of the contents of the **verse_words** array, with each array element on its own line:

```
i   1▾  <script>
    2       var verse = "I love to hear her speak,"
    3           + " yet well I know "
    4           + "That music hath a far more "
    5           + "pleasing sound;";
    6
    7       var verse_words = verse.split(" ");
    8       for(var i = 0; i < verse_words.length;
    9▾         i++) {
    10          document.write(verse_words[i]);
    11          document.write('<br>');
    12      }
    13  </script>
    14
    15
    16
    17
    18
    19
    20
    21
    22
    23
    24
```
I
love
to
hear
her
speak,
yet
well
I
know
That
music
hath
a
far
more
pleasing
sound;

A new type of for loop

We can now introduce a new type of loop that is often useful when going over an array. This loop is also a **for** loop, but it uses a special syntax in the conditional:

```
i  1 ▾ <script>
   2      var verse = "I love to hear her speak,"     I
   3          + " yet well I know "                    love
   4          + "That music hath a far more "          to
   5          + "pleasing sound;";                     hear
   6                                                    her
   7      var verse_words = verse.split(" ");          speak,
   8 ▾    for(var i in verse_words) {                  yet
   9        document.write(verse_words[i]);            well
  10        document.write('<br>');                    I
  11      }
  12  </script>
```

The above loop does exactly the same thing as the earlier loop. You can think of it as something of a shorthand that is easier to type. The meaning of **for (var i in verse_words)** is: "for each element in **verse_words**, do the following, while using **i** to represent the index value of the current element".

Catching words

We are now ready to perform operations on the **verse_words** array. Below, I have updated the loop to print out words starting with "h":

```
i  1 ▾ <script>
   2      var verse = "I love to hear her speak,"     hear
   3          + " yet well I know "                    her
   4          + "That music hath a far more "          hath
   5          + "pleasing sound;";
   6
   7      var verse_words = verse.split(" ");
   8
   9 ▾    for(var i in verse_words) {
  10        var current_word = verse_words[i];
  11        if(current_word[0] === 'h' ||
  12 ▾         current_word[0] === 'H') {
  13            document.write(current_word);
  14            document.write('<br>');
  15        }
  16      }
  17  </script>
```

On line 10, I put the current array element into a new variable named **current_word**. On lines 11-12, I check whether the first letter of **current_word** is a lowercase or uppercase "h". **current_word[0]** means "the first character of the string" when we are dealing with a string, as has been covered before.

On lines 11-12 we need to do two checks rather than one because in JavaScript an "h" is different from an "H". If we had only written **if(current_word[0] === 'h')**, this would not have caught any words starting with an "H". The condition therefore says: "If the word's first character is a lower case "h", OR if it is an uppercase "H", then do this".

As can be seen in the preview area, the loop detected three words that started with an "h".

The charAt() function

Programmers generally reserve accessing variables by index (as in **my_var[0]**) for arrays. It is confusing and unusual to use it on a string. We have done it so far for simplicity's sake. The better and safer method is to use the **charAt()** string function, as follows:

```
 1 ▾ <script>
 2       var verse = "I love to hear her speak,"
 3           + " yet well I know "
 4           + "That music hath a far more "
 5           + "pleasing sound;";
 6
 7       var verse_words = verse.split(" ");
 8
 9 ▾     for(var i in verse_words) {
10           var current_word = verse_words[i];
11           var first_letter = current_word.charAt(0);
12           if(first_letter === 'h' ||
13 ▾             first_letter === 'H') {
14               document.write(current_word);
15               document.write('<br>');
16           }
17       }
18  </script>
```

```
hear
her
hath
```

Above, on line 11 I create a new variable named **first_letter**. I use **current_word.chartAt(0)** to extract the first character of **current_word**. The zero refers to index 0 of the string.

We can simplify the **if** statement as follows:

```
i   1▾  <script>
    2       var verse = "I love to hear her speak,"      hear
    3           + " yet well I know "                     her
    4           + "That music hath a far more "           hath
    5           + "pleasing sound;";
    6
    7       var verse_words = verse.split(" ");
    8
    9▾      for(var i in verse_words) {
   10           var current_word = verse_words[i];
   11           var first_letter = current_word.charAt(0);
   12           first_letter = first_letter.toLowerCase();
   13▾          if(first_letter === 'h') {
   14               document.write(current_word);
   15               document.write('<br>');
   16           }
   17       }
   18   </script>
```

On line 12, I use **toLowerCase()** to convert **first_letter** to a lower case letter. Now a single check on line 13 is sufficient: we only need to check for "h" rather than having to check for "H". Regardless of whether the first letter is "h" or "H", since we are forcing it to always become an "h" on line 12, on line 13 we only need to check for lowercase "h". We *never* run into an uppercase "H" on line 13 because line 12 prevents that.

Instead of doing **toLowerCase()** on its own line, we can do it right inside the **if** statement:

```
i   1▾  <script>
    2       var verse = "I love to hear her speak,"      hear
    3           + " yet well I know "                     her
    4           + "That music hath a far more "           hath
    5           + "pleasing sound;";
    6
    7       var verse_words = verse.split(" ");
    8
    9▾      for(var i in verse_words) {
   10           var current_word = verse_words[i];
   11           var first_letter = current_word.charAt(0);
   12▾          if(first_letter.toLowerCase() === 'h') {
   13               document.write(current_word);
   14               document.write('<br>');
   15           }
   16       }
   17   </script>
```

Above on line 12 **first_letter.toLowerCase()** forces every first letter to become lowercase right before the comparison.

We can even do away with **first_letter** variable, as follows:

```
i  1 ▾ <script>
   2        var verse = "I love to hear her speak,"
   3            + " yet well I know "
   4            + "That music hath a far more "
   5            + "pleasing sound;";
   6
   7        var verse_words = verse.split(" ");
   8
   9 ▾    for(var i in verse_words) {
  10          var current_word = verse_words[i];
  11          if(current_word.charAt(0).toLowerCase()
  12 ▾            === 'h') {
  13              document.write(current_word);
  14              document.write('<br>');
  15          }
  16      }
  17   </script>
```
```
hear
her
hath
```

On line 11, we do everything in one step. We get the first letter of **current_word** using **charAt()**, then we immediately turn it to lower case, then we compare it to "h".

We can even go further by eliminating the **current_word** variable, as follows:

```
i  1 ▾ <script>
   2        var verse = "I love to hear her speak,"
   3            + " yet well I know "
   4            + "That music hath a far more "
   5            + "pleasing sound;";
   6
   7        var verse_words = verse.split(" ");
   8
   9 ▾    for(var i in verse_words) {
  10          if(verse_words[i].charAt(0).toLowerCase()
  11 ▾            === 'h') {
  12              document.write(verse_words[i]);
  13              document.write('<br>');
  14          }
  15      }
  16   </script>
```
```
hear
her
hath
```

Now on line 10 we get the current array element of **verse_words** using **verse_words[i]**, then we get its first character using **chartAt(0)**, then we convert it to lowercase, then we do the comparison, all inside the **if** statement's condition.

The above code is terser and cleverer, but it is not necessarily better. Sometimes it is better to use an intermediate variable (such as **current_word**), which makes it easier to understand the code. Right now a reader has to spend a while looking at line 10 before they understand what is going on. By using intermediate variables like **current_word** and **first_letter**, we make it easier for humans to understand it, even if it makes no difference to the end result.

When reading code written by experienced programmers you often run into examples like line 10 above, where multiple operations are chained together. Unless you have spent a lot of time reading and writing code, it is natural for these chains to be confusing and difficult to understand.

Nested loops

Below, we have a new piece of code that finds every word that contains the letter "i" or "I" at any point (not just the beginning of the word):

```
1 ▾ <script>
2       var verse = "I love to hear her speak,"
3           + " yet well I know "
4           + "That music hath a far more "
5           + "pleasing sound;";
6
7       var verse_words = verse.split(" ");
8
9 ▾    for(var i in verse_words) {
10         var current_word = verse_words[i];
11         for(var j = 0; j < current_word.length;j++)
12 ▾       {
13             current_letter = current_word.charAt(j);
14             current_letter = current_letter.toLowerCase();
15 ▾           if(current_letter === 'i') {
16                 document.write(current_word);
17                 document.write('<br>');
18             }
19         }
20     }
21  </script>
```

I
I
music
pleasing

We have a nested loop above, meaning one loop inside another. First we loop over all of the array elements, and inside of that, we loop over every character of every word. The first thing to notice is that on line 11, we are using **j** inside the inner for loop rather than **i**, because the variable name **i** is already being used by the outer loop. Using the same variable name in both loops would not make sense and would lead to errors.

In order to make it easier to understand what is going on in the code, below I have added some extra **document.write()** statements:

```
i  1 ▾ <script>
   2        var verse = "I love to hear her speak,"
   3            + " yet well I know "
   4            + "That music hath a far more "
   5            + "pleasing sound;";
   6
   7        var verse_words = verse.split(" ");
   8
   9 ▾    for(var i in verse_words) {
  10            var current_word = verse_words[i];
  11            document.write('Currently at word: ' + current_word);
  12            document.write('<br>');
  13            for(var j = 0; j < current_word.length;j++)
  14 ▾          {
  15                current_letter = current_word.charAt(j);
  16                current_letter = current_letter.toLowerCase();
  17                document.write(current_letter + ' / ');
  18 ▾            if(current_letter === 'i') {
  19                    document.write('<br>Found an i in the word: ');
  20                    document.write(current_word);
  21                }
  22            }
  23            document.write('<br>');
  24        }
  25  </script>
```

Here is a sample of the result in the preview area:

```
Currently at word: I
i /
Found an i in the word: I
Currently at word: love
l / o / v / e /
Currently at word: to
t / o /
Currently at word: hear
h / e / a / r /
Currently at word: her
h / e / r /
Currently at word: speak,
s / p / e / a / k / , /
Currently at word: yet
y / e / t /
Currently at word: well
w / e / l / l /
Currently at word: I
i /
Found an i in the word: I
Currently at word: know
```

In the outer loop we print out which word we are currently processing (on line 11). In the inner loop, we print out each letter we are processing followed by a slash, in order to separate it from the letter that comes after it. If the inner loop finds any occurrences of the letter "i", it prints out "Found an i…" on line 19. Once the inner loop is done, we print out a new line on line 23.

At that point, the code goes back to the top of the outer loop, which will process the next word, and so on and so forth.

Notice that on line 15 we wrote **chartAt(j)** rather than **chartAt(0)** because **j** changes with each inner loop, starting at 0 and going up to the final index of the string.

Searching strings with indexOf()

We can accomplish what the previous code did with only one loop by using **indexOf()**. We will first look at a simple example:

```
1 ▾ <script>
2       var verse = "I love to hear her speak,"
3          + " yet well I know "
4          + "That music hath a far more "
5          + "pleasing sound;";
6
7       document.write(verse.indexOf('love'));
8   </script>
```

2

The **indexOf()** function tells us the index of the string we are checking. On line 7, we are requesting the index of the word "love". The result is 2, meaning that the word "love" starts at index 2 of the **verse** variable.

Below I check for the index of the letter "i":

```
1 ▾ <script>
2       var verse = "I love to hear her speak,"
3          + " yet well I know "
4          + "That music hath a far more "
5          + "pleasing sound;";
6
7       document.write(verse.indexOf('i'));
8   </script>
```

50

The result is 50 because this is only searching for lowercase occurrences of "i", which happens to be the "i" in "music".

Back to the previous example where we were checking for words containing "i":

```
i  1 ▾ <script>
   2       var verse = "I love to hear her speak,"     i
   3           + " yet well I know "                    i
   4           + "That music hath a far more "          music
   5           + "pleasing sound;";                     pleasing
   6
   7       var verse_words = verse.split(" ");
   8
   9 ▾     for(var i in verse_words) {
   10          var current_word = verse_words[i];
   11          current_word = current_word.toLowerCase();
   12 ▾        if(current_word.indexOf('i') !== -1) {
   13              document.write(current_word);
   14              document.write('<br>');
   15          }
   16      }
   17 </script>
```

Above, I have removed the inner loop and replaced it with an if statement that uses **indexOf()** to check if **current_word** contains an "i" or not. First, on line 11 I turn current_word to lowercase to avoid having to check for both uppercase and lowercase occurrences of the letter "i". On line 12, we have something new. I am checking whether the index of the letter "i" equals -1 or not. That is because **indexOf()** returns the index of the letter if it finds it, but if it does not find it, it returns -1. Here is a simple illustration of this:

```
i  1 ▾ <script>
   2       document.write("love".indexOf('e'));    3
   3       document.write("<br>");                 -1
   4       document.write("love".indexOf('i'));
   5 </script>
```

Above, on line 2 we print out the index of the letter "e" inside the string "love", which happens to be 3. On line 4 we print out the index of the letter "i". But since the word "love" does not contain the letter "i", **indexOf()** returns -1. The negative index tells us that **indexOf()** failed to find what we were looking for.

Back to the main example, on line 12 we can check whether current_word contains the letter "i" or not by asking the question: Does the index of "i" inside this variable equal -1 or not? If it equals -1, it means it does not contain an "i", if it does not equal negative one, it contains an "i".

Below is a further illustration:

```
i  1 ▾ <script>
   2        var verse = "I love to hear her speak,"
   3            + " yet well I know "
   4            + "That music hath a far more "
   5            + "pleasing sound;";
   6
   7        var verse_words = verse.split(" ");
   8
   9 ▾      for(var i in verse_words) {
  10            var current_word = verse_words[i];
  11            current_word = current_word.toLowerCase();
  12            document.write(current_word + ' ');
  13            document.write(current_word.indexOf('i'));
  14            document.write('<br>');
  15        }
  16    </script>
  17
  18
  19
  20
  21
  22
  23
  24
```

```
i 0
love -1
to -1
hear -1
her -1
speak, -1
yet -1
well -1
i 0
know -1
that -1
music 3
hath -1
a -1
far -1
more -1
pleasing 5
sound: -1
```

Above, I print out each word along with the index of the letter "i" inside that word. That words that do not contain an "i" all show a negative index, while the ones that contain it either show zero or a positive number.

Joining array elements

We have already covered the **split()** function that turns a string into an array by splitting it up. The **join()** function performs the opposite function. It joins the elements of an array and gives us a string back:

```
i  1 ▾ <script>
   2        var verse = "I love to hear her speak,"
   3            + " yet well I know "
   4            + "That music hath a far more "
   5            + "pleasing sound;";
   6
   7        var verse_words = verse.split(" ");
   8
   9        document.write(verse_words.join(' / '));
  10    </script>
```

I / love / to / hear / her /
speak, / yet / well / I / know /
That / music / hath / a / far /
more / pleasing / sound:

Above, on line 7 we split the **verse** string in to an array as usual. On line 9, we use **join()** to turn it back into a string. Since the argument to the **join()** function is **' / '**, the array elements are separated by spaces and slashes. This argument could be anything we want. Below I have chosen an asterisk and space:

```
i   1 ▾ <script>
    2       var verse = "I love to hear her speak,"
    3           + " yet well I know "
    4           + "That music hath a far more "
    5           + "pleasing sound;";
    6
    7       var verse_words = verse.split(" ");
    8
    9       document.write(verse_words.join('* '));
   10   </script>
```

I* love* to* hear* her* speak,* yet* well* I* know* That* music* hath* a* far* more* pleasing* sound:

The argument could even be a **
** tag to make each array element appear on its own line:

```
i   1 ▾ <script>
    2       var verse = "I love to hear her speak,"
    3           + " yet well I know "
    4           + "That music hath a far more "
    5           + "pleasing sound;";
    6
    7       var verse_words = verse.split(" ");
    8
    9       document.write(verse_words.join('<br>'));
   10   </script>
   11
   12
   13
   14
   15
```

I
love
to
hear
her
speak,
yet
well
I
know
That

We can also do the splitting and joining on one line as follows:

```
i   1 ▾ <script>
    2       var verse = "I love to hear her speak,"
    3           + " yet well I know "
    4           + "That music hath a far more "
    5           + "pleasing sound;";
    6
    7       document.write(
    8           verse.split(" ").join(" - ")
    9       );
   10   </script>
```

I - love - to - hear - her - speak, - yet - well - I - know - That - music - hath - a - far - more - pleasing - sound:

Reading line 8 from left to right: we first have the **verse** string variable, then using the **split()** function it is split at the spaces into an array, next using the **join()** function it is joined back together into a string with the array elements separated by spaces and dashes.

Analyzing students' names

In this example, we have the first and last names of 14 students in an array. Our task is to find out the master common first names among them. Writing a program to analyze a mere 14 names is unnecessary, but imagine working for the census office and having to analyze millions of names. That is when programming skills are indispensable.

```
1 ▾ <script>
2       var student_names =
3 ▾         ['Sophia Johnson', 'Noah Smith', 'Emma Davis',
4             'Liam Williams', 'Mason Brown', 'Ava Garcia',
5             'Jacob Jones', 'William Miller', 'Liam Anderson',
6             'Olivia Wilson', 'Emma Jacobson', 'Olivia Young',
7             'Liam Wright', 'Sophia Baker'];
```

In order to proceed with our analysis, we first create a new array **first_names** that will only hold the first names (line 8 below).

```
1 ▾ <script>
2       var student_names =
3 ▾         ['Sophia Johnson', 'Noah Smith', 'Emma Davis',
4             'Liam Williams', 'Mason Brown', 'Ava Garcia',
5             'Jacob Jones', 'William Miller', 'Liam Anderson',
6             'Olivia Wilson', 'Emma Jacobson', 'Olivia Young',
7             'Liam Wright', 'Sophia Baker'];
8       var first_names = [];
```

Below is the loop we will use to go over the names:

```
1 ▾ <script>
2       var student_names =
3 ▾         ['Sophia Johnson', 'Noah Smith', 'Emma Davis',
4             'Liam Williams', 'Mason Brown', 'Ava Garcia',
5             'Jacob Jones', 'William Miller', 'Liam Anderson',
6             'Olivia Wilson', 'Emma Jacobson', 'Olivia Young',
7             'Liam Wright', 'Sophia Baker'];
8       var first_names = [];
9 ▾     for(var i in student_names) {
10          student_full_name = student_names[i];
11          document.write('current name: ' + student_full_name);
12          document.write('<br>');
13          student_split_name = student_full_name.split(' ');
14          document.write('split name: ' + student_split_name.toString());
15          document.write('<br>');
16          student_first_name = student_split_name[0];
17          document.write('first name only: ' + student_first_name);
18          document.write('<br>');
19          first_names.push(student_first_name);
20      }
```

Seeing all of that code in one loop can be a little overwhelming, but there is actually nothing new in it that we have not already covered. I have added **document.write()** statements in various places in order to show what is going on inside the loop. Here is what gets printed out in the preview area:

```
current name: Sophia Johnson
split name: Sophia,Johnson
first name only: Sophia
current name: Noah Smith
split name: Noah,Smith
first name only: Noah
current name: Emma Davis
split name: Emma,Davis
first name only: Emma
current name: Liam Williams
split name: Liam,Williams
first name only: Liam
current name: Mason Brown
split name: Mason,Brown
first name only: Mason
current name: Ava Garcia
split name: Ava,Garcia
first name only: Ava
current name: Jacob Jones
split name: Jacob,Jones
first name only: Jacob
```

Try to read the code to see if you can understand everything that is going on before I explain it below.

Below is the loop with the **document.write()** statements removed:

```
 9 ▾      for(var i in student_names) {
10             student_full_name = student_names[i];
11             student_split_name = student_full_name.split(' ');
12             student_first_name = student_split_name[0];
13             first_names.push(student_first_name);
14         }
```

On line 10 we place the current student's name in the **student_full_name** variable. On line 11 we split this variable at the spaces and place the result inside the array variable **student_split_name**. On line 12, we get the first element of the **student_split_name** array using the zero index and place it inside the **student_first_name** string variable. On line 13 we use the **push()** function to place the value of this variable inside the **first_names** array.

Below I use **document.write()** and **toString()** to print out the contents of the **first_names** array after the loop is done:

```
 9 ▾     for(var i in student_names) {
10           student_full_name = student_names[i];
11           student_split_name = student_full_name.split(' ');
12           student_first_name = student_split_name[0];
13           first_names.push(student_first_name);
14       }
15       document.write(first_names.toString());
```

Here is the result:

Sophia,Noah,Emma,Liam,Mason,Ava,Jacob,William,Liam.

There is more inside the array than can be seen above since the preview area is not large enough to show all of the contents. Below on line 15 we use **join()** rather than **toString()** to turn the **first_names** array into a string with the elements separated by spaces and slashes:

```
 9 ▾     for(var i in student_names) {
10           student_full_name = student_names[i];
11           student_split_name = student_full_name.split(' ');
12           student_first_name = student_split_name[0];
13           first_names.push(student_first_name);
14       }
15       document.write(first_names.join(' / '));
```

Here is the result:

Sophia / Noah / Emma / Liam / Mason / Ava / Jacob /
William / Liam / Olivia / Emma / Olivia / Liam / Sophia

Let us know go on with our analysis. Below we use a new function and a new to proceed with counting the names:

```
15 ▾     function countOccurrences(word, array_of_words) {
16           var count = 0;
17 ▾         for(var i in array_of_words) {
18 ▾             if(word === array_of_words[i]) {
19                   count++;
20               }
21           }
22           return count;
23       }
24 ▾     for(var i in first_names) {
25           var first_name = first_names[i];
26           var count = countOccurrences(first_name, first_names);
27           document.write(first_name + ' ' + count + '<br>');
28       }
```

461

Here is the result:

```
Sophia 2
Noah 1
Emma 2
Liam 3
Mason 1
Ava 1
Jacob 1
William 1
Liam 3
Olivia 2
Emma 2
Olivia 2
Liam 3
Sophia 2
```

Inside the new loop (lines 24-28) we use the new function **countOccurrences()** to count the number of times each name occurs in the **first_names** array. The **countOccurrences()** function works by going over the **array_of_words** variable that we pass to it and increasing the **count** variable by one each time it detects the value of the **word** variable inside the **array_of_words** array.

Below I have added extra **document.write()** statements to the **countOccurrences()** function in order to show how it works:

```
15 ▾    function countOccurrences(word, array_of_words) {
16           var count = 0;
17           document.write('current word: ' + word + '<br>');
18 ▾        for(var i in array_of_words) {
19               document.write('will compare ' + word +
20                   ' with ' + array_of_words[i] + '<br>');
21
22 ▾            if(word === array_of_words[i]) {
23                   count++;
24                   document.write('match detected!' + '<br>');
25                   document.write('current count: ' + count + '<br>');
26               }
27           }
28           return count;
29       }
```

Here is the output when this function analyzes the name Sophia:

```
current word: Sophia
will compare Sophia with Sophia
match detected!
current count: 1
will compare Sophia with Noah
will compare Sophia with Emma
will compare Sophia with Liam
will compare Sophia with Mason
will compare Sophia with Ava
will compare Sophia with Jacob
will compare Sophia with William
will compare Sophia with Liam
will compare Sophia with Olivia
will compare Sophia with Emma
will compare Sophia with Olivia
will compare Sophia with Liam
will compare Sophia with Sophia
match detected!
current count: 2
```

Back to our analysis, you may have noticed that in the earlier output some names are unnecessarily shown multiple times:

```
Sophia 2
Noah 1
Emma 2
Liam 3
Mason 1
Ava 1
Jacob 1
William 1
Liam 3
Olivia 2
Emma 2
Olivia 2
Liam 3
Sophia 2
```

That is because our new loop at lines 24-28 does not care whether it has already checked the number of occurrences of the name it is seeing. If it sees Sophia multiple times, it will analyze it each time and show its count:

```
24 ▾    for(var i in first_names) {
25           var first_name = first_names[i];
26           var count = countOccurrences(first_name, first_names);
27           document.write(first_name + ' ' + count + '<br>');
28       }
```

Using includes() and the continue statement

We can make the loop smarter by making it avoid re-analyzing names it has already analyzed.

```
24       var analyzed_names = [];
25 ▾    for(var i in first_names) {
26           var first_name = first_names[i];
27           var count = countOccurrences(first_name, first_names);
28           document.write(first_name + ' ' + count + '<br>');
29           analyzed_names.push(first_name);
30       }
```

Above, on line 24 we declare a new array named **analyzed_names**. On line 29 we push each name we analyze inside this array.

Next we add an **if** statement to check whether the name has already been analyzed or not (lines 27-29):

```
24       var analyzed_names = [];
25 ▾    for(var i in first_names) {
26           var first_name = first_names[i];
27 ▾        if(analyzed_names.includes(first_name)) {
28               continue;
29           }
30           var count = countOccurrences(first_name, first_names);
31           document.write(first_name + ' ' + count + '<br>');
32           analyzed_names.push(first_name);
33       }
```

Inside the loop, on line 27 we use a new built-in JavaScript function called **includes()**. This function checks whether an array contains a certain value or not. We are checking if **analyzed_names** contains the **first_name** we are currently analyzing. If it contains it, it means we have already analyzed the name. If so, we want to tell JavaScript to not run the analysis again. In order to do so we use the new **continue** statement on line 28. This statement causes the loop to stop executing and to go back to the top onto the next item. This means that if the name we are checking has already been analyzed previously, the **continue** statement on line 28 causes the statements on lines 30-32 to be ignored.

Here is the result:

Sophia 2
Noah 1
Emma 2
Liam 3
Mason 1
Ava 1
Jacob 1
William 1
Olivia 2

As you can see, there are no duplicate names anymore.

Here is the complete code. I recommend that you read it from top to bottom and try to understand each statement. Reading code and trying to make sense of it is an important part of learning programming:

```
1 <script>
2     var student_names =
3         ['Sophia Johnson', 'Noah Smith', 'Emma Davis',
4         'Liam Williams', 'Mason Brown', 'Ava Garcia',
5         'Jacob Jones', 'William Miller', 'Liam Anderson',
6         'Olivia Wilson', 'Emma Jacobson', 'Olivia Young',
7         'Liam Wright', 'Sophia Baker'];
8     var first_names = [];
9     for(var i in student_names) {
10         student_full_name = student_names[i];
11         student_split_name = student_full_name.split(' ');
12         student_first_name = student_split_name[0];
13         first_names.push(student_first_name);
14     }
15     function countOccurrences(word, array_of_words) {
16         var count = 0;
17         for(var i in array_of_words) {
18             if(word === array_of_words[i]) {
19                 count++;
20             }
21         }
22         return count;
23     }
24     var analyzed_names = [];
25     for(var i in first_names) {
26         var first_name = first_names[i];
27         if(analyzed_names.includes(first_name)) {
28             continue;
29         }
30         var count = countOccurrences(first_name, first_names);
31         document.write(first_name + ' ' + count + '<br>');
32         analyzed_names.push(first_name);
33     }
34 </script>
```

This page intentionally left blank

19. Objects

At this point in this book, you have already mastered the basics of programming. From here on we will discuss more advanced topics that will expose the nitty-gritty of programming to you and will take you from a novice to an intermediate learner. Some of the concepts covered from here on are going to be rather advanced and will strongly depend on the things you have already learned. It might be a good idea to review the previous chapters before proceeding.

We have come to the final important data type in JavaScript, objects. Not all languages have this data type. It is, however, one of the most useful data types in JavaScript and it is essential for building large-scale JavaScript programs.

In order to speak about objects, we will start by looking at an example array:

```
i  1 ▾ <script>
   2 ▾     var student_data = ['Sophia Davis', '2', '85220',
   3           'Emma Davis', 'James Davis'];
   4   </script>
```

Above, the **student_data** holds information about a student named Sophia Davis. The problem with this data is that you cannot be exactly sure what the different values stand for. The second element of the array is the number "2", which probably stands for her grade. The next element looks like a ZIP code, and the next two elements look like the student's mother and father names. Now imagine if there were fifty more elements in the array. It could become unmanageably difficult to make sense of the array.

Below is an object named **student_data** that holds the same data as before:

```
i  1▾ <script>
   2▾     var student_data = {
   3           'full_name' : 'Sophia Davis',
   4           'grade' : '2',
   5           'zip_code' : '85220',
   6           'mother_full_name' : 'Emma Davis',
   7           'father_full_name' : 'James Davis'
   8       };
   9  </script>
```

Above **student_data** is now an object. Objects are declared using curly braces **{}**. An object is made up of what are known as key-value pairs. They key "full_name" is associated with the value "Sophia Davis".

Both arrays and objects are like tables, but with a crucial difference. An array is like a table with numbers as its first column. You find each item by looking up its number:

```
student_data = [
```

0	'Sophia Davis',
1	'2',
2	'85220',
3	'Emma Davis',
4	'James Davis'

```
];
```

But an object is like a table with descriptive labels as its first column rather than numbers, making it possible to look up each value by a label (or key) rather than a number:

```
student_data = {
```

'full_name'	'Sophia Davis',
'grade'	'2',
'zip_code'	'85220',
'mother_full_name'	'Emma Davis',
'father_full_name'	'James Davis'

```
};
```

Below is an example of accessing an object's value by a key:

```
i   1 ▾ <script>
    2 ▾     var student_data = {
    3           'full_name' : 'Sophia Davis',
    4           'grade' : '2',
    5           'zip_code' : '85220',
    6           'mother_full_name' : 'Emma Davis',
    7           'father_full_name' : 'James Davis'
    8       };
    9       document.write(student_data.full_name);
   10   </script>
```

Sophia Davis

On line 9, using the statement **student_data.full_name**, we access the value we associated with the **full_name** key on line 3. The key-value pair is called a "property". For example we say that **full_name** is a property of the **student_data** object whose key is **full_name** and whose value is "Sophia Davis".

Objects can be nested, which allows us to create highly readable and useful ways of representing our data:

```
i   1 ▾ <script>
    2 ▾     var student_data = {
    3           'full_name' : 'Sophia Davis',
    4           'grade' : '2',
    5           'zip_code' : '85220',
    6 ▾         'mother' : {
    7               'full_name' : 'Emma Davis',
    8               'phone_number' : '12345678',
    9           },
   10 ▾         'father' : {
   11               'full_name' : 'James Davis',
   12               'phone_number' : '23456789',
   13           }
   14       };
   15       document.write(student_data.mother.full_name);
   16   </script>
```

Emma Davis

Above, I have removed the **mother_full_name** key. Instead, we now have a **mother** key that refers to a new object with two keys, **full_name** and **phone_number**. It is the same for the father's data. On line 15 I use **student_data.mother.full_name** to get the student's mother's full name.

Another way to declare objects is to declare an empty object then add stuff to it later on:

```
i   1 ▾ <script>
    2       var student = {};
    3       student.full_name = 'Liam Smith';
    4       student.father = {};
    5       student.father.full_name = 'Jeffrey Smith';
    6       document.write(student.father.full_name);
    7   </script>
```

Jeffrey Smith

Above, note that only the **student** variable needs to be declared with a **var**. The rest of the declarations do not need a **var**.

Below we have an object variable named city that represents the city of Ann Arbor in Michigan:

```
i  1▾ <script>
   2       var city = {};
   3       city.name = 'Ann Arbor';
   4       city.county = 'Washtenaw';
   5       city.population = '121000';
   6▾      city.zip_codes = [
   7           48103, 48104, 48105, 48106, 48107,
   8           48108, 48109, 48113
   9           ];
```

We use an array to represent the city's eight ZIP codes, meaning that **zip_codes** is an array that is inside the **city** object. We can use this array like any other array, as follows:

```
i  1▾ <script>                                              48103
   2       var city = {};                                   48104
   3       city.name = 'Ann Arbor';                         48105
   4       city.county = 'Washtenaw';                       48106
   5       city.population = '121000';                      48107
   6▾      city.zip_codes = [                               48108
   7           48103, 48104, 48105, 48106, 48107,           48109
   8           48108, 48109, 48113                          48113
   9           ];
  10▾      for(var i in city.zip_codes) {
  11           document.write(city.zip_codes[i] + '<br>');
  12       }
  13   </script>
```

The above is the same as the below.

```
i  1▾ <script>                                              48103
   2       var city = {};                                   48104
   3       city.name = 'Ann Arbor';                         48105
   4       city.county = 'Washtenaw';                       48106
   5       city.population = '121000';                      48107
   6▾      city.zip_codes = [                               48108
   7           48103, 48104, 48105, 48106, 48107,           48109
   8           48108, 48109, 48113                          48113
   9           ];
  10       var zip_codes = city.zip_codes;
  11▾      for(var i in zip_codes) {
  12           document.write(zip_codes[i] + '<br>');
  13       }
  14   </script>
```

Above I create a new variable named **zip_codes** on line 10 and put the **city.zip_codes** array inside it, then I use the new **zip_codes** variable inside the loop.

The coffee robot

In this section we will discuss a simple system for communicating with a coffee-making robot using an object. This is something that can actually work in the real world, provided that you have a friend who works as a "back-end" programmer and knows how to write software that can understand requests sent from JavaScript.

We will start by declaring a new object that represents the cup of coffee we want the robot to make:

```
i  1▾ <script>
   2       var my_coffee = {};
   3  </script>
```

Next we will declare what kind of cup of coffee we want:

```
i  1▾ <script>
   2       var my_coffee = {};
   3▾      my_coffee.attributes = {
   4           'origin' : 'Chiapas',
   5           'organic' : 'Yes',
   6           'grind' : 'Rough',
   7           'roast' : 'Medium',
   8           'creamer' : 'None',
   9           'sweetener' : 'None',
  10       };
  11  </script>
```

Next we will declare a function that sends the order to the robot:

```
i  1▾ <script>
   2       var my_coffee = {};
   3▾      my_coffee.attributes = {
   4           'origin' : 'Chiapas',
   5           'organic' : 'Yes',
   6           'grind' : 'Rough',
   7           'roast' : 'Medium',
   8           'creamer' : 'None',
   9           'sweetener' : 'None',
  10       };
  11▾      my_coffee.order = function() {
  12
  13       };
  14  </script>
```

Above I have declared a function named **order** on lines 11-13. As you can see, an object can hold functions. This function can be called by writing **my_coffee.order()**. Note the way we declared the function on line 11, which is different from the way we have done it before. Normally you would write **function order() { }**. But here, we are using a different method of defining functions, which is to declare it "anonymously" (without specifying a name for it) then put it inside a variable, in this case the **my_coffee.order** variable. Even though this function is technically nameless, since we have put it inside a variable, we can use it like any other function by using the variable's name.

The function is at present empty. The first thing we need is a way to access the attributes of the cup of coffee so that we can send them to the robot. In order to do that, we use a new concept known as **this**.

```
11 ▾    my_coffee.order = function() {
12          var cup_properties = this.attributes;
13      };
```

The **this** keyword is used to refer to the current object. When we write **this.attributes** on line 12, JavaScript knows that we mean **my_coffee.attributes** since we are inside a function that is inside this object. Think of **this** as meaning "the current object we are inside of" and it should make sense.

Next we will define the part of the function that actually communicates with the robot, on lines 14-24:

```
11 ▾    my_coffee.order = function() {
12          var cup_properties = this.attributes;
13
14 ▾        $.ajax('http://0.0.0.0/robot/orders', {
15              data: cup_properties,
16 ▾            success: function () {
17                  document.write('The robot successfully '
18                      'received the order!');
19              },
20 ▾            error: function () {
21                  document.write('There was an error '
22                      + 'connecting to the robot');
23              }
24          });
25      };
```

Explaining what is going above is beyond the scope of this book, it is merely there to show readers that JavaScript is not merely a toy, it can actually communicate with real-world machines and control them. What we are doing is sending an "AJAX" request using something called jQuery to the robot's Internet address. On line 15 we have **data: cup_properties**, this means that when we communicate with the robot, we send it the details of the type of cup of coffee we declared earlier. Note that running this code on your local machine will not work since the Internet address defined on line 14 is not a real address.

Above we have only declared the function. If we run the code nothing happens since we are not actually calling the function. The final step would therefore be to call the **order** function:

```
27      my_coffee.order();
28  </script>
```

If everything works correctly, running the code would cause the preview area to show the following message:

> The robot successfully received the order!

Text Analyzer

In this section, we will build a simple JavaScript program that we will call Text Analyzer. We will use an object variable named **text_analyzer** to hold the program.[21]

```
i  1 ▾ <script>
   2 ▾ var text_analyzer = {
   3      current_text : '',
   4 ▾    get_words_array : function() {
   5          var text = this.current_text;
   6          var split_text = text.split(' ');
   7          return split_text;
   8      }
   9  };
  10
  11  text_analyzer.current_text =
  12      'And this is Dorlcote Mill. I must '
  13      + 'stand a minute or two here on the bridge '
  14      + 'and look at it, though the clouds are '
  15      + 'threatening, and it is far on in the afternoon. '
  16      + 'Even in this leafless time of departing February '
  17      + 'it is pleasant to look at,-perhaps the chill, '
  18      + 'damp season adds a charm to the trimly kept, '
  19      + 'comfortable dwelling-house, as old as the elms '
  20      + 'and chestnuts that shelter it from the '
  21      + 'northern blast. ';
  22  </script>
```

The **text_analyzer** program currently has only one function named **get_words_array** which splits the string inside **text_analyzer.current_text** and returns the resulting array. On lines 11-21 we place a relatively long string inside **text_analyzer.current_text** taken from George Eliot's 1860 novel *The Mill on the Floss*.

---

[21] Visit my personal website for the code for Text Analyzer and other functions developed throughout this book: http://hawramani.com/?p=67000

Notice that when declaring the **get_words_array** on line 4, we are using a colon not an equal sign because we are inside an object and we are declaring the object's keys and values, which are separated by colons. In this case the key is **get_words_array** and the value is an anonymous function.

We will now add a new function to **text_analyzer** that counts the number of words we give the program:

```
i   1 ▾  <script>
    2 ▾  var text_analyzer = {
    3        current_text : '',
    4 ▾      get_words_array : function() {
    5            var text = this.current_text;
    6            var split_text = text.split(' ');
    7            return split_text;
    8        },
    9 ▾      count_words : function() {
   10            return this.get_words_array().length;
   11        }
   12   };
   13
   14   text_analyzer.current_text =
   15        'And this is Dorlcote Mill. I must '
   16        + 'stand a minute or two here on the bridge '
   17        + 'and look at it, though the clouds are '
   18        + 'threatening, and it is far on in the afternoon. '
   19        + 'Even in this leafless time of departing February '
   20        + 'it is pleasant to look at,-perhaps the chill, '
   21        + 'damp season adds a charm to the trimly kept, '
   22        + 'comfortable dwelling-house, as old as the elms '
   23        + 'and chestnuts that shelter it from the '
   24        + 'northern blast. ';
   25   document.write(text_analyzer.count_words());
   26   </script>
```

75

The new function is named **count_words** (lines 9-11). This function makes use of the previously defined function **get_words_array** to get the string as an array, then simply returns the length property of the array. On line 25 we use the **count_words()** function and the result, seen in the preview area, is 75.

To explain what is going on line 10, below I break it down into three lines:

```
    9 ▾      count_words : function() {
   10            var words_array = this.get_words_array();
   11            var length = words_array.length;
   12            return length;
   13        }
```

In the shorter version of the function, writing **this.get_words_array().length** returns the length of the *result* of the **get_words_array()** function. The brackets in **this.get_words_array().length** are crucial. It is a common mistake to forget the brackets so that one writes **this.get_words_array.length**. This leads to a wrong result because JavaScript gets confused into thinking we are trying to get the length of the function's code.

Below are two statements to clarify the issue of the brackets. The first on line 27 uses **count_words** with brackets, while the second one on line 29 does not use the brackets.

```
27    document.write(text_analyzer.count_words());
28    document.write('<br>');
29    document.write(text_analyzer.count_words);
```

Here is the result:

```
75
function () { var words_array =
this.get_words_array(); var length =
words_array.length; return length; }
```

The statement on line 27 works as expected. The statement on line 29, however, returns the function's code. It is the brackets right after the function's name that tells JavaScript to run the function. Without the brackets, JavaScript thinks we are simply referring to the function definition.

Below we add a third function named **get_average_word_length** that analyzes the text to find out the average length of the words in the text.

```
14 ▾     get_average_word_length : function() {
15          var all_word_lengths = 0;
16          var words_array = this.get_words_array();
17 ▾       for(var i in words_array) {
18              var current_word = words_array[i];
19              all_word_lengths = all_word_lengths +
20                  current_word.length;
21          }
22          return all_word_lengths / words_array.length;
23      },
24  };
25
26  text_analyzer.current_text =
27      'And this is Dorlcote Mill. I must '
28      + 'stand a minute or two here on the bridge '
29      + 'and look at it, though the clouds are '
30      + 'threatening, and it is far on in the afternoon. '
31      + 'Even in this leafless time of departing February '
32      + 'it is pleasant to look at,-perhaps the chill, '
33      + 'damp season adds a charm to the trimly kept, '
34      + 'comfortable dwelling-house, as old as the elms '
35      + 'and chestnuts that shelter it from the '
36      + 'northern blast. ';
37  document.write(text_analyzer.get_average_word_length());
38  </script>
```

```
4.386666666666667
```

In the **get_average_word_length()** function we use **all_word_lengths** to sum up the length of all the words in the text. On line 22 we divide this sum by the number of words in the text to get the average, which as seen in the preview area is 4.386. This average is not fully accurate because our code counts punctuation as part of the word that comes before it. For example "kept," is counted as 5 letters in length. There are ways to fix this but that is a topic for later chapters.

We next add a function for finding out the longest word in the text:

```
24    get_longest_word : function() {
25        var longest_length_seen_so_far = 0;
26        var longest_word = '';
27        var words_array = this.get_words_array();
28        for(var i in words_array) {
29            var current_word = words_array[i];
30            if(current_word.length >
31                longest_length_seen_so_far) {
32                longest_word = current_word;
33                longest_length_seen_so_far =
34                    current_word.length;
35            }
36        }
37        return longest_word;
38    },
39 };
40
41 text_analyzer.current_text =
42    'And this is Dorlcote Mill. I must '
43    + 'stand a minute or two here on the bridge '
44    + 'and look at it, though the clouds are '
45    + 'threatening, and it is far on in the afternoon. '
46    + 'Even in this leafless time of departing February '
47    + 'it is pleasant to look at,-perhaps the chill, '
48    + 'damp season adds a charm to the trimly kept, '
49    + 'comfortable dwelling-house, as old as the elms '
50    + 'and chestnuts that shelter it from the '
51    + 'northern blast. ';
52 document.write(text_analyzer.get_longest_word());
53 </script>
```

dwelling-house,

The **get_longest_word()** function uses what is known as a "high watermark algorithm" to find out the longest word in the text's array of words. In the **for** loop on lines 28-36, each time we see a word that is longer than the ones seen before, we store it in **longest_word** while also storing its length in **longest_length_seen_so_far**. Once the loop is done, **longest_word** ends up containing the longest word in the entire array.

Below I have added a new **document.write()** statement on lines 33-34 to clarify how the **get_longest_word()** function works:

```
24 ▾    get_longest_word : function() {                    ▲
25           var longest_length_seen_so_far = 0;
26           var longest_word = '';
27           var words_array = this.get_words_array();
28 ▾        for(var i in words_array) {
29              var current_word = words_array[i];
30              if(current_word.length >
31 ▾                longest_length_seen_so_far) {
32                  longest_word = current_word;
33                  document.write('longest '
34                     + 'word: '
35                     + longest_word + '<br>');
36                  longest_length_seen_so_far =
37                     current_word.length;
38              }
39           }
40           return longest_word;
41       },
```

longest word: And
longest word: this
longest word: Dorlcote
longest word: threatening.
longest word: dwelling-house.
dwelling-house.

As the function runs, at first it considers "And" to be the longest word, since the check **current_word.length > longest_length_seen_so_far** compares 3 with zero. Next time the loop runs it compares the length of "this" with the length of the previously seen "And". Again, since the new word is larger, **longest_word** ends up containing "this". The next word that is checked is the word "is". Since this is shorter than "this", the condition becomes false so that **longest_word** continues to contain "this". In this way each time a word is seen that is longer than the word stored in **longest_word**, **longest_word** is updated to contain the new word. In the end "dwelling-house," wins as the longest word.

Bracket notation and dynamic properties

We have already seen how an object property can be accessed using dot notation, as in **student.full_name**. There is another way of accessing the same property by using bracket notation, as in **student["full_name"]**:

```
i  1 ▾  <script>
   2    var student = {};
   3    student.full_name = "Sophia Davis";
   4    document.write(student.full_name);
   5    document.write('<br>');
   6    document.write(student["full_name"]);
   7    </script>
```

Sophia Davis
Sophia Davis

Above, on line 4 we access the **full_name** property of the **student** object using dot notation, while on line 6 we use bracket notation. The result is the same in both cases.

Below we have an array that contains fruit names. We want to convert this array into an object with the keys as the fruit names and the values as the length of each fruit name:

```
1  <script>
2  var fruits_array = ['banana', 'apple',
3         'orange'];
4
5  </script>
```

Here is an illustration of the object we want to create based on the above array, with each fruit name on the left, and the length of each fruit name on the right as its value:

```
fruits_object = {
    'banana' : 6,
    'apple' : 5,
    'orange' : 6
}
```

Below is the code we use to create just such an object from the array:

```
1  <script>
2  var fruits_array = ['banana', 'apple',
3         'orange'];
4  var fruits_object = {};
5  for(var i in fruits_array) {
6      var current_fruit = fruits_array[i];
7      fruits_object[current_fruit]
8          = current_fruit.length;
9  }
10 </script>
```

Above, we first declare an empty **fruits_object** on line 4. On line 5 we loop over the **fruits_array**. On lines 7-8 is where the interesting stuff happens. By writing fruits_object[current_fruit], we are telling JavaScript to create a property inside the fruits_object that has a key of the value inside **current_fruit**. The first time the loop runs, **fruit_object[current_fruit]** is interpreted by JavaScript as **fruit_object["banana"]**, the second time as **fruit_object["apple"]**, and the third and last time as **fruit_object["orange"]**. These properties do not actually exist inside the object, but by accessing them here and setting them equal to **current_fruit.length**, we create them and put a value inside them all in one step.

You may wonder why instead of using a loop we cannot just write out each property we want to create, as follows:

```
i   1▾ <script>
    2▾ var fruits_array = ['banana', 'apple',
    3            'orange'];
    4   var fruits_object = {};
    5   fruits_object.banana = "banana".length;
    6   fruits_object.apple = "apple".length;
    7   fruits_object.orange = "orange".length;
    8   </script>
```

The above accomplishes exactly the same thing as before. The difference is that the earlier code can handle arrays of any length. Imagine if **fruits_array** had hundreds of words in it. You would then either have to write a relatively simple loop, or you would have to write a hundred lines to deal with each separate word.

Below we add a new loop to print out the contents of the **fruits_object**:

```
i   1▾ <script>                              banana 6
    2▾ var fruits_array = ['banana', 'apple',  apple 5
    3            'orange'];                   orange 6
    4   var fruits_object = {};
    5▾ for(var i in fruits_array) {
    6        var current_fruit = fruits_array[i];
    7        fruits_object[current_fruit]
    8            = current_fruit.length;
    9   }
   10▾ for(var i in fruits_object) {
   11        document.write(i + ' ' +
   12            fruits_object[i]);
   13        document.write('<br>');
   14   }
   15   </script>
```

Above, we have a normal-looking **for** loop on line 10, but this time we are looping over an object not an array. The value of i is not going to be a number, it is going to be one of the keys of the object. The first time the loop runs, **i** contains the word "banana" while **fruits_object[i]** contains the number 6, as if we had an object defined as follows:

```
fruits_object = {
    "banana" : 6
}
```

It can be difficult for even experienced programmers to intuitively make sense of the fact that **i** contains keys and **some_bject[i]** contains values. To avoid confusion, it can help to create variables at the top of the loop with more descriptive names:

```
i   1▾ <script>
    2▾ var fruits_array = ['banana', 'apple',
    3           'orange'];
    4   var fruits_object = {};
    5▾ for(var i in fruits_array) {
    6       var current_fruit = fruits_array[i];
    7       fruits_object[current_fruit]
    8           = current_fruit.length;
    9   }
   10▾ for(var i in fruits_object) {
   11       var current_key = i;
   12       var current_value = fruits_object[i];
   13       document.write(current_key);
   14       document.write(' ' + current_value);
   15       document.write('<br>');
   16   }
   17   </script>
```

banana 6
apple 5
orange 6

Printing objects

We cannot use **object.toString()** to print out the contents of an object. Doing so will always cause JavaScript to display **[object Object]** regardless of what the object contains:

```
i   1▾ <script>
    2▾ var car = {
    3       'maker' : 'Honda',
    4   };
    5   document.write(car.toString());
    6   </script>
```

[object Object]

In this section we will create our own object printing function. The second loop shown earlier already showed how to do this.

```
i  1 ▾ <script>
   2 ▾ function print_object(the_object) {
   3 ▾     document.write('{<br>');
   4 ▾     for(var i in the_object) {
   5           var key = i;
   6           var value = the_object[i];
   7           document.write('"' + key + '"');
   8           document.write(' : ');
   9           document.write(value);
   10          document.write('<br>');
   11      }
   12      document.write('}<br>');
   13  }
   14
   15 ▾ var car = {
   16      'maker' : 'Honda',
   17      'year' : '2018',
   18  };
   19  print_object(car);
   20  </script>
```

```
{
"maker" : Honda
"year" : 2018
}
```

Above, the new **print_object** function takes an object and prints out its contents. On line 3 we print out an opening curly brace and a new line. On line 12 we print out a closing curly brace and a new line. These curly braces are not necessary, they are simply for presentation purposes to help a reader immediately know that what is shown is an object's contents. On line 7 we write out **'"' + key + '"'**. This prints out the **key** with a double quotation mark before it and a double quotation mark after it. In the preview area you can see that "maker" and "year" have quotation marks. The strange syntax **'"'** simply means "a string that contains a double quotation mark". The single quotation marks before and after it are used to enclose the string, similar to the way the string **'Apple'** has a single quotation mark before it and after it to tell JavaScript where the string starts and where it ends. To clarify further, below I have temporarily changed line 7 so that it now puts asterisks rather than quotation marks before and after each key:

```
i  1 ▾ <script>
   2 ▾ function print_object(the_object) {
   3 ▾     document.write('{<br>');
   4 ▾     for(var i in the_object) {
   5           var key = i;
   6           var value = the_object[i];
   7           document.write('*' + key + '*');
   8           document.write(' : ');
   9           document.write(value);
   10          document.write('<br>');
   11      }
   12      document.write('}<br>');
   13  }
```

```
{
*maker* : Honda
*year* : 2018
}
```

Printing nested objects

The above printing function only works on simple objects. If we pass it an object that contains another object, the following happens:

```
i   1 ▾ <script>
    2 ▾ function print_object(the_object) {
    3 ▾     document.write('{<br>');
    4 ▾     for(var i in the_object) {
    5           var key = i;
    6           var value = the_object[i];
    7           document.write('"' + key + '"');
    8           document.write(' : ');
    9           document.write(value);
   10           document.write('<br>');
   11       }
   12       document.write('}<br>');
   13   }
   14
   15 ▾ var car = {
   16       "maker" : "Honda",
   17       "year": 2018,
   18 ▾     "model_details" : {
   19           "name" : "Accord",
   20           "length" : '192"',
   21           "width" : '73" W',
   22           "height" : '57" H',
   23       }
   24   }
   25   print_object(car);
   26   </script>
```

```
{
"maker" : Honda
"year" : 2018
"model_details" : [object Object]
}
```

As you can see, the **model_details** property is printed out as **[object Object]**. This is because on line 9 the **document.write(value)** statement forces JavaScript to interpret the nested object as a string. Since JavaScript is not designed to handle this, it simply tells us that we are trying to force an object to become a string.

In order to make **print_object** handle nested objects, we use a technique known as recursion:

```
i   1 ▾ <script>
    2 ▾ function print_object(the_object) {
    3 ▾     document.write('{<br>');
    4 ▾     for(var i in the_object) {
    5           var key = i;
    6           var value = the_object[i];
    7           document.write('"' + key + '"');
    8           document.write(' : ');
    9 ▾         if(typeof value != 'object') {
   10               document.write(value);
   11           }
   12 ▾         else {
   13               print_object(value);
   14           }
   15           document.write('<br>');
   16       }
   17       document.write('}<br>');
   18   }
```

```
{
"maker" : Honda
"year" : 2018
"model_details" : {
"name" : Accord
"length" : 192"
"width" : 73" W
"height" : 57" H
}

}
```

On line 9 we use the new **typeof** operator, which is used to check the data type of a variable. The check **if(typeof value != 'object')** means "if the data type of the **value** variable is not the object data type". We are saying if the current property we are dealing with is not an object, then do the normal thing on line 10, which is to use **document.write()** to print out its contents. But if it *is* an object, meaning if we are dealing with a nested object, then instead the **else** part runs. In the **else** part we do something wonderful that programming allows us to do, which is to use a function inside itself. If we are printing a nested object, we simply call a new instance of the **print_object** function to print that nested object. This means that even if we had a dozen objects nested in one another, this function could handle them. Each time it sees a nested object, it passes control to a new version of the **print_object** function that deals specifically with the nested object.

When the loop inside **print_object()** function reaches the **model_details** property, the **else** part runs. The value variable that we pass into the second **print_object()** function on line 13 is actually an object, as if we had written:

```
else {
    print_object(
        {
            "name" : "Accord",
            "length" : '192"',
            "width" : '73" W',
            "height" : '57" H',
        }
    );
}
```

JavaScript starts a new separate instance of the **print_object()** function that deals solely with this nested object, not caring about the previous **print_object()** function that is also running. However, since JavaScript executes code line by line, the inner **print_object()** function has to finish like any other statement before JavaScript goes on with the loop in the outer **print_object()** function.

Recursion is relatively complicated and programmers rarely use it in their day-to-day work. But there are some situations that it is ideally suited for.

An object can also contain an array, and that array could in turn contain objects. Our function cannot handle such situations. Well, it can handle them, but it mistakenly thinks arrays are objects, as follows:

483

```
20 ▾ var car = {
21       "maker" : "Honda",
22       "year": 2018,
23 ▾     "model_details" : {
24           "name" : "Accord",
25           "length" : '192"',
26           "width" : '73" W',
27           "height" : '57" H',
28       },
29 ▾     "configurations" : [
30 ▾         {
31               'name': 'LX',
32               'msrp': '23570',
33           },
34 ▾         {
35               'name' : 'Sport CVT',
36               'msrp' : '25780',
37           },
38 ▾         {
39               'name' : 'Sport Manual',
40               'msr' : '25780'
41           }
42       ],
43   }
44   print_object(car);
45   </script>
46
```

```
{
"maker" : Honda
"year" : 2018
"model_details" : {
"name" : Accord
"length" : 192"
"width" : 73" W
"height" : 57" H
}

"configurations" : {
"0" : {
"name" : LX
"msrp" : 23570
}

"1" : {
"name" : Sport CVT
"msrp" : 25780
}
```

The reason it works is that **for** loops work on both arrays and objects. But as you can see in the preview area, the **configurations** property is printed with curly braces after it even though its value is an array.

Let us update it so that it can handle them. First we need a **print_array()** function for printing arrays:

```
19 ▾ function print_array(the_array) {
20 ▾     document.write('[<br>');
21 ▾     for(var i in the_array) {
22           var value = the_array[i];
23 ▾         if(Array.isArray(value)) {
24               print_array(value);
25           }
26 ▾         else if(typeof value === 'object') {
27               print_object(value);
28           }
29 ▾         else {
30               document.write(value + ',');
31           }
32       }
33       document.write(']<br>');
34   }
```

The principles used in this function are similar to those in **print_object()**. However we now have three checks inside the loop. We first use **Array.isArray()**, which is a special JavaScript function that checks if something is an array or not. In the **else if** part on line 26 we use the already-seen **typeof** operator to check if the **value** is an object. And if it is anything else we print it out normally.

We now have to update the **print_object()** function as well to recognize arrays. The original check was as follows:

```
 9 ▾        if(typeof value != 'object') {
10              document.write(value);
11          }
12 ▾        else {
13              print_object(value);
14          }
```

The **typeof** operator returns "object" for arrays as well, so it is useless for determining whether something is an array or an object. This is why we used **Array.isArray()** above to check if something is an array. We have to do the same here:

```
 9 ▾        if(Array.isArray(value)) {
10              print_array(value);
11          }
12 ▾        else if(typeof value === 'object') {
13              print_object(value);
14          }
15 ▾        else {
16              document.write(value);
17          }
```

We first have to check whether value is an array or not. If we put the **typeof value === 'object'** check first, that would stop our code from working properly, because **typeof value === 'object'** is true regardless of whether **value** is an array or an object. So first we have to check if it is an array. If it is not an array but it is an object according to **typeof**, it means it really is an object. Lastly we have an **else** statement for printing plain variables.

Below I have used the new code to print the cars object:

```
{
"maker" : Honda
"year" : 2018
"model_details" : {
"name" : Accord
"length" : 192"
"width" : 73" W
"height" : 57" H
}

"configurations" : [
{
"name" : LX
"msrp" : 23570
}
{
"name" : Sport CVT
"msrp" : 25780
}
{
"name" : Sport Manual
"msr" : 25780
}
]
```

As you can see, the **configurations** property is correctly recognized as an array, while the objects inside it are recognized and printed as objects.

Converting Arrays to Objects

In this section we will add functions (in addition to **print_object()** and **print_array()**) to turn arrays into an objects. Arrays are one-dimensional, while objects are two-dimensional. This gives us multiple options for converting arrays to objects:

```
39   var my_array = ['a', 'b', 'c'];
40 ▾ var my_first_object = {
41       'a' : '',
42       'b' : '',
43       'c' : '',
44   };
45 ▾ var my_second_object = {
46       0 : 'a',
47       1 : 'b',
48       2 : 'c',
49   };
50 ▾ var my_third_object = {
51       1 : 'a',
52       2 : 'b',
53       3 : 'c',
54   }
```

Above, on line 39 we have an array that contains three strings. Below that we have three ways of putting these strings into objects. In the first method we create an object whose keys are the same as the array elements, but whose values are empty strings. In the second method, we create an object whose keys are the same as the array index numbers, and whose values are the strings. In the method, we create an object whose keys start from 1 rather than zero, because the keys can be anything we want.

```
39 ▾ function array_to_object_1(my_array) {
40       var my_object = {};
41 ▾     for(var i in my_array) {
42           var the_element = my_array[i];
43           my_object[the_element] = '';
44       }
45       return my_object;
46   }
47
48   var my_array = ['a', 'b', 'c'];
49   print_object(array_to_object_1(my_array));
50   </script>
```

Above I have added a function to convert arrays to objects using the first method. Here is the result in the preview area:

```
{
"a" :
"b" :
"c" :
}
```

Below is a function to convert arrays to objects using the second method. The function is only slightly different from the previous one:

```
39 ▾ function array_to_object_1(my_array) {
40        var my_object = {};
41 ▾      for(var i in my_array) {
42            var the_element = my_array[i];
43            my_object[the_element] = '';
44        }
45        return my_object;
46    }
47
48 ▾ function array_to_object_2(my_array) {
49        var my_object = {};
50 ▾      for(var i in my_array) {
51            var the_element = my_array[i];
52            my_object[i] = the_element;
53        }
54        return my_object;
55    }
56
57    var my_array = ['a', 'b', 'c'];
58    print_object(array_to_object_2(my_array));
```

Here is the result:

```
{
"0" : a
"1" : b
"2" : c
}
```

Here is the third function:

```
57 ▾ function array_to_object_3(my_array) {
58            var my_object = {};
59 ▾      for(var i in my_array) {
60            var the_element = my_array[i];
61            var the_key = i + 1;
62            my_object[the_key] = the_element;
63        }
64        return my_object;
65    }
66
67    var my_array = ['a', 'b', 'c'];
68    print_object(array_to_object_3(my_array));
```

And here is the result:

```
{
"11" : b
"21" : c
"01" : a
}
```

Oops! We have a problem. On line 61, when we write **var the_key = i + 1**, JavaScript mistakenly thinks we are trying to concatenate two strings instead of adding two numbers. The result is that when i contains "1", JavaScript thinks **"1" + 1** equals **"11"**, similar to the way **"a" + 1** equals the string **"a1"**. To fix this error, we need a way to force JavaScript to interpret **i** as a number rather than as a string.

The simplest way to make JavaScript interpret a variable as a number is to multiply the variable by 1. Since multiplication only works on numbers, JavaScript is forced to see the variable as a number:

```
57 ▾ function array_to_object_3(my_array) {
58           var my_object = {};
59 ▾     for(var i in my_array) {
60           var the_element = my_array[i];
61           var the_key = (i * 1) + 1;
62           my_object[the_key] = the_element;
63       }
64       return my_object;
65  }
```

Above, on line 61 we multiply **i** by 1. This does not change the value of i but makes JavaScript see it as a number. The brackets are not necessary, but they help make it clear what we are doing. The function now works properly:

```
{
"1" : a
"2" : b
"3" : c
}
```

Calculating Word Frequencies

We will now go back to the Text Analyzer program to add a new function to it. This new function will calculate how many times each word occurs in the text. We already did something similar with students' first names. This time, now that we have access to objects, we can do things much more efficiently. First, I move the text to the top of the code since it is taking up a lot of screen space. On line 15 I put the **text** variable inside **text_analyzer.current_word** to keep things just as before:

```
i  1▾ <script>
   2   var text =
   3       'And this is Dorlcote Mill. I must '
   4       + 'stand a minute or two here on the bridge '
   5       + 'and look at it, though the clouds are '
   6       + 'threatening, and it is far on in the afternoon. '
   7       + 'Even in this leafless time of departing February '
   8       + 'it is pleasant to look at,-perhaps the chill, '
   9       + 'damp season adds a charm to the trimly kept, '
  10       + 'comfortable dwelling-house, as old as the elms '
  11       + 'and chestnuts that shelter it from the '
  12       + 'northern blast. ';
  13
  14▾ var text_analyzer = {
  15       current_text : text,
  16▾      get_words_array : function() {
```

Below we add the new **get_word_frequencies()** function on lines 51-69:

```
  51▾     get_word_frequencies : function() {                     And: 1
  52          var words_array = this.get_words_array();           this: 2
  53          var word_frequencies = {};                          is: 3
  54▾         for(var i in words_array) {                         Dorlcote: 1
  55              var current_word = words_array[i];              Mill.: 1
  56▾             if(! (current_word in word_frequencies)) {      I: 1
  57                  word_frequencies[current_word] = 1;         must: 1
  58              }                                               stand: 1
  59▾             else {                                          a: 2
  60                  var previous_frequency =                    minute: 1
  61                      word_frequencies[current_word];         or: 1
  62                  var new_frequency = previous_frequency      two: 1
  63                      + 1;                                    here: 1
  64                  word_frequencies[current_word] =            on: 2
  65                      new_frequency;                          the: 7
  66              }                                               bridge: 1
  67          }                                                   and: 3
  68          return word_frequencies;                            look: 2
  69      },                                                      at: 1
  70  };                                                          it.: 1
  71                                                              though: 1
  72  var frequencies = text_analyzer.get_word_frequencies();    clouds: 1
  73▾ for(var i in frequencies) {
  74      document.write(i + ': ' + frequencies[i] + '<br>');
  75  }
  76  </script>
  77
  78
  79
```

The **get_word_frequencies()** function goes over all of the words in the text one by one and uses the object **word_frequencies** to keep track of how many times each word is seen in the loop. On line 56 we use something we have not seen before to check whether the **word_frequencies** object has a particular property or not. When the **current_word** variable contains the word "And", the check **if(! (current_word in word_frequencies))** is interpreted by JavaScript as **if(! ("And" in word_frequencies))**, which checks whether the **word_frequencies** object has a property named **And** or not. Since the condition starts with an exclamation mark, that makes the whole condition negative, meaning the check is if *not* **And** exists in **word_frequencies**. We write it this way because we want the code below it to create the property if it does not exist, so we are saying *if it does not exist, then do this.*

If the property does not exist, then we create it using **word_frequencies[current_word] = 1** on line 57. This means that when **current_word** is "And", **word_frequencies["And"]** is created and set to 1 in one statement, as the following illustration shows:

```
if(! ("And" in word_frequencies)) {
    word_frequencies["And"] = 1;
}
```

As the loop goes on, the **word_frequencies** object is gradually filled up. Each element in the **words_array** is turned into a property of the **word_frequencies** object. They keys are all from the array, while all the values are 1. Here is a simple illustration of what we are creating with this loop:

```
var my_array = ["a", "b", "c"];
var my_object = {
    "a" : 1,
    "b" : 1,
    "c" : 1
}
```

However, if we see a word that we have already seen before, then the check on line 56 fails because **word_frequencies** will contain a key that is the same as that word, so that the **else** part of our code runs:

```
56 ▾    if(! (current_word in word_frequencies)) {
57          word_frequencies[current_word] = 1;
58      }
59 ▾    else {
60          var previous_frequency =
61              word_frequencies[current_word];
62          var new_frequency = previous_frequency
63              + 1;
64          word_frequencies[current_word] =
65              new_frequency;
66      }
```

If, for example, **word_frequencies["is"]** has already been seen once in the past, if we see it again, in the **else** part we first get the number of times it has been seen in the past using the statement **previous_frequency = word_frequencies[current_word]** on lines 60-61. We then add 1 to this number. Then we update **word_frequencies["is"]** so that it contains the new number. Below is a simple illustration of what is going on. The array **my_array** contains the string "a" three times, but all three "go into" the same key on **my_object**, while the value is increased to 3 to reflect how many times "a" is in **my_array**:

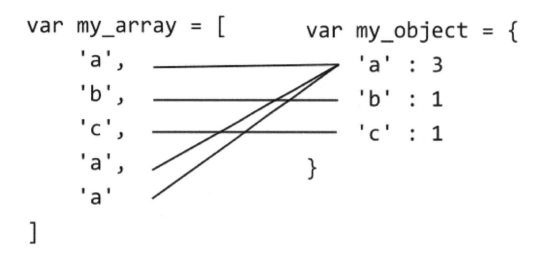

At this point we have finished explaining how the **get_word_frequencies()** function works. Below I use the **print_object()** function to print out the object returned by the function:

```
109  var frequencies = text_analyzer.get_word_frequencies();
110  print_object(frequencies);
111  </script>
```

Here is the result (partially shown due to being too long):

```
{
"And" : 1
"this" : 2
"is" : 3
"Dorlcote" : 1
"Mill." : 1
"I" : 1
"must" : 1
"stand" : 1
"a" : 2
"minute" : 1
"or" : 1
"two" : 1
"here" : 1
"on" : 2
"the" : 7
"bridge" : 1
"and" : 3
"look" : 2
"at" : 1
```

We can also use **get_word_frequencies()** to check the number of times one particular word occurs rather than printing out all of the results, as follows:

```
109   var frequencies = text_analyzer.get_word_frequencies();
110   document.write(frequencies['on']);
```

Here is the result:

```
2
```

We can shorten the above two lines into one line:

```
109   document.write(text_analyzer.get_word_frequencies()['on']);
```

At this point we have covered the basics of objects. If you find objects confusing, feel free to forget about them for now and review them days or weeks later. You can create any program you can imagine without using objects. But once you are used to them, you will find many uses for them.

This page intentionally left blank

20. Regular Expressions

Regular expressions enable us to use patterns to do search and replace within a piece of text. You may have used "wildcards" in programs like Microsoft Word. Below is an example in which we put the wildcard **c?t** in Word's Find and Replace dialog:

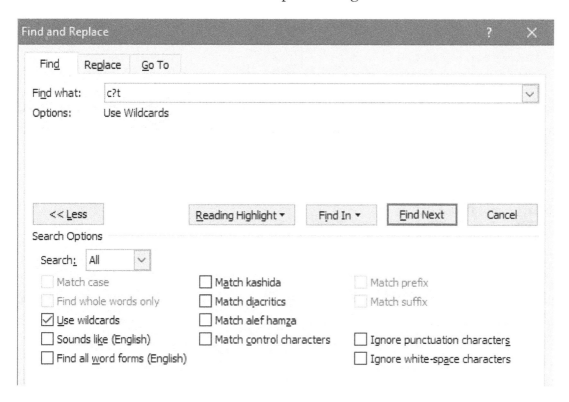

In Word, doing a wildcard search for **c?t** finds any 3-character string that starts with a c and ends with "t", such as "cat" and "cot".

In JavaScript, regular expressions help us achieve the same kind of thing. Below we use a regular expression to check whether the string variable **text** contains the string "is a":

```
1 ▾ <script>
2    var text = 'It is a good day';
3
4    var my_regular_expression = /is a/;
5    document.write(my_regular_expression.test(text));
6  </script>
```

true

The regular expression is on line 4. It starts with a forward slash and ends with a forward slash. Regular expressions are not strings, arrays, plain objects or any other data type. They are their own independent thing. On line 5, we use the **test()** function (which only works on regular expressions) to test whether the text variable satisfies the regular expression or not. The result is a boolean "true" as seen in the preview area, meaning that the text variable does indeed satisfy the **/is a/** regular expression (since it contains "is a").

Below we change the regular expression to test whether the string contains "it" or not:

```
1 ▾ <script>
2    var text = 'It is a good day';
3
4    var my_regular_expression = /it/;
5    document.write(my_regular_expression.test(text));
6  </script>
```

false

The result is false because the variable **text** contains "It", not "it". We can make our regular expression case-insensitive so that it will match both uppercase and lowercase characters as follows:

```
1 ▾ <script>
2    var text = 'It is a good day';
3
4    var my_regular_expression = /it/i;
5    document.write(my_regular_expression.test(text));
6  </script>
```

true

Above, I have added an **i** after the regular expression's ending slash on line 4. This is called a "modifier", it modifies how the regular expression works. The **i** stands for insensitive, making the regular expression insensitive to the difference between upper and lower case characters so that it matches both.

Since the **test()** function returns a boolean **true** or **false**, we can use it in if statements as follows:

```
i  1 ▾ <script>
   2    var text = 'It is a good day';
   3
   4    var my_regular_expression = /day/i;
   5 ▾ if(my_regular_expression.test(text)) {
   6        document.write('The string has '
   7        + '"day" in it!');
   8    }
   9    </script>
```

The string has "day" in it!

We can also use a regular expression directly without putting it in a variable:

```
i  1 ▾ <script>
   2    var text = 'It is a good day';
   3
   4 ▾ if(/day/i.test(text)) {
   5        document.write('The string has '
   6        + '"day" in it!');
   7    }
   8    </script>
```

The string has "day" in it!

Besides the **test()** function, we also have the more interesting **match()** function. This function is actually a string function, meaning that it has to be called on strings rather than regular expressions, so that using this function is reverse of the way we used the test() function.

```
i  1 ▾ <script>
   2    var text = 'It is a good day';
   3
   4    var my_regular_expression = /good/;
   5    var matches = text.match(my_regular_expression);
   6    document.write(matches.toString());
   7    </script>
```

good

The **text.match()** function returns an array that contains all the strings matched by the regular expression we give to it. Above, we search for "good", and unsurprisingly, the matches array contains "good" as its only element when we print it out.

Below I update the text variable so that it now contains another passage from *The Mill on the Floss*. I have made the whole passage fit on one line in the code in order to save space. On line 3 I have printed out the **text** variable so that you can see part of the string in the preview area.

```
i  1▾ <script>
   2  var text = 'The rush of the water and the booming
   3  document.write(text);
   4  var my_regular_expression = /good/;
   5  var matches = text.match(my_regular_expression);
   6  document.write(matches.toString());
   7  </script>
   8
   9
  10
  11
  12
  13
  14
  15
  16
  17
  18
  19
  20
```

The rush of the water and the booming of the mill bring a dreamy deafness, which seems to heighten the peacefulness of the scene. They are like a great curtain of sound, shutting one out from the world beyond. And now there is the thunder of the huge covered wagon coming home with sacks of grain. That honest wagoner is thinking of his dinner, getting sadly dry in the oven at this late hour; but he will not touch it till he has fed his horses,—the strong, submissive,

I now remove the **document.write()** statement on line 3. The code shown earlier actually causes an error in JavaScript when we run it. When looking at the console we see the following:

```
▶Uncaught TypeError: Cannot read property 'toString' of null
   at <anonymous>:6:23
```

This cryptic error message is telling us we have used the **toString()** function on line 6 on something that is **null**. What it actually means is that the **matches** array is not actually an array, it is **null**. This is because the new string inside **text** does not contain the word "good" that we are searching for. The **match()** function on line 5 returns **null**. This means that the **matches** variable contains **null**, so that using **toString()** on it leads to an error and breaks our code, since **toString()** is not designed to be used on variables that contain **null**. To avoid this error, we have to check whether the **matches** array is null or not before we try to print it out:

```
i  1▾ <script>
   2  var text = 'The rush of the water and the booming
   3
   4  var my_regular_expression = /good/;
   5  var matches = text.match(my_regular_expression);
   6▾ if(matches === null) {
   7      document.write('No matches found!');
   8  }
   9▾ else {
  10      document.write(matches.toString())
  11  }
  12 </script>
```

No matches found!

Above, we check if **matches** is **null** on line 6. If so, we print out a helpful message. If it is not **null**, then we use **toString()** to print out its contents on line 10.

Below, we update the regular expression to search for " the " (a space followed by "the" followed by a space):

```
 i   1 ▾ <script>
     2   var text = 'The rush of the water and the booming      the
     3
     4   var my_regular_expression = / the /;
     5   var matches = text.match(my_regular_expression);
     6 ▾ if(matches === null) {
     7       document.write('No matches found!');
     8   }
     9 ▾ else {
    10       document.write(matches.toString())
    11   }
    12   </script>
```

In the preview area only one " the " gets printed out even though the **text** variable obviously contains multiple occurrences of the word "the". This is caused by the fact that JavaScript regular expressions by default stop searching once they find a single match. In order to find all occurrences of a word, we have to use the **g** modifier (which stands for "global"), as follows:

```
 i   1 ▾ <script>
     2   var text = 'The rush of the water and the booming      the , the , the , the , the , the , the ,
     3                                                           the , the , the , the , the , the , the ,
     4   var my_regular_expression = / the /g;                   the , the , the , the , the , the , the ,
     5   var matches = text.match(my_regular_expression);        the , the
     6 ▾ if(matches === null) {
     7       document.write('No matches found!');
     8   }
     9 ▾ else {
    10       document.write(matches.toString())
    11   }
    12   </script>
```

Now all occurrences of " the " are printed out. That is not very useful at the moment. One use of this code however would be to find out how many times the string we are searching for occurs in the text, as follows:

```
 i   1 ▾ <script>
     2   var text = 'The rush of the water and the booming      23
     3
     4   var my_regular_expression = / the /g;
     5   var matches = text.match(my_regular_expression);
     6 ▾ if(matches === null) {
     7       document.write('No matches found!');
     8   }
     9 ▾ else {
    10       document.write(matches.length)
    11   }
    12   </script>
```

Above, I have changed line 10 to print out the length of the matches array, which equals 23, meaning that " the " occurs 23 times inside the **text** variable.

499

We can now move on to the more interesting part of regular expression, wildcards. The following regular expression matches all 3-character-long strings starting with an "a":

```
1 ▾ <script>
2   var text = 'The rush of the water and the booming
3
4   var my_regular_expression = /a../g;
5   var matches = text.match(my_regular_expression);
6 ▾ if(matches === null) {
7       document.write('No matches found!');
8   }
9 ▾ else {
10      document.write(matches.toString())
11  }
12  </script>
```

```
ate.and.a d.amy.afn.ace.are.a g.at
.ain.ago.ack.ain.at .ago.adl.at .ate.as
.ast.anc.are.ach.at .at .ack.at .at
.awf.ann.as .at .ard.all.aus.are.ar .at
.and.agg.at .asp.art.at .ati.avy.ar..at
.aun.ar
.ard.arn.and.arn.age.are.and.aga.at .a
s.ace.and.arc.ago.app.ars.at
```

The regular expression **/a../g** means "a string starting with a, followed by any character, followed by any character". Inside regular expressions dots stand for "any character". The preview area shows us a large number of matches. The results are messy because the regular expression matches inside words and between words. The first match is "ate", which is from the word "water". JavaScript does not care that this match is in the middle of a word since we have not told it to care. There is also the match "a g" ("a" followed by a space followed by a "g") which is from the string "a great". The dot wildcard matches spaces too, so this is a perfectly good match.

We can improve the results we get by updating the regular expression to have a space before and after it:

```
i 1 ▾ <script>
  2   var text = 'The rush of the water and the booming
  3
  4   var my_regular_expression = / a.. /g;
  5   var matches = text.match(my_regular_expression);
  6 ▾ if(matches === null) {
  7       document.write('No matches found!');
  8   }
  9 ▾ else {
  10      document.write(matches.toString())
  11  }
  12  </script>
```

```
and . are . are . all . are . and . are .
and . and
```

Above, I have changed **/a../g** to **/ a.. /g**. The meaning of the new regular expression is "a space, followed by an a, followed by any character, followed by any character, followed by a space".

The next wildcard we will look at is the question mark wildcard. This wildcard makes the pattern that comes before it optional.

```
 1▾  <script>
 2    var text = 'The rush of the water and the booming
 3
 4    var my_regular_expression = / a?.. /g;
 5    var matches = text.match(my_regular_expression);
 6▾   if(matches === null) {
 7        document.write('No matches found!');
 8    }
 9▾   else {
10        document.write(matches.toString())
11    }
12   </script>
```

of , and , of , to , of , are , of , is , of . of , is , of , in , at , he , it , he , are , at , he , at , in , as , up , all , are , at . to , at , of , at , of , to , of , and , are . and , go , at , and , of , at

Above I have added a question mark right after the "a" in the regular expression on line 4. The result is that we now have many more matches. The regular expression **/ a?.. /g** means: "(a space)('a' or nothing)(any character)(any character)(a space)". The question mark after the "a" makes the "a" optional, so that the regular expression will match any string that matches the rest of the pattern whether or not the "a" is present at that place. The result is that "of" is the first match we get.

Below I move the question mark behind the last dot:

```
 1▾  <script>
 2    var text = 'The rush of the water and the booming
 3
 4    var my_regular_expression = / a..? /g;
 5    var matches = text.match(my_regular_expression);
 6▾   if(matches === null) {
 7        document.write('No matches found!');
 8    }
 9▾   else {
10        document.write(matches.toString())
11    }
12   </script>
```

and , are , at , are , at , at , as , all . are , at , at , at , and , are , and , at , and , at

The new regular expression means: "(a space)(an 'a')(any character)(any character or nothing)(a space)". The result is that it matches all two and three-character-long strings that start with a.

Regular expressions are like a programming language within a programming language. They have their own syntax and logic, for this reason it will take learners a long time to familiarize themselves with them and master them. Like everything else in programming, reading and writing code is the best way to learn how to use regular expressions.

Replacing strings

The **replace()** function allows us to use patterns to replace one part of a string with something else. This function takes two arguments. The first argument is a pattern. The second argument is the string we want to replace the pattern with:

```
i  1▾ <script>
   2    var text = 'The rush of the water and the
   3    text = text.replace(/r/, 'b');
   4    document.write(text);
   5    </script>
   6
   7
```

The bush of the water and the booming of the mill bring a dreamy deafness, which seems to heighten the peacefulness of the scene.

Above, we have given the regular expression **/r/** as the first argument to **replace()**. The second argument is the string 'b'. This tells JavaScript to replace the string that matches **/r/** with the string "b". The result is that the word rush is now "bush" in the preview area. Below I add the **g** modifier to the regular expression, so that it now replaces *all* of the matches of the pattern not just the first one:

```
i  1▾ <script>
   2    var text = 'The rush of the water and the
   3    text = text.replace(/r/g, 'b');
   4    document.write(text);
   5    </script>
   6
   7
```

The bush of the wateb and the booming of the mill bbing a dbeamy deafness, which seems to heighten the peacefulness of the scene.

Above, you can see that the word "water" has become "wateb" in the preview area, since we are now replacing all r's with b's.

Now onto a useful example; what if your boss gave you a list of 10,000 names and asked you to turn every middle name to an initial (for example Henry Newton Smith would become Henry N. Smith)? We can accomplish this in a few relatively simple lines. In our example, we will use the names of three American economists to simply the example:

```
i   1▼  <script>
    2▼  var american_economists = [
    3           'Henry Charles Carey',
    4           'Erasmus Peshine Smith',
    5           'George Ernest Barnett',
    6       ];
    7
    8   var shortened_names = [];
    9
   10▼  for(var i in american_economists) {
   11       var economist
   12           = american_economists[i];
   13       var shortened =
   14           economist.replace(/ ([A-Z])[a-z]+ /,
   15           ' $1. ');
   16       shortened_names.push(shortened);
   17   }
   18
   19   document.write(shortened_names.join('<br>'));
   20   </script>
```

Henry C. Carey
Erasmus P. Smith
George E. Barnett

The code should be self-explanatory except for lines 14 and 15. An illustration is perhaps the best way to explain the regular expression on line 14:

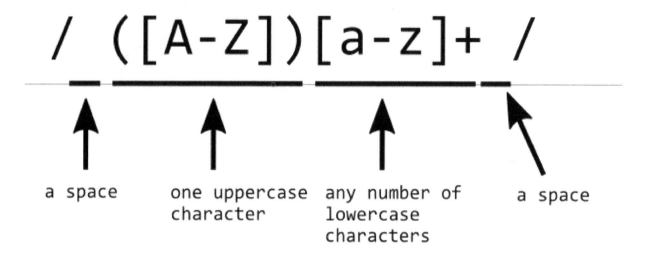

We have a number of new concepts in this regular expression. The first one is the stuff in the square brackets, such as **[A-Z]**. This is known as a character class and means "any character between uppercase A and uppercase Z". We also have another character class **[a-z]** which means "any character between lowercase a and lowercase z". The first character class is inside round brackets **([A-Z])**. Inside regular expressions brackets have a very special meaning and the stuff inside them is known as a "capturing group". They tell JavaScript to store the stuff in the brackets in a variable that we can later refer to using a dollar sign and a number (that is what the **$1** on line 15 does).

503

The other new thing is the plus sign after the second character class. This sign means "one or more of the preceding pattern". In other words, **[a-z]+** means "one or more lowercase characters.

The regular expression as a whole matches middle names, since middle names have a space before them, start with an uppercase character and have any number of lowercase characters after that and have a space after them.

The second argument of the **replace()** function is **' $1. '**. This means "a space, followed by whatever was matched by the capturing group, followed by a space. If the regular expression on line 14 had matched " Charles ", since the capturing group on line 14 only captures the first character of the name, all of the string " Charles" is replaced by " C. ".

All of lines 14 and 15 can be interpreted as "find a middle name, save the first character of the middle name in a variable named **$1**, then replace all of the middle name with the value inside this variable, followed by a dot."

Comments

In programming, comments are pieces of text inside our code that do nothing. They are just there for the benefit of programmers to help them understand the code better. Below I have added a comment on line 13:

```
10 ▾ for(var i in american_economists) {
11       var economist
12           = american_economists[i];
13       var shortened = // the middle initial
14           economist.replace(/ ([A-Z])[a-z]+ /,
15           ' $1. ');
16       shortened_names.push(shortened);
17   }
```

The comment on line 13 starts with a double forward slash. This tells JavaScript this is a comment. Anything after the double slashes will be ignored by JavaScript, but programmers reading the code will have an easier time understanding what the code does, since it will not be obvious even to an experienced programmer what the regular expression does unless they wait for a few seconds to decipher it. But if they see the comment, they can instantly realize that it is trying to get the middle initial of the name.

The above type of comment is known as a single line comment. We also have mutli-line comments that allow us to write whole paragraphs of text as a comment:

```
 9 ▾ /*
10    This loop goes through the full names
11    and initializes the middle names
12    while leaving the first and last names
13    intact.
14    */
15 ▾ for(var i in american_economists) {
16        var economist
17            = american_economists[i];
18        var shortened = // the middle initial
19            economist.replace(/ ([A-Z])[a-z]+ /,
20            ' $1. ');
21        shortened_names.push(shortened);
22    }
```

A multi-line comment starts with a slash followed by an asterisk (line 9) and ends with an asterisk followed by a slash (line 14).

Instead of using a multi-line comment we can use multiple single line comments as follows:

```
10    // This loop goes through the full names
11    // and initializes the middle names
12    // while leaving the first and last names
13    // intact.
14 ▾ for(var i in american_economists) {
15        var economist
16            = american_economists[i];
17        var shortened = // the middle initial
18            economist.replace(/ ([A-Z])[a-z]+ /,
19            ' $1. ');
20        shortened_names.push(shortened);
21    }
```

It is always best to write your code to be self-explanatory so that it will not require comments. By giving your variables and functions easy-to-understand names, the code will be easy to understand. Regular expressions, however, are an exception. It is almost always a good idea to write a comment explaining what the regular expression does, otherwise if you are reading your own code months later you may have no idea what the regular expression is meant to do and may waste many precious minutes deciphering its purpose.

Counting Names

In this section we will examine a real-world file and run some JavaScript on it. The file we will use is the entire text of the novel *The Mill on the Floss* by George Eliot, freely available at the Project Gutenberg website. Below is a screenshot of the novel as opened on my computer in the Chromium web browser:

In order to use JavaScript on this document we have to open the console (you can right click on an empty area in the document click "Inspect" or something similar, as explained in chapter 2). With the console open, I click the "Console" tab, which currently shows up as a blank area:

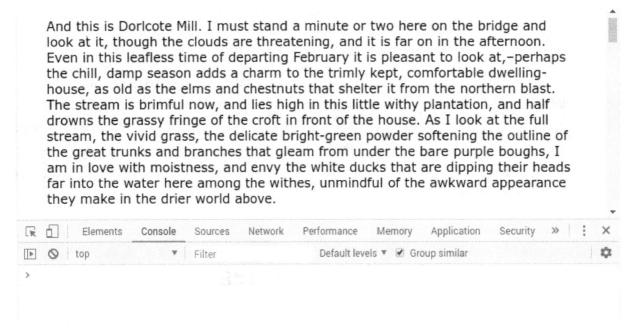

The first thing to do is to put the entire text of the novel inside a single variable. To do so we use the statement shown below:

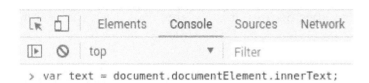

```
> var text = document.documentElement.innerText;
```

The property **document.documentElement.innerText** is a special JavaScript variable that retrieves all of the text in the document. Once we press Enter (or similar), the console runs the code and prints out "undefined":

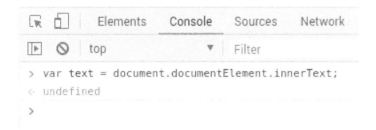

```
> var text = document.documentElement.innerText;
< undefined
>
```

The "undefined" in this case simply means our statement returned nothing. This is not a bad thing. Since we putting one variable inside another, there is nothing to print out yet.

The console works on a line-by-line basis. You write one statement, press Enter, then go to onto the next statement. You can also write multiple statements by pressing Shift+Enter to create a new line.

Below, I use the **match()** function to attempt to find the full names of all the characters mentioned in the novel:

```
> text.match(/[A-Z][a-z]+ [A-Z][a-z]+/g);
< (964) ["The Project", "The Mill", "George Eliot", "United States", "Project Gutenberg", "United States"
  , "The Mill", "George Eliot", "Posting Date", "Release Date", "First Posted", "Curtis Weyant", "David M
  addock", "The Mill", "George Eliot", "Outside Dorlcote", "Dorlcote Mill", "Declares His", "Riley Gives"
  , "His Advice", "Tom Is", "Tom Comes", "The Aunts", "Uncles Are", "Tulliver Shows", "His Weaker", "To G
  arum", "Maggie Behaves", "Worse Than", "She Expected", "Maggie Tries", "Her Shadow", "Tulliver Further"
  , "First Half", "The Christmas", "The New", "The Young", "Second Visit", "The Golden", "Gates Are", "Th
  e Downfall", "What Had", "Household Gods", "The Family", "Vanishing Gleam", "Tom Applies", "His Knife",
  ▶ "Popular Prejudice", "Hen Takes", "An Item", "Family Register", "The Valley", "Protestantism Unknown",
  "The Torn", "Nest Is", "Red Deeps", "Aunt Glegg", "The Wavering", "Another Love", "The Cloven", "The H
  ard", "Won Triumph", "The Great", "First Impressions", "Confidential Moments", "Showing That", "Tom Had
  ", "Philip Re", "New Light", "The Spell", "Seems Broken", "Family Party", "Borne Along", "The Final", "
  The Return", "Passes Judgment", "Showing That", "Old Acquaintances", "Are Capable", "Surprising Us", "T
  he Last", "Outside Dorlcote", "Dorlcote Mill", "Dorlcote Mill", "Dorlcote Mill", "Declares His", "Lawye
  r Wakem", "John Gibbs", "As Mrs", "If Mr", "Exit Maggie", "Riley Gives", "His Advice", "Old Harry", "Ol
  d Harry", "Even Hotspur", "Daniel Defoe", "Jeremy Taylor", "Holy Living", "But Stelling", …]
```

The regular expression I use is **/[A-Z][a-z]+ [A-Z][a-z]+/g**, which means "an uppercase word followed by a space followed by an uppercase word". When we run the statement, the console immediately prints out the result. The number 964 at the beginning tells us how many elements are in the returned array, meaning that our regular expression had 964 matches.

The console does not show us the fully array of matches because it is so large. But if we click on it, it will expand it as follows, showing us the index values:

```
▶ [0 … 99]
▶ [100 … 199]
▶ [200 … 299]
▶ [300 … 399]
▶ [400 … 499]
▶ [500 … 599]
▶ [600 … 699]
▶ [700 … 799]
▶ [800 … 899]
▶ [900 … 963]
  length: 964
▶ __proto__: Array(0)
```

Clicking on one of these number ranges further expands them:

```
▼ [800 … 899]
    800: "If Maggie"
    801: "Miss Tulliver"
    802: "Miss Tulliver"
    803: "Miss Tulliver"
    804: "When Maggie"
    805: "Showing That"
    806: "Old Acquaintances"
    807: "Are Capable"
    808: "Surprising Us"
    809: "When Maggie"
    810: "Then Mrs"
    811: "While Mrs"
    812: "But Tom"
```

Many of the values in the array are repetitions. We can fix that by creating a function that filters out all repeated values from an array. Below I define a new function, **get_unique_only()** right inside the console. The function is on multiple lines. As I mentioned earlier, to write a new line without the console running the code, you have to use Shift+Enter. Pressing Enter alone will make the console try to execute the incomplete code.

```
> function get_unique_only(my_array) {
      var my_set = new Set(my_array);
      var my_unique_array = Array.from(my_set);
      return my_unique_array;
  }
```

The function uses a clever trick to get all the unique values from an array. It first converts the array into a set (a set is a special data type in JavaScript inspired by mathematical sets, and it can only contain unique values) using **var my_set = new Set(my_array)**. It then converts the set back to an array using **Array.from(my_set)**. And that is all. This conversion back-and-forth conversion causes all duplicate values to wither away.

After writing out the function, I press Enter to make JavaScript run the code. The word "undefined" is printed out again, because I have only *defined* a function, I have not used it yet, so there is no return value. But the function remains there behind the scenes to be used later on.

```
>  function get_unique_only(my_array) {
       var my_set = new Set(my_array);
       var my_unique_array = Array.from(my_set);
       return my_unique_array;
   }
<  undefined
>
```

If you remember, earlier when I ran the **text.match(/[A-Z][a-z]+ [A-Z][a-z]+/g);** function I did not put the result inside a variable. Even though the console printed out the resulting array, the array is no longer available to me. I will run the code again but this time I will put the array inside its own variable:

```
>  var array_full_of_duplicates = text.match(/[A-Z][a-z]+ [A-Z][a-z]+/g);
<  undefined
```

Next I will declare a new array build using the new **get_unique_only()** function:

```
>  var unique_array = get_unique_only(array_full_of_duplicates);
<  undefined
```

And now, to actually show the result, we write the new array's name in the console then press Enter:

```
>  unique_array
<  (379) ["The Project", "The Mill", "George Eliot", "United States", "Project Gutenberg", "Posting Date",
    "Release Date", "First Posted", "Curtis Weyant", "David Maddock", "Outside Dorlcote", "Dorlcote Mill",
    "Declares His", "Riley Gives", "His Advice", "Tom Is", "Tom Comes", "The Aunts", "Uncles Are", "Tulliv
    er Shows", "His Weaker", "To Garum", "Maggie Behaves", "Worse Than", "She Expected", "Maggie Tries", "H
    er Shadow", "Tulliver Further", "First Half", "The Christmas", "The New", "The Young", "Second Visit",
    "The Golden", "Gates Are", "The Downfall", "What Had", "Household Gods", "The Family", "Vanishing Gleam
    ", "Tom Applies", "His Knife", "Popular Prejudice", "Hen Takes", "An Item", "Family Register", "The Val
  ▸ ley", "Protestantism Unknown", "The Torn", "Nest Is", "Red Deeps", "Aunt Glegg", "The Wavering", "Anoth
    er Love", "The Cloven", "The Hard", "Won Triumph", "The Great", "First Impressions", "Confidential Mome
    nts", "Showing That", "Tom Had", "Philip Re", "New Light", "The Spell", "Seems Broken", "Family Party",
    "Borne Along", "The Final", "The Return", "Passes Judgment", "Old Acquaintances", "Are Capable", "Surp
    rising Us", "The Last", "Lawyer Wakem", "John Gibbs", "As Mrs", "If Mr", "Exit Maggie", "Old Harry", "E
    ven Hotspur", "Daniel Defoe", "Jeremy Taylor", "Holy Living", "But Stelling", "Ask Mr", "Walter Stellin
    g", "Mudport Free", "De Senectute", "Louisa Timpson", "Thus Mr", "Animated Nature", "Master Tom", "Prod
    igal Son", "Sir Charles", "Round Pool", "Thus Maggie", "Tom Tulliver", "Great Ash", …]
```

Let's now check how many times the name of the heroine is used throughout the novel:

```
> text.match(/Maggie/g);
  (1402) ["Maggie", "Maggie", "Maggie", "Maggie", "Maggie", "Maggie", "Maggie", "Maggie", "Maggie", "Magg
  ie", "Maggie", "Maggie", "Maggie", "Maggie", "Maggie", "Maggie", "Maggie", "Maggie", "Maggie", "Maggie"
  , "Maggie", "Maggie", "Maggie", "Maggie", "Maggie", "Maggie", "Maggie", "Maggie", "Maggie", "Maggie", "
  Maggie", "Maggie", "Maggie", "Maggie", "Maggie", "Maggie", "Maggie", "Maggie", "Maggie", "Maggie", "Mag
  gie", "Maggie", "Maggie", "Maggie", "Maggie", "Maggie", "Maggie", "Maggie", "Maggie", "Maggie", "Maggie
  ", "Maggie", "Maggie", "Maggie", "Maggie", "Maggie", "Maggie", "Maggie", "Maggie", "Maggie", "Maggie",
  "Maggie", "Maggie", "Maggie", "Maggie", "Maggie", "Maggie", "Maggie", "Maggie", "Maggie", "Maggie", "Ma
  ggie", "Maggie", "Maggie", "Maggie", "Maggie", "Maggie", "Maggie", "Maggie", "Maggie", "Maggie", "Maggi
  e", "Maggie", "Maggie", "Maggie", "Maggie", "Maggie", "Maggie", "Maggie", "Maggie", "Maggie", "Maggie",
   "Maggie", "Maggie", "Maggie", "Maggie", "Maggie", "Maggie", "Maggie", "Maggie", …]
```

Apparently it is 1402 times. Since there is no point in seeing all those repeated Maggies printed out, we can simply get the length of the array:

```
> text.match(/Maggie/g).length;
< 1402
```

Let's now get the total number of words in the novel:

```
text.match(/ [A-Za-z]+ /g);
  (92332) [" Project ", " EBook ", " The ", " on ", " by ", " eBook ", " for ", " use
  ", " anyone ", " in ", " United ", " and ", " parts ", " the ", " at ", " cost ",
  " with ", " no ", " You ", " copy ", " give ", " away ", " it ", " the ", " Project
  ", " License ", " with ", " eBook ", " online ", " If ", " are ", " located ", " t
  he ", " check ", " laws ", " the ", " where ", " are ", " before ", " this ", " The
   ", " on ", " George ", " September ", " January ", " set ", " START ", " THIS ", "
  GUTENBERG ", " THE ", " ON ", " FLOSS ", " by ", " Weyant ", " David ", " Mill ",
  " the ", " of ", " Boy ", " Dorlcote ", " of ", " Declares ", " Resolution ", " Ril
  ey ", " His ", " Concerning ", " School ", " Is ", " Comes ", " Aunts ", " Uncles "
  , " the ", " and ", " Tulliver ", " His ", " Garum ", " Behaves ", " Than ", " Trie
  s ", " Run ", " from ", " and ", " Glegg ", " Tulliver ", " Entangles ", " Skein ",
   " Christmas ", " New ", " Young ", " Second ", " Golden ", " Are ", " The ", " Had
   ", " at ", " or ", " Family ", " Vanishing ", " Applies ", " Knife ", …]
```

The result of 92332 is not perfect, but something of an approximation. The regular expression this time uses **[A-Za-z]+**, which means "one or more uppercase or lowercase characters". This means it will match "START", "anyone", "Garum", and any other mix of uppercase and lowercase characters.

Below I use the earlier **get_unique_only()** function to the number of unique words in the novel:

```
get_unique_only(text.match(/ [A-Za-z]+ /g));
  (7731) [" Project ", " EBook ", " The ", " on ", " by ", " eBook ", " for ", " use
  ", " anyone ", " in ", " United ", " and ", " parts ", " the ", " at ", " cost ", "
  with ", " no ", " You ", " copy ", " give ", " away ", " it ", " License ", " onli
  ne ", " If ", " are ", " located ", " check ", " laws ", " where ", " before ", " t
  his ", " George ", " September ", " January ", " set ", " START ", " THIS ", " GUTE
  NBERG ", " THE ", " ON ", " FLOSS ", " Weyant ", " David ", " Mill ", " of ", " Boy
  ", " Dorlcote ", " Declares ", " Resolution ", " Riley ", " His ", " Concerning ",
  " School ", " Is ", " Comes ", " Aunts ", " Uncles ", " Tulliver ", " Garum ", " B
  ehaves ", " Than ", " Tries ", " Run ", " from ", " Glegg ", " Entangles ", " Skein
  ", " Christmas ", " New ", " Young ", " Second ", " Golden ", " Are ", " Had ", "
  or ", " Family ", " Vanishing ", " Applies ", " Knife ", " to ", " Prejudice ", "
  a ", " Takes ", " Item ", " Variation ", " Protestantism ", " Torn ", " Voice ", "
  Wheat ", " Wavering ", " Cloven ", " Day ", " Duet ", " That ", " Spell ", " Along
  ", " Return ", " Passes ", …]
```

If we want to show the number only, we can again use the **length** property at the end of the statement:

```
> get_unique_only(text.match(/ [A-Za-z]+ /g)).length;
< 7731
```

At this point you have been exposed to a few regular expressions to help you see what they are. We only scratched the surface of what regular expressions can do as it is not within the scope of this book to cover them comprehensively.

This page intentionally left blank

21. Sorting and Filtering

In this chapter we will discuss two common operations in programming; sorting and filtering.

The **sort()** function sorts an array from the lowest value to the highest value:

```
1 ▼ <script>
2     var numbers = [1, 5, 3, 4, 2];
3     var sorted_numbers = numbers.sort();
4     document.write(sorted_numbers.join('<br>'));
5   </script>
6
7
```

```
1
2
3
4
5
```

On line 2 we have an array that contains a mix of numbers. On line 3 we use **numbers.sort()** to sort the numbers. The result, as seen in the preview area, is that the numbers are now sorted from smallest to largest.

Sorting of numbers will not work properly if the numbers are strings, as follows:

```
1 ▼ <script>
2     var numbers = ["1", "11", "2", "25"];
3     var sorted_numbers = numbers.sort();
4     document.write(sorted_numbers.join('<br>'));
5   </script>
6
```

```
1
11
2
25
```

The difference is that on line 2 the numbers now have quotation marks around them. Even though they are numbers, because of the quotation marks JavaScript sees them as strings. And that means when it sorts them, it will sort them as if they are strings, so 1 is shown right before 11 the way that a will be shown before aa. In order to make the sorting take place properly, we have to use a custom function:

```
1 ▾ <script>
2 ▾ function my_custom_sort(a, b) {
3          // convert both to true numbers
4          a = a * 1;
5          b = b * 1;
6
7 ▾      if( a > b) {
8              return 1;
9          }
10 ▾     else if(a < b) {
11             return -1;
12         }
13 ▾     else {
14             return 0;
15         }
16     }
17     var numbers = ["1", "11", "2", "25"];
18     var sorted_numbers =
19         numbers.sort(my_custom_sort);
20     document.write(sorted_numbers.join('<br>'));
21     </script>
```

```
1
2
11
25
```

Above, **my_custom_sort** is a custom sorting function. All custom sorting functions take two values (**a** and **b**), compare them, then return a positive number, 0 or a negative number depending on how we want the sorting to be done. The value of these positive and negative numbers does not matter, all that JavaScript cares about is whether they are positive or negative. We use 1 and -1 in the example. What JavaScript does is get the first pair of values in the array (such as "1", "11", passes them to **my_custom_sort()**, then if the return value is -1, it means the first one should be first, if it is 0 it means they are equal and it does not matter which one is first, and if it is 1 it means the second one should be first. The first two lines of the function (4 and 5) convert the variables to "true" numbers by multiplying them by 1. This allows us to compare them as numbers rather than strings.

Below is an illustration of how JavaScript uses **my_custom_sort()** to do the sorting:

```
unsorted: ["1", "11", "2", "25"]
1st pass: my_custom_sort(1, 11).
    Return: -1.
    The array now: [1, 11, 2, 25]
2nd pass: my_custom_sort(11, 2).
    Return: 1.
    The array now: [1, 2, 11, 25]
3rd pass: my_custom_sort(11, 25).
    Return: -1.
    The array now: [1, 2, 11, 25]
Complete!
```

In reality we do not know how JavaScript does the sorting behind the scenes because there are various advanced algorithms used behind the scenes to speed up sorting. But when it comes to us programmers, all that we need to know is that custom sorting functions take two arguments and return either 1, 0 or -1.

On line 19 we have **numbers.sort(my_custom_sort)**. Even though **my_custom_sort** is a function, here we are using it without the usual parentheses because we are only telling JavaScript the function's name, we do not want the function to be run on that line. JavaScript will run the function behind the scenes when it wants.

Custom sorting is an advanced part of programming and many programmers will have to use the Internet to look up the proper way to do it.

Instead of using a named function for sorting, we can use an anonymous function:

```
i  1 ▾ <script>
   2    var numbers = ["1", "11", "2", "25"];
   3    var sorted_numbers =
   4 ▾      numbers.sort(function(a, b) {
   5            // convert both to true numbers
   6            a = a * 1;
   7            b = b * 1;
   8
   9 ▾          if( a > b) {
  10                return 1;
  11            }
  12 ▾          else if(a < b) {
  13                return -1;
  14            }
  15 ▾          else {
  16                return 0;
  17            }
  18        });
  19    document.write(sorted_numbers.join('<br>'));
  20    </script>
```

```
1
2
11
25
```

The sorting function can be shortened as follows. This is in fact how experienced programmers write sorting functions:

```
 3    var sorted_numbers =
 4 ▾      numbers.sort(function(a, b) {
 5            // convert both to true numbers
 6            a = a * 1;
 7            b = b * 1;
 8
 9            return a - b;
10        });
```

515

Below is the same illustration as before updated to show how the shorter method works:

```
unsorted: ["1", "11", "2", "25"]
1st pass: function(1, 11).
    Return: 1 - 11 (-10).
    The array now: [1, 11, 2, 25]
2nd pass: function(11, 2).
    Return: 11 - 2 (9)
    The array now: [1, 2, 11, 25]
3rd pass: function(11, 25).
    Return: 11 - 25 (-14)
    The array now: [1, 2, 11, 25]
Complete!
```

Even though the numbers are now different, their positivity or negativity is exactly the same as before, and that is what matters.

In order to sort the numbers from largest to smallest, we can simply switch the places of the two variables in the sorting function:

```
1  <script>
2    var numbers = ["1", "11", "2", "25"];
3    var sorted_numbers =
4      numbers.sort(function(a, b) {
5          // convert both to true numbers
6          a = a * 1;
7          b = b * 1;
8
9          return b - a;
10     });
11   document.write(sorted_numbers.join('<br>'));
12 </script>
```

```
25
11
2
1
```

Below is an illustration of how this reverse sorting works:

```
unsorted: ["1", "11", "2", "25"]
1st pass: function(1, 11).
    Return: 11 - 1 (10).
    The array now: [11, 1, 2, 25]
2nd pass: function(1, 2).
    Return: 2 - 1 (1)
    The array now: [11, 2, 1, 25]
3rd pass: function(1, 25).
    Return: 25 - 1 (24)
    The array now: [11, 2, 25, 1]
4th pass: function(2, 25).
    Return: 25 - 2 (23).
    The array now: [11, 25, 2, 1]
5th pass: function (11, 25).
    Return: 25 - 11 (14).
    The array now: [25, 11, 2, 1]
Complete!
```

This time five passes were needed to complete the sort because the number 25 at the end has to be brought to the beginning one step at a time. Depending on the sorting algorithm used behind the scenes, a different number of passes could be needed.

Sorting arrays of objects

Below we have an array of objects representing a number of economists:

```
39 ▾ var economists = [
40 ▾     {
41          "name" : "Henry Charles Carey",
42          "death_year" : 1879,
43      },
44 ▾     {
45          "name" : "Erasmus Peshine Smith",
46          "death_year" : 1882,
47      },
48 ▾     {
49          "name" : "Adam Smith",
50          "death_year" : 1790,
51      },
52 ▾     {
53          "name" : "George Ernest Barnett",
54          "death_year" : 1938
55      }
56  ];
```

Below is our function to sort these economists by their names:

```
58  var sorted_by_name = economists.sort(
59 ▾     function(a, b) {
60 ▾         if(a.name < b.name) {
61              return -1;
62          }
63 ▾         else if(a.name > b.name) {
64              return 1;
65          }
66 ▾         else {
67              return 0;
68          }
69      }
70  )
71  print_array(sorted_by_name);
```

Here is the result:

```
[
{
"name" : Adam Smith
"death_year" : 1790
}
{
"name" : Erasmus Peshine Smith
"death_year" : 1882
}
{
"name" : George Ernest Barnett
"death_year" : 1938
}
{
"name" : Henry Charles Carey
"death_year" : 1879
}
]
```

Inside our sort function, we do not compare **a** and **b** directly. We compare **a.name** and **b.name**, because **a** and **b** represent individual objects inside the array and we interested in their **name** properties. Using the greater and small than signs with strings makes JavaScript compare the strings alphabetically, with "a" being "smaller" than "b", "b" being smaller than "c" and so on. Below is a simplified illustration of how the sorting is done:

```
unsorted: [{name: Henry}, {name: Erasmus}, {name: Adam}, {name: George}]
1st pass: function({name: Henry}, {name: Erasmus}).
    Henry is greater than Erasmus. Return 1.
    The array now: [{name: Erasmus}, {name: Henry}, {name: Adam}, {name: George}]
2nd pass: function({name: Henry}, {name: Adam}).
    Henry is greater than Adam. Return 1.
    The array now: [{name: Erasmus}, {name: Adam}, {name: Henry}, {name: George}]
3rd pass: function({name: Henry}, {name: George}).
    Henry is greater than George. Return 1.
    The array now: [{name: Erasmus}, {name: Adam}, {name: George}, {name: Henry}]
4th pass: function({name: Erasmus}, {name: Adam}).
    Erasmus is greater than Adam. Return 1.
    The array now: [{name: Adam}, {name: Erasmus}, {name: George}, {name: Henry}]
5th pass: function ({name: Erasmus}, {name: George}).
    Erasmus is smaller than Adam. Return -1.
    The array now: unchanged
6th pass: function ({name: George}, {name: Henry}).
    George is smaller than Henry. Return -1.
    The array now: unchanged
Complete!
```

Next we will sort the economists by their death dates:

```
44 ▾         {
45                  "name" : "Erasmus Peshine Smith",
46                  "death_year" : 1882,
47          },
48 ▾         {
49                  "name" : "Adam Smith",
50                  "death_year" : 1790,
51          },
52 ▾         {
53                  "name" : "George Ernest Barnett",
54                  "death_year" : 1938
55          }
56     ];
57
58     var sorted_by_death_year = economists.sort(
59 ▾         function(a, b) {
60                  return a.death_year - b.death_year;
61          }
62     )
63     print_array(sorted_by_death_year);
64     </script>
65
66
67
```

```
[
{
"name" : Adam Smith
"death_year" : 1790
}
{
"name" : Henry Charles Carey
"death_year" : 1879
}
{
"name" : Erasmus Peshine Smith
"death_year" : 1882
}
{
"name" : George Ernest Barnett
"death_year" : 1938
}
]
```

Since we are comparing numbers, **a.death_year - b.death_year** on line 60 suffices for comparing them. If **a**'s death year is greater than **b**'s death, a positive number is returned, making **a** sorted after **b**. If **a**'s death year is smaller, a negative number is returned, making **a** get sorted before **b**. And if they are equal, 0 is returned, causing no change to their sorting. We can cause the economists to be sorted from the latest death to the earliest by changing line 60 as follows:

```
44 ▾         {
45                  "name" : "Erasmus Peshine Smith",
46                  "death_year" : 1882,
47          },
48 ▾         {
49                  "name" : "Adam Smith",
50                  "death_year" : 1790,
51          },
52 ▾         {
53                  "name" : "George Ernest Barnett",
54                  "death_year" : 1938
55          }
56     ];
57
58     var sorted_by_death_year = economists.sort(
59 ▾         function(a, b) {
60                  return b.death_year - a.death_year;
61          }
62     )
63     print_array(sorted_by_death_year);
64     </script>
65
66
67
```

```
[
{
"name" : George Ernest Barnett
"death_year" : 1938
}
{
"name" : Erasmus Peshine Smith
"death_year" : 1882
}
{
"name" : Henry Charles Carey
"death_year" : 1879
}
{
"name" : Adam Smith
"death_year" : 1790
}
]
```

Filtering arrays

Filtering arrays allows us to filter out some of the elements of an array so that only those that we want will remain. We can do this using **for** loops, but the **filter()** function can be far more convenient and useful. Below we have an array of bird names and we only want the ones that start with a g:

```
 1 ▾ <script>
 2 ▾ var birds = ['duck', 'goose', 'swan', 'nene',
 3       'teal', 'pintail', 'scaup', 'eider',
 4       'scoter', 'maleo', 'chachalaca', 'guan',
 5       'curassow', 'partridge', 'grouse'];
 6
 7 ▾ var g_birds = birds.filter(function(bird) {
 8 ▾     if(bird[0] === 'g') {
 9           return true;
10       }
11 ▾     else {
12           return false;
13       }
14    });
15    document.write(g_birds.toString());
16    </script>
```

goose.guan.grouse

Similar to the **sort()** function, the **filter()** function can take an anonymous function that does the filtering for us. If this function returns true, it means the value should go through the filter. But if it returns false, it means the value should be filtered out.

Above, inside the anonymous function we check if the first character of bird is a g. If it is, we let it go through the filter. Otherwise we filter it out. The result is that **g_birds** ends up containing only those bird names that begin with g.

Below we have the economists from before. I have added a new property, **nationality**. We want to create a new array that has only the American economists:

```
39 ▾ var economists = [
40 ▾     {
41              "name" : "Henry Charles Carey",
42              "death_year" : 1879,
43              "nationality" : 'American',
44         },
45 ▾     {
46              "name" : "Erasmus Peshine Smith",
47              "death_year" : 1882,
48              "nationality" : 'American',
49         },
50 ▾     {
51              "name" : "Adam Smith",
52              "death_year" : 1790,
53              "nationality" : 'British',
54         },
55 ▾     {
56              "name" : "George Ernest Barnett",
57              "death_year" : 1938,
58              "nationality" : 'American',
59         }
60 ];
61 var american_economists = economists.filter(
62 ▾     function(single_economist) {
63              if(single_economist.nationality
64 ▾             === 'American') {
65                  return true;
66         }
67 ▾         else {
68                  return false;
69         }
70     }
71 );
72 print_array(american_economists);
73 </script>
```

```
[
{
"name" : Henry Charles Carey
"death_year" : 1879
"nationality" : American
}
{
"name" : Erasmus Peshine Smith
"death_year" : 1882
"nationality" : American
}
{
"name" : George Ernest Barnett
"death_year" : 1938
"nationality" : American
}
]
```

Next we will filter the economists to create an array of 19ᵗʰ century economists:

```
61 var 19_century_economists = economists.filter(
62 ▾     function(single_economist) {
63              if(single_economist.death_year >=
64              1800 && single_economist.death_year
65 ▾             <= 1900) {
66                  return true;
67         }
68 ▾         else {
69                  return false;
70         }
71     }
72 );
```

The above code actually causes an error:

⊗ ▸Uncaught SyntaxError: Invalid or unexpected token   VM10106:61

The error message is not very helpful. But since it gives us a line number on the far right (61), we know we have to look carefully at line 61. The problem on line 61 is that the variable **19_century_economists** has an invalid name because variable names cannot start with a number. Below is the corrected code:

```
55 ▾      {
56             "name" : "George Ernest Barnett",
57             "death_year" : 1938,
58             "nationality" : 'American',
59         }
60    ];
61    var nineteenth_century_economists =
62         economists.filter(
63 ▾          function(single_economist) {
64                 if(single_economist.death_year >=
65                     1800 && single_economist.death_year
66 ▾                  <= 1900) {
67                         return true;
68                 }
69 ▾              else {
70                     return false;
71                 }
72             }
73    );
74    print_array(nineteenth_century_economists);
75    </script>
```

```
[
{
"name" : Henry Charles Carey
"death_year" : 1879
"nationality" : American
}
{
"name" : Erasmus Peshine Smith
"death_year" : 1882
"nationality" : American
}
]
```

This page intentionally left blank

22. Events

When a user clicks on a word, button or image on a webpage, that click is seen by the browser and transmitted to JavaScript. In JavaScript, we can detect this "event" and do something in response to it.

There are many kinds of events, the most commonly used one being the **click** event. When you move your mouse over a webpage that is a **mousemove** event. When you scroll down a webpage, that is a **scroll** event. When your mouse enters the space above a certain HTML element (such as an image), that is a **mouseenter** event. In this chapter we will see the most important events in action.

In order to demonstrate events, we will start by creating a rectangle using HTML and CSS:

```
i  1 ▾ <div id="my-rectangle" style="height:
   2      50px; width:50px;
   3      border:5px solid #000;">
   4
   5  </div>
   6
   7
```

Above, I have used an HTML **<div>** element. I have given the element an **id** attribute of "my-rectangle". I could have called it "my-square" since it is a square. I chose to call it "my-rectangle" because later on we make changes to it that make it stop being a square.

In this way I have given this HTML element an "id" which allows me to refer to it later using JavaScript. Using the **style** attribute, I have also added some styling to the element (a border, a height and a width) to make it look like a rectangle. On line 4 we can add contents inside the **<div>** element, as follows:

```
i  1▼ <div id="my-rectangle" style="height:
   2      50px; width:50px;
   3      border:5px solid #000;">
   4      Hello world!
   5  </div>
   6
```

Now I will add a **<script>** tag below the **<div>** in order to add some JavaScript. The **<script>** tag has to be placed after the **<div>** because the code we write requires that the **<div>** should exist first. If your JavaScript code tries to deal with an HTML element that does not exist yet, you get an error.

```
i  1▼ <div id="my-rectangle" style="height:
   2      50px; width:50px;
   3      border:5px solid #000;">
   4      Hello world!
   5  </div>
   6
   7▼ <script>
   8      var my_rectangle = document.getElementById("my-rectangle");
   9  </script>
```

Above, on line 8 I use the built-in **document.getElementById()** function to get a hold of the **<div>** element I created earlier. As the name of the function suggests, it helps you "get" an "element" by its "id" in the "document". I place the element inside a variable named **my_rectangle**. The **my_rectangle** variable acts a bridge between JavaScript and HTML. When we do things to it, things happen to the HTML element in the document.

Next I will define a function that I will use later on:

```
   7▼ <script>
   8      var my_rectangle = document.getElementById("my-rectangle");
   9
  10▼     function write_out_a_response() {
  11          document.write('You just clicked the rectangle!');
  12      }
  13
  14  </script>
```

Above, the function on line 10-12 doesn't do anything yet. It is just a function definition that can be called later on.

Now, I will add the JavaScript code that watches out for clicks on the rectangle:

```
 7 ▾ <script>
 8       var my_rectangle = document.getElementById("my-rectangle");
 9
10 ▾   function write_out_a_response() {
11          document.write('You just clicked the rectangle!');
12       }
13
14       my_rectangle.addEventListener("click", write_out_a_response);
15
16  </script>
```

Our code is complete now. Above, I used the built-in **addEventListener()** function to tell JavaScript to run the **write_out_a_response** function when the user clicks on the rectangle. The **addEventListener()** function can only be used on a variable that contains a reference to an HTML element, as in the case of **my_rectangle**, which refers to the HTML element with the **id** of "my-rectangle".

The **addEventListener()** takes two arguments. The first one is the type of event we want to watch out for, in our case it is a **click** event. The second argument is the name of a function that we want to run when the event takes place. Note the way the function name does not have quotes around it. This is because we are giving **addEventListener()** the very function itself, not just its name. This will be made clearer later on.

Now, when I click the rectangle in the preview area, this is what happens:

You just clicked the rectangle!

The rectangle disappears and in its place we see the above message.

We now have an interactive program. A user clicks on something, the program respond's to the user's action.

The reason we no longer see the rectangle is that the **document.write()** statement on line 11 overwrites the entire document. The reason for this is technical but it is as follows for those interested: This did not happen in our past examples because those examples executed the **document.write()** statements as part of the document as it loaded. But if we delay the statement until a user action happens, for example until a user clicks on something as in the present example, then JavaScript ends up replacing the whole document with whatever the **document.write()** prints out. This is a problem with **document.write()** that makes it unfit for use with events.

At any rate, we need a better way of outputting stuff that does not overwrite the document. There are all kinds of ways of achieving this. For the present we will do it be inserting information write into the rectangle itself when a user clicks on it:

```
10 ▾    function write_out_a_response() {
11          var the_rectangle = document.getElementById("my-rectangle");
12          the_rectangle.innerHTML = 'You just clicked me!';
13      }
```

Above, I have updated the **write_out_a_response()** function to get a hold of the **my-rectangle <div>** element and to put some text inside it. On line 12 we use **the_rectangle.innerHTML**. This is how we refer to the inside contents of an HTML element when writing JavaScript code. The statement therefore means "replace the inner contents of the **my-rectangle** HTML element with the string **You just clicked me!**".

Here is the result in the preview area when I click the rectangle:

The text "overflows" outside the rectangle because the browser continues to respect the width and height we defined for the rectangle. If we try to put some stuff inside it that is too big, it will simply flow out of it. Below I have updated the HTML so that the rectangle now has a width of 100 pixels and no height definition:

```
i   1 ▾ <div id="my-rectangle" style="width:100px;
    2        border:5px solid #000;">
    3        Hello world!
    4    </div>
```

Hello world!

By not giving it a height, the browser automatically decides its height according to its contents. Now when I click on it, the rectangle expands to contain the full message:

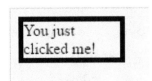

Below I have updated the **write_out_a_response()** function to do something a little more interesting:

```
 9 ▾    function write_out_a_response() {
10          var the_rectangle = document.getElementById("my-rectangle");
11          var old_contents = the_rectangle.innerHTML;
12          var new_contents = "You just clicked me!";
13          the_rectangle.innerHTML = old_contents + new_contents;
14      }
```

On 11 we get the contents of the rectangle and put it in a variable. On 12 we create a new variable, and on line 13 we put the two together and put them back inside the rectangle. This means that every time we click the rectangle, the sentence "You just clicked me!" is added to whatever is already inside it. Below is the result in the preview area after I clicked the rectangle four times:

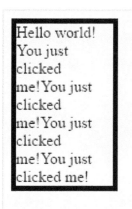

Next, we will change **write_out_a_response()** to clone the rectangle every time a user clicks on it:

```
10 ▾    function write_out_a_response() {
11          var the_rectangle = document.getElementById("my-rectangle");
12          var new_rectangle = the_rectangle.cloneNode();
13          document.body.appendChild(new_rectangle);
14      }
```

On line 12 above we use **the_rectangle.cloneNode()** to create a "clone" of the rectangle element and we put it inside **new_rectangle**. This only creates a clone in JavaScript, nothing happens to the HTML document yet. We next have to tell JavaScript where to put the clone that we just created. We do that on line 13 using **document.body.appendChild()**. This function takes an HTML element and places it at the end of the document. Line 13 therefore inserts the cloned rectangle into the document at its very end. Here is the result when I click the rectangle twice:

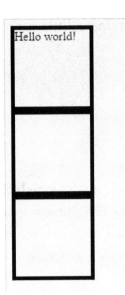

The reason the cloned rectangles are empty and do not contain the "Hello world!" sentence is because the **cloneNode()** function only copies the element itself, not its *contents*. In order to also copy the contents, we have to pass a boolean **true** to it as follows:

```
12        var new_rectangle = the_rectangle.cloneNode(true);
```

Here is the result:

A real-world program

In this section we will discuss how to build a small interactive program using what we have learned so far. Here is the code that we will start with:[22]

```html
 1 ▾ <html>
 2 ▾     <head>
 3 ▾         <script>
 4 ▾         function submit() {
 5               document.getElementById("output").innerHTML =
 6               'You just clicked submit!';
 7           }
 8
 9         </script>
10     </head>
11 ▾   <body>
12         <textarea id="input"></textarea>
13         <br>
14         <button onclick="submit()">Submit</button>
15         <br>
16         <div id="output"></div>
17     </body>
18   </html>
```

Here is the result when we run the code:

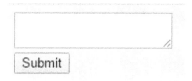

Submit

You can put the above code in a file ending with the html extension in order to use it in a browser, as follows (I have named it program.html):

1	10/6/2018 1:31 PM	File folder	
program.html	10/6/2018 1:30 PM	Chrome HTML Do...	1 KB
text_analyzer.txt	10/1/2018 5:32 PM	Text Document	3 KB

When opening this file in Chrome, here is the result:

---

[22] You can copy this code from my website at http://hawramani.com/?p=67000

If you put the code in a file and open it in a browser as shown above, you will have to click the reload button every time you make a change to the code.

The code we have is mostly HTML code that creates a text area and a button. This is not the place to explain how HTML works, but if you look at the code for the button on line 14, you will notice that it has an **onclick** property that refers to a JavaScript function:

```
14          <button onclick="submit()">Submit</button>
```

We already covered how to add an event listener to an HTML element using the **addEventListener()** function. The above accomplishes the exact same thing; it is just another way of adding an event listener to an HTML element, but rather than having to do it in a JavaScript section of code, we add the event as an attribute of the HTML element itself. Note that the attribute is "onclick" rather than "click".

The **submit()** function is defined above it on lines 4-7:

```
4 ▾        function submit() {
5              document.getElementById("output").innerHTML =
6              'You just clicked submit!';
7          }
```

This **submit()** function will be run every time a user clicks on the button. What the code of the function does on lines 5-6 is find an HTML element with the id of "output" (see line 16) then it replaces its contents with the text "You just clicked submit!".

Below is what shows up in the preview area when I click the submit button:

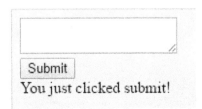
You just clicked submit!

Below I have updated the **submit()** function to print out the current date and time when someone clicks the Submit button:

```
4 ▼        function submit() {
5              var date_string = new Date().toLocaleString();
6
7              document.getElementById("output").innerHTML =
8              'Current date and time: '
9                  + date_string;
10         }
```

On line 5, we create a JavaScript **Date** object using the special **new** "operator". **Date** is a built-in JavaScript construct that allows us to access functionalities related to date and time. The statement **new Date()** means "create a **Date** object and return it." But instead of putting this returned object in a variable, we immediately access a function that the object has, which is the **toLocaleString()** function, which returns a string that represents the current date and time.

To clarify further, below is line 5 broken into two lines:

```
var date_object = new Date();
var date_string = date_object.toLocaleString();
```

Here is the result when we click Submit:

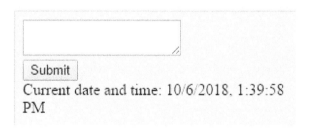

Current date and time: 10/6/2018, 1:39:58 PM

Moving on, we update the **submit()** function so that it greets the user if they put their name in the empty box you see in the preview area:

```
4 ▼        function submit() {
5              var input = document.getElementById("input").value;
6              document.getElementById("output").innerHTML =
7              'Hello ' + input + '!';
8         }
```

Below I put my first name in the box then clicked Submit:

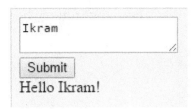

The statement **document.getElementById("input").value** retrieves whatever text is in the empty box. We have already seen **document.getElementById()** before. In this case we are retrieving the HTML element that has an id of "input", then we are accessing the **value** property of this retrieved element. Note that only a few HTML elements have a **value** property.

Below I wrote "Fred Flintstone" in the input box and press Submit:

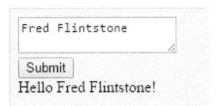

Below I update **submit()** so that it is now a function that converts a person's height to centimeters. The user is supposed to enter a height in feet and inches and will be shown their height in centimeters once they click Submit:

```
4 ▾    function submit() {
5          var input = document.getElementById("input").value;
6          var measures = input.split(" ");
7          var feet = measures[0];
8          var feet_numbers = feet[0];
9          var inches = measures[1];
10         var inches_numbers = inches.replace('"', '');
11         var inches_numbers = inches_numbers * 1;
12         var total_inches = (feet_numbers * 12) + inches_numbers;
13         var centimeters = total_inches * 2.54;
14         var centimeters_rounded = Math.floor(centimeters);
15
16         document.getElementById("output").innerHTML =
17         'Your height in centimeters: ' + centimeters_rounded ;
18    }
```

Here is the result when I enter a height and click Submit:

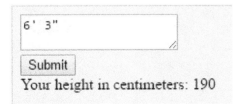

Below is the same function with explanatory comments added:

```
4 ▾    function submit() {
5          var input = document.getElementById("input").value;
6          // split 6' 3" into an array
7          var measures = input.split(" ");
8          // feet contains the string 6'
9          var feet = measures[0];
10         // feet_numbers contains 6 (we get first character)
11         var feet_numbers = feet[0];
12         // 3"
13         var inches = measures[1];
14         // 3 (we replace quotation mark with nothing to delete it)
15         var inches_numbers = inches.replace('"', '');
16         // multiply by number to force JavaScript to
17         // treat it as a number
18         var inches_numbers = inches_numbers * 1;
19         var total_inches = (feet_numbers * 12) + inches_numbers;
20         var centimeters = total_inches * 2.54;
21         var centimeters_rounded = Math.floor(centimeters);
22
23         document.getElementById("output").innerHTML =
24         'Your height in centimeters: ' + centimeters_rounded ;
25     }
```

On line 15 we use the **replace()** function without using a regular expression, as this function can also take strings as its first argument. The statement **replace('"', '')** makes JavaScript find all double quotation marks and replace them with nothing, meaning that they all get deleted. When we pass a string to **replace()** rather than a regular expression, the replacement will be done globally, so there is no need for the **g** modifier. In fact we cannot use modifiers in **replace()** unless we are using regular expressions.

Mouseover and mouseout events

In JavaScript we can attach multiple events to the same element. In this section we will use the **mouseover** and **mouseout** events on the rectangle from earlier. The **mouseover** event takes place when a user's mouse enters the space occupied an HTML element, while the **mouseout** event is its opposite; it takes place (or "fires") when the user's mouse leaves the space occupied by an element. Below is the code we will use:

```
 7 ▾  <script>
 8 ▾      function say_in() {
 9             the_rectangle = document.getElementById("my-rectangle");
10             the_rectangle.innerHTML = 'Mouse is inside';
11         }
12 ▾      function say_out() {
13             the_rectangle = document.getElementById("my-rectangle");
14             the_rectangle.innerHTML = "Mouse is outside.";
15         }
16
17         var my_rectangle = document.getElementById("my-rectangle");
18         my_rectangle.addEventListener("mouseover", say_in);
19         my_rectangle.addEventListener("mouseout", say_out);
20
21     </script>
```

Above, we attach two separate events to the rectangle on lines 18 and 19. Each event calls one of the functions defined above. Here is what the rectangle looks like originally, when the page first loads:

When I hover my mouse above the rectangle, the rectangle's text changes as follows:

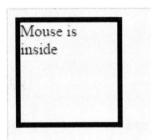

And as soon as my mouse leaves the rectangle, the text changes as follows:

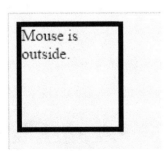

JavaScript menus

Many websites use menus that integrate JavaScript functionality. Below is a screenshot of the Open Library website. When I click "Browse", the vertical menu that you see opens up.

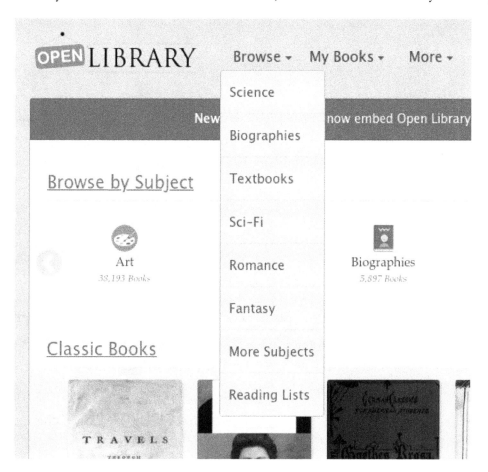

 We will now recreate a very simple replica of the above menu. Below we have two HTML elements, a "browse-button" element that will function as our button, and a "sub-menu" element that will function as the menu that opens up when a user clicks "Browse". In a real menu the menu items (like "Science") would be links to other webpages. But to keep things simple we will merely write "Science" and so on without worrying about links.

```
i  1   <div id="browse-button">Browse</div>
   2 ▾ <div id="sub-menu">
   3       Science<br>
   4       Biographies<br>
   5       Textbooks<br>
   6   </div>
   7
```

Browse
Science
Biographies
Textbooks

As you can see in the preview area, currently everything shows up. We want only "Browse" to show up, so that a user can click it to view the rest of the words. In order to achieve that, we will add a **style** attribute to the "sub-menu" element (line 3 below):

```
i  1   <div id="browse-button">Browse</div>        Browse
   2 ▾ <div id="sub-menu"
   3       style="display:none;">
   4       Science<br>
   5       Biographies<br>
   6       Textbooks<br>
   7   </div>
```

As you can see in the preview area, now only the word "Browse" shows up. The "sub-menu" element exists; it is just hidden at the moment. We will JavaScript to make up show up when we want. Below I have added the JavaScript to accomplish that:

```
 9 ▾ <script>
10       var browse_button = document.getElementById('browse-button');
11 ▾    browse_button.addEventListener('click', function() {
12           var sub_menu = document.getElementById('sub-menu');
13           sub_menu.style.display = 'block';
14       });
15   </script>
```

On lines 11-14, we use the **addEventListener()** to attach a click event to the "Browse" button. Instead of passing it a function's name as its second argument, we pass it an anonymous function. This does not make a difference to its functionality; it is just more convenient since it helps you avoid the task of having to name your function.

Inside the anonymous function we get a hold of the "sub-menu" element and on line 13 we change its **style.display** attribute to **block**. This causes it to show up.

Here is the result when click "Browse":

```
Browse
Science
Biographies
Textbooks
```

We are only half-way done. In order for it to be a proper menu, the sub menu should go away when a user clicks "Browse" again. In order to accomplish that we make the following changes to the anonymous function:

```
11 ▾     browse_button.addEventListener('click', function() {
12          var sub_menu = document.getElementById('sub-menu');
13 ▾        if(sub_menu.style.display === 'none') {
14              sub_menu.style.display = 'block';
15          }
16 ▾        else if(sub_menu.style.display === 'block') {
17              sub_menu.style.display = 'none';
18          }
19      });
```

Above, inside the anonymous function we now have conditional blocks. On line 13 we check if the sub menu is not showing up, in which case we cause it to show up on line 14. But if it is already showing up, we cause it to stop showing up on line 17. In this way we "toggle" the menu.

Below I have changed the menu so that now the sub menu shows up when a user's mouse is over the word "Browse". When they take their mouse away, the sub menu goes away. To accomplish that I have used two event listeners:

```
 9 ▾ <script>
10      var browse_button = document.getElementById('browse-button');
11 ▾    browse_button.addEventListener('mouseover', function() {
12          var sub_menu = document.getElementById('sub-menu');
13          sub_menu.style.display = 'block';
14      });
15 ▾    browse_button.addEventListener('mouseout', function() {
16          var sub_menu = document.getElementById('sub-menu');
17          sub_menu.style.display = 'none';
18      });
19 </script>
```

Note that the above code is not sufficient to make a functioning menu because as soon as a user moves their mouse pointer to the sub menu (for example if they were intending to click "Science") the sub menu goes away, so that they never get the opportunity to actually click anything in the sub menu. In order to make it function properly we will need to use some complex logic which is beyond the scope of this book.

Using "this" with events

We saw the **this** keyword in the coffee robot example. This keyword is extremely useful when dealing with events. Below we have some CSS and HTML that creates four rectangles as can be seen in the preview area. The **<style>** tag at the top allows us to add "styling" to HTML elements. In this case we are adding borders, margins and other styling using the CSS language which is beyond the scope of this book.

```
i   1 ▾ <style>
    2 ▾     div {
    3             border:5px solid #000;
    4             float:left;
    5             margin: 10px;
    6             padding:10px;
    7         }
    8   </style>
    9
   10 ▾ <div>
   11         Rectangle 1
   12   </div>
   13 ▾ <div>
   14         Rectangle 2
   15   </div>
   16 ▾ <div>
   17         Rectangle 3
   18   </div>
   19 ▾ <div>
   20         Rectangle 4
   21   </div>
```

Next we will add a JavaScript statement to get a hold of all the rectangles in one variable:

```
23 ▾ <script>
24       var all_rectangles = document.querySelectorAll('div');
25
26   </script>
```

Above, we are using **document.querySelectorAll()**. This function retrieves all HTML elements that share a certain characteristic. In this case, we are retrieving all HTML elements that are **<div>** tags.

Next we will define the function that we want to run when a user clicks on any of the rectangles:

```
25 ▾     function change_background() {
26           this.style.background = 'red';
27       }
```

The **change_background()** function simply changes the background color of the clicked element to red. On line 26 we use **this** to refer to the currently clicked element without caring what element it is. You will see why this is useful below.

We next add event listeners to the rectangles using a **for** loop:

```
29 ▾     for(var i = 0; i < all_rectangles.length; i++) {
30           all_rectangles[i].addEventListener("click", change_background);
31       }
```

The loop goes over the **all_rectangles** variable and adds an event listener to each rectangle using the **addEventListener()** function. We pass **change_background** to the

addEventListener() function as its second argument on line 30, meaning that the **change_background()** function will run whenever a user clicks on any of the rectangles.

Below is the result in the preview area when I click on the first rectangle:

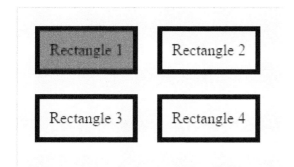

Below I have clicked on the fourth rectangle after clicking the first one:

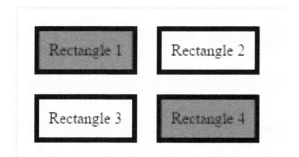

Thanks to using **this** inside the **change_background()** function, JavaScript intelligently applies the background change to the rectangle we have clicked and not to the other ones.

Below I have updated the JavaScript so that now the background of a rectangle changes when a user hovers their mouse pointer over it. However, I have also added the twist that when a user's mouse pointer leaves a rectangle, the background of the rectangle is reset to transparent:

```
23 ▾ <script>
24      var all_rectangles = document.querySelectorAll('div');
25 ▾    function change_background() {
26          this.style.background = 'red';
27      }
28 ▾    function reset_background() {
29          this.style.background = 'transparent';
30      }
31
32 ▾    for(var i = 0; i < all_rectangles.length; i++) {
33          all_rectangles[i].addEventListener("mouseover", change_background);
34          all_rectangles[i].addEventListener("mouseout", reset_background);
35      }
36
37  </script>
```

On line 33 we pass **change_background** to **addEventListerner()**, while on line 34 we pass the new function **reset_background**. Try to take the time to read the above code carefully until you fully understanding how it works.

23. Cookies

You may have seen those annoying notifications on certain websites that tell you that the site uses cookies. Those notifications are required by European Union privacy laws. Cookies allow websites to store information about the current user on the user's own machine. For example, a news website may allow you to change the size of the text in their articles and store your preference in a cookie. When you come back to their site the next day, the site uses its cookie to remember your preferred text size. In this way you do not have to go through the hassle of changing the text size every time you visit the site. The site "remembers" your preferred size. There is nothing sinister about this type of cookie. There is however another type of cookie known as a "third-party cookie" that is used by sites like Facebook and Google to track your online activities *even when you are not on their website*. We will not go into further details about that since it is beyond the scope of this book.

Below, we have the first sentence of George Eliot's *Middlemarch* in a **<p>** tag:

```
1  <p>Who that cares much to know the history of man, and how the
2     mysterious mixture behaves under the varying experiments of Time,
3     has not dwelt, at least briefly, on the life of Saint Theresa,
4     has not smiled with some gentleness at the thought of the little
5     girl walking forth one morning hand-in-hand with her still
6     smaller brother, to go and seek martyrdom in the country of
7     the Moors?
8  </p>
```

We will now add buttons to enable the user to increase or decrease the size of the text. We will not use anything fancy, just unstyled **<div>** tags as follows:

```
9   <div>+ Increase size</div>
10  <div>- Decrease size</div>
```

Here is what the preview area looks line now:

> Who that cares much to know the history of man, and how the mysterious mixture behaves under the varying experiments of Time, has not dwelt, at least briefly, on the life of Saint Theresa, has not smiled with some gentleness at the thought of the little girl walking forth one morning hand-in-hand with her still smaller brother, to go and seek martyrdom in the country of the Moors?
>
> + Increase size
> - Decrease size

We will start our JavaScript with a variable that keeps track of the current size setting in pixels. It is currently set to 16, because that is the font size that the preview area uses by default.

```
12 ▾ <script>
13     var current_size_setting = 16;
```

We will next add the function that changes font sizes when a user clicks on either of the two buttons.

```
15 ▾ function change_size() {
16       var the_paragraph = document.querySelectorAll('p')[0];
17    }
```

Above, we have a barebones function for now that only retrieves the paragraph without doing anything to it yet. It uses the **querySelectorAll()** function to retrieve all **<p>** tags in the document. But since we are dealing with only one **<p>** tag, at the end of the statement we have put a **[0]** to access the first and only element returned by the function (since the function always returns an array-like result even if there is only one element). To clarify, here is the same statement broken into two lines:

```
15 ▾ function change_size() {
16       var all_paragraphs = document.querySelectorAll('p');
17       var the_paragraph = all_paragraphs[0];
18    }
```

Next, we will put **this** into a new variable just for clarity;

```
15 ▾ function change_size() {
16       var all_paragraphs = document.querySelectorAll('p');
17       var the_paragraph = all_paragraphs[0];
18
19       var current_button = this;
20    }
```

The **current_button** variable refers to the button the user has clicked, which is going to be either the "Increase size" button or the "Decrease size" button. Putting this inside a variable does not change how it works, but it makes the code easier to read since **this** is vague and can be hard to interpret, especially if you are dealing with a long piece of code.

Next we will add an **if** statement to the function:

```
19      var current_button = this;
20 ▾    if(current_button.innerHTML === '+ Increase size') {
21
22      }
23 ▾    else {
24
25      }
```

In the if statement's condition we check the **innerHTML** attribute of the button to find out whether the current button is the button for increasing or decreasing text size (since we are going to be using the **change_size()** function for both increasing and decreasing text size). Any code we place on line 21 will run when the user clicked on "Increase size", while any code we put on line 24 will run if the user clicked on "Decrease size".

Below we have added the finishing touches to **change_size()**:

```
12 ▾ <script>
13    var current_size_setting = 16;
14
15 ▾  function change_size() {
16        var all_paragraphs = document.querySelectorAll('p');
17        var the_paragraph = all_paragraphs[0];
18
19        var current_button = this;
20 ▾      if(current_button.innerHTML === '+ Increase size') {
21          current_size_setting = current_size_setting + 2;
22          the_paragraph.style.fontSize = current_size_setting + 'px';
23        }
24 ▾      else {
25          current_size_setting = current_size_setting - 2;
26          the_paragraph.style.fontSize = current_size_setting + 'px';
27        }
28    }
```

On line 21 we are using the **current_size_setting** variable that was defined *outside* the function (note how there is no **var** in front of it). This is important because by having this variable outside the **change_size()** function, the variable continues to exist even after the function ends. Next time the **change_size()** function runs, it will still access the very same **current_size_setting** variable from before. The **current_size_setting** variable continues to "live" behind the scenes as long as the document is open in a browser.

On line 21 we increase the **current_size_setting** variable's value by 2. We could have increased it by 1 instead, but 2 causes is a more visible change in the font size. On line 22 we update the font size of the paragraph using **the_paragraph.style.fontSize**. Note that this will not work if we merely pass it a number. It has to end with a unit, such as "px" (which stands for pixels, which is a unit of measurement for text sizes and other things). This is why we have **+ 'px'** at the end of the statement.

On lines 25-26 we have the counterpart for the above code, this time for decreasing the font size.

Next we have the code for attaching the event listeners to the buttons:

```
30    var change_size_buttons = document.querySelectorAll("div");
31
32 ▾  for(var i = 0; i < change_size_buttons.length; i++) {
33        change_size_buttons[i].addEventListener("click", change_size);
34    }
35    </script>
```

Here is the result in the preview area after I clicked "Increase size" once:

Who that cares much to know the history of man, and how the mysterious mixture behaves under the varying experiments of Time, has not dwelt, at least briefly, on the life of Saint Theresa, has not smiled with some gentleness at the thought of the little girl walking forth one morning hand-in-hand with her still smaller brother, to go and seek martyrdom in the country of the Moors?

+ Increase size
- Decrease size

If I click it again, the size increases more:

Who that cares much to know the history of man, and how the mysterious mixture behaves under the varying experiments of Time, has not dwelt, at least briefly, on the life of Saint Theresa, has not smiled with some gentleness at the thought of the little girl walking forth one morning hand-in-hand with her still smaller brother, to go and seek martyrdom in the country of the Moors?

+ Increase size
- Decrease size

We now have a fully functional system for allowing users to increase and decrease the text size of this paragraph.

Next we will use cookies to store the user's text size preference so that even if they close the page and open it again, the document continues to remember the text size they set the paragraph at.

Note that not all browsers all you to set cookies when dealing with local files. If you are using JS Tinker, cookies will only work if you have accessed JS Tinker through a website. If download JS Tinker and open it locally, cookies will not work except in certain browsers (such as version 53 of Firefox).

First, here is a function I have added to the top of the script to check whether cookies are enabled or not:[23]

```
12 ▾ <script>
13 ▾     function areCookiesEnabled() {
14           document.cookie = "verify=1";
15           if(document.cookie.length >= 1
16 ▾           && document.cookie.indexOf("verify=1") !== -1) {
17               return true;
18           }
19           return false;
20       }
21 ▾     if(areCookiesEnabled()) {
22           document.write('We have cookies!');
23       }
```

---

[23] You can copy the code from my website at http://hawramani.com/?p=67000

Above, we use the function **areCookiesEnabled()** to check whether we can create cookies or not. This function tries to create a cookie on line 14 and on lines 15-16 checks whether the cookie was created or not.

The statement **document.cookie = "verify=1"** on line 14 creates a cookie with the name of **verify** and with the value of **1**. On line 15, the condition **document.cookie.length >= 1** checks whether any cookies exist at all. On line 16, we specifically check whether a cookie exists with the name of **verify** and the value of **1**.

Here is the result in the preview area when I run the above code:

Who that cares much to know the history of man, and how the mysterious mixture behaves under the varying experiments of Time, has not dwelt, at least briefly, on the life of Saint Theresa, has not smiled with some gentleness at the thought of the little girl walking forth one morning hand-in-hand with her still smaller brother, to go and seek martyrdom in the country of the Moors?

+ Increase size
- Decrease size
We have cookies!

Note the sentence "We have cookies!" at the bottom.

The **document.cookie** variable is actually just a simple string variable that holds all cookies. We can even print it out, as follows:

```
25      document.write('<br>');
26      document.write(document.cookie);
```

Here is the result:

+ Increase size
- Decrease size
We have cookies!
verify=1

As you can see above, **document.cookie** merely contains the string **verify=1**. Which was created by **areCookiesEnabled()** earlier.

We will next add a function for creating cookies. We already saw that we can create cookies merely by writing **document.cookie = "cookie_name=cookie_value "**. The problem with cookies created this way is that they are deleted once the user leaves the document, which rather defeats the purpose of cookies. In order to create proper cookies, we will use a **setCookie()** function as follows:

```
26 ▾      function setCookie(name,value,days) {
27            var expires = "";
28 ▾         if (days) {
29                var date = new Date();
30                date.setTime(date.getTime() + (days*24*60*60*1000));
31                expires = "; expires=" + date.toUTCString();
32                console.log(expires);
33            }
34 ▾         if(!value) {
35                value = "";
36            }
37            cookie = name + "=" + value  + expires + "; path=/";
38            document.cookie = cookie;
39        }
```

Dealing with cookies is such a tiresome business that programmers simply copy a few good cookie-related functions from the Internet without bothering about how they work. I will try to explain how the function works, but you shouldn't worry too much about it since you can use it whether you understand it or not. Some of the discussion will get quite technical, so feel free to merely skim the explanations on how cookie functions work. The **setCookie()** function takes three arguments: the name of the cookie, its value, and the number of days the cookie should be stored on the user's computer. On lines 28-32 the function creates a string that represents the cookie's expiry date. The expiry date is calculated based on the number of days that are passed to the function. On lines 33-35 we set the **value** variable to an empty string if it is a "falsy" value like **null**, **NaN**, zero or **false**. This helps avoid unexpected behavior that comes about if you try to store such values in cookies. Note that this means you cannot store the number zero in a cookie. If you are storing numbers in a cookie, if you have to store zero then simply store an empty string and later check if the cookie's value is an empty string. If so, you can then assume it is a zero.

On line 36 we store the actual cookie. Here is what the **cookie** would look like if we were to print it out after calling the function as **setCookie("cookie_name", "cookie_value", 365)**:

```
cookie_name=cookie_value; expires=Fri, 22 Nov 2019 17:36:22 GMT; path = /
```

If we print out **document.cookies** now to see the cookies we have, here is what we get:

```
+ Increase size
- Decrease size
We have cookies!
verify=1; cookie_name=cookie_value
```

Even though we created an expiry date and a "path" for the cookie in **setCookie()**, when printing out the cookies we only see the cookie's name and value because, for whatever reason, JavaScript is designed to prevent us from accessing cookies' expiry dates and paths.

The path determines which pages of a website the cookie will apply to. If the path is a forward slash as it is above, that means the cookie will apply to the entire website, meaning that every page of the website will be able to access the cookie and update it.

Next we will discuss the **getCookie()** function that we will use for getting the values of cookies we have already stored:

```
40 ▾       function getCookie(name) {
41             var result = document.cookie.match("\\b" + name + "=([^;]*)\\b");
42 ▾         if(result) {
43                 return result[1];
44             }
45 ▾         else {
46                 return null;
47             }
48         };
```

The above uses a sophisticated regular expression on line 41 to find out whether the **document.cookie** variable contains a cookie with that matches the **name** argument passed to the function. Explaining how the regular expression works is beyond our scope.

On line 42 we check if we have a **result**, and if so, we return the first match using **result[1]**. And if there is no result, meaning we did not find a cookie with that name, then we return **null** on line 46.

We will now update the **change_size()** function to store the user's size preference in a cookie:

```
52 ▾    function change_size() {
53           var all_paragraphs = document.querySelectorAll('p');
54           var the_paragraph = all_paragraphs[0];
55
56           var current_button = this;
57 ▾         if(current_button.innerHTML === '+ Increase size') {
58               current_size_setting = current_size_setting + 2;
59               the_paragraph.style.fontSize = current_size_setting + 'px';
60           }
61 ▾         else {
62               current_size_setting = current_size_setting - 2;
63               the_paragraph.style.fontSize = current_size_setting + 'px';
64           }
65           setCookie('size-preference', current_size_setting, 365);
66       }
```

On line 65 we are storing a cookie named size-preference and in it we store the value of **current_size_setting**. This means that every time the user changes the size of the text, we update the cookie to reflect the new size.

We now need a way to restore the user's size preference when they first open the page. Remember that above the **change_size()** function we defined the original value for **current_size_setting**, as follows:

```
50       var current_size_setting = 16;
51
52 ▾     function change_size() {
```

We will now add a cookie-related section underneath line 50:

```
50       var current_size_setting = 16;
51       var cookie_value = getCookie('size-preference');
52 ▾     if(cookie_value !== null && cookie_value !== "") {
53           current_size_setting = cookie_value;
54           current_size_setting = current_size_setting * 1;
55           var all_paragraphs = document.querySelectorAll('p');
56           var the_paragraph = all_paragraphs[0];
57           the_paragraph.style.fontSize = current_size_setting + 'px';
58       }
59
60 ▾     function change_size() {
```

On line 51 we try to retrieve the cookie's value. On line 52 we check if the cookie is not null and not an empty string, and if so we use its value. On line 54 we multiply **current_size_setting** by 1 in order to force it to become a number (since all values from cookies are strings by default). On lines 55-58 we update the paragraph's **style.fontSize** property in order to contain the size preference we got from the cookie.

Note that the above cookie-related code only runs once; when the page loads.

Now each time I increase or decrease the text size, if I type **document.cookie** in the JavaScript console I can see the new size reflected there:

```
>>   document.cookie;
←    "verify=1; size-preference=26"
>>   document.cookie;
←    "verify=1; size-preference=24"
>>   document.cookie;
←    "verify=1; size-preference=22"
>> document.cookie;|
```

Deleting cookies

Deleting a cookie is as simple as changing its expiry date so that the browser thinks the cookie has expired:

```
49 ▾       function deleteCookie(name) {
50              var past_date = new Date(1976, 8, 16);
51              var expired_string = 'expires=' + past_date.toUTCString();
52              var expired_cookie = name + '=; ' + expired_string + '; path=/';
53              document.cookie = expired_cookie;
54          }
```

Above on line 50 we use **new Date()** to create a JavaScript **Date** object set to represent a day in 1976. On line 51 we create a string variable that contains the full cookie-format definition for the expired date. On line 52 we create the full expired cookie. Note the "path" at the end, this has to exactly match the path the cookie was created with. The cookie value does not matter, note that it is empty above.

On line 53 we perform the deletion by storing the expired cookie, which causes the original cookie to be replaced by the expired cookie, which is then immediately deleted by the browser. Note that **document.cookie** is a special variable, as we have already seen when we write **document.cookie =** this only affects one cookie at a time.

24. Combining HTML, CSS and JavaScript

In this final chapter we will be looking into more convenient and advanced ways of using JavaScript with HTML and CSS.

We will start with a simple reading journal that lists three books with their authors and publication years:

```
1 ▼  <style>
2 ▼      .title {
3             font-style:italic;
4        }
5 ▼      .publication-year {
6             font-size:90%; padding-left:1em;
7        }
8     </style>
9     <h1>My Reading Journal</h1>
10 ▼  <ul>
11 ▼      <li>
12            <span class="author">Rebecca Stott</span>, <span class="title">
13            Darwin's Ghosts: The Secret History of Evolution</span> <span
14            class="publication-year">2012</span>
15        </li>
16 ▼      <li>
17            <span class="author">David W. Deamer</span>, <span class="title">
18            First Life: Discovering the Connections Between Stars, Cells, and
19            How Life Began</span> <span class="publication-year">2011</span>
20        </li>
21 ▼      <li>
22            <span class="author">Alister E. McGrath</span>, <span class="title"
23            >Dawkins' God: From The Selfish Gene to The God Delusion</span>
24            <span class="publication-year">2015</span>
25        </li>
26    </ul>
```

Here is what it looks like in the preview area:

My Reading Journal

- Rebecca Stott, *Darwin's Ghosts: The Secret History of Evolution* 2012
- David W. Deamer, *First Life: Discovering the Connections Between Stars, Cells, and How Life Began* 2011
- Alister E. McGrath, *Dawkins' God: From The Selfish Gene to The God Delusion* 2015

We will begin by making the publication year smaller and separating it a bit from the book titles:

```
5 ▾    .publication-year {
6          font-size:90%; padding-left:1em;
7      }
```

Here is the result:

- Rebecca Stott, *Darwin's Ghosts: The Secret History of Evolution*　　2012
- David W. Deamer, *First Life: Discovering the Connections Between Stars, Cells, and How Life Began*　　2011
- Alister E. McGrath, *Dawkins' God: From The Selfish Gene to The God Delusion*　　2015

Next we will add each book's ISBN as a special attribute on each **<li>** tag. This is something we have not seen before, but it is used commonly by web applications:

```
11 ▾    <li data-isbn="9780679604136">
12          <span class="author">Rebecca Stott</span>, <span class="title">
13          Darwin's Ghosts: The Secret History of Evolution</span> <span
14          class="publication-year">2012</span>
15      </li>
16 ▾    <li data-isbn="9780520258327">
17          <span class="author">David W. Deamer</span>, <span class="title">
18          First Life: Discovering the Connections Between Stars, Cells, and
19          How Life Began</span> <span class="publication-year">2011</span>
20      </li>
21 ▾    <li data-isbn="9781118964781">
22          <span class="author">Alister E. McGrath</span>, <span class="title"
23          >Dawkins' God: From The Selfish Gene to The God Delusion</span>
24          <span class="publication-year">2015</span>
25      </li>
26  </ul>
```

Above, on lines 11, 16 and 21 we have added the **data-isbn** attributes. Custom attributes start with the word **data** followed by a dash. After the dash we can write anything we want, similar to variable names. The attributes, as is obvious, represent each book's ISBN (International Standard Book Number), a unique number that is associated with each book.

We will next add some JavaScript:

```
28 ▾  <script>
29 ▾      var books = {
30 ▾          '9780679604136' : {
31                 'publisher' : 'Random House Publishing Group',
32                 'pages' : '432',
33             },
34 ▾          '9780520258327' : {
35                 'publisher' : 'University of California Press',
36                 'pages' : '271',
37
38             },
39 ▾          '9781118964781' : {
40                 'publisher' : 'John Wiley & Sons',
41                 'pages' : '208',
42             },
43         };
44  </script>
```

The JavaScript defines a single variable named **books**. The variable is an object with three objects inside that provide additional information for each book. Each inner object represents a book. The keys are the ISBNs for each book.

We will now add event code in order to provide additional information about each book when a user clicks on its title:

```
45      var all_book_list_items = document.querySelectorAll('li');
46 ▾    for(var i = 0; i < all_book_list_items.length; i++) {
47 ▾        all_book_list_items[i].addEventListener('click', function() {
48
49         });
50      };
```

Above, we go through all the list items and attach a click event to each. The anonymous function on lines 47-49 currently does nothing. What we will do is fetch the book's publisher and page number from the books variable we defined earlier. We will then place them inside the list item for that book when it is clicked.

```
46 ▾    for(var i = 0; i < all_book_list_items.length; i++) {
47 ▾        all_book_list_items[i].addEventListener('click', function() {
48             var isbn = this.getAttribute('data-isbn');
49             var book_object = books[isbn];
50             this.innerHTML = this.innerHTML + '<br>'
51                 + '<span class="extras">Publisher: ' + book_object.publisher
52                 + '. Page count: ' + book_object.pages + '</span>';
53         });
54      };
```

Above, on line 48 we retrieve the list item's **data-isbn** attribute using the **getAttribute()** function. The statement **this.getAttribute('data-isbn')** means "get the **data-json** attribute of the current element." As previously explained, inside functions dealing with events, **this** refers to the element to which the event happened. In this case, it refers to the list item that was clicked by the user.

555

On line 49 we use this retrieved ISBN to access the book's information inside the **books** object, since the **books** object uses ISBNs as keys. We cannot write **books.isbn**, it has to be **books[isbn]**. Line 49 causes that specific book's information to be placed inside **book_object**. On lines 50-52 we update the list item with the information inside the **book_object** variable. Here is the result when I click the first list item:

My Reading Journal

- Rebecca Stott, *Darwin's Ghosts: The Secret History of Evolution*   2012
  Publisher: Random House Publishing Group. Page count: 432
- David W. Deamer, *First Life: Discovering the Connections Between Stars, Cells, and How Life Began*   2011
- Alister E. McGrath, *Dawkins' God: From The Selfish Gene to The God Delusion*   2015

And below I have clicked the third list item:

My Reading Journal

- Rebecca Stott, *Darwin's Ghosts: The Secret History of Evolution*   2012
  Publisher: Random House Publishing Group. Page count: 432
- David W. Deamer, *First Life: Discovering the Connections Between Stars, Cells, and How Life Began*   2011
- Alister E. McGrath, *Dawkins' God: From The Selfish Gene to The God Delusion*   2015
  Publisher: John Wiley & Sons. Page count: 208

This allows user to see more information about the book when they click its list item.

There is a problem however. If we click a list item multiple times, the extra information is printed out multiple times. Below is what happens when I click the first list item three times:

My Reading Journal

- Rebecca Stott, *Darwin's Ghosts: The Secret History of Evolution*   2012
  Publisher: Random House Publishing Group. Page count: 432
  Publisher: Random House Publishing Group. Page count: 432
  Publisher: Random House Publishing Group. Page count: 432
- David W. Deamer, *First Life: Discovering the Connections Between Stars, Cells, and How Life Began*   2011
- Alister E. McGrath, *Dawkins' God: From The Selfish Gene to The God Delusion*   2015

In order to prevent that, we add the following three lines to the beginning of the anonymous function:

```
47     all_book_list_items[i].addEventListener('click', function() {
48         if(this.querySelectorAll('.extras').length) {
49             return;
50         }
51         var isbn = this.getAttribute('data-isbn');
52         var book_object = books[isbn];
53         this.innerHTML = this.innerHTML + '<br>'
54             + '<span class="extras">Publisher: ' + book_object.publisher
55             + '. Page count: ' + book_object.pages + '</span>';
56     });
57 };
```

On line 48 we use **querySelectorAll()** in two new ways. First, we are not writing **document.querySelectorAll()**, which would have retrieved everything from the document. Instead we are writing **this.querySelectorAll()**, which means that the function will only look inside **this** to find what we are trying to retrieve, instead of looking at the whole document. The second new thing is that instead of passing a tag name to **querySelectorAll()** as its argument, we are passing a CSS selector. That is right, you can use CSS selectors with **querySelectorAll()**, which is extremely handy. The selector is **.extras**, which refers to the new span we added on line 54 inside of which we placed the information on the publishers and page counts.

The statement **this.querySelectorAll('.extras').length** retrieves the number of elements inside this which have a class name of **extras**. If there is no such element, it will return zero, therefore the **if** condition will fail. But if there is already an element with the class name of **extras**, the **if** condition will succeed and therefore the function will return (line 49) without doing anything. In this way, the extra information is only printed out once no matter how many times the user clicks the list item. The first click causes the whole function to run, while the second click and after will run headlong into the **return** statement on line 49, causing the function to finish prematurely without doing anything more.

There is, however, another interesting thing we could do. We could cause the extra information to be deleted on the second click. This would mean the first click on a list item would show the extra information and the second click would hide the information. This creates an "expanding and collapsing" effect that is used by many web applications to show and hide extra information upon user clicks. In order to accomplish that, we simply update the **if** statement from earlier:

```
48    if(this.querySelectorAll('.extras').length) {
49        var the_extras_span = this.querySelectorAll('.extras')[0];
50        this.removeChild(the_extras_span);
51    }
```

Above, on line 49 we retrieve the extras element. On line 50 we use **this.removeChild()**, which is a function that deletes an element from the document. This function can only be called on a variable that contains an HTML element, and it can only take another HTML element. As the name suggests, it removes a "child" element, meaning an element that is inside **this**.

Here is the result when I click the first list item twice:

- Rebecca Stott, *Darwin's Ghosts: The Secret History of Evolution*   2012
- David W. Deamer, *First Life: Discovering the Connections Between Stars, Cells, and How Life Began*   2011
- Alister E. McGrath, *Dawkins' God: From The Selfish Gene to The God Delusion*   2015

You do not actually see any difference because the second click causes the added information to be removed, so the original state is restored.

We are done with implementing this functionality. There is however an issue which is useful to look into. If I click any of the list items many times, a space starts to appear underneath them. This is what the list looks like after I click the first item six times in succession:

- Rebecca Stott, *Darwin's Ghosts: The Secret History of Evolution*   2012

- David W. Deamer, *First Life: Discovering the Connections Between Stars, Cells, and How Life Began*   2011
- Alister E. McGrath, *Dawkins' God: From The Selfish Gene to The God Delusion*   2015

Unexpected issues like the above are known as "bugs". What is causing the above is the fact that when we remove the extras **<span>**, we are leaving behind a **
** tag. This means we are not actually restoring the list item to its original state after each second click. Below is what the first list item looks like when I look at it in the Chrome inspector. Notice the extra **
** tags at the end.

```
▼<li data-isbn="9780679604136">
    <span class="author">Rebecca Stott</span>
    ", "
    <span class="title">
        Darwin's Ghosts: The Secret History of Evolution</span>
    <span class="publication-year">2012</span>
    <br>
    <br>
    <br>
</li>
```

Below is our function. The issue is being caused on line 55. Each time a user clicks the list item, line 55 adds a **
** tag to the end of it, then adds the extras **<span>** tag. This means that when we later remove the extras span, the **
** gets left behind.

```
47 ▼        all_book_list_items[i].addEventListener('click', function() {
48 ▼            if(this.querySelectorAll('.extras').length) {
49                 var the_extras_span = this.querySelectorAll('.extras')[0];
50                 this.removeChild(the_extras_span);
51                 return;
52             }
53             var isbn = this.getAttribute('data-isbn');
54             var book_object = books[isbn];
55             this.innerHTML = this.innerHTML + '<br>'
56                 + '<span class="extras">Publisher: ' + book_object.publisher
57                 + '. Page count: ' + book_object.pages + '</span>';
58        });
```

To fix this "bug", we need a way to also remove the **
** when we delete the **<extras>** span. One simple solution would be to put the **
** inside the **<extras>** span, so that when the **<extras>** span is deleted, the **
** is deleted along with it:

```
55             this.innerHTML = this.innerHTML + '<span class="extras">'
56                 + '<br> Publisher: ' + book_object.publisher
57                 + '. Page count: ' + book_object.pages + '</span>';
58        });
```

Above, the **
** is now on line 56 and inside the **<span>**. The problem is solved.

We will next look into creating a way to add a special style to the list item clicked by a user. First we create the CSS for it:

```
1 ▾  <style>
2 ▾      .title {
3            font-style:italic;
4        }
5 ▾      .publication-year {
6            font-size:90%; padding-left:1em;
7        }
8 ▾      .active-list-item {
9            border:1px solid #000;
10       }
11   </style>
```

Above I have added an **.active-list-item** class selector on lines 8-10 that adds a 1 pixel black border.

```
49 ▾      for(var i = 0; i < all_book_list_items.length; i++) {
50 ▾          all_book_list_items[i].addEventListener('click', function() {
51 ▾              if(this.querySelectorAll('.extras').length) {
52                   var the_extras_span = this.querySelectorAll('.extras')[0];
53                   this.removeChild(the_extras_span);
54                   this.className = '';
55                   return;
56               }
57               this.className = 'active-list-item';
58               var isbn = this.getAttribute('data-isbn');
59               var book_object = books[isbn];
60               this.innerHTML = this.innerHTML + '<span class="extras">'
61               + '<br> Publisher: ' + book_object.publisher
62               + '. Page count: ' + book_object.pages + '</span>';
63           });
```

Above I have added two new lines. The first one is line 54. This line sets the list item's class name to an empty string, meaning that its class is removed. This what we want to happen upon a second click on the list item. On line 57 we have the second new line, which is what happens when the user first clicks a list item. By setting **this.className** to **active-list-item**, the list item acquires a class of **active-list-item** and any CSS defined on this class will automatically be shown on the list item.

Below is the result when I click on the first list item:

- Rebecca Stott, *Darwin's Ghosts: The Secret History of Evolution*   2012
  Publisher: Random House Publishing Group. Page count: 432
- David W. Deamer, *First Life: Discovering the Connections Between Stars, Cells, and How Life Began*   2011
- Alister E. McGrath, *Dawkins' God: From The Selfish Gene to The God Delusion*   2015

Above, you can see that two things now take place. The old functionality we created where the extra information is show on click is still there. But now the element also acquires the style we defined for it in the CSS. If we click the list item again, the border goes away and the extra information is removed.

We will now add a new piece of functionality that displays information about the author when their name is clicked. To start, we will create a new authors variable that holds information about the authors. In the real world you would not code in this variable by yourself. You would instead use what is known as a web API to retrieve the information from a database that may hold information about thousands of authors. If you ever find yourself writing information about people or places (or other real-world items) in JavaScript or another programming language, you are doing it wrong. Such information should always be stored in a database unless you are dealing with something extremely small and simple.

```
48 ▾    var authors = {
49 ▾        'Rebecca Stott' : {
50              'born' : '1964',
51              'degree' : 'PhD',
52              'profession' : 'Professor at the University of East Anglia',
53              'other-works' : ['Ghostwalk (2007)', 'The Coral Thief (2009)'],
54          },
55 ▾        'David W. Deamer' : {
56              'born' : '1939',
57              'degree' : 'PhD',
58              'profession' : 'Research professor at UCSC',
59              'other-works' : ['Membrane Structure (2012)'],
60          },
61 ▾        'Alister E. McGrath' : {
62              'born' : '1953',
63              'degree' : 'PhD',
64              'profession' : 'Professor at Oxford University',
65              'other-works' : ['Mere Theology (2010)', 'C. S. Lewis, A Life (2013)']
66          }
67      }
```

Next we will add the code for attaching event listeners to the author names. This time we will use a new and much better way of adding event listeners:

```
87 ▾    document.body.addEventListener('click', function(event) {
88          var clicked_element = event.target;
89 ▾        if (clicked_element.classList.contains("author")) {
90              var author_name = clicked_element.innerHTML;
91
92          }
93      });
```

Above we have added a click event on the HTML **<body>** element, which is the top HTML element in the document, using the special **document.body** syntax. Since <body> is the top-level element, whenever you click on *anything* inside the document, you also click on **<body>** whether you want to or not. This enables us to add an event listener on **<body>** then check which element it was that was clicked and do something special based on that. Above, on line 88 we access the clicked element using **event.target**, which is a special variable that JavaScript makes available to us. Note that you can only use this if you put the word **event** as the anonymous function's argument, as we have done so on line 87. There is no need to worry about how this works exactly. You do not need to use the word **event**, it can be any variable name. Some programmers use the letter **e** as a short and handy variable name for the event object (in which case you would write **e** on line 87 instead of **event** and access the target by writing **e.target**).

On line 89 we use **clicked_element.classList.contains()** to check whether the clicked element has a class of "author". Since an element can have many classes, this is the proper way to check for the existence of a class. If the clicked element has the "author" class, the code inside the **if** statement runs. On line 90 we access the author's name using **clicked_element.innerHTML**. Since we put the author names inside **<span>** tags with the class of "author", the **innerHTML** property of these elements allows us to get each author's name when it is clicked.

Next we will access the author object for that specific author:

```
87 ▾    document.body.addEventListener('click', function(event) {
88          var clicked_element = event.target;
89 ▾        if (clicked_element.classList.contains("author")) {
90              var author_name = clicked_element.innerHTML;
91              var author_object = authors[author_name];
92
93          }
94      });
```

On line 91, we are accessing the **authors** object that we defined in the JavaScript earlier. Since the **authors** object uses each author's name as a key, writing **authors[author_name]** allows us to access the nested object that contains that particular author's information.

To verify that everything is working correctly, we can do a **console.log()** as follows:

```
87 ▾    document.body.addEventListener('click', function(event) {
88          var clicked_element = event.target;
89 ▾        if (clicked_element.classList.contains("author")) {
90              var author_name = clicked_element.innerHTML;
91              var author_object = authors[author_name];
92              console.log(author_object);
93          }
94      });
```

We won't get any output, however, until we click an author name, since this function only runs when an event takes place. Below is the output I get in the console when I click Alister McGrath's name in the preview area:

```
▸ Object {born: "1953", degree: "PhD", profession: "Professor at
  Oxford University", other-works: Array(2)}
```

As can be seen, everything is working correctly, since we got the information for the Alister McGrath.

Next we will create a brand new **<div>** tag to contain the extra information about the author:

```
87    document.body.addEventListener('click', function(event) {
88        var clicked_element = event.target;
89        if (clicked_element.classList.contains("author")) {
90            var author_name = clicked_element.innerHTML;
91            var author_object = authors[author_name];
92
93            var bio_div = document.createElement('div');
94            bio_div.innerHTML = '<h2>' + author_name + ' ('
95                + author_object.degree + ')</h2>';
96            bio_div.innerHTML += '<h3>' + author_object.profession + '</h3>';
97            bio_div.innerHTML += '<div>Born: ' + author_object.born + '<br>';
98            bio_div.innerHTML += 'Other works: '
99                + author_object['other-works'].join(', ');
100           bio_div.innerHTML += '</div>';
101
102           document.getElementsByTagName('body')[0].appendChild(bio_div);
103       }
104   });
```

On line 93 above we use **document.createElement()** to create a new **<div>** element (note that we pass only **'div'** and not **<div>** to the **createElement()** function). On the lines that follow we add the extra information about the author inside this new **<div>** tag by accessing its **innerHTML** attribute. The first time we use this attribute we use an equal sign (line 94), but from then on we use the plus equal sign (lines 96-100) in order to append new information to its contents rather than overwriting them (remember that **a += b** is the same as **a = a + b**).

When we create an element using **createElement()**, the element is only create inside JavaScript and will not be shown in the document. We need to "append" it to the document for it to be displayed. We take this step on line 102. We first use **document.getElementsByTagName('body')[0]** to get a hold of the **<body>** tag, then we use **appendChild(bio_div)** to place the **<div>** tag inside the **<body>** tag.

Note that instead of using the ugly syntax **getElementsByTagName('body')[0]**, we could have written:

```
document.querySelector('body').appendChild(bio_div);
```

Or even:

```
document.body.appendChild(bio_div);
```

These are all ways of achieving the same thing.

563

Below is the result in the preview area when I click on Rebecca Stott's name:

My Reading Journal

- Rebecca Stott, *Darwin's Ghosts: The Secret History of Evolution*   2012 Publisher: Random House Publishing Group. Page count: 432
- David W. Deamer, *First Life: Discovering the Connections Between Stars, Cells, and How Life Began*   2011
- Alister E. McGrath, *Dawkins' God: From The Selfish Gene to The God Delusion*   2015

Rebecca Stott (PhD)

Professor at the University of East Anglia

Born: 1964
Other works: Ghostwalk (2007), The Coral Thief (2009)

Above, at the end of the document we have the new **<div>** that we created. Clicking on Alister McGrath's name causes his information to be appended to the end of the document:

Rebecca Stott (PhD)

Professor at the University of East Anglia

Born: 1964
Other works: Ghostwalk (2007), The Coral Thief (2009)

Alister E. McGrath (PhD)

Professor at Oxford University

Born: 1953
Other works: Mere Theology (2010), C. S. Lewis, A Life (2013)

The information for Rebecca Stott remains because we are appending to the end of the document rather than replacing its contents.

Clicking on an author's name multiple times causes it to be appended multiple times:

Alister E. McGrath (PhD)

Professor at Oxford University

Born: 1953
Other works: Mere Theology (2010), C. S. Lewis, A Life (2013)

Alister E. McGrath (PhD)

Professor at Oxford University

Born: 1953
Other works: Mere Theology (2010), C. S. Lewis, A Life (2013)

Alister E. McGrath (PhD)

Professor at Oxford University

We can now use some CSS to cause this information to "pop up" rather than to be shown at the bottom of the preview area. To do that we first add a class name to the **\<div\>** after creating it:

```
93          var bio_div = document.createElement('div');
94          bio_div.className = 'bio';
```

Below we have the new CSS:

```
11 ▾    .bio {
12          position:absolute;
13          top:5%;
14          left:5%;
15          margin:5%;
16          padding:2% 5%;
17          border-radius:10px;
18          box-shadow: 5px 5px 5px #000;
19          background:#fff;
20          border:1px solid #ccc;
21      }
```

Here is the result when I click on Rebecca Stott's name now:

My Reading Journal

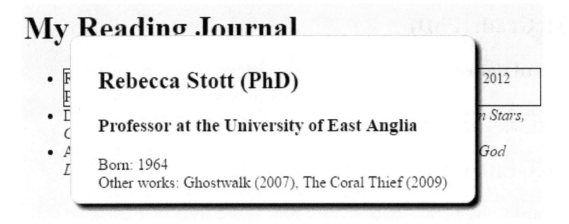

There is currently no mechanism for hiding the information once it is shown. Let's add such a mechanism. We will be adding it inside the event listener's function:

```
98 ▾   document.body.addEventListener('click', function(event) {
99          var clicked_element = event.target;
100 ▾       if (clicked_element.classList.contains("author")) {
101             var author_name = clicked_element.innerHTML;
102             var author_object = authors[author_name];
103
104             var bio_div = document.createElement('div');
105             bio_div.className = 'bio';
106             bio_div.innerHTML = '<h2>' + author_name + ' (' 
107                 + author_object.degree + ')</h2>';
108             bio_div.innerHTML += '<h3>' + author_object.profession + '</h3>';
109             bio_div.innerHTML += '<div>Born: ' + author_object.born + '<br>';
110             bio_div.innerHTML += 'Other works: '
111                 + author_object['other-works'].join(', ');
112             bio_div.innerHTML += '</div>';
113
114 ▾           bio_div.addEventListener('click', function() {
115                 this.parentElement.removeChild(this);
116             });
117
118             document.getElementsByTagName('body')[0].appendChild(bio_div);
119
120         }
121   });
```

Above, on lines 114-116 we are defining a new event listener inside the original event listener. This new event listener will be attached to the new **\<div\>** element just as it is created. On line 115, when we write **this**, this time it refers to the new **\<div\>** since it is inside the anonymous function for the event attached to the **\<div\>**. When seeing a **this** anywhere in JavaScript code, you have to use the context to judge what it is referring to. Line 115 causes the \<div\> to be deleted. As has been mentioned, we cannot delete an element unless we call the **removeChild()** function on *its parent* rather than on itself. Therefore we need to access its parent using **this.parentElement**.

Actually since the parent of this **\<div\>** is the **\<body\>** element, we could have also grabbed the **\<body\>** tag (such as by using **document.body**) and called **removeChild()** on that, as follows:

```
114 ▾        bio_div.addEventListener('click', function() {
115              //this.parentElement.removeChild(this);
116              document.body.removeChild(this);
117          });
```

Above, I have used a double slash on line 115 to "comment out" the earlier code. This is a convenient way of disabling a line of code without deleting it. On line 116 I call **removeChild()** on **document.body** and the result is the same.

However, it is always best to use this instead, because you may make a change to your code that causes the \<div\> to become the child of some other element. If that happens, this event listener will stop working, because it will expect the **\<div\>** to be a child of **\<body\>**. By writing **this.parentElement.removeChild(this)**, we are always sure to be calling it the right way regardless of where the element is in the document structure.

This page intentionally left blank

Where to go next...

At this point, you have acquired a basic training in HTML, CSS and JavaScript and you are ready to create your own website. A website must be "hosted" on a "server" for people to be able to see it on the internet. In my book *Cloud Computing for Complete Beginners* I teach how to create a website on a server that you yourself own and control. If your goal is to acquire the skills needed for a career in web design and development, then that book teaches the professional way for doing things.

And if you merely wish to have your own personal website and do not expect a huge amount of traffic, then you can do a web search for "how to host my own website" and you will find various tutorials for signing up for a "web host" and transferring your HTML, CSS and image files to the server via something called FTP.

Many web hosting services provide you with a "WordPress plan". This allows you to quickly get a beautiful and easy-to-manage website going while also giving you a lot of control over the HTML and CSS.

To go on to develop sophisticated websites with databases, you will need to learn a server scripting language, such as PHP, Ruby or Python. You will also need some knowledge of the database language SQL.

WordPress (note that I am speaking of WordPress.org, rather than the simple blogging service WordPress.com) is a great system for beginners who want to build websites. It already has everything set up (HTML, CSS, JavaScript, PHP and MySQL) and it can allow you to get a website up and running in minutes. I highly recommend using WordPress or another framework as a learning tool because tinkering with already-built systems is a great way of mastering programming. My *Cloud Computing for Complete Beginners* teaches how to get your very own Linux web server and get a WordPress-based website working on it. If you want to do some "real" web development work then this is a great place to start, since once you are done you will have a fully functional website on the Internet.

If you want to build games to be played on Android and iOS devices, you can check out the Unity framework. This is a program that allows you to build a game using visual tools and the C# (C-Sharp) language. When the game is ready, it can be "exported" to both Android and iOS without having to worry too much about the differences between these two systems.

If your goal is to build apps (not games) for mobile devices, React Native is the most popular tool right now and uses JavaScript as its basis and is used by some of the biggest tech companies.

If you are some sort of business manager and wish to put your new programming skills to good use, you can import spreadsheets into Google Spreadsheets then use JavaScript to run little programs on the spreadsheet to do all sorts of advanced calculations (do a web search for "google spreadsheet scripting").

If you are interested in a more academic study of programming, you can search for books on object oriented programming, data structures and algorithms.

This page intentionally left blank